IN GOOD COMPANY

IN GOOD COMPANY.

An Account of the 6th Machine Gun Company
A.I.F. in search of Peace 1915-19.

by

LIEUTENANT W. A. CARNE

---

with a Foreword by
Major-General Sir John Gellibrand, K.C.B., D.S.O.

The Naval & Military Press Ltd

Published by

The Naval & Military Press Ltd
Unit 5 Riverside, Brambleside
Bellbrook Industrial Estate
Uckfield, East Sussex
TN22 1QQ England

Tel: +44 (0)1825 749494

www.naval-military-press.com
www.nmarchive.com

In reprinting in facsimile from the original, any imperfections are inevitably reproduced and the quality may fall short of modern type and cartographic standards.

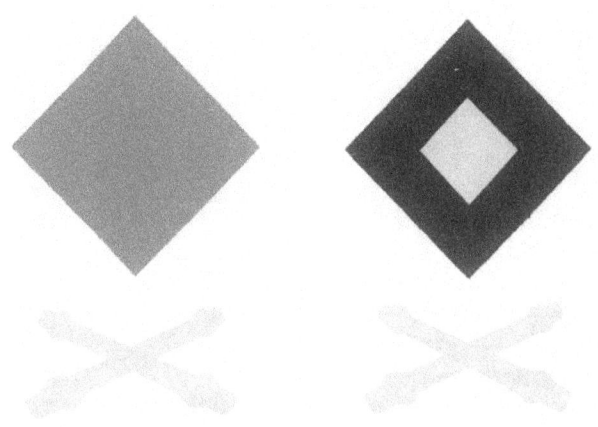

DEDICATED TO
THE MEMBERS OF THE
6th MACHINE GUN COMPANY
A.I.F.

FOREWORD.

By MAJOR-GENERAL SIR JOHN GELLIBRAND K.C.B., D.S.O.

It is both inevitable and regrettable that Military History should deal only with matters of high importance to the conduct of operations and the campaign in general, whilst subsiduary records, such as memoirs, recollections, and experiences present an essentially individual point of view. On the other hand, purely regimental history which deals with life and events within the limited horizon of a unit, is of very definite value in bringing to light many otherwise unrecorded experiences and lessons of military service, day by day. Put into other words, the General Staff work interests the troops on one day out of twenty, whilst the Administrative Staff's labours concern them from the first day to the last.

For many reasons, the records of the smaller units are of surpassing value in gaining an insight to the ways and means, the methods, and the spirit of the force to which they belong. Cause and effect are easily traced on account of their smaller numbers, and because their work is under constant observation by critics of no mean standing or ability—their comrades in the larger units. Whatever factors affect the progress and value of a small unit may safely be assumed to be of importance to the whole force.

In particular, the history of an Australian Machine Gun Company offers many features of special interest. The majority of their ranks were born, so to speak, in the Light Horse and Infantry, whilst the nature of their training and work imbued them with many of the characteristics of Artillery.

No more welcome task could have fallen to my lot than this one of taking part in the Record of the 6th Machine Gun Company. I knew the component Sections as part of their Battalions on Gallipoli, and later watched their transition to independent existence as a Company in Egypt, as well as their development during the first years on the Western Front.

In the early days of the Company's existence, strongly

resembling chaos, a three party covenant was entered into between its Commander, Major L. F. S. Hore, the Battalion Commanders, and Brigade Headquarters, on the following lines: the Company to receive every conceivable assistance, advantage, and privilege, and in return was to "deliver the goods on demand" at any time and under all circumstances. This covenant had the merit that it worked without breach, either in the letter or the spirit, and I cannot call to mind any incident giving rise to adverse comment, or in which it was reasonable to expect more from Major Hore and his men. Nor can I recall any cause for what is called disciplinary action. There was certainly the matter of a duck, I think at La Vicogne, but the weight of evidence was in favour of a verdict of "felo de se." The bird wilfully obstructed a machine-gun horse, was trodden on in the execution of military duty, and was then, in accordance with Brigade Orders, directing the war to be won economically, eaten by the officers. Unfortunately, the duck was a drake of many years' standing in the owner's family, and the incident closed with a subscription of 30 francs towards a monument. Another matter was the rust spot discovered by an inspecting officer on the mounting of a gun—at Flers!—in the winter of 1916! Those who remember the time and place will understand why the caustic reprimand featuring "Unsoldierly slovenliness" was not allowed to go beyond Brigade Headquarters.

It was no easy matter to join the ranks of the 6th Machine Gun Company, since under the covenant, the Company had the call of any man of the required rank in any of the four Battalions, and a candidate had to be asked for. It would no doubt have been easier to get out of the Company, but this is a matter of surmise, as cases seldom occurred (except as casualties). The personnel was, of necessity, composed solely of men who wanted to serve together, and there were no "passengers."

The system underlying the Company work in the line and in billets was designed to give all hands the fullest scope for initiative within the horizon of Company aims and methods. Any one of the officers could well have exercised the functions of command, and the greater number of N.C.O.'s would have been welcome as officers. The most difficult position in military life is that of Second in Command, with all the disadvantages and temptations that beset heirs apparent. To fill this position adequately and loyally, and then to succeed to the command with the unit marching on with unchanged pace and direction, commands the highest qualities of character from the individual

FOREWORD.

concerned and from the unit. That is Drummond's record in the 6th Machine Gun Company. Command without worries enabled Major Hore to devote his energies and abilities to the development of the most effective co-operation with the Battalions, who were not slow in appreciating the value of the work. In this respect the only discordant note was the first one when, owing to a lamentable error or misprint in a text book, the first night firing resulted in a sentry falling slightly wounded off the Boutillerie wall at Fleurbaix, and using his C.O., who was passing, as a landing ground. As Major Hore pointed out, no one was much the worse, and, but for the incident, much valuable ammunition would have been wasted. The enemy held other views, which they are known to have expressed in vigorous terms at Pozieres, Mouquet Farm, and Bullecourt. The sequel is possibly not without interest. Some one, probably Major Hore, was struck with the splendour of a succession of sudden thoughts. Why not appeal to the friendly sentiments and technical knowledge of Colonel H. W. Lloyd, who commanded the Artillery supporting the Brigade, with a view to training officers and N.C.O.'s in the technique of indirect fire. The mission was entrusted to the largest subaltern, a man of unprepossessing appearance, but endowed with a capacity common to settlers in the Wimmera, to suffer rebuffs of fortune, and yet to win through in the end. A strenuous course of instruction was arranged, the guns were fitted with true planes, clinometers were bought in London, the 6th Machine Gun Company stressed the GUNNER part of their designation, the infantry ceased from troubling, and the enemy had many an occasion for grief.

The tragedy and tedium of war are sensibly mitigated by the company one keeps, and where men, minds, and matters function without friction on the same lines for a common cause; where duty is done decently for personal satisfaction, even war has its bright spots. Undoubtedly small numbers have an important bearing on the standard of a unit, both for the highest summits of success and the lowest depths of failure—for the simple reason that the personality of the Commander is in closer contact with all ranks of the unit. In the case of the 6th Machine Gun Company, there was an ideal combination under Hore, and later under Drummond, which was bound to create a "happy band of brothers"—happy in their own close association, happy in the esteem of the units they worked with, happy in the consciousness that in every branch of their work they had exerted their utmost powers of mind and body. To the novice in war, the only thing that counts is service in the front line, but the older hands give transport and quartermaster work their full due of equality in merit. I doubt whether any unit can show a better record of reliability and capacity in the service of their comrades in this respect.

I am well aware that, at this point, the 6th Machine Gun Company reader will say: "Why not have said something of this sort at the time, instead of waiting 20 years?" The answer is, that men who do their work well and faithfully are invariably capable of assessing its value, and they are in no doubt whatever as to the opinions of those whose views are of any importance to them. The highest praise given by the greatest Commander runs: "Soldiers! I am content with you." I could not say it, so I thought it.

—JOHN GELLIBRAND.

PREFACE.

To those who were engaged in raising, training, and leading the troops recruited by Australia in the Great War, the reasons for describing in detail the experiences of a small unit will, no doubt, be adequate. To others, the sphere of action and the relative importance of the activities of a machine-gun company may seem so infinitesimal and insignificant as to render any detailed account of their life history more a matter of sentiment than of practical value. Nevertheless, it is hoped that the present account will contribute its share towards a fuller understanding of the difficulties common to most units of the A.I.F. as well as of the characteristic qualities of the men, and of the bitter-sweet experiences in the field.

This volume is, therefore, a serious attempt to record the formation, experiences, achievements, and failures of a relatively small "specialist" unit of the Australian Imperial Force; the 6th Machine Gun Company, a component part of the 2nd Australian Division. It is based on the official diaries and records of the Company and associated units, the writer's diary and those kept by members of the Company, as well as such letters as could be made available. While in no sense a history of that now famous Force, it seeks to record a part of the whole, and in so doing, to present an intimate and detailed narrative which is not possible in the story of large formations or of the Force itself. To those it is supplementary, and in the nature of an adjunct. Constant reference to associated units has been made, but only with the purpose of showing the Company's part in perspective.

Primarily, the compiler of such a narrative is faced with enormous difficulties; a fact which probably explains why no history of a machine-gun unit of the A.I.F. has, so far, appeared. As was found, there had been no preliminary preparation; no research; no careful filing of detailed records for future historians. The existing official records, while usually continuous, are generally sketchy and impersonal, and oftimes are more notable for what they omit than for what they reveal; further, occasional errors intrude themselves. No criticism is implied by these allusions; such a result might be expected when those concerned were preoccupied with the pressing tasks of helping to win the war rather than with the more deliberate matter of recording the doings of the unit and its members. The difficulties are further increased by the passing of the years; diaries and letters—treasure trove to the historian—become lost or destroyed, and memories—except for particular incidents—fade and break down under cross-examination. And who is to write the history? No officer or man served in every engagement of the Company, and if one did, he could see but part, and often a small one at that. The horizon of each individual was usually strictly limited. Generally he was so concerned with his own and his party's difficulties and problems as to leave little or no time to observe his neighbours. In these pages, many ex-Company members will, doubtless, learn for the first time, the doings of their comrades in engagements in which they themselves took part. This aspect will be better understood when it is realised that the Company's activities usually ranged over the whole area of an infantry brigade; normally half a divisional sector. In such circumstances, any narrative which aims at completeness must, of necessity, be in the nature of a patchwork. The compiler's secondary difficulty is to weave the patches—large and small—into something like unity.

To such an undertaking, the writer committed himself for the chief reason that it appeared that no other ex-member of the Company had sufficient spare time for the task. To him—as, doubtless, to others—it is a matter of deep regret that so few—comparatively speaking—A.I.F. unit histories have appeared to supplement the noble and monumental work of the Official Historian. Further, the passing of each year renders any such project more difficult of achievement. These considerations became sufficiently pressing to induce him to overcome a natural reluctance to venture into the domain of literature—unqualified by any previous experience—for the sake of the object, and to pay tribute to his old unit, for which he—and many others—retains a deep and lasting affection.

To supplement the paucity of detail, it became necessary to obtain from individual members (preferably participants and eye-witnesses) accounts of their experiences. This involved the writer in an amount of correspondence which became voluminous, the compilation of many and varied questionnaires, and much cross-examination of evidence, oftimes based on memories of events which happened up to 20 years before. A preliminary search for ex-members of the unit, now scattered over the Commonwealth and beyond, became necessary. However, these difficulties have, in the main, been overcome by persistence on the one hand, and on the other (in nearly every case of inquiry), by painstaking replies. The unrivalled friendships formed oversea, and the esprit de corps towards the old unit ensured a willing response to the prosaic task of penning replies to the numerous questions of an importunate seeker of information. Every known and/or likely source of information has been fully explored, and it is believed that the record is as complete as it is now possible to make it.

As to the narrative itself, the writer has endeavoured to indicate the problems attendant on the raising of a "specialist" unit from enthusiastic but unskilled volunteers, and likewise the transition of novices to skilled machine-gunners. The latter process required constant mental effort and no small degree of physical exertion to meet the continuous developments in machine-gunnery. Nor was the enemy the only opponent to contend with, as all those who served with the unit through the bitter and unforgettable winter of 1916-17 will testify. The writer has essayed to show individual and collective reactions to both contenders, as well as the remarkable growth of the "team" spirit which was such a potent factor in the success of the A.I.F. It may be doubted whether that spirit reached a greater degree of intensity than it did in the Company. At the same time, the various increases in the ratio of Vickers machine-guns to infantry strength has been noted, as well as the extensions of the gun's usefulness. Primarily a weapon of defence, the earlier "settled" conditions of trench warfare on the Western Front led to the application of the principles and practice of indirect fire, and a consequent fresh field for exploitation. Concurrently, changes in tactical control and developments in methods of administration have been set out. Save for one instance, no deed of desperate defence or rear-guard action marks the story, for the simple reason that the Company was never involved in repelling a major attack or in the covering of a retiring force. As a consequence, particularly effective work and outstanding individual or collective performances were mainly confined to the more restricted field (for the Vickers gun) of advances in infantry attacks. Every recorded death and wounding has been noted, and in nearly every case the circumstances are stated; diligent enquiry has, however, failed to ascertain a few of the latter. All decorations and mentions in despatches appear, likewise the deeds for which they were awarded. Details as to personnel and other items appear in the Appendix. So far as it is possible and fair, the descriptions and personal comments are those of the war years.

No attempt at fine writing has been made, but the compiler has been to considerable pains to ensure the strict accuracy of every phase of the narrative and, at the same time, to present one without colour or exaggeration. Space has been given to happenings which, to the uninitiated, may appear commonplace, but it should be borne in mind that the topsy-turveydom of war often relegates the heroic to the commonplace, and elevates the trivial to a point of importance in the every-day life of the soldier. It is hardly necessary to say that the glorification of war is not intended; a more ghastly and devilish method of settling differences cannot be imagined. Nevertheless, history demands a record of the reactions of the youthful manhood of this young Commonwealth during the world-shaking convulsion of 1914-18. Therein is enshrined the responses to the call of Justice and of our Blood, and in the process our national traditions acquired their greatest and richest inheritance.

The writer acknowledges with grateful thanks the assistance of many helpers. To Lieutenant R. C. Callister he is deeply indebted for his generous contributions of valuable matter, comments, suggestions, and careful reading of the whole of the manuscript. Over a period of eight years his stimulating support was an abiding inspiration. In a long list of contributors of matter, the following should be mentioned:—Captain D. F. Rae, Lieutenants A. P. Hitchcock, R. F. Bennett, H. A. Robinson, W. S. Clayton, F. L. Wright, G. A. Jeffery, N. F. Wilkinson, J. N. Myers, R. Dodgshun, T. F. Turnbull, and H. J. Bennett; Sergeants J. P. Adam, J. N. Spittle, S. A. Greaves, R. C. Trevan, A. McDonald, F. L. Fitzpatrick, A. E. Cameron, A. Payton; Corporals V. G. Esmond, J. W. Findlay, A. E. Coe, W. E. Peters, N. C. Hammon, E. D. Saker, W. N. Riley, H. G. Black, S. H. Deakin, R. L. M. Cox, W. Sharp, J. J. Passeri; Lance Corporal A. Chitty; Signaller D. C. Howard; Driver E. J. Nash; Privates H. E. Horner, A. V. Caldwell, and D. Lazarus. The references to the operations of the Australian Army Corps in the latter chapters are based mainly upon Lieutenant-General Sir John Monash's "The Australian Victories in France in 1918." The poem, "Up and Down the Duckboards," is published by courtesy of "The Herald." Thanks are also due to Major-General Sir John Gellibrand, for reading the manuscript, valuable sugges-

PREFACE.

tions, and his generous Foreword; to the Official Historian (Dr. C. E. W. Bean), for contributions from enemy records; to the Director and staff of the Australian War Memorial, for access to records and courteous assistance; to Miss W. R. Joy, for much of the incidental typing (including questionnaires and drafts); to Lieutenant N. F. Wilkinson and Quartermaster-Sergeant R. W. Watt, for reading the proofs; to Quartermaster-Sergeant R. W. Watt, Lieutenant A. H. Wardrop (5th Pioneer Battalion); Mr. A. Cousins and Mr. A. Kerr, for preparing the maps; to the Trustees of the Anzac Book Fund for financial assistance; likewise to those ex-members of the Company who loaned photographs and maps, and to those who helped to establish a Publishing Fund.

Finally, the writer ventures to hope that the volume now presented will be adjudged an acceptable contribution to the stirring and growing literature appertaining to those splendid Crusaders, the members of the Australian Imperial Force.

W.A.C.

Glenhuntly,
    Victoria,
        22/8/36.

CONTENTS

Chap.		Page.
	FOREWORD	7
	PREFACE	11
	1915-6.	
I	PRE-COMPANY RECORDS	19
	1916.	
II	FORMATION OF THE COMPANY	31
III	ACROSS THE MEDITERRANEAN	41
IV	EARLY DAYS IN FRANCE: FLEURBAIX—ERQUINGHEM	43
V	EARLY DAYS IN FRANCE: BOIS GRENIER	65
VI	POZIERES	76
VII	RESPITE AND RETURN TO POZIERES: MOUQUET FARM	99
VIII	YPRES, 1916	113
IX	THE FIRST WINTER IN FRANCE: FLERS	122
X	THE FIRST WINTER IN FRANCE: FLESSELLES—LE TRANSLOY—RIBEMONT	134
	1917.	
XI	THE GERMAN WITHDRAWAL TO THE HINDENBURG LINE	150
XII	BULLECOURT	172
XIII	THE LONG REST	190
XIV	THE BATTLE OF MENIN ROAD	206
XV	YPRES, 1917: BROODSEINDE RIDGE	230
XVI	YPRES, 1917: DAISY WOOD	241
XVII	YPRES, 1917: PASSCHENDAELE	257
XVIII	THE WINTER OF 1917-8: LOCRE—NEUVE—EGLISE—WARNETON—WATTERDAL	262
	1918.	
XIX	FORMATION OF THE 2ND MACHINE GUN BATTALION	277
XX	THE FINAL MOVE TO THE SOMME	282
XXI	VILLE-SUR-ANCRE	289
XXII	JUNE, 1918: FRANVILLERS—VILLE-SUR-ANCRE—QUERRIEU	299
XXIII	HAMEL AND ITS AFTERMATH	307
XXIV	THE BEGINNING OF THE END: 8th, 9th, and 11th AUGUST	323
XXV	MONT ST. QUENTIN	350
XXVI	THE LAST FIGHT: MONTBREHAIN	367
	1918-9	
XXVII	LAST DAYS	384
	APPENDIX	399

LIST OF MAPS AND DIAGRAMS.

Map.	Page
Pozieres	91
Bullecourt	173
Diagram of Result of Indirect Fire	199
Battle of Menin Road: Machine Gun Barrage of 2nd Division. Facing	216
Ypres 1917: Broodseinde Ridge	233
Ypres, 1917: Daisy Wood	243
Ville-Sur-Ancre	293
Attack by 2nd Division: 8th August	325
Attack by 2nd Division: 9th August	336
Attack by 2nd Division: 11th August	343
Mont St. Quentin	356
Montbrehain	369
Illustration of the Vickers Machine Gun	426

LIST OF PHOTOGRAPHS.

Sir John Gellibrand, K.C.B., D.S.O.	Facing	46
The Three Commanding Officers	,,	62
The Two Senior Lieutenants	,,	94
First Billets in France, German machine-gun Instruction, The Company cooker	,,	110
Guns Mounted for Anti-aircraft Duty	,,	158
Zambuck Post, Warneton, Company Members in Malt Trench Support	,,	174
No. 2 Section	,,	206
No. 1 Section	,,	222
Horse Lines at Warlencourt, Company Headquarters at Hannebeke Wood, Company Officers at Watterdal	,,	254
Winning Team (Tug-o'-War) 6th Brigade Sports	,,	270
Company Officers (Official photograph)	,,	302
Company N.C.O.'s (Official photograph)	,,	318
Transport Section	,,	366
No. 4 Section	,,	382

CHAPTER I.

Pre-Company Records.

January, 1915—February, 1916.

According to official records, the 6th Machine Gun Company, A.I.F., was formed at Moascar, in the Canal Zone, Egypt, on the 1st March, 1916, by the amalgamation of the existing Machine Gun Sections of the 21st, 22nd, 23rd and 24th Battalions, which constituted the 6th Infantry Brigade of the 2nd Australian Division.

The date is noteworthy in so far as it records a phase in the development of machine-gunnery in the 2nd Division (and incidentally in the A.I.F.), but any survey of the experiences of the new Company must extend further back than the time indicated. Indeed, it should commence in the early months of 1915, when the Military authorities in Victoria were engaged in the task of forming the 6th Infantry Brigade, which later, formed one of the three Brigades of the 2nd Division.

For the reason stated, this narrative will follow, in outline, the experiences of the four Battalion Machine Gun Sections until their detachment from their respective Battalions, and subsequent formation of a new Brigade unit, the 6th Machine Gun Company.

The 6th Infantry Brigade was raised in Victoria from volunteers who enlisted in that State, and was maintained from the same territory. As a result, the Sections, and later formed Company, were originally, and remained except for a few transfers in the last stages, a purely Victorian unit.

The pre-occupations of the approaching wheat, wool, and fruit harvests at the outbreak of the War caused an appreciable number of men from country districts to defer enlistment until the yearly task was completed. These men were not available for the ranks of the 1st Division, but formed an appreciable contribution to the later formed 2nd Division. In due course, some found their way into the Battalion Machine Gun Sections.

Country men, or men from country districts, appear to have comprised nearly half the personnel, and they certainly gave the new formations the imprint of their sturdy personalities—characteristics which the Sections and Company retained to the last.

During the formation of the Brigade at Broadmeadows, the Sections were, in most cases, constituted by the calling for volunteers from the Depot companies. Those responsible for the selection had no dearth of applicants, so a discriminating selection was possible. At the very outset, it was possible to "pick and choose" as to personnel; a policy which was maintained to the end as far as the Sections and Company were concerned. By this means a high mental standard was attained. The fact that the "specialists" were dubbed the "Suicide Club" did not deter alert men from forsaking the Infantry, or "Footsloggers," and entering a unit which required special duties. It was felt that, while its popular title promised an early demise, the new formations offered an escape from some of the comprehensive and strenuous tasks allotted to the Infantryman. Subsequent experiences vindicated the soundness of their judgment.

The existing Battalion Establishment provided for 2 Maxim machine-guns (with accessories), 1 limber, 1 officer, 1 sergeant, 1 corporal, 12 gunners, 2 drivers and 1 batman.

With the exception of the 24th Battalion Section, this Establishment was, with respect to personnel, completed in due course. The men were keen to learn the "ins and outs" of the weapon, but scarcity of guns and skilled instructors greatly hampered training. Until shortly before embarkation, the 23rd Battalion Section was without guns, and as a makeshift for the purposes of gun drill, used a large stone for a tripod and a piece of timber for a gun. Generally a few officers and non-commissioned officers who had attended a course at Liverpool (N.S.W.) supervised what instruction was given in the all-important subject of mechanism. The 22nd Battalion Section was more fortunate than the others in so far that a Reserve Section was formed, and the teams had actual firing experience at the Williamstown rifle range.

Owing to the very late formation of the 24th Battalion (which was organised largely from raw recruits, and equipped for embarkation overseas on just over one week's notice), the Section was hastily formed without any gun training and embarked with one obsolete gun. The other Sections obtained their complement of guns, but the 21st was the only Section to depart with a limber. No horses were taken.

Officers on embarkation were:—21st Battalion: Lieutenant C. M. Bartels, Sergeant W. J. Darley, Corporal Williamson. 22nd Battalion: Lieutenant R. B. Sewell, Sergeant E. Matthews, Corporal A. Palling. 23rd Battalion: Lieutenant E. E. King, Sergeant C. Chase, Corporal T. Bentley. 24th Battalion: Lieutenant V. Hyndes, Sergeant M. Andrews, Corporal O. H. Bailey.

Such, in brief, were the Machine Gun Sections of the 6th Brigade upon embarkation. With some knowledge of gun drill and little or none of mechanism, it cannot be said that the teams had received even an elementary training. No blame is implied by this statement. The facilities for the training of machine-gunners in Victoria did not, apparently, exist, and the military authorities were fully occupied with the organisation and despatch of large bodies of troops which suddenly grew beyond the capacity of existing staffs. While the teams left Australia in the raw state referred to, they possessed, on the other hand, high spirits, enthusiasm, and the priceless gift of youth—factors which helped enormously in the shaping of what subsequently became a highly efficient fighting unit.

The Brigade marched out of Broadmeadows Camp on the 8th May, and entrained for Port Melbourne for embarkation. The 21st and 22nd Sections, with their respective Battalions, were allotted to the transport "Ulysses," and the 23rd and 24th to the "Euripides." No secrecy was observed, and in consequence a very large crowd of relatives and friends gathered at the wharf to say farewell.

By next day both transports were clear of the Heads, and made the long voyage together. Sea-sickness soon made itself felt, and some men were thus early, temporarily "out of action." On the 14th, the last glimpse of Australian shores was seen. The door closed upon the days of peaceful citizenship, and during four years in foreign lands, among strange peoples, the Sections gave many lives and much strenuous service to the Cause for which they had enlisted.

During the voyage the weather was uniformly good. The teams made a closer acquaintance with the mechanism of the gun, and practised gun drill. Various games and sports helped to pass the leisure time away. Both transports lost men through death from illness, and to whom a burial at sea was accorded. In the circumstances, the strikingly beautiful form of the Burial Service assumed a deeper sense of solemnity.

Colombo was reached on the 25th May. Those on the "Ulysses" went ashore and stretched their legs in a rather strenuous route march. That experience did not fall to the lot of those on the "Euripides," and only a few who took "unofficial" leave got ashore. At Colombo, a 4.7 naval gun was mounted on the "Euripides," and placed in charge of an ex-naval gunner. The 23rd Battalion Section were put through a course of training, and acted as a team for the gun.

The passage through the Suez Canal was very interesting. Precautions were taken in the way of protection from enemy snipers by the erection of steel plates and sandbags, but the transports were not molested. Some months later interest in the historic waterway was revived when the Brigade took up defensive lines some miles east of the Canal, after an exhausting march.

Alexandria was reached on the 9th June by the "Ulysses," and some time later the "Euripides" steamed in. From the boatside the Brigade entrained for Heliopolis, and in due course detrained at Zietoun and Helmiah. The railway journey of five or six hours was done in exceedingly hot weather, and all ranks found the march to the camp at Heliopolis, in their first practical experience of full gear and marching order, a very trying one.

In company with their respective Battalions, the Sections at once settled down to circumstances that were very different from the more congenial camp at Broadmeadows. Tents were provided for living quarters, and large, flimsy, wooden huts for meals and lectures. The sand was all pervading, and the heat intense. Physical training on empty stomachs was soon discontinued, and the programme was arranged as follows: 5 a.m., Reveille; 5.15, Tea and bread and jam; 5.30, Fall in; 5.45, on the Battalion parade ground, drill till 8.30 a.m., then breakfast; 11 to noon, Lectures, then dinner. 3.30, bread and jam and tea; 4 p.m., Fall in. Finish up about 8-9.30 for tea. Lights out at 10 p.m. The heat was at times terrific. Some measure of relief was afforded by the issue of pith helmets and cotton "shorts" or knickers for use instead of breeches.

The training was thorough in a physical sense. The Sections indulged in a considerable amount of "battle practice" with their Battalions, and soon hardened up to heat and sand; could run a mile with the gun and tripod, and as one of the men expressed it, "could control one's thirst to some extent." At times, but not often, Battalion Transport Limbers were used. The teams soon learned gun handling with considerable speed and precision. Range finding practice, infantry training, and musketry were not neglected. On the other hand, the more technical side did not receive the attention necessary. There was not enough assembling and dissembling of the mechanical parts of the gun or sufficient "stoppage" rectification. Opportunity was taken to train "Reserve" Sections composed of men drawn from the respective Battalions. This precaution proved to be a wise one.

The deficiency in mechanical training was remedied to some extent when a proportion (in some cases, all) of the Sections were sent to a Machine Gun School of Instruction at Zietoun. This school was staffed by Imperial Officers, and was commanded by Lieutenant-Colonel Coulston, of the Coldstream Guards, and assisted by Captain Clarke (Adjutant), Sergeant Major Jones, and a staff of Instructors. The instruction accorded was conscientious and thorough, and high marks were gained by all the participants. One result of the course was the offer made to retain some of the trainees for service as Instructors, but the inducements failed to attract a single applicant. The School training was supplemented by a short course of firing at the Abbassia Rifle Range, when most of the teams fired their guns for the first time.

Egypt has much to offer to the visitor. While it cannot be said that the Australian Forces entered the country under the designation of tourists, the Brigade certainly lived up to the reputation which earned for the 1st Australian Division the title of "six bob a day tourists." It should be added that that reputation was never lost. Cairo, the Pyramids, and all points of interest in the surrounding country were explored with a thoroughness that left nothing to be desired. A shrewd observer at the time remarked that the Australians were a "crowd of tourists who did a bit of fighting in between whiles as a hobby." The observation was accurate as to the first part, but did not indicate that grim and remarkable efficiency with which they afterwards carried out the main purpose of their mission. Suffice it to say, that the Machine Gun Sections made full use of their opportunities to acquaint themselves, in their own peculiar fashion, with what historic and material Egypt had to offer. "I will pass this way but once; let me gather while I may," seemed to be their motto.

Such, in brief, was the preparation accorded by the sojourn in Egypt. Physically, the men were hardened and improved. They had become accustomed, to some extent, to the inexorable routine demanded by active service, but the full acceptance of those conditions was not yet in sight; neither was that mutual trust and dependence on one another, so essential to team work. Off parade, they were left almost entirely to themselves. Especially at meal times was noticeable the lack of "give and take," when clamourous and noisy ones were much in evidence. Leaders had yet to be evolved to control the internal economy.

Certain changes in the Sectional commands took place. In the 21st, Lieutenant Bartels became ill just before departure for Gallipoli, and his place was taken by Sergeant W. J. Darley, who was promoted to 2nd Lieutenant; Lance Corporal Stone became Sergeant. In the 22nd, Lieutenant Sewell returned to Australia, and Lieutenant P. Stewart assumed command, assisted by Lieutenant A. N. McLennan. Lieutenant King, in the 23rd, gave way to Lieutenant Drummond (shortly before departure), who afterwards succeeded to the command of the Company. In the 24th, Lieutenant Hyndes was followed by Lieutenant J. Needham.

Towards the end of August, orders were received to embark and, on the 29th August, the Brigade entrained for Alexandria, which was reached after a weary journey in open trucks. By next morning, the Sections with their Battalions were aboard their respective transports. The 21st embarked on the ill-fated "Southland," the 22nd on the "Scotian," and the 23rd on the "Haverford," and the 24th on the fast steamer "Nile."

The voyage to Lemnos was uneventful except in the case of the "Southland." In addition to the 21st Battalion, this transport carried 2nd Division and 6th Brigade Headquarters, "B" Company of the 23rd Battalion, and some details. The trip was pleasant till within ten miles of Lemnos; then it became interesting, but not pleasant. In common with other transports, the Maxim guns were mounted for action and continuously manned in view of the submarine menace. About 10.15 a.m. on 2nd September, just after the guns had been cleaned and overhauled—they were mounted amidships—Lieutenant Darley dashed up to the port gun shouting: "Load that gun; torpedo; look." It was seen coming, perhaps 400 yards away, well under water. It struck fairly well forward, and a number of men were killed by the explosion. A long and careful search was made for the submarine, but it was not sighted.

The members of the Machine Gun Section were taken off in different boats, but it was 11.45 a.m. when the remainder, consisting of Lieutenant Stone, Lance Corporals F. Windsor, and R. C. Callister, Corporal Williamson, and Private E. A. Burtonclay were ordered off on to rafts. Their zeal for the safety of their two guns led them to try to save their weapons by getting them on to rafts. Alas, for their efforts, the rafts capsized and the guns were lost. The Section had the mortification of realising afterwards that its zeal was misdirected, because the "Southland" was able to make port under her own steam.

The "Nile" and "Scotian" were ahead of the "Southland," but much concern was felt on the "Haverford," which was in the rear. A diarist in the 23rd Section (Private W. S. Clayton) recorded his impressions as follows: "About noon, came up to the transport 'Southland,' and ascertained that she had been torpedoed. She had a decided list to port. All the soldiers had disembarked into boats and rafts, and dozens of men were swimming about also. The men in the boats and on the rafts were, apparently, in great spirits; singing and cheering alternately. They seemed determined to be cheerful, anyhow. Two boats were floating bottom up, the keels laden with soldiers sitting astride, and they looked like so many school kids having a joyful time, rather than men who were momentarily in danger of being pitched into the sea and drowned. We picked up the 'crew' of one of the up-turned boats, and several others who were swimming about and on the rafts. Others were picked up by the hospital ship 'Neuralia,' and a British gun boat and destroyer, all of which were in attendance when we came up. Other destroyers were 'flying' around searching for the submarine, having apparently been summoned by wireless. It was a sight worth seeing to watch their rapid manoeuvering over the water. The 'Southland,' meanwhile, was moving very slowly, but still able to move off under her own steam at about 1.30 p.m."

When it was ascertained that the stricken vessel was not sinking, a number of volunteers—6 officers and 12 men—entered the stokehold and discharged the duties of firemen until she reached Lemnos. In the party was Private C. M. Bowden, a member of "A" Company, 21st Battalion. Bowden afterwards became a respected and valued member of the 21st Machine Gun Section, and later, of the Company, from which he was sent to a Cadet School for Officers in England. Upon his return to France, he was posted to the 22nd Battalion, and achieved the notable distinction of being the only Officer in that Battalion to meet his death during the attack on Ville-sur-Ancre in May, 1918.

After a short stay at Lemnos, the Sections were moved to Gallipoli; the 21st and 24th per the "Abbasieh," the 22nd per the "Osmanieh," and the 23rd per the "Partridge." By the 8th September, all had landed, and after a brief stay in Rest and other gullies, moved into the line.

All ranks were deeply shocked at the appearance of the men of the 1st Division who were relieved by the Brigade. Their wasted frames, gaunt faces, bespoke of the hardships they had endured. They were obviously delighted to get away to Lemnos shortly after for a well earned rest.

The 21st took over from the 5th and 8th Battalions, and manned no less than 8 guns in different positions at Courtney's and Steel's Posts. The 22nd relieved 4 gun teams at Johnson's Jolly. The 23rd (4 guns), and 24th (5 guns), took over from positions in, and close to, Lone Pine. Without any alteration in the Section Establishment, the disposition was arranged in accordance with the tactical requirements and the guns available. The allotment necessitated the absorption of the reserve Sections and, in addition, men from the Battalions were taken on strength and gradually trained as gunners. In this way the personnel was strengthened to meet the Machine Gun Defence of the Brigade front.

All the guns were zoned to give cross-fire to the frontage held. In some instances they were emplaced in "secret" positions with orders not to open fire except in cases of attack. Sometime later, the Pine guns were administered as a "Lone Pine Defensive Unit," the duties of C.O. being shared by Lieutenants J. H. Drummond and J. Needham. Another change was the appointment of Lieutenant W. J. Darley as Brigade Machine Gun Officer, the subsequent vacancy in the 21st being filled by the promotion of Sergeant J. E. Stone to Second Lieutenant.

PRE-COMPANY RECORDS.

The Sections soon settled down to the novel conditions which made no great demands beyond the daily routine of cleaning their guns and rifles, the constant repair of trenches necessitated by shell-fire, and improvements and some alterations to positions. With the end of the major and costly operations by the 1st Division during the previous month, offensive operations had definitely ceased, and upon the newcomers devolved the duties of garrison troops. On the whole, very little firing was done. No. 2 Section fired but one gun, and that was but a burst during the last week of occupation when a "silent stunt" was in progress. A Turkish patrol approached Lance Corporal A. Payton's gun, whereupon he opened fire and killed one or two. For this action he was placed under open arrest, but subsequently exonerated. No. 1 Section was not encouraged to fire, their guns fired but rarely, and only at long intervals. Some of the "Pine" guns joined in occasionally during "demonstrations," but the intention was almost entirely in the way of tests as to firing capabilities. At one point, the 23rd's No. 2 gun could engage enemy parties, and some shooting was done by one of the 24th, which caused observed casualties.

In one respect, the Sections differed from their Battalions in so far that, while the latter maintained frequent and regular reliefs out of the line, the Sections did not. It was possible for a man to obtain leave for a few hours to visit the beach for a much needed bath, but apart from that, the positions were manned continuously day and night by the same teams. At times, some teams "side-slipped" to other positions, but the inexorable routine went on.

It is not surprising that, in common with the rest of the garrison, the health of the men deteriorated sharply. The monotonous food—of which "bully beef" formed an appreciable part—the confinement, the presence of numerous bodies buried in the parapet and often disturbed by bursting shells, the presence of lice and millions of flies, many fleas, and a shortage of water, all combined to lower the vitality of the men. Small cuts and sores quickly became septic, and digestive troubles were common.

The complaint was made that, while the Infantry were being sent away with jaundice and similar ailments, men in the Sections similarly afflicted had to remain. This measure was doubtless due to the shortage of trained men and the importance attached to the Machine Gun Defence Scheme. A keen observer has recorded: "Our second reinforcements arrived six weeks after us, and I was amazed to see how full-faced and fresh complexioned they were by comparison with the rest of us."

The "blizzard" which swept over Gallipoli on the 27th November affected severely the men in the physical condition described. It is true the deep trenches afforded some measure of protection, but many were caught wearing the depleted clothing of the earlier and warmer months. They shivered in the unofficial "shorts" with which many were clad, and wondered what the advancing winter would be like. Some looked on snow for the first time, and marvelled at the transformation wrought by it. The low temperature brought other problems affecting the guns, and these called for immediate attention. To prevent the freezing of the water in the barrel casing (which would have made the gun unworkable) short bursts were fired at intervals. Some teams managed to secure a quantity of glycerine from the beach, which was placed, with water, in the barrel casing, to retard freezing. Others used fat lamps for the same purpose. The measures taken appeared to have been successful, but no extended trial, in the circumstances, was necessary. The "blizzard" was, fortunately, of short duration, and had the beneficial effect of killing off many of the flies which so sorely tried the troops, and reducing the high rate of sickness.

On the 29th November, the Division experienced its first severe bombardment, when heavy shells, up to 11 inch calibre, fell for two hours and a half, mainly upon Lone Pine. The 23rd and 24th Battalions suffered over 100 casualties, in which the Machine Gun Sections shared. The heavy shelling brought about the collapse of the walls of the deep trenches, and many of the garrison were trapped thereby and suffocated. The 24th Battalion Section retained very vivid memories of the strenuous service rendered by a stretcher bearer of the 12th Field Ambulance, named S. H. Kirby, and others, who dug out many of their buried comrades.

After the bombardment on the 29th November, it was recognised that the holding of the line would be seriously affected by the growing weight of the enemy artillery. Work on "winter quarters" was proceeded with, but no one guessed that evacuation was contemplated. When the announcement was made, it met with receptions varying according to the temperament of the individual. In accordance with the policy of depletion, some teams and guns were withdrawn into the

Plugge's Plateau garrison. These took the packs of their comrades remaining on post. The night of the final stage (19th December) found a proportion of the teams in the line with Sections of infantry, who were the last to leave. All guns and tripods and spare parts were brought out, but the ammunition had, perforce, to be left behind. No mishap marred the final stages, and with a deep feeling of thankfulness the last teams clambered into the waiting boats. All ranks were greatly impressed by the smoothness and precision with which the admirable Military and Naval Staff arrangements were carried out, which enabled a bloodless and successful withdrawal from under the noses of an alert and watchful enemy.

The Battalions, which had been disjointed during the evacuation, re-assembled at Lemnos, where the first Christmas away from home was celebrated, a notable event being the issue of Australian Christmas "billies." The 22nd Battalion Section felt aggrieved because the "billies" issued to it were not of Victorian origin. They paraded to Colonel R. Smith, who promptly put them on fatigue work—cleaning up the lines—for their pains.

Early in the New Year, the Sections, in conformity with their respective Battalions, returned to Egypt, and disembarked at Alexandria. The 21st and 22nd were taken by the "Ascanius," and the 23rd and 24th on the "Minnewaska." Some of the guns were mounted on both vessels for possible action against enemy submarines, but the return voyage was uneventful in both cases.

Such, briefly, were the experiences of the Machine Gun Sections on Gallipoli. In surveying the general results, it must be said that little had been learned in the use of the gun as a weapon; it was left to a wider and more exacting theatre to develop a high standard of excellence. On the other hand, much had been learned, and permanently absorbed, of the incidentals of trench warfare. These may be summarised as: The effects of shell-fire, the use of cover, how to deal with enemy snipers, the digging and erection of gun positions, the maintenance of guns and ammunition in a state of instant readiness, the working of regular and continuous shifts, the care and distribution of water and rations by teams, and attention to wounded comrades. The three months' sojourn in trenches had developed a certain measure of the "team" spirit, and was accompanied by a larger acceptance of the unrelenting routine of an army in the field. Another outcome was the gradual emergence of leaders to whom the control of the internal economy could be safely entrusted, and to some extent the elimination of the incompetent and the physically unfit. It will be observed that the foundations of the new Company's personnel had been tried and tested as far as the exigencies of the days in Egypt and Gallipoli permitted.

CHAPTER II.

FORMATION OF THE COMPANY.

1st-18th March, 1916.

Upon arrival at Alexandria, the Battalions immediately entrained for Cairo, and thence to Tel-el-Kebir on the Cairo-Ismailia railway, and in due course entered the very large concentration camp then in process of formation on the battlefield of that name. In this camp, perhaps two miles long, was gathered practically all of the then rapidly expanding A.I.F. Thousands of reinforcements from Australia were awaiting absorption, and the great "meeting of the waters" provided many interesting experiences. Brothers and friends among the later arrivals sought out their connections among those who had passed their baptism of fire, with some degree of respect as for a higher order. Their eager questions did not fall on deaf ears, and the "veterans" were nothing loath to relate more or less actual experiences to the "greenhorns," and, at the same time, carefully preserve a wide imaginary line between themselves and the newcomers. Reorganisation on a wholesale plan was afoot; new theatres of war, other lands and experiences loomed ahead, and all ranks felt the throb of life at its fullest flow and the lure of distant fields.

General training was at once resumed. The long confinement in deep trenches on Gallipoli had induced a certain slackness in deportment and dress. The latter was corrected by the issue of deficiencies in clothing and equipment, and the former by squad, platoon, and company drill. The older men were grimly amused when they were called on to do saluting by numbers and other elementary drill. The Machine-Gun Sections completed their establishments. A few reinforcements were taken on strength, but vacancies were filled almost entirely by drawing upon the older men in their respective Battalions.

In a very short time all ranks showed a marked improvement in health and appearance. A reinforcement who had managed to get a transfer into the 23rd Battalion Section, recorded his impressions when the Brigade arrived from Gallipoli: "The returned have a worn, quiet look; evidently they have been tamed and have finally settled down to the life—something we have to learn." With renewed enthusiasm, all hands became expert at gun drill, mechanism, rectification of gun stoppages, and finally a course of actual firing at large earthen bricks. Reserve Sections were also trained.

The adjacent battlefield, where Lord Wolseley had inflicted a notable defeat on Arabi Pasha during the revolt in 1882, was an object of much interest. The old trenches were still in existence, and some men unearthed Martini Henry cartridges and other relics. The nearby cemetery, containing the graves of the British dead who fell in the fighting, was visited, and a silent tribute paid to the red-coats by the khaki-clad men from the South.

Other memories of Tel-el-Kebir include the "two up" schools, which flourished exceedingly. Never before or since in the history of the A.I.F., were such numbers seen devoted to the pastime which was often carried on at night by the aid of lamps and torches. "Crown and Anchor" came in for its share, and others, to whom the gambling spirit did not appeal, found much interest in listening to the glib patter of the proprietors of the boards. One enterprising individual was wont to declare to sundry listeners, "You come here paupers and you go away millionaires."

A restricted amount of leave to Cairo—distant about 70 miles by railway—was given. This was supplemented by some who absented themselves for a few days, and were quite content, upon return, to have a fine entered in their pay books, and to endure a term of "C.B." "It was well worth it" declared more than one delinquent.

Some evidence of the reorganisation and training was observed on the 15th January, when General Murray, British Commandant in Egypt, inspected the 1st and 2nd Australian Divisions formed up in mass. About 15,000 men, newly equipped and clothed, were on parade. They presented a magnificent spectacle of bronzed and virile manhood.

Speculation and discussion as to the next move was a daily subject. It was obvious that such large bodies of troops would not be held in comparative idleness very long. The spectacle of trains laden with material which ran eastwards day and night, suggested a move to the Suez Canal. No great surprise was felt

FORMATION OF THE COMPANY.

when the announcement was made that the famous waterway would be the scene of the next operations.

At the end of January and early February, the Brigade entrained for Ismailia, and from thence moved to a point about ten miles east of the Canal, where defensive positions were taken up in conformity with the very extensive lines of defence laid down by the British Army Authorities. Although the march did not exceed 20 miles, in three stages, the route was over deep, undulating sand, and it proved very exhausting. In addition to marching order, each man carried a blanket, 150 rounds of ammunition, and two days' rations.

As part of the scheme of defence, a proportion of the guns was mounted in selected positions, for which gun pits and belt filling chambers were built in the all-pervading sand. Sand-bags and wooden frames, over which canvas was stretched, were used. The high winds caused much movement in the sand—so much so that on a number of occasions positions dug overnight were completely filled and covered by morning, necessitating a search for them.

Meanwhile the daily gun training went on. The Reserve Sections received considerable attention and gradually became efficient. At this time, the Lewis automatic rifle or machine-gun was issued to the Infantry Battalions, and the advent of that weapon resulted in the transfer, from the Machine Gun Sections, of a number of skilled officers and men. These transfers necessitated the filling of vacancies and the training of fresh men.

Out in the vast desert, with little but sand and sky to look upon, the Battalions were thrown very much on themselves. The time passed happily, nevertheless. Concerts (without the accompaniment of musical instruments), and boxing contests, helped to pass the time. At first, rations were light, but soon increased in quantity as to appear ample, being supplemented by the Australian Comforts Fund. Supplies were delivered daily over the final stages by means of camel teams. The appearance of those teams was carefully looked for each morning. It meant that the limited quantity of water could be consumed for another day at least. Men became expert in the matter of a bath with one quart of water.

With the approach of summer, the danger of a Turkish attack quickly faded. With its disappearance, the next move became a much-debated subject. Some favoured Salonica, others various thrusts at the Turk in Asia Minor, but France had support. Finally, all doubts were set at rest when General Legge announced a move to France. Soon after, on the 7th March, a New Zealand Brigade took over the sector, and the Brigade marched in, in good order, to Ferry Post to complete its internal arrangements before proceeding to the Western Front.

In view of an early departure, certain changes in Brigade organisation were taken in hand and expedited. One of these was the detachment from the Infantry Battalions of their Maxim machine-gun sections, and the formation of those sections into brigade machine-gun companies, controlled from Brigade headquarters. The formation of machine-gun companies marked a definite change in the administration and development of machine-gunnery in the A.I.F., and was followed by further developments during the campaign in France.

Instructions as to formation were received from 2nd Divisional Headquarters on the 27th February, and preliminary steps were taken next day to comply with the order. Captain W. J. Darley, who had acted as Brigade Machine Gun Officer on Gallipoli was appointed to command the new Company, and arrangements were made to assemble the component parts at Ferry Post on the Suez Canal. The 22nd Battalion Section was the first to be detached from its parent Battalion on the 2nd March. The others followed some days later. On the morning of the 9th, the now assembled Company crossed the Canal, marched to Ordnance Stores at Ismailia, handed in its Maxim guns, spare parts, and Mark VI rifles, and received in exchange 16 Vickers Light Guns, spare parts, and Mark VII rifles. The Mark IV tripods were retained. From Ismailia, the Company, in proud possession of its new weapons, marched to Moascar and camped.

Ten days were spent at Moascar. The first steps were to organise the Company on the lines laid down. The establishment provided for a personnel of 10 officers and 142 other ranks, and certain equipment which will be noted. The personnel was apportioned as follows:—

FORMATION OF THE COMPANY.

	Officers.	Other Ranks.
Company Headquarters. †		
Commanding Officer (Major or Captain)*	1	
Company Sergeant-Major (Warrant Officer, Class II)		1
Quartermaster Sergeant		1
Signallers		4
Artificer		1
Cook		1
Storeman		1
†*Four Gun Sections, each of four gun teams.*		
Commanding Officer (Lieutenant)	4	
Second in Command (Lieutenant)	4	
Sergeants (2)		8
Corporals (2)		8
Gunners (including batmen)		88
Transport Section.		
Sergeant		1
Corporal		1
Lance Corporals		2
Farrier		1
Saddler		1
Cook		1
Drivers		22
	9	142

To give effect to the foregoing, certain changes in officers and non-commissioned officers were made. In the 21st Battalion Section, Lieutenant J. E. Stone was transferred (at his own request) to the newly-formed Lewis Gun Section of that Battalion, and Sergeants R. C. Callister and F. Windsor were promoted to Second Lieutenant. In the 22nd Battalion Section, Lieutenant P. Stewart was transferred to another command, and Sergeant J. D. Campbell was promoted to Second Lieutenant. From the 23rd Battalion, Lieutenant A. J. Noall came to the Company. In the 24th, Lieutenant R. F. Bennett had succeeded Lieutenant J. Needham, and Sergeant F. J. Blenkarn was promoted to Second Lieutenant. The first officers and non-commissioned officers in the Company were:—

* A Second in Command (Captain) was authorised in May, 1916.
† A Company Clerk (Corporal) was authorised in August, 1916.

Company Headquarters.

Officers.
Captain W. J. Darley.

Non-Commissioned Officers.
No. 1028 C.S.M. A. Palling.
No. 1615 C.Q.M.S. H. L. Smith.
No. 1567 Cpl. R. W. Watt (Coy. Clerk).
No. 1059 Cpl. R. H. E. Dixon (Signallers).

No. 1 Section.

2nd Lieut. R. C. Callister.
2nd Lieut. F. Windsor.

No. 32 Sgt. J. E. Hopper.
No. 301 Sgt. R. D. Desmond.
No. 928 Cpl. E. Moffatt.
No. 198 Cpl. J. L. Stapleton.
No. 701 L./Cpl. F. J. Nixon.
No. 2107 L./Cpl. R. A. Armstrong.
No. 144 L./Cpl. W. Dutton.
No. 703 L./Cpl. H. G. Oldham.

No. 2 Section.

2nd Lieut. A. N. McLennan.
2nd Lieut. J. D. Campbell.

No. 70 Sgt. C. F. Murrell.
No. 1761 Sgt. M. Quinn.
No. 700 Cpl. J. W. Torrens.
No. 656 Cpl. A. L. Newlands.
No. 586 L./Cpl. R. Dodgshun.
No. 826 L./Cpl. S. F. Hall.
No. 371 L./Cpl. A. E. Fair.
No. 7 L./Cpl. A. Payton.

No. 3 Section.

Lieut. J. H. Drummond.
Lieut. A. J. Noall.

No. 62 Sgt. G. Woodburgess.
No. 60 Sgt. H. L. Wilhelm.
No. 148 Cpl. F. Hickey.
No. 457 Cpl. J. W. Taylor.
No. 4 L./Cpl. W. H. Butterworth.
No. 1123 L./Cpl. J. T. Milnes.
No. 1200 L./Cpl. G. B. Crerar.
No. 1039 L./Cpl. A. G. Stevens.

FORMATION OF THE COMPANY.

No. 4 Section.

2nd Lieut. R. F. Bennett.
2nd Lieut. F. J. Blenkarn.

No.   11 Sgt. O. H. Bailey.
No. 105 Sgt. E. J. Bice.
No.   19 Cpl. A. P. Hitchcock.
No. 1534 Cpl. A. P. Earle.
No. 1753 L./Cpl. M. J. O'Brien.
No.   15 L./Cpl. A. E. Coe.
No.   20 L./Cpl. E. Mackley.
No. 993 L./Cpl. J. Brandebura.

Transport Section.

2nd Lieut. J. D. Campbell
(transferred from No. 2)

No.   57 Sgt. T. Smith.
No. 3318 Cpl. C. Callaghan.
No. 564 L./Cpl. P. D. Bell.
No. 1768 L./Cpl. J. J. Passeri.

The Company Establishment provided for equipment as follows:—

Material.

16 Vickers Light Machine-Guns, with spare parts, ammunition-belts, and belt boxes.
16 Tripods, Mark IV.
   Artificers' Tools.
 8 Four-horse Limbers (Gun Limbers).
 4 Two-horse Limbers (Ammunition Limbers).
 1 Water Cart.
 1 Cook's Cart.
   Signallers' Telephones, with wire and tools.
 4 Bicycles.

Animals.

*43 Light Draught Horses.
* 9 Riding Horses.

   * Increased in the following August to 11 Riding and 45 Light Draughts.

The Transport Section was not formed until arrival in France; its advent will be noted later. The four gun sections were constituted by maintaining the old Battalion sections practically unchanged; an arrangement which had the merit of convenience without disturbing the well-established camaraderie in the various gun teams. Each Section was thus enabled to continue its internal economy without a break. Officially the Sections were designated Nos. 1, 2, 3, and 4, but it was not until after the fighting at Pozieres that the Battalion numbers finally ceased to be used and the Company emerged a coherent body; its Battalion memories and traditions, superimposed by a new Company spirit, outlook, and a jealously guarded reputation.

It should be said that the formation of the new unit was not accompanied by any enthusiasm. Regret was felt and expressed that the association with the Battalions had come to an end. The men were mainly indifferent, though some were resentful at the change made. As one of the 21st said: "We had done a lot towards making the reputation of the red and black diamond, and now had to make a fresh start in a smaller unit." It was recognised that no appeal could be made, so little time was lost in repining. "Make the best of it" was a fairly general conclusion.

The new weapons sufficed to hold the close attention of all ranks during the next few days. The teams were drilled in gun mounting and instructed in the internal mechanism. It was noted that no radical difference existed as compared with the older Maxim, but the difference in weight (24 lbs.) was much appreciated.† Some of the thoughtful ones desired to know why the same economy of metal was not extended to the tripod. As soon as the first stage of instruction had been passed, the guns were put to the actual test of firing. Except for one instance of a bulged barrel, they emerged successfully.

An amusing incident was witnessed at that first firing practice. One officer was firing, evidently for the first time, and another observing. On the range being reported short, the temporary gunner merely raised the tangent sight and resumed firing. Again the range was reported short, again the sight was raised. The operation was repeated for the third time before it dawned on the gunner or his observer that the gun had not been elevated.

---

† See Appendices J and K for illustration and short specification of the Vickers machine-gun.

FORMATION OF THE COMPANY.

Meanwhile, all clothing had been treated by a steam bath in the Foden fumigator, with the object of destroying all vermin. One definite result was that each man received back a collection of pathetic looking articles, which he proceeded to resume with a certain degree of sorrow. Another precaution taken was to innoculate everyone with Mixed Typhoid, Paratyphoid A, and Paratyphoid B Vaccines.

A more popular event was the daily swimming parade in the Bitter Lakes. The sight of thousands of nude, athletic Australians disporting themselves as school boys was a picture to remain long in the memory.

On the 18th March, H.R.H. the Prince of Wales and General Birdwood inspected the troops in the Moascar area. The great majority of those present saw the Prince for the first time, and at once expressed their appreciation of the Heir to the Throne. After viewing the units, the Prince made an informal inspection of the Camp and was informally welcomed, though none the less enthusiastically, by large crowds who greeted him with many remarks of a homely nature, while all the rules of military discipline went by the board for the time being. The unaffected demeanour of the Prince won the hearts of those who saw him that day—a regard which ensured him a hearty welcome in later days when he came in contact with Australian troops.

In accordance with the colour patch scheme of the A.I.F., the Company was allotted the red diamond of the 6th Brigade as its distinguishing badge. The patch did not come into general use till a few weeks later, but reference may be made here. It cannot be said that it was favourably received Indeed, in some cases, it met a hostile reception. Objection was raised, not against the red diamond as such, but because it superseded the Battalion colours to which the men had become attached. Protests were, of course, useless, and the new emblem was adopted with very bad grace. It is interesting to note that two years later, when the red diamond was in turn superseded, the order regarding the change was stubbornly and calmly ignored and men had to be individually and specifically ordered to make the change. During those two years, they had conceived a deep and lasting affection for the one-time unwelcome stranger.

By this time, the new Company had, to external appearances, shaken down to something like a coherent body. The daily Company parades, the settling of numerous details, the wider outlook, and the excitement of adventures in fresh fields, all combined to inculcate the beginning of that intense "family" spirit which subsequently became the Company's outstanding characteristic. Three evacuations due to sickness took place during this period, but all returned after a few days at field ambulance.

Thus was the Company duly formed. In the land of one of the oldest civilisations, and upon historic ground, these youthful crusaders from the youngest nation were brought together to handle the deadliest weapon in modern warfare.

CHAPTER III.

Across the Mediterranean.

19th-24th March, 1916.

On the night of the 18th March, the members of the newly-formed Company commenced their final departure from Egypt. Camp was struck at 11 p.m., and in company with other Brigade units, entrainment was made at 2 a.m. on the 19th, for Alexandria.

Rain is an unusual event in Egypt, and, as if to mark the departure of the sojourners, a steady downpour of an hour's duration was accorded the speeding guests. Open trucks had been provided, and, as a result, the remainder of the night was spent in dire misery. A wet, bedraggled, and tired Company huddled together on the floor of the jolting trucks and tried in vain to sleep. Fortunately, the morning broke fine. The train then presented an extraordinary appearance owing to the wet blankets being attached to all points of vantage and flying in the wind. The natives were quick to take advantage of the opportunity for trading, especially as they enjoyed a strong tactical position owing to the troops being confined to the trucks—a position which they exploited to the full. The stops made were of uncertain length, and only the venturesome essayed a short sortie after a native who made off with the "change" due from a transaction in dates, fruit, and the inevitable "eggs-a-cook." In most cases the "Gippos" had the last word.

Alexandria was reached at 11 a.m. on the morning of the 19th, and embarkation was at once made on the now familiar "Minnewaska." Other troops were 6th Brigade Headquarters, 21st Battalion, Field Artillery, and some horses. The chief topic for discussion was the port of destination. The rest of the day was spent on board, and the Company had ample opportunity for studying the city from the transport. The Company strength on embarkation was stated (officially) at nine officers, 141 other ranks, and two horses.

Next day the leaden coloured "Minnewaska" steamed out at 10 a.m. alone and unescorted — a fact which made everyone realise that serious business lay ahead and that the comparatively easy days in Egypt were gone forever. Enemy submarines were active in the Mediterranean; a fact which, however, did not unduly depress the spirit of the troops. That the danger was real was evidenced by the torpedoing of the "Minneapolis" on the morning of the 23rd, when a wireless message was received to that effect. The "Minneapolis" was returning empty from Marseilles, after landing the first batch of Australians at that port. She eventually sank near Malta.

As some sort of precaution, eight of the Company's guns were mounted in various parts of the transport, and crews stood on guard throughout the day and night. Lifebelts were worn during the day and generally used as pillows at night. The "Minnewaska" was a roomy ship, but little provision was made for sleeping accommodation. The men lay about on the floors and tables. No lights were allowed at night, consequently the changing of guards and teams was a matter of great difficulty to both outgoing and incoming men. In moving across the crowded floor, many unintentional and undeserved kicks were given and received—events which usually called forth forcible comment. If, in the search for his "place," a man struck a match, the comments were more forcible, and were often accompanied by threats of grievous bodily violence. The prospect of a watery grave on a dark night did not appeal to anyone.

Although the weather was fine, some seasickness was reported, but generally speaking, the troops were able to enjoy a good passage, admire the blue water of the Mediterranean, and express some wonder at its dimensions. Some speculation was indulged in as to how much longer the journey was rendered by the continual zig-zagging course of the ship—a measure taken to counter a possible torpedo attack. The day before arrival at port, another inoculation had to be endured, the same vaccines being used as noted in the previous chapter.

Historic France at last! Marseilles was reached at 4 p.m. on the 24th March, after a voyage of four days. The approach on a fine afternoon afforded all hands an excellent opportunity of studying the breakwater, docks, and shipping of the port. With that distant view they had to be content, although a few enterprising ones managed to get ashore.

CHAPTER IV.

EARLY DAYS IN FRANCE: FLEURBAIX-ERQUINGHEM.

25th March-10th June, 1916.

It has been said that first impressions are lasting. When they are accompanied by circumstances of beauty and novelty, the effect is increased a hundredfold. The entry of the Company into the "Western Front" was an unforgettable experience for those who entered it by way of Marseilles and the Rhone Valley.

Of Marseilles, little was seen as the troops marched from the boat to the train. Departure was made at 9.15 a.m. on the 25th March, so all day was available for those first impressions. To eyes that so long had dwelt on the barren hillsides of Gallipoli and the vast stretches of the sandy deserts of Egypt and Sinai, the view presented was one of continuous delight. Centuries of toil, it appeared, had combed the land into cultivated beauty then flushed with the tender green of Spring. It came upon the beholders that the unfolding scene was something they had only dimly comprehended from old-world pictures which had appeared artificial and unreal. Here was the reality, fresh and living. To the north-east, the distant Alps formed a blue and fitting background, and as the train sped northwards, enchanting glimpses of the stately Rhone were obtained. "All day long," wrote one diarist, "we passed through scenes that were perfectly lovely in their sylvan beauty. Many miles of farms, homesteads, olive groves, vineyards, interspersed with cities and towns connected by good roads; houses built of stone and tiled—two or more stories high—so quaint with their settings of gardens and trees; everything trim and clean, it looked like a vast estate presided over by one mind. Every bit of land was under cultivation. Away in the distance, a great mountain range gave a fitting background to the picture, which, however, had another side. The whole country appeared deserted except for women and children and a few old men. Many of the women were in black and all appeared subdued. In the towns passed through, all we saw at the stations were a few railway employees; in some cases women were at work in the goods-sheds."

The effect on the men was that of an intoxicant. Crowding at the windows of the carriages, they cheered the inhabitants, the country, and themselves. Struggling with their very limited French, they sought to explain their delight by adding a strange mixture of Australian slang and tags of Arabic. It is certain that the residents understood little of the spoken word, but of the purport they could have little doubt. With their unfailing courtesy, they acknowledged everything. It was the first contact of Australian troops with the French people, who were delighted by the appearance of their new and unconventional allies.

As night approached, the eight occupants of the tiny compartments of third class railway carriages — burdened with rifles, packs, and gear — realised that little, if any, sleep would be possible. Such proved to be the case. The long train jogged along in fits and starts and the tired and cramped men slept in like fashion.

A closer study of the towns, next day, emphasised the fact that no able-bodied men were to be seen. Old men and women were at work in the fields, assisted by children, and women were doing the manual work in the towns.

As the train moved northwards and approached the industrial areas, the landscape underwent a modification. It was apparent that Winter held sway; grey skies, bare trees, and hedges, and a wet countryside, took the place of the warmer and smiling South. The approach to Paris caused many eyes to turn in that direction, but the delectable city was passed—at some distance—during the night.

The city of Amiens was reached on the third day of the railway journey. Continuing northward and gradually approaching the "Front," signs of occupation by the British army were observed. The presence of "Tommies" in billets, army transport on the roads, and the recurring sounds of distant explosions combined to blot out the earlier impressions of a smiling countryside, and to substitute an atmosphere in which grim war held sway.

To the intense relief of everyone, the town of Aire was reached at 4 p.m. on the afternoon of the 27th March, and the long and tedious railway journey of three days and two nights came to an end. With darkening skies and a wintry atmosphere, the Company set out for billets at Rincq. Soon after starting, rain fell and continued in a steady downpour. No great distance had to be traversed, but the guide lost his bearings while taking a short cut down a lane. Here the Company made its first acquaintance with the mud of Flanders—fortunately not much over ankle deep. Captain Darley led the party and Lieutenant Drummond began his many practices in French upon the bystanders. For the first time was heard in France, the comment, "O-Oh! out come the maps—lost again!" It was a rain-soaked and mud-spattered Company which reached its destination at dusk. Billets were arranged which, though large and draughty, offered welcome relaxation after the close confinement of small railway carriages.

The next few days were very cold, and some snow fell. The uncongenial weather, however, did not check the spirits of the Australian abroad. He slipped into the role of tourist automatically, as it were. The towns and villages of the adjacent countryside were at once thoroughly explored, the "estaminets" tested as to their liquor stocks, and all available avenues of food supply closely investigated. With their large appetites and liberal pay, they fairly took away the breath of the local populace by their demands for eggs, chips, and excellent coffee. Madam was distinctly embarrassed when these strange big men from the Antipodes swarmed into her kitchen and made themselves at home with their playful ways and light hearts. What they lacked in knowledge of the language, they made up with a strange medley of Australian slang, tags of Arabic, and odds and ends of French. France — or rather that part of it — was indeed subjected to another invasion.

The men soon became aware of a marked similarity in billets in the villages of Northern France. Nearly all seemed to possess —in addition to the farmhouse—a large barn and stables built round a wide, shallow pit for stable refuse, a well and pump immediately adjoining, and in some cases a large dog whose chief function appeared to be to operate a treadmill which actuated a butter churn. The men were quartered in the barns or stables, sometimes with straw for bedding, sometimes without; the officers were given rooms in the dwelling, sometimes with beds, sometimes without. Other points of uniformity were the large white Percheron horses—large of body but small of head—the small holdings worked by horse and hand labour, and the methods of intense cultivation. These and other matters were objects of much interest during the first days in France while billeted with the civilian populace. The men were quick to appreciate the comparative comfort of troops in reserve positions, after the experience of Egyptian camps and the cramped areas of Gallipoli. The free and easy ways of the Australian at this time appeared to be in sharp contrast to established military customs, and Brigade Headquarters devoted some of its attention to matters of dress and the saluting of officers, the Company duly receiving its share.

Training in the handling of the new weapon was at once resumed, and all ranks gradually became familiar with its construction. In addition to gun mounting, rectification of stoppages and mechanism, some firing was done against a high bank in an adjacent lane, which was used as a short range. A few days later, gas helmets were issued. Known officially as P.H.G., they were made of flannelette, U-shaped, and when placed over the head the bottom end was tucked inside the collar of the tunic. Large goggle-like eyes allowed a limited field of vision through mica "glasses," which were apt to become cloudy after short use. Inward breathing was done from the air which passed through the chemically impregnated flannelette, while the exhausted air was expelled through a rubber mouthpiece. The inmate was always conscious of partial suffocation, and at those first trials many fervent hopes were expressed that incarcerations would never be of long duration. At this time, Lieutenant R. C. Callister was detached for instruction in anti-gas measures, at an Army School, and subsequently became Company Gas Officer. In that capacity he inflicted much conscientious gas drill on a long-suffering Company, but he had his reward in so far that it is believed that not a single gas casualty was suffered that could have been prevented by the use of a gas-mask.

On the 1st April, Captain W. J. Darley returned to the 21st Battalion, and was succeeded by Captain L. F. S. Hore—late 8th Light Horse Regiment—as Commanding Officer. The newcomer was not a machine-gunner, and made that fact clear in his first address to the Company. All ranks, however, paid him the compliment of taking him for what he appeared to be, i.e., an officer and a gentleman, and they were not disappointed. His success in moulding his untried charge will be referred to later.

Company duties were not onerous at first. After the daily routine was completed, the nearby old-fashioned town of Aire was often visited. Its shops and estaminets functioned much as usual, although it was entirely drained of men of military age—a

Sir John Gellibrand, K.C.B., D.S.O.

feature of all French towns and villages. During one of these visits, some members of the Company witnessed an inspection of the 21st and 22nd Battalions by Lord Kitchener.

After eight days at Rincq, the Company—in conformity with the move of the 6th Brigade—marched out in the early afternoon of the 4th April for Haverskerque. The distance traversed was about eleven miles, in four and a half hours. Several stretches of the march were done over cobblestones, which provided painful experience for feet rendered soft by contact with the sands of Egypt and Sinai. Cobblestones, in later days, always conjured up memories of their first acquaintance, and the utter distress of that first day.

The march was resumed next morning. Sailly was reached in the afternoon—14 miles distant. The cobblestones did not appear so painful, nevertheless the Company was glad to reach its destination. The marches of the two preceding days had brought the Brigade in close proximity to the British Front. Preliminary arrangements for taking over a Brigade Sector were made, while similar details were arranged by the 7th Brigade for the first entry of Australian troops into the Western Front. The Company had a day's rest at Sailly, and had ample opportunity to listen to the steady but continuous explosions by day and at night, the rattle of machine-gun and rifle fire, and the regular discharge of the brilliant illuminating flares from the German line, which rose always at the same angle, poised momentarily high in the air, and curved with a graceful sweep to earth.

Next evening (the 7th) the Company marched to Port A'Clous farm on the outskirts of the village of Fleurbaix, and billeted there. Although the final stage was done after nightfall to a reserve position, elaborate precautions against noise and smoking were taken—precautions which, in later days, would have given rise to considerable hilarity. During the day, one gun Section had moved into front line positions and relieved gunners of the 101st Brigade of the 34th Division. It so happened that the 7th Machine Gun Company sent its first relieving Section in on the previous day, and thus claimed—by a few hours—to be the first Company to enter the Western Front. It subsequently happened that in the last engagement of the A.I.F. the 6th Company was the last Machine Gun Company to leave the line, and thus narrowly missed the double distinction of being the first and last to engage in hostilities,

Fleurbaix was close to the front line, deserted by its inhabitants, but most of its houses were still standing. The roads leading to the village were grass-grown, but many of the adjacent fields were tilled by the peasantry. Artillery lines were often sited in the open, but did not appear to be disturbed by the enemy. Transport in the forward areas by day was forbidden. No movement by large parties of men was permitted, and as a further precaution men had to walk close to houses and hedges and not reveal themselves to the observers in the stationary balloons which rose daily at intervals along the whole of the front that was visible.

During the next few days, the relief by the 6th Brigade was completed, and the Company's guns were disposed as follows:—

Brigade Left Sector: Four in front line emplacements, two at Jay Post.
Reserve Sector. One at Smith's Villa, one at Elbow Farm.
Brigade Right Sector: Two in front line emplacements, one at M.O. House, one at Brick Kiln Post.
In reserve at Port A'Clous Farm: Four.

Internal reliefs gave about four or five days in the line and reserves. The Section at Port A'Clous Farm did the usual Company fatigues and carried the rations forward daily.

The first entry to trenches in France was naturally a subject of absorbing interest. After the deep trenches dug out of the hard earth of Gallipoli, the men looked disdainfully at the built-up breastworks—in places without a parados—and frail shelters of the front line, and had much unfavourable comment to offer. Later, however, they realised that in that dank, low-lying country, excavation was not possible in the waterlogged earth. At the time of the Company's entry, trench warfare was still the order of the day, and the existing lines had been evolved from the days when the opposing armies, in a fruitless endeavour to outflank each other, had settled down to a stalemate. Front line conditions, however, were comfortable. Cooking was done therein, and smoke from the fires ascended from both sides without molestation. The various "bays" were numbered and locations could be found easily. The front gun positions were armoured, but they were suspected of being traps in an emergency. As far as the Company was concerned, reliefs were conducted with ease and in daylight; the relatively small unit of a gun team permitting it, a distinct advantage over the Infantry Battalions who, perforce, had to change under cover of darkness. Duckboards were laid along the trench floors, and fire-steps permitted a view across No Man's Land, which was seldom less than 200 yards across. Certain points in rear of the breastworks were marked, "Do not linger here—fixed rifle," an intimation that German thoroughness had selected that point upon which to discharge occasional shots from a fixed rifle.

At night the continual discharge of flares from the German line was a distinct novelty, and the operations of German machine-guns, which swept parapets and approaches with unfailing regularity, naturally appealed to the men of the Company. One gun in particular was both regular and accurate, and was known as "Parapet Joe." A member of No. 3 Section had cause to remember his first night in the line. After watching the regular and graceful rise and fall of the enemy flares, avoiding the periodic sweep of "Parapet Joe," and sensing that, after all, it was but the nightly routine, he laid his rifle on the parapet and "gave Fritz five rounds rapid." As he refilled the magazine, with some faint feelings of satisfaction, hurried footsteps were heard stumbling along the duckboards from the left. "S-s-stop firing!" gasped an excited infantryman, "Stop firing, we have a listening post out in front and you nearly shot us!"

Artillery activity was confined—by both sides—mainly to the shelling of houses and suspected observation posts in rear, and the front line enjoyed almost total immunity. Sniping by those set aside was practised daily, but the teams were occupied with the daily cleaning of guns, distribution of rations, and minor improvements in their quarters. The weather continued cold and showery, with occasional sleet and snow.

On the 13th April, Lieutenants Callister and Windsor, with Captain Nicholls of the 7th Machine Gun Company and others, attended a meeting at Croix du Bac, when the principles of indirect overhead fire from machine-guns were explained by an English Cyclist Machine Gun Unit. The method of shooting from maps, safety limits, etc., was explained, and elevation tables and graphs were supplied. Indirect overhead fire from machine-guns was in use by both sides in France, but the practice was entirely new to the Company. Briefly stated, the method was as follows:—The gun position and target having been located on the Army map, distance was determined by measurement, and the bearing from gun to target by means of a protractor. The next step was to ascertain, preferably by graph, whether the "cone of fire," i.e., the flight of bullets, conformed to the safety margin laid down by the Army authorities—a precaution rendered necessary because firing was invariably done over the heads of our own troops. Assuming the clearance was sufficient, the gun was laid on the bearing by means of a prismatic compass and then "levelled" by the aid of a clinometer, which was really a graduated spirit level. The gun was then regarded as being at "zero," and a marked stick was fixed a few yards in front as an aiming mark. The clinometer having been adjusted to the required angle, it was laid on the bed of the tangent sight of the gun, and the latter elevated to the desired point indicated on the clinometer. Assuming correct calculations, the gun was then in a position to open fire on the target. If the target was a road which could be enfiladed, the gunner had merely to elevate and depress in order to "search" for a given distance. If the target was a trench running at right angles to the gun, "traversing" was resorted to. A brass graduated dial was affixed to the tripod and a pointer on the gun indicated the degree of sweep or "traverse" by any lateral movement on the part of the gunner. Before firing, the legs of the tripod were braced with sandbags filled with earth to ensure a stable position, and further, to counteract the vibration during firing. As a precaution, the gun was depressed to the lowest safety point and a "stop" placed at that point to prevent it being, by any chance, brought below the margin of safety.

Like most innovations, the new idea was viewed with mixed feelings by the Company officers, who were the first to come in contact with it. However, preliminary steps were taken to carry out the first practices; maps were studied, targets and gun positions selected, and calculations worked out. The first venture was made on the 16th April, when three guns fired on a suspected German Headquarters and a tramway, both some little distance in rear of the enemy's front line. The distances varied from 1650 to 2000 yards. 3450 rounds were fired, and the only item recorded was the breaking of the muzzle-cups of the guns used, due probably to being clamped too tightly. After the first trial, the practice was continued almost daily and nightly. Observation of one target was possible, when an enemy working party was dispersed. The same day, however, the gun position was demolished by shell fire, fortunately without damage to gun or team. Firing was at first restricted to daylight hours, but after a few days the guns were "laid" during the day and fired at night as well. The early targets involved some searching, but it was some time before combined "searching" and "traversing" was used, the absence of traversing dials precluding the latter practice at night. For night work, a flame extinguisher was attached to the barrel and a further precaution taken to erect a hessian screen directly in front of the gun, through which the bullets only passed, care being taken to exclude nails or metal, which would cause deflection in the flight of the bullets.

It cannot be said that the early practices were an unqualified success. Indeed, on two occasions, bullets fell into our own front line, inflicting slight casualties on the garrison. These mishaps caused much consternation in the infantry battalions in the Brigade, and it was some time before their nervousness disappeared and they became accustomed to indirect machine-gun fire from their rear. After the mishaps, it became the usual custom to notify the infantry beforehand, and the Section Officer in the line would stand under the cone of fire and watch for shorts; but even the spectacle of the officer standing on the front parapet in a direct line with the gun, failed to carry conviction to the neighbouring infantry. It is but fair to record that the Company never again committed the error described. From that unpropitious commencement, however, it developed the practice with such precision and confidence that, some months later, the whole of the Company's guns were grouped in batteries, firing Creeping and S.O.S. barrages, and switching fire on to given targets at the sign of S.O.S. or the receipt of a telephone message—a proceeding which heartened the attacking infantry and earned their cordial appreciation.

The new use of the Vickers gun had the effect of changing it, in a large measure, from a weapon primarily of defence to one of offence. In stationary warfare, it became possible to harass the enemy when otherwise the guns would have had to remain silent. In offensive operations, its supporting fire became a regular feature in the preliminary stages. The altered functions affected very considerably the subsequent activities of the Company, and the development of which called for a greater degree of intelligence and responsibility on the part of officers and men, much toil in the transport of large quantities of ammunition, and the discharge of uninteresting duties in conditions of weather and circumstances which taxed their skill and endurance to the uttermost. That development will be noted in due course.

Towards the end of April, the weather gradually improved. The improvement was accompanied by aerial activity on both sides. The daring way in which the British airmen patrolled the lines pursued by bursting shells from the German anti-aircraft batteries, was a source of continuous interest and admiration. At times the interest was turned to sudden apprehension by the descent of shell-cases and shell fragments. Each side, as if by tacit agreement, refrained from shelling the front trench, so, all things considered, a tour of the line, though interesting and novel, was not particularly dangerous. The only loss was sustained on 26th April, when Private J. M. R. Taylor was wounded by shrapnel, and thus earned the distinction of being the first casualty in the line.

On the night of the 27th, the first gas alarm was sounded. That it was a false one did not detract from the excitement. Klaxon horns and gongs joined in a weird chorus, to which the artillery of both sides added its share. The suffocating helmets were donned for the first time in earnest, and the inmates peered through the dim eye-glasses to watch the brilliant effects caused by bursting shells and the rapid discharge of flares by the enemy. One diarist wrote, "We 'stood to' for an hour or more, prepared, but the storm subsided. Rather awe-inspiring flares rising, artillery, machine-guns, and rifles joining in one continuous crash."

The first tour of line duty came to an end on the 29th April, when the Brigade was relieved by the 2nd Australian Brigade of the 1st Division, which was then making its first acquaintance with the line. The Company was relieved without mishap by the 2nd Machine Gun Company, and marched to huts in Erquinghem, a village on the outskirts of Armentieres. By this change, the Brigade passed into Divisional reserve.

The Sections were fairly comfortable in Army huts, with boarded floors, upon which they slept. Headquarters were in an adjoining farm house, and the officers in neighbouring dwellings. Here the Company settled down to the most comfortable and easiest period of its existence. Almost immediately, Spring came with a burst of mild, warm weather, and effected a wondrous change in the countryside. The transformation came as by magic —trees and hedges burst into leaf and crops appeared. The change was reflected in the men—their health and spirits rose accordingly.

Company training was undertaken with thoroughness and regularity. Some fast times in gun-mounting were established. The usual gun work was varied with map reading, target indication, judging distance (in which Barr and Stroude range-finders were used for checking), and gun-mounting with gas helmets on.

Lieutenant Callister conscientiously put the Sections through much gas helmet drill.

A welcome innovation were the bathing parades. Sections in turn marched to the Dye Works in Armentieres and disported themselves as so many schoolboys. The large vats and ample equipment for the supply of hot water, were admirably suited for the purpose. Hardy members ventured into the River Lys during the first week in May. Their numbers were greatly augmented with the sudden advent of Spring. Private H. F. ("Tod") Nicholson was foremost in acquatic sport, for which he was famous.

More popular was the inauguration of English leave, although the issue was a restricted one; two men from the Company at intervals, which the Sections in turn balloted for. It was twelve months since the majority had left Australia, so the first instalment was overdue. One of the first to leave was "Bill," the Company cook. His departure would have been noteworthy in any case, but when he appeared arrayed for the journey, it was noticed that a great transformation had taken place. Smoked clothes had given way to a new uniform, and a fresh and hitherto unsuspected colour appeared in the much altered face of the best known member of the Company. The unofficial "send off" tendered was of a very hearty nature. Interest was revived a few days later when a report came through that "Bill" had got halfway to Paris before he discovered that he was heading for the delectable city instead of the Channel ports.

On the 14th May, the Company received a notable "issue" of material, when twelve limbers and 42 light draft horses were received and put into commission. This accession to the Company's strength—to be followed later by ten riding horses, a water cart and officers' mess cart—completed the establishment as then provided, and enabled the Company to carry out its own internal transport requirements. The personnel required to man this arm was drawn entirely from the Sections. As the Company's strength comprised a proportion of men who had enlisted from country districts in Victoria, first class material was available. The men were particularly suitable for the work, and under Lieutenant J. D. Campbell and Sergeant J. McGaffin at once settled down to their new duties. In a short time, the Company's Section became and remained, one of the most efficient in the Brigade. During its formation, Captain Hore utilised his Light Horse experience in exercising the teams in Cavalry movements on the far side of the Lys River.

On the evening of 5th May, a heavy bombardment broke out on the Divisional Front occupied by the 5th Brigade. In response to an urgent order, the Company, gathered hurriedly from the huts and village, fell in on its parade ground and "stood by" for three hours. It was subsequently ascertained that the enemy had raided the Bridoux Salient, and carried off two of the newly issued Stokes mortars. The loss of those mortars remained a long and live memory, and led to a surprising retort when an Australian passed the time-honoured greeting to a Tommy: "Have you any kangaroo feathers, Chum?" Reply: "Have you any more trench mortars, Aussie?"

The Company soon realised that its status as a specialist unit conferred on it distinct advantages. After the day's training was over—usually about 4.30 or 5 p.m.—the men were free till the next morning, and had ample opportunity to observe and comment upon the spectacle of the infantry battalions of the Brigade marching off to the lines, at dusk, to carry out pick and shovel and other laborious work.

The large town of Armentieres was within easy walking distance, and although close to the line contained a proportion of civilians and shops where articles suitable as souvenirs could be obtained. Eggs, chips, and coffee were easy of access, and food of a more delectable nature could be obtained at prices which were rarely encountered in later days.

Sunday was invariably observed as a holiday after Church Parade had been held. Padre A. P. Bladen, of the 23rd Battalion, usually officiated. His addresses were always in conformity with the dictum laid down by one of the Company that "A good sermon should be short and a bad one shorter." The Padre was highly esteemed for his sterling qualities and his generous tolerance of the virile and high-spirited members of his charge—an esteem which had its foundations in Gallipoli days. The best tribute that can be paid to the Padre is that texts—in some cases sermons—were remembered for years after. Individuals had other causes to remember his kindly services.

Certain sporting fixtures were carried through. Inter-Section competitions were held. A tournament was arranged with a neighbouring Artillery Unit, in which the Company carried off all the honours save one. The 22nd Battalion was met and defeated at football.

Notwithstanding the easy conditions, some ardent spirits

found the times unenterprising and irksome. One of these was Private Herbert Heyne ("The Swede"). His murmurings and criticism of the High Command's conduct of affairs on the Western Front led to a mock Court Martial, at which he was charged with "Traitorous Conduct and Seditious Language." Everybody entered into the spirit of the joke and a lot of fun resulted Private W. S. Clayton was the prosecuting officer. His reference —at the end of much evidence—to the accused's having "Consorted with certain dissentient spirits," was regarded as the culmination of a masterly bit of eloquence, and was applauded in defiance of all laws of procedure. It should be recorded that, after such an oration, of which only one gem has been recorded, the Court had no hesitation in finding a verdict of "guilty" and remanding the prisoner for sentence.

At this time, a new method of promotion to commissioned rank came into vogue in the A.I.F. Units in France were directed to submit names of non-commissioned officers and men who were considered to possess qualities of leadership and educational qualifications. If the nominee passed the scrutiny of the Brigadier, he was sent to A.I.F. Headquarters in London, and from there was posted to one of the Officer Cadet Battalions in England for training as an infantry officer. These Battalions were the training centres from which the British Army supplied its requirements in commissioned officers. Australians entered on terms of equality with the British entrants who were invariably in the great majority. It was obligatory for all machine-gun nominees to pass the infantry course, and, if successful, to proceed to Grantham to qualify as machine-gun officers. If unsuccessful as machine-gunners, they were sent to France to infantry battalions, a course which was disliked intensely. At the outset, the infantry course extended over three months, and the machine-gun course one month. Later, the gun section was extended to two months, and the infantry course was also lengthened. In both cases, the courses were thorough, and a rigid routine of discipline and conduct was insisted upon. Some of the more fortunate ones found themselves posted to the Battalions established in Oxford and Cambridge. At those places, the hitherto well-defended citadels of English University life were opened to the training of the arts of war instead of the pursuits of peace. British Army officers who had had service oversea comprised the instructional staff, and were assisted in the details of infantry drill by British Army non-commissioned officers. Thus it was that men, who some months before had led civilian lives in Australia, found themselves quartered in famous Colleges, dining in halls from whose walls portraits of students, now famous men, looked down upon them; and demonstrating the sporting prowess of their country on the charming fields and rivers of those historic centres. It should be said that the oversea men were not, in any way, daunted by their surroundings. On the parade-ground and in the examination room, they showed to great advantage. In athletics, they dominated the various sports in which they took part. Almost every nominee from the Company passed all tests and eventually returned to his old unit as a commissioned officer. By this method most of the Company's subsequent requirements were met. Company Sergeant-Major A. Palling, who left at this time, was the first Company nominee. He was followed by others at intervals until the signing of the Armistice.

Before leaving Erquinghem, the Company received its complement of steel helmets, better known as "tin hats." The shallow crown and general strangeness led to much hilarity on their first appearance on the heads of the wearers. Later, as one member described it, "They came into their own in the presence of the enemy." Every man felt a sense of protection from shell splinters, shrapnel, and even bullets while it rested on his head—a sensation that was noticeably absent if by any mischance the hat was missing. Other issues included an "auxiliary mounting" for the gun, a small three-legged mount clamped to the barrel casing, and designed for firing over the top of a trench, or for quick mounting against a fleeting target. It was rarely used, and soon fell into disuse. A more acceptable addition was the graduated brass plate known as the "traversing dial." It was attached to the top of the tripod and a pointer on the gun indicated the degree of "traverse." This became a permanent and useful attachment for use in indirect fire. The fitting of the 16 guns with this dial provided Company Artificer A. E. Burtonclay with his first official task.

The pleasant stay of six weeks at Erquinghem came to an end on the 10th June, when the Company marched out and relieved the 7th Machine Gun Company in the Division's left Brigade Sector. In later days, the weeks at Erquinghem came to be regarded as the best in the Company's experience. That is, judged from the soldiers' standard, which looked for good quarters adjacent to the diversions of a large town, sufficient food, not too much drill, not turned out too early nor kept out late, pleasant weather and surroundings. During the period covered by this chapter, eleven other ranks were evacuated "sick." In most cases the complaint was not of a serious nature and the individual rejoined after a short spell at field ambulance. The only line casualty (wounded) has been noted.

One effect of the easy conditions was that the Company came to know itself. Its establishment was completed, and its duties and responsibilities in the main understood. The privileges and advantages of a small compact specialist unit were emphasised by the exemption from many duties of the infantry battalions— a consideration which led men to value their place in the Company, and to avoid breaches of conduct or duty which might lead to their removal to an infantry battalion—a course sanctioned by General Gellibrand. Isolated cases did occur in later days involving transfers for disciplinary reasons, but they were rare. On the other hand, the infantry of the Brigade was not slow to appreciate the favoured position of the members of the Company. When vacancies had to be filled from their ranks, there was never a dearth of applicants, so the Company was in the happy position of being able to pick and choose—a satisfactory arrangement for the Company, but the Battalions must have regretted the loss of some of their best men.

Another effect was that the Company came to know and appreciate its own members, and to respond to the influence of those responsible for its moulding and fashioning. Some reference will now be made to its leaders, and a few of the outstanding personalities, of which the Company possessed more than its share.

The Company was fortunate in the allotment of one who was to be virtually its first Commanding Officer. Captain L. F. S. Hore was born at Muree, India, and at the time of joining the Company was 46 years of age. Previous to enlistment, he had practised as a solicitor in London and Hobart. Leaving Australia as a Captain in the 8th Light Horse Regiment, he served on Gallipoli with that unit, and was one of the few survivors of the tragic charge made by the Regiment at The Nek on the 7th August previous. In the attack, he was wounded in the leg and still limped as a result and invariably carried a stick. Although not qualified by experience in machine-gunnery, he applied himself to his new duties with energy and enthusiasm, and under his control the Company steadily progressed in efficiency and cohesion. On the personal side, the results he achieved were probably out of all proportion to his apparent talents. From a military point of view, his orderly room procedure was at times appalling, but he obtained the results he sought and on very few occasions did he resort to the statutory military punishments. Justice was always tempered with mercy—ofttimes much mercy—and the welfare of his charges was his constant care. All ranks agreed that their Commanding Officer was an officer and a gentleman, and consequently gave him their respect and loyalty, and it is not too much to say, their affection, feeling sure of a "fair deal" from him. The Captain's promotion to Major just after the Pozieres operations was a welcome announcement, but it was a regretful Company that witnessed his departure for a machine-gun school in England late in the year. He subsequently became First Anzac Corps Machine Gun Officer during 1917-18, with the temporary rank of Lieutenant-Colonel. In that capacity he directed the Corps machine-gun activities during the Ypres fighting in the Autumn of 1917, to which reference will be made later. In March, 1918, he was appointed second in command of the 2nd Machine Gun Battalion, upon its formation. The man Hore was a cheerful and social being, and widely known. He was abstemious in his habits, and possessed of a disposition to always speak of the best side and character of men, even when well aware of their failings. His general clean living and clean mind, and his enthusiasm, probably helped him greatly in his associations with General Gellibrand, with whom, and with his staff, he was much in contact. With all his enthusiasm and keenness to quickly bring the war to a successful conclusion, there were few less militaristic minds engaged as combatants.* During the struggle, one son served in the Royal Navy and another in the Royal Australian Navy.

In its second in command the new Company was equally fortunate. Lieutenant J. H. Drummond was born in Somerset East, Cape Colony, of English parentage, on 21/12/1890. Leaving his occupation of bank clerk, he was at sea on his way to Australia when war broke out. Enlisting at Sydney soon after arrival, he was posted to artillery reinforcements, but secured an entry to an officers' school at Broadmeadows in Victoria. There he obtained his commission, and sailed on the "Euripides" in charge of the first reinforcements of the 23rd Battalion. Shortly before the 6th Brigade left for Gallipoli, he was given charge of the Maxim Machine Gun Section of the 23rd Battalion and served with that unit, as previously related. Narrow-faced, spare of build, and laconic in manner, he resembled in many ways his new-found comrades. On the transfer of Major Hore in November,

---

* After discharge from the Army, he held the positions of chief judge and Crown law officer in New Guinea before managing his own plantation at Kavieng. He died at Kavieng, New Ireland, on 1/9/35.

1916, he assumed command of the Company, and except for absences due to wounds, sickness, and detachments, continued in command almost to the end. In the early days of the Company, he provided an excellent foil to Captain Hore. The Captain had the imagination and enthusiasm, while his subordinate possessed the cold common-sense to cull out the best of the ideas and develop them, at the same time getting the less suitable and superfluous put aside and forgotten. By no means a stickler for regimental details, he nevertheless insisted on the performance of essentials and steadily persevered in his efforts to obtain the desired ends. In doing so, he left the details of training to his subordinates, only correcting when he found them leaning to some phases and neglecting others. He seemed above favouritism, but could be unforgiving to those whom he thought failed to uphold his endeavours. Careful planning and forethought on his part had much to do with the smooth working of the Company's internal economy; a smoothness which became accepted as the normal state of affairs. His forethought and care were carried into his poker playing, with results very satisfactory to himself, yet in games—cricket, etc.—was much disposed to "have a go." He always persisted with the horses he rode until they cantered to his satisfaction, and, while a keen student of languages, especially of French, seemed invariably successful in finding feminine instructresses. In line work he possessed considerable judgment in locating gun positions and in anticipating probable enemy-shelled areas, and in active operations was usually so far forward as to be on the spot when difficult business was in hand. At these times, his coolness and nonchalance under fire set an example to his admiring observers. The Transport Section was looked upon by him as a useful adjunct to the gun sections, especially when in the line. Those in charge were strongly encouraged to push the horses and limbers far forward to save undue exertion by the gun-teams even though it meant running some risks. The possession in such large measure of the requisites of successful leadership naturally obtained the all-important result; the leader received his reward in the whole-hearted loyalty of his non-commissioned officers and men, and the unquestioning support and affection of his officers.

When Captain Drummond succeeded Major Hore as commanding officer, no official second-in-command was appointed for some time. In fact, it was not until the beginning of July, 1917 (eight months after), when Lieutenant D. F. Rae was transferred from the 5th Machine Gun Company, that the position was definitely filled. His entry (due to conditions which were none of his making or choosing) was in circumstances which would have daunted many But, in spite of the initial difficulty, he applied himself to his new duties so thoroughly that his outlook became and remained that of a member of the 6th Company; furthermore, his memories, records, and pride were mainly connected with his second unit. Temperate in his habits, he never hesitated to make an extra effort if it would add to the efficiency of the Company and work towards winning the war. About a month after arrival in the Company, he was promoted to Captain, and during the absences of Captain Drummond assumed command, and by quiet persistence succeeded in obtaining his interpretations of orders and instructions and maintaining the Company's efficiency. The barrage gun-drill as a preparation for the highly developed machine-gun barrages which were a feature of the Autumn offensives near Ypres in 1917, was initiated in the Company by him; it was a subject in which he was well versed. While he maintained the prejudice of a Rugby Union player against the Australian Rules game, his ability as a sprinter in competitive sports brought laurels to the Company.

No. 1 Section had an initial advantage in having two excellent officers, who remained with it for a considerable time. Lieutenant Windsor served his apprenticeship as Corporal and Sergeant in the machine-gun section of the 21st Battalion on Gallipoli, and on the formation of the Company, was promoted to commissioned rank. He was an Englishman who had spent some years in various parts of Australia. Always disinclined to discuss himself, he gave an impression of reserve, but possessed great self-control and the will to do anything that appeared necessary, stoically and efficiently. This faculty carried him through dangers and difficulties with apparent unconcern, and with a determination that nothing daunted. He was always in favour of aggressive action, and was himself a good gunner. "A great soldier" was the fervent verdict of more than one of his Section, and, it should be added, a great leader. In the succeeding narrative, mention will be made of his unsparing services given in such whole-hearted measure as doubtless caused his death after discharge.

Lieutenant Windsor's colleague was Lieutenant R. C. Callister. He was born at Ballarat East on 10/10/89, and was a metallurgist at the time of his enlistment. He also served as Corporal and Sergeant in the machine-gun section of the 21st Battalion, and was promoted to commissioned rank on the formation of the Company. His natural thoroughness, analytical mind, studious nature, patience, and retentive memory, fitted him admirably for a machine-gun officer. Men, guns, and the continuous development in machine-gunnery were objects to him for profound study as a contribution to winning the war, and, in the process, he became probably the Company's greatest authority; although he would be the last to claim that distinction. To these qualifications was added a degree of self-control under fire which suggested complete indifference. To move about with their officer in the forward area was not a task that was sought after by his men. While his own conduct of life was above reproach, he maintained a discriminating tolerance towards the high-spirited individuals in his charge. At intervals during 1916, 1917, and again in 1918, he acted as Second in Command of the Company. In 1918 (July) he commanded the Company while holding the temporary rank of Captain. Later he acted both as Adjutant and Assistant Adjutant to the 2nd Machine Gun Battalion. His storehouse of knowledge was freely made available to the writer of this volume, which bears many imprints both of his whole-hearted service and generous assistance.

Lieutenant F. J. Blenkarn served his apprenticeship with the 24th Battalion on Gallipoli, and was a Sergeant at the Evacuation. On the formation of the Company, he was promoted to commissioned rank, and continued with his comrades in No. 4 Section. No parade, tour of duty, march, or relief was quite dull while "Blank," as he was invariably known, was present. His long limbs and quizzical expression always suggested amusement to the beholder. To a literary summing-up of a situation, he added a flair for uncommon words and sentences, which ofttimes relieved a difficult situation. Some of those words and sentences became incorporated in the jargon of the Company, and their authorship was never attributed to anyone else. What member of No. 4 Section, who was present, has forgotten a relief on a certain dark night, when, after a long and fruitless effort to find their objective, their leader came to the emphatic conclusion that they had "certainly wandered off the map."

No. 2 Section was happily supplied in its two first officers, although the subject of this reference did not remain with it very long. Lieutenant J. D. Campbell hailed from the Warrnambool district, where he was engaged in farming pursuits when he enlisted. He also graduated through his machine-gun section (22nd Battalion) and received his commission on the Company's formation. Known affectionately as "Cam," his genial and debonair manner considerably smoothed his way. In addition, his was a great capacity to say the right few words, tactfully and at the right time, in order to get his way, and also to obtain a great deal of work from those about him. Early in the proceedings he was transferred to the Transport Section to take control on its formation. Under his command, the Section soon became and remained the most efficient in the Brigade, and was his joy and pride. During the winter of 1916-17, and the following spring, he was Second in Command of the Company, and his administration of the rear headquarters relieved Captain Drummond of much worry. At one stage he might have had quick promotion, through influence offering to push him, but he decided to earn such as came his way. On two occasions he voluntarily went into the line with gun-teams when the Company needed officers. The circumstances leading to his death were characteristic of him, and will be noted in due course.

The other foundation officer of No. 2 Section was Lieutenant A. N. McLennan. He was commissioned before the 6th Brigade left Australia, and was transferred to the Machine Gun Section of the 22nd Battalion in Egypt. He was possibly the best turned-out officer in the Company and managed his Section efficiently and smoothly. After Pozieres, he was transferred to the 22nd Battalion for a time, but returned to the Company before being appointed to command the newly-formed extra machine-gun company in the Division, the 22nd. It says much for his ability and application that he was able to resume his legal studies after the four-years' break at the war and to complete them successfully.

In the internal economy of the Company, the two focal points around which much of the "family" life eddied, were the cook-house (?) and the quartermaster's store. An army cook's fire is not usually regarded as a spot to attract or to interest, whether it be a row of dixies over fires in the open or a travelling kitchen installed in a draughty shed. But when an important culinary department is presided over by such a notable character as it was, the Company's cook-house was elevated to a place of perennial interest and amusement. Private Herbert ("Bill") Wormald's claim (he never thought to make one) to a place among the notables, does not rest on his culinary abilities. "Bill's" civil occupation as a cab-driver in Ballarat did not qualify him as a cook, neither did his natural inclinations; rather the reverse. How he stuck it, on the one hand, and how the Company did on the other, was one of the wonders of the war. In the early days especially, it must have been a trial of the flesh for both parties, but in the

Capt. J. H. Drummond, M.C., Major L. F. S. Hore, M.C., Capt. D. F. Rae, M.C.
(The three Commanding Officers).

process "Bill" progressed to reasonable efficiency and the Company learned to appreciate the efforts to discharge a truly thankless job, and one which required enormous patience to meet the ever-varying conditions of an army in the field. It says much for his grit that he remained at his post (except when on leave) until the end of 1918, and in the meantime was one of a handful who never went sick. In person, "Bill," with his walrus moustache, was not unlike his great prototype so graphically portrayed by Captain Bruce Bairnsfather. A gruff manner was not improved by the constant chaffing and good-natured abuse received, but a word or two of appreciation always brought the kinder side to light. It was, however, "Bill's" limited vocabulary of strong language and unconscious humour that ofttimes delighted the bystanders, and his occasional lapses from the strict line of duty were told and re-told with a relish never accorded his dishes. To a Company grown war-weary such episodes came as a tonic, and more than one member wondered if they were not worth the price. A few of the best-remembered will be found in these pages.

No reference to "Bill" would be complete without a mention of his assistant, or, in Army parlance, "offsider," as he was known. Private J. W. Purchase held the doubtful honour, and his great qualification was the admirable foil he accorded his senior. Somewhat short in stature, his consistent good temper and perpetual grin were always looked for and rarely failed. His long and good service is remembered with gratitude.

If the cook's fire did not dissipate the visitor's ennui, a call at the quartermaster's store hardly ever failed. The Company was well served by the three successive occupants (Quartermaster Sergeants) who held the position—H. L. Smith with his disarming smile, R. W. Watt by his tact and efficiency, and A. H. ("Boss") Smith. As assistant (private) for two years and then in charge, the latter will always be most readily associated with the store. He was always in it and of it. Over 40 years of age, grey haired, ruddy of face, blue-eyed and erect of form, he would impress at once; when in action, doubly so. Always a decided and fearless individualist, he possessed extraordinary powers of fluent and sustained speech which held all debaters and tied them, in the end, to impotent silence. To the older hands, grown wary by experience, it was an interesting diversion to bring a newcomer to the door of the store and artfully contrive to involve him in a wordy bout with the occupant. The result was always the same. In the early days "Boss" seemed unnecessarily bitter in his judgments of men and things—almost dangerously so—but the passing of the years and doubtless a better realisation on his part of the services of those associated with him, mellowed his outlook and judgment, and he became one of the warmest advocates of the Company personnel, and withal kindly and considerate. Though a strong talker, he was also a great worker, and as he fought for and served the men in the line in the earlier days, so he battled for the Company in his later capacity, and by his forceful tact and "give and take" received a good deal of consideration in the receipt of stores. His promotion to Quartermaster-Sergeant in March, 1918, was a tribute to the judgment of Captain Drummond, as "Boss's" earlier free speech and criticisms had been sufficient to warrant his being passed over. The decision was fully justified. Before the Company disbanded, he was presented by the other ranks with an inscribed silver watch and a gold locket in appreciation of his services; an act of recognition which must be unique in the records of quartermasters.

To second his efforts with the Transport Section, Lieutenant Campbell had a worthy assistant in Sergeant J. A. McGaffin. It could be said with truth that he was born to the job. For many years his father had been associated with horses in the Eastern States, and in his time must have broken in a great number. His son followed in his steps, and became a past-master in judging, breaking, riding, and handling horses. To quote an observer, "He was even tolerant of donks." Furthermore, he would dare to ride any outlaw, and invariably succeeded. Other units with problems on their hands often called for his services. He carried a quiet voice and manner with his job as Transport Sergeant, and got his work done effectively. His remarkable fleetness of foot soon earned him a reputation as a sprinter.

CHAPTER V.

EARLY DAYS IN FRANCE: BOIS GRENIER.

10th June-26th July, 1916.

The 7th Brigade had been holding the Divisional Left Sector since early April, and now, upon its relief by the 6th Brigade, passed into Divisional Reserve. In conformity with the change, the Company took over the outgoing Company's headquarters and billets in Rue Marle—adjacent to Armentieres—and gun positions in the line at Bois Grenier. The guns were disposed, four in each of front, support, and reserve lines, while four were kept in reserve in billets at Rue Marle. The relief was carried through without incident and completed on the 10th June, a portion of each gun team having, as a preliminary step, moved in on the previous day. After a few days in each position, the teams changed over with each other, the teams in reserve carrying forward the daily rations, and providing quartermaster's, cook's, and incidental fatigues.

General trench conditions were similar to those experienced at Fleurbaix. Duckboards, however, appeared to be everywhere, and the improved weather made the area dry and pleasant. Spring was well advanced and helped to hide some of the scars of war by a thick growth of grass between the trenches, and leaves appeared on the trees which remained. The skylark daily ascended with his song of joy; the only jarring notes were those produced by man himself. In places, strawberries were gathered from the remains of untended gardens. The teams enjoyed a measure of leisure which was duly appreciated, and was devoted to letter-writing, watching the increasing aerial activities, and some minor improvements to quarters. Sergeant J. E. Hopper employed several morning hours in taking a live German pineapple bomb completely to pieces, and in removing nose caps from large "dud" shells—a practice quite contrary to orders.

The 7th Machine Gun Company had done an immense amount of indirect fire, which the Company immediately resumed. Enemy roads and communications were fired upon regularly, much of it being done at night when it was presumed he would be moving more freely. The interesting information was obtained from German prisoners taken at Bois Grenier, that the indirect fire of the Australian machine-guns on the roads in their back area was harassing, and caused a good number of casualties. At one point, observation of the effect of the fire of one gun was possible. The Company signallers had established an observation post in Dead Cow Farm, from whence they could observe Distillery Road. On movement being observed, "pip pip" was sent over a specially laid telephone wire, and a long burst would be fired. The arrangement provided some interesting shooting. On the morning of the 22nd June, fire was opened on a small party, and three men were seen to fall. Shortly after, another party came into view, when a belt was fired causing five to fall, of which three arose and took shelter. Next morning, at the same point, a party turned back when fire was opened. A little later they again attempted to pass, but were again turned back. During the afternoon, another party was scattered very hurriedly. The first shooting was also noticed by the 22nd Battalion and reported by them. Most of the indirect fire was done from positions sited in the open, but no molestation by the enemy was recorded. Due regard for concealment in sitting positions had, however, been observed.

Soon after the Brigade's occupancy of the Sector, relations with the enemy underwent a decided change. As a prelude to the opening of the Somme offensive, and intended as a diversion, the British front became very active. The English papers featured "Great Activity on the British Front." Due, doubtless, to the effect of a one-sided censorship, the reader received the impression that the reported activity emanated from one side only. But the man in the line had quite a different story to tell. Bombardment by both sides became almost a daily and nightly occurrence. Raids, and rumours of raids, gas alarms, and aerial activities, added to the excitement. The teams had many narrow escapes, but no fatal casualties were sustained until two days before the tour ended. Thus, a 4.2 shell entered a breastwork dugout in which Lance Corporal W. Dutton and Private A. St. G. Tuohy were sheltering. Out of the smoke and dust, their comrades were surprised to see them emerge, black-faced and shaken, but uninjured. The two right-hand teams of No. 3 Section were just finishing the midday meal when a terrific bombardment opened on their sector without the slightest warning. Rushing to a flank—fortunately the safe one—they escaped annihilation by seconds. In the circumstances, the front line teams had little rest. A diary extract from a member of No. 3 Section reads: "Friday, 23rd June: Day fairly quiet, but what a night! At 11 p.m. our artillery opened heavily—a fearsome sight watching the Hun line torn with high explosive, and slashed with shrapnel. Hell, indeed! Of course, the reply came, then WE hugged Mother Earth, and endured the same thing as hopefully as we could. Oh! that merciless, whistling shrapnel! After the storm came the calm, then a gas alarm—helmets hastily put on; then no gas reported—helmets taken off. At 1 a.m. tried to sleep, but was awakened at 2 a.m. Orders were that no man was to sleep in dug-outs because the wind was favourable for cloud gas attack. 'Stand to' about 3 a.m. to 4 a.m. Slept awhile, then on post from 6 to 8, then slept till breakfast at 9.30. As I write the skylark is singing aloft from its nest in 'No Man's Land' and all is quiet." The same writer remarked, "These French nights are very short. Dusk at 9 p.m., dawn at about 3 a.m." After such nights as those described by the diarist, both sides apparently slept the sleep of exhaustion, and for some hours after dawn, almost unbroken calm descended on the front.

Further diary entries read: "Sunday, 25th June: Intermittent shelling. At about 11.30 p.m. raids on our right by the 5th Brigade, and on our left by the New Zealanders, with artillery accompaniment. The usual reply. Some shrapnel came pretty close. During the day our Stokes trench mortars fired from a salient on our immediate left."

"Monday, 26th June: The reply came to the shooting by our Stokes mortars about 4.30 p.m.—the most intense bombardment I have seen. Our cooking recess holed our four feet. Four Hun balloons fired by our aeroplanes—smart work!—great excitement watching the airman going for his target and daring the hostile anti-aircraft batteries. No rest at night—up and down—stunts every half-hour, which brought the inevitable replies. To complete our discomfort, it rained steadily. Such is modern warfare, nerve-racking in the extreme!"

Speaking of the experiences of No. 1 Section, Lieutenant Callister said: "No. 1 Section went to the front line with the right gun position at the head of Park Row, and on the junction of the 5th and 6th Brigades, with the Bridoux salient on the right. There was also a salient in the 6th Brigade sector, but it was held by Lewis guns. I had two guns on the Park Row side of this salient, and Lieutenant F. Windsor the other two on the further side. One night, about 9 p.m., Lance Corporal F. J. Nixon's gun, with Corporal J. L. Stapleton, nearest to the salient, was enclosed in a 'box barrage.' Nixon was on the gun and the emplacement was hit several times that evening by 4.2 shells, which shifted the structure, but without material damage. Stapleton was on the fire step, sitting down to avoid the large number of flying missiles, while I was observing from one corner of the fire-bay and a 22nd Battalion Company Sergeant-Major from the other. Things seemed to be approaching a climax—heavy fire, flares, etc.—when a quiet voice enquired, 'How are things?' It was Windsor, who, having found himself and teams outside the 'box,' had calmly come through the fire curtain to see whether he could help, and I think because the pandemonium was such he feared we were all out of action. However, no one was hurt, but I think most of us could always remain occupied outside of those 'box barrages' until compelled to enter."

Patrolling of "No Man's Land" at this time by the Brigade became very active. When the patrols were out, the front line teams were advised, to prevent their being fired on. On a number of occasions the guns opened on, and scattered, enemy working parties, on receipt of reports from the patrols.

Sniping by both sides also added its quota to the varied activities. This did not come within the scope of the Company's duties, but it led to an amusing experience which befell Sergeant J. E. Hopper, while trying out a new fangled periscope of small dimensions. He took a look through it, pulled it down to readjust, put it up again and was immediately knocked off the fire step on to the trench floor. With Hopper, gear, tin hat, and periscope all coming down five feet, there was a great clatter and some alarm to his mates. Hopper, however, very red and annoyed, picked himself up and decided he was not hit or hurt. A sniper's bullet from 300 yards had hit the periscope, dented it, flung it hard against Hopper's tin hat, and the force and surprise had knocked him off the fire step. The bullet was picked up and the periscope used again.

The art of writing poetry could hardly be expected to flourish during such times as those described. Nevertheless, those strenuous days produced at least one poem. Lance Corporal George Brown Crerar, of No. 3 Section, was a member of a gun team which occupied a reserve position in a trench which contained the usual duckboards. Towards evening 4.2 shells commenced to fall in that particular sector during drizzling rain. The bombardment was not heavy, but persistent. The first shell landed close to the gun position, and was followed by another. The teams moved some little distance along the trench, but the shells followed. Further movements took place, with the shells always following as if possessed of uncanny knowledge, but with the teams just out of danger. Between the rushes from point to point, Crerar was observed busily writing in a notebook. Each time the party crouched against the parapet, further noting took place, the writer grinning the while, and ignoring the facetious comments as to "writing a farewell message to his girl" and so forth. The wildest guesses as to the writer's activity did not include verse, but it was during this brief but stressful half-hour that the following lines were written:—

Up and Down the Duckboards.

Up and down the duckboards, up and down again,
   Blinkin' at the star shells fallin' in the rain;
Thinkin' of the rations, if they're gettin' wet,
   Thinkin' if there's any rum and how much we'll get.
Thinkin' if a bullet hurts, if there's any pain.
      Yow! Here comes a bleedin' bomb;
      Up and down again.

Up and down the duckboards, screwin' at the moon,
   Musin' on the bally strafe we got this afternoon;
Thinkin' how explosives make you jump and sweat,
   Thinkin' how you duck and run and hug the parapet.
Thinkin' of the next one, if it's joy or pain.
      Hell. It's getting hotter;
      Duck, and off again.

Up and down the duckboards, good and bad and worn,
   From "stand to" in the evenin' till "carry on" at morn;
Thinkin' all the bloomin' things you never thought before,
   Thinkin' of the "stunt" last night and feelin' pretty sore.
Thinkin' you'll chuck thinkin' up, before you turn insane.
      Two whizz-bangs and a nine point two,
      And then you think again.

Following the activities described, the first raid of the 6th Brigade took place on the night of 29th-30th June. The raid—the most important of the Anzac series—was undertaken by a party made up from all Battalions in the Brigade, and was equal to the strength of an infantry company. Captain A. R. L. Wiltshire, of the 22nd Battalion, was in command, and the raiders underwent a thorough system of training for the event. From air photographs, the German lines to be entered were reconstructed some distance in rear, and over the ground the large party practised nightly the various and numerous parts that had to be undertaken. Several members of the Company volunteered their services and went over with the attackers. They were Privates A. C. Chalmers and A. G. Elliott (No. 2 Section), H. L. Heyne and J. N. Myers (No. 3 Section), J. F. Gribble and Lance Corporal M. J. O'Brien (No. 4 Section). The artillery programme involved an expenditure of 8000 shells and about 1000 trench mortar bombs; the latter mainly for the purpose of cutting the enemy wire. In conjunction with the artillery, two of the Company's guns fired indirectly on enemy trenches and communications. The venture was successful; some of the enemy garrison were killed and prisoners taken from the 50th (Prussian) Reserve Division. The raiders sustained losses amounting to eight killed, twenty-one wounded, and three missing. Among the killed was Private Gribble, who thus earned the distinction of being the first man in the Company to fall. Before leaving the front trench, Lance Corporal O'Brien was rather badly wounded in the left wrist, but notwithstanding the injury he went over with the raiders, and on entering the enemy trenches compelled three men to surrender, passed them back, and entered a dug-out where he shot three Germans, but was badly wounded by a fourth and brought away unconscious. For his part in the night's work he received the Serbian Gold Medal, and was thus the first Company member to be decorated.

The return of the raiding party led to some amusing reactions. Brigade headquarters (under the temporary command of Colonel C. H. Brand) was in a very hospitable mood and served light refreshments with a liberal rum issue. Naturally everyone relaxed from the previous highly-strung state, and the details of the venture were fought over again. Private Myers was in a happier mood than ever, and sought to relate incidents to Captain Norman of the Brigade staff. He found great difficulty, however, in getting past his opening remark, "You know, it was like this, Norman." Nevertheless, he essayed with many repetitions, each time placing a blackened hand on the shoulder of his listener. The bystanders roared with delight as various black marks appeared on the light-coloured tunic of the immaculate staff captain. Before dawn the details were related to the very sleepy occupants of one of the Company's billets by Private Heyne, who was full of the exploits of the night. His drowsy audience, however, did not respond to his lengthy and very vehement account, so he became more vehement, personal and threatening. The spectacle of a blackened and excited raider waving a live Mills grenade thoroughly roused and alarmed everyone, and in various stages of night attire they rushed from the billet to the open fields, one scared member crashing through a thin partition in his anxiety to reach a safer spot.

No. 4 Section sustained further loss when Private K. J. McKenzie was killed by shell-fire on the 2nd July. He was a member of a team in charge of a gun mounted in an armoured emplacement situated in the front line. It was the practice to cover the steel loop-hole with a steel plate—disguised with a sandbag—by day, and to remove it at night. In the evening, after the plate had been removed, McKenzie and Lance Corporal A. E. Coe were sitting, one each side of the gun, talking and watching. Without any warning, a "whizz-bang" (77 millimetre shell) entered the loop-hole and exploded at the foot of the gun. The barrel casing was badly riddled and McKenzie received the full force of the explosion. Coe very luckily escaped with a bad shaking and was relieved from duty.

After a tour lasting 25 days, the Brigade was relieved on the night of 3rd-4th July by the New Zealand Rifle Brigade. The Company was relieved by the machine gun company of that unit. The "change over" proceeded very smoothly until it was disturbed by enemy action. It so happened that the 14th Battalion of the newly arrived 4th Australian Division occupied the frontage adjoining the 6th Brigade's right flank, and, by mutual arrangement, the Company's extreme right-hand gun had been mounted in the territory of the 14th to obtain enfilade fire along the 6th Brigade's front. On the night of 2nd-3rd July, the 14th Battalion raided the German lines opposite their front, and on the night following the Germans retaliated by a raid directed against the front held by the 14th Battalion. Part of the preliminary bombardment, which lasted over an hour and was particularly intense, fell on the right of the 6th Brigade and greatly disturbed the relief in progress. Great anxiety was felt as to the right-hand gun team. When Lieutenant Blenkarn moved round to investigate, he found that a large minenwerfer shell had landed close to the gun, killing Privates B. E. Gale, E. O'Neill, A. F. and H. H. Matthews, and badly wounding Sergeant O. H. Bailey. The place was wrecked, but Corporal F W. H. Matthews was discovered (assisted by a

New Zealander as his No. 2), firing into the raiding party in No Man's Land—the tears streaming down his face, but the very personification of courage and determination. His action had, doubtless, much to do with the limited success of the raiders. A very regrettable fact was that all three Matthews were brothers. H. H. Matthews had joined the Company but four days before his death. All three clamoured to be allotted to the same gun team — a request to which both Captain Hore and Lieutenant Blenkarn reluctantly agreed, much against their better judgment. A. F. Matthews was wounded the day after landing on Gallipoli while with the 9th Battalion, but returned before the evacuation and joined the 24th Battalion Machine Gun Section. F. W. H. Matthews also served on Gallipoli, with the 24th Battalion, where he was wounded in the foot. After eight months in hospital, he rejoined the Company ten days before the incident related. Later he also met his death in the line at Flers on the 9th of the following November. All three were fine specimens of young Australian manhood, and their loss came as a grievous blow to their comrades. Sergeant Bailey's wounds led to his discharge. The losses for this period were six other ranks killed in action, two wounded, and three evacuated sick. One officer (Lieutenant Drummond) was also evacuated sick.

On the afternoon following—the 4th July—the Company left its billets in Rue Marle and marched to quarters in Steenwerck. "Rained at the start and all the way" wrote one diarist. "Wet through, but a dry barn and NO shells were ample compensations. Slept soundly after about a five-mile march." The foregoing was doubtless, the feeling of all the Company who left the line with intense relief that a strenuous period was over.

Four days were spent at Steenwerck, devoted mainly to overhauling guns, gear, and equipment. The weather was close and sultry, with intermittent showers which had a marked effect on the green and luxuriant wheat and root crops to which the area was given up. The wheat appeared to grow before the eyes; progress which drew forth many comments from those accustomed to cultivation in a dryer land and under a warmer sun. "Great growing weather," wrote a diarist, "everything green and fresh, cherries ripe, very picturesque country."

On the 8th July, the Company left Steenwerck and marched to Strazeele, where the night was spent. Next day march was resumed to Renescure through country that was picturesque, gently undulating, and very green. Two pleasant days were passed at

Renescure. Billets were good, and tramps to the old-world abbey town of St. Omer were welcome diversions. Trouble over the saluting of officers again cropped up, and thereafter the red diamond was distinguished from other Brigade units by the addition of a blue bar worn horizontally across the centre of the colour patch. Some months later the blue bar was discontinued, and a yellow cloth representation of crossed machine-guns was issued and worn over the diamond. Still later, the crossed guns were ordered to be worn about an inch below the colour patch. This arrangement continued in force until the last months of the war, when the Company emblem was superseded by the new patch of the 2nd Machine Gun Battalion.

At this time, a most persistent rumour was in circulation that the whole Division was to leave for England, there to train as a "Mobile Division." The idea was scouted by many, but it served to keep everyone in a state of expectation. Lengthy newspaper accounts of the Somme offensive were coming through. These accounts—owing to the censorship—gave the one-sided impression of wide and continued progress, but little reference to the tragic cost. The successes appeared, to the hopeful ones, to indicate that mobile units would be required for the looked-for "break-through," and gave colour to the rumour. The dreadful days and nights of Pozieres lay ahead, but as yet cast no shadow, so the optimists—and they were many!—held sway.

Reveille was fixed for 3 a.m. on the morning of the 11th, but the sentries on the horse lines of the Transport Section slept, so the Company started, very late and annoyed, for Arques (near St. Omer), three miles away, where entrainment took place at 8 a.m. When the train moved slowly in a north-westerly direction towards Calais, excitement, arising out of the rumour referred to, reached fever heat. As the train approached that historic town, men hung on to every vantage position and watched the engine proceed from point to point until it seemed as if it would certainly turn to the right and run down to the wharf. Long betting odds were offered on the destination being England, but there were no takers. Alas! for the high hopes. Instead of turning to the right, the engine turned to the left. England faded out of the mental horizon, and the Somme came into view.

Leaving Calais and the fleeting prospect of England behind, the train journey was resumed southwards. The route lay through a countryside that was very beautiful in its Spring dress, and all ranks realised how lovely unravaged France was. Passing through

IN GOOD COMPANY.

Boulogne, Etaples, and Abbeville, Amiens was reached in the evening, when the Company disentrained and marched to the village of St Sauveur on the Somme, where billets were found. After a journey of 19 hours, a very weary Company soon fell asleep on the wire netting bunks with which most of the billets were provided.

The Company stayed four days at St. Sauveur. Training was continued in pleasant weather, and the guns received a good deal of polishing and oiling, and officers were issued with revolvers. Some tactical movements were practised in conjunction with the Infantry Battalions of the Brigade. Swimming in the Somme Canal was much in evidence. The fine city of Amiens was distant but six miles, and received much attention from all ranks. At that time, it was quite undamaged by the ruthless hand of war, its population was in residence, trams ran in the streets, all of which afforded welcome diversions to men grown weary of sojourning in billets in small French country villages. The city's glorious Cathedral was a prominent landmark, and a never-ending joy to those who cared for beauty and majesty as expressed in such architectural magnificence. The daily tramp to and from the city lay through undulating country covered with ripening cornfields, which were made gay with a profusion of red poppies and blue cornflowers. Distant rumbling from the Somme battlefield could be heard day and night; but, in true Australian fashion, the men resumed the role of tourists, bought postcards and other souvenirs, and ignored the menacing sounds that came floating to their ears from the East.

The move eastwards was commenced on the 16th July, when march was made to Rainville, where two days were spent, thence to Toutencourt for two days' stay, then on to Varennes. At Rainville, the old proprietor of one billet complained that one or two rungs of a ladder leading up to a loft were missing, and successfully claimed for the sum of 20 francs. He was most jubilant when the claim was paid, until some of the men decided that, as the ladder was paid for, they were entitled to some much-needed firewood, and thereupon it was chopped up. The proprietor was furious, but the French liaison officer decided that as his claim had been fully met, he had no further interest in the ladder. He remained unable or unwilling to see the humour of the situation.

In accordance with the custom of the British Expeditionary Force, the remaining blanket (one of the two on issue, had been withdrawn about the 1st June), was returned to Store, leaving the men with only their ground-sheet and overcoat for their "bed" at night. The first night after the withdrawal was cool—so much so that few slept. In spite of the uncongenial conditions, good humour prevailed. At 2 a.m., a very hearty chorus was heard proceeding from one billet, the burden of which was "We want to go home." Representations were made for the return of one blanket, and some time later it was restored.

Varennes was about eight miles from the battlefield of the Somme—then in its fourth week of activity—and it was obvious that the Company was destined to participate therein. From the village could be seen the effect of large shell bursts in the great masses of smoke and dust thrown up. Keen discussions took place daily as to the part the Company would be called on to play, and how it would perform in its first offensive action. The discussions received a fresh impulse on the 20th, when sixteen men from each of the four Infantry Battalions in the Brigade marched in and were "attached" to the Company, primarily to serve as ammunition carriers and runners. These men were taken in hand at once, and, during the next six days, were instructed in the mounting, loading, and firing of the guns; also stoppage rectification. They had volunteered for the transfer and were, in the main, sturdy and reliable. In the subsequent operations they proved their worth. The Company was able to retain some of them, although the majority were recalled to their Battalions to make up for the heavy losses they had sustained.

Six days were spent at Varennes. Ample time was thus available to complete final arrangements for the move that was daily expected. All ranks settled down to the preparations necessary with a quiet confidence that the Company would do well in its first "hop-over"; the seriousness of which was not underestimated. An "offensive" atmosphere was everywhere in evidence. The prevailing fine weather, the constant movement of troops to and from the front; the daily and nightly bombardments; a string of fifteen captive observation balloons, and the presence of newly-captured Germans in cages—who were duly inspected and commented upon—were obvious signs of offensive operations on a large scale! At the Company Church Parade on Sunday, 23rd July, Padre Bladen delivered an eloquent and appropriate sermon based on the text, "Be ye faithful unto death." That evening, when the news came through of the success of the 1st Australian Division in taking Pozieres, it was felt that the time for participation had duly arrived.

CHAPTER VI.

Pozieres.

26th July-7th August, 1916.

The name Pozieres must be indelibly inscribed in the memories of the survivors of those thousands of members of the A.I.F. who passed through the inferno which raged in and around the hitherto obscure French village during the months of July, August, and September, 1916. It was at Pozieres that the 1st, 2nd, and 4th Australian Divisions, after some intensive training and an introduction to the methods of trench warfare, received their fiery baptism on the Western Front on making their entry in the Somme offensive. And such a baptism it was! All the conditions conspired to make supreme and unprecedented demands on the young manhood engaged, and the magnificent response to those demands must surely register one of the high-water marks of human endeavour. The records of endurance and achievement of those days should rank among the most treasured possessions of this young nation. No other square mile of French soil—taking in Pozieres, the Ridge, and Mouquet Farm—has been so richly consecrated by valour and sacrifice, and holds so much of all that is mortal of the brave men and boys who fought thereon.

The Battle of the Somme — which lasted four and a half months—had been in progress nearly three weeks when the 1st Australian Division became involved in it on the night of 19th-20th July. When fifteen British Divisions attacked simultaneously on a twenty-mile front—in conjunction with an eight-mile advance by the French on their right—it was by far the greatest and most ambitious effort of the British Army. After months of careful preparation, it was launched with high hope on the morning of the 1st July. The German defensive zone selected for the thrust had been carefully chosen with respect to natural advantages, and nearly two years of industrious labour expended on trenches, dug-outs, and barbed wire obstacles had enormously strengthened those advantages. Against such a barrier, the new armies threw themselves with unstinted valour, but it was on only about seven miles of the southern end that the forward line of the zone was breached. In spite of its losses, General Rawlinson's Fourth Army continued to exploit its successes, and by mid-July, culminating in a great attack on the 16th, had broken through the German second line. At this point, the Reserve Army was brought in on the left of the breach. It was as part of the Reserve Army that the 1st Australian Division took its place in the front line and found itself opposite the fortified straggling agricultural village of Pozieres, located on the main Albert-Bapaume road. Up till that time, the village had successfully resisted several attacks by British units, and as a result of bombardments had been reduced to ruins. Pozieres was not included in the German second line—which ran along the edge of the ridge in its rear—but had been incorporated as a bastion of that line by a trench (Pozieres Trench) running south-west and joining another running north, known as Kay Trench. It was obvious that Pozieres must be captured before the line proper on the ridge in rear could be assaulted.

By the 26th July, the whole of the village was in the safe custody of the 1st Australian Division, and on that night the 6th Brigade of the 2nd Australian Division relieved the 2nd Brigade (both Victorian) of the former, as part of an inter-Divisional relief. The area taken over by the 6th Brigade comprised the much demolished village itself, from Kay Trench on the left to a point near the Albert-Bapaume road. On the right was the 5th Brigade, and on the left the 48th (British) Division.

At this time, the holding of the line by what was afterwards known as "distribution in depth" was not fully understood, consequently, into a frontage of 800 yards, the Brigade crowded its front line and immediate supports by sending in the 22nd and 24th. Battalions, half its fighting strength. The Company attempted to do the same.* By the early morning of the 27th, the "change over" was complete. From the front line, on the forward edge of the village, the newcomers gazed up the gently sloping ground to the trench-crowned ridge in front. Looking across the shell-pitted earth, from which most of the herbage had disappeared, no movement or sign of life was visible. But every man knew that from that ridge unseen observers watched, and a

* On a Brigade being relieved, all orders, dispositions and responsibility rested with the old Brigadier till "relief complete." The new Brigadier could hardly alter dispositions until he had an opportunity of sizing up the situation. In the present instance, a reduction in the number of troops in the line was subsequently made.

few words from them over a telephone line to hidden batteries in rear would turn their holding into a belching volcano. And such it proved to be; a dreadful illustration of the application of science to the art of warfare. A hot sun shone down from a clear blue sky as the enemy shells pounded and re-pounded the crumbling trenches and dusty earth. Telephone wires were continuously destroyed, so runners carried messages, ration parties transported food and water, and stretcher-bearers carried their human burden through the artillery barrages that the struggle might be continued. Men fought and many died without once having seen an opponent, while those that survived lived with the dead. Night brought no relief, because the same guns—firing on registrations obtained in daylight—continued their devastating work. It was a hellish contest; human flesh and will contending with the diabolical combination of engineer, chemist, and mathematician. In spite of it all, human will prevailed. At tragic cost the ground was held, the ridge—a key position—twice attacked, and finally wrested from the enemy in an undertaking which involved the Division in ten days and nights of stark horror.

To return to the thread of the Company narrative. On the morning of 26th July, the Company marched out of Varennes at 5 a.m., and by 8.30 a.m. had reached the outskirts of Albert. There, the rest of the day was spent in rather idle fashion, except for the completion of a few minor items of preparation and the stacking of packs in Albert, while "tin hats" displaced the more comfortable felt headgear. During the day, Lieutenant Clive M. Williams was transferred to the Company from the 23rd Battalion and Lieutenant Drummond rejoined from hospital. With the latter was Private A. Anders, who also reported from hospital. While at Camieres, Anders had met his officer, then on his way to rejoin the Company, and hearing that active operations were afoot prevailed on Lieutenant Drummond to accept him temporarily as his batman to ensure an immediate return to the Company. Meanwhile, the men had ample opportunity for inspecting the deserted and somewhat damaged town of Albert, with its great red brick church, from whose high and damaged tower a huge gilded statue of the Virgin and Child hung suspended at an acute angle. Popular report had it that the French held the belief that when the statue fell from its precarious position the war would end. More interesting, however, was the presence in the immediate vicinity of some of the battle shattered battalions of the 1st Australian Division, who had been relieved in the front line during the previous night after the successful storming of the village of Pozieres. Soon after the

Company arrived, moving scenes were enacted, when the remnants of the former gay and splendid battalions of the 3rd Brigade were aroused from deep sleep to attend the roll call. Members of the Company listened in silence when the long lists of names were called with but few responses. They were greatly impressed by the eloquent tale which the appearance of the survivors bespoke. Haggard, weary, dust-covered, bloodshot of eye and bent of frame, they appeared to have emerged from some terrible ordeal. One diarist wrote, "Some of the 1st Division are here; that is, the remnants of different battalions. Poor fellows, they have had a trial; worn, dirty wrecks of humanity; their tale is one of triumph except for the artillery fire." Much of the morning was spent interrogating the survivors as to their experiences, all of which served to indicate what the Company might expect. Even in their distressed state, the true Australian spirit flamed up. Asked how he was, one red-eyed and weary individual replied, "Two or three good feeds and sleeps, and I'll be ready to have another go at those bastards."

After such a preparation, members were naturally somewhat subdued when the Company set off, section by section, for the line. A diarist recorded: "About 6.30 p.m. we marched out in 'fighting order'; quietly resolved, not looking too far ahead—the neighbouring battalions are too significant—but buoyed up by the hope that springs eternal in the human breast. We will do the best that Australians are capable of." Passing through Albert, along the Bapaume road, and turning to the right, it was dusk when the Company reached Sausage Valley after a fast and rather fatiguing march. Sausage Valley was the gateway through which the 2nd Division entered to relieve the 1st, and was a revelation of the activity involved in the rear section of a great offensive. The wide valley seemed to be full of artillery batteries—some were firing at the time — cookers, dumps of material, and all the attendant accessories of a modern battle. Vague figures were moving about in casual fashion, but a grim, business-like air rested over everything. The atmosphere was dust-laden, and the burst of an occasional enemy shell added a different note to the clamour, while the sickly-sweet odour of 'tear-gas' brought the gas masks into use at times. On the narrow roadway leading to the head of the Valley, the two-way traffic struggled to pass. Battalions of the 1st Division were coming out as the men of the 2nd Division moved in, and as the shadowy figures passed each other, occasional enquiries were made as to what unit was passing. At one point, an incident, amusing to the onlookers, served to indicate the crowded state of affairs. The Company Transport Section brought the guns and gear well forward to minimise carrying. One limber was in charge of Driver R. J. V. Smith, and was drawn by horses who chose that particular moment to indulge in their jibbing propensities. Presently a very emphatic voice came out of the darkness, requesting the driver to move on, accompanied by the announcement, "We are about to fire." Looking round, Smith discovered, by the aid of a "flash" from a nearby battery, that he was looking down the barrel of a big gun. It is recorded that he called on Heaven and Earth to aid him in moving the refractory animals, at the same time imploring the battery crew to hold their hands.

While still in Sausage Valley, the guns and gear were taken from the limbers and the teams waited by the roadside while Captain Hore sought 2nd Brigade headquarters for information as to the relief of the teams of the 2nd Machine Gun Company. It seemed a very long time to the waiting and impatient men before the preliminaries were arranged, and even then the information was not precise.

No. 1 Section was directed to relieve a Section of the 2nd Company, but the location — to quote one of the recipients — "seemed from vague to unknown." However, a start was made and the Section, led by Lieutenants F. Windsor and R. C. Callister, and accompanied by its 16 "attached" men, set out, carrying guns and a collection of gear that would in later days have caused considerable hilarity. It should be noted, however, that the Section was entering its first major enterprise, with little experience and no advice to guide it. It was fortunate in one important respect, in that it had been provided with an efficient guide, who conducted his charge past the Chalk Pits, through Pozieres, to the 2nd Company position on the forward edge of the roadway running north-west past the village cemetery. The location was on the left of the Brigade frontage. There was much traffic en route, and though dark the dreadful effects of the previous bombardments were observable in the ruined roads and village and the numerous dead lying around. On the way, several bursts of shrapnel were encountered, and though some men were struck by pellets, none were wounded or incapacitated. The 2nd Company teams departed with great celerity after showing the deep dug-outs in Rail Trench adjacent where the reserve men were at once placed for protection. "We had only the vaguest ideas," said Lieutenant Callister, "as to the general whereabouts of the Germans and our own people, were thoroughly tired, and the shelling, though continuous and persistent, was mostly falling on ground just behind us."

No. 2 Section was directed to relieve teams of the 2nd Company, which were located on the right of the Brigade front in a place known as the Orchard. Like No. 1, the whole of the Section, with its four guns, gear, and sixteen "attached" men set out. Lieutenant A. N. McLennan was in charge, and Captain Hore decided to accompany the party. All went well till the strong concrete block-house, known as "Gibraltar," was reached. Here Captain Hore called a halt, and while resting, Lieutenant McLennan fell to the ground, evidently struck by a fragment from a shell-burst. Fortunately, he was not injured. At that stage, the guide confessed he was lost, so Captain Hore ordered the party to fall back to the Chalk Pits, just off the road leading to the rear of Pozieres, while he reported to Brigade headquarters. Meanwhile, some men became detached in the darkness, and, moving forward with the ingoing infantry, reached the front line. A few walked into No Man's Land before realising their position; while two or three—following a call for "machine-gunners"—joined infantry parties, only to discover that Lewis gunners had been called. The detached ones took refuge in shell-holes or remained with the infantry and rejoined their comrades when dawn appeared. With the approach of daylight, Lieutenant McLennan, with Sergeant A. L. Newland, Corporal H. A. Robinson, and two teams and guns, made a second attempt. An infantry guide was obtained. The man was just about done—he had been in and out of the line many times, and the look in his eyes plainly told of an imminent break-down—but when McLennan asked him if he would take the party in he undertook to do so. While taking a brief spell, Lance-Corporal A. E. Fair was severely wounded in the back, an injury which led to his discharge. McLennan's batman, Private F. W. Johnson, was also wounded at this stage. Without further loss the anxiously waiting 2nd Company teams were relieved, and the men detached overnight rejoined their comrades; some being sent out as more than sufficient were available for the two guns. No dug-outs were in the vicinity, so the party proceeded to dig narrow slits in a bank, such as their experience suggested would give them the best protection in the circumstances against shell-fire.

Nos. 3 and 4 Sections were sent to reserve positions, the former to the rear edge of Bailiff Wood and the latter to the Chalk Pits. No loss was sustained in reaching the positions, but the guide appointed took No. 3 over a long and circuitous journey and it was 2.30 a.m. on the 27th before they finally settled down. "I shall never forget that journey," said one. "It was my first entry under shell-fire. There was little shelling after leaving the road, but we trailed through various trenches in which numerous signallers' wires were hung along the sides, on the bottom, and across the top. I carried two petrol tins of water, and to leave my hands free had slung my rifle across my back. In the darkness the wires were invisible, and every now and then I was almost precipitated on to the bottom of the trench owing to tripping over them. Then, as a variation, the piling swivel of my rifle caught an overhead wire and I was jerked violently backwards. I determined to get through with those tins, and succeeded. After reaching our destination, we settled down, but had very little sleep owing to the continuous noise of the artillery of both sides." Thus by the early morning of the 27th the 2nd Machine Gun Company had been relieved and the 6th Company established in the area of the 6th Brigade.

The narrative now follows the experiences of the left (Cemetery) and right (Orchard) positions separately until the night of the 4th August, when the second attack made by the 2nd Division brought about a re-arrangement.

No. 1 Section, established overnight in an advanced position in front of the Cemetery, was not sorry when the first signs of daylight appeared. Meanwhile, the teams had dug narrow slits into the forward bank of the roadway for the purpose of cover. The four guns were grouped close together; one to give crossfire with a gun at the Orchard on the right; two to cover the left flank, and one for frontal fire. They did not have long to wait. At dawn, a large party of the enemy were observed moving obliquely across the front. Lieutenant F. Windsor, acting as No. 1, fired a belt into them and they dispersed hurriedly. Later, 42 bodies were counted by the 23rd Battalion, who, in reporting the matter, referred to them as "Mr. Windsor's men." When daylight appeared, the two officers reconnoitred their surroundings and located their immediate neighbours, the 24th Battalion. During the day, they were visited by patrols from the Warwickshire Regiment on the left as well as the 24th Battalion. Heavy and effective shelling continued during the day. The 24th Battalion in Kay Trench and holding the line to the Orchard suffered severely, but the teams dug in, in their advanced position, escaped casualties. To quote from Lieutenant Callister's account, "The shelling smashed up the Cemetery and Pozieres into still smaller dust without materially harming us." A very disturbed night followed. Several times the teams were straddled by salvoes from 4.2 in. guns, and a number were hit by small fragments. Lance Corporal H. G. Oldham's gun was blown up and damaged although still capable of firing. While some of the "attached" men were assisting the 24th Battalion wounded, an unlucky shell fell among them, wounding Privates W. E. Spark, J. C. Ritson, A. R. Brien, and A. Hunt, the latter mortally. About 2 a.m. on the 28th, large detachments of the 24th Battalion, while digging "jumping-off" trenches in No Man's Land, were compelled to return to the front line owing to the heavy shelling. About 5 a.m., the shelling along the roadway became intense. Lieutenant Windsor was severely wounded and was carried out via Rail and Kay Trenches, by Privates A. E. Noonan and B. H. Johnston, for which action they both received the Military Medal. The same shell that hit Windsor put nine splinters in Lieutenant Callister, but that imperturbable individual carried on and did not deem such a dose worthy of evacuation. Others were wounded, but carried on, namely, Sergeant J. E. Hopper and Lance Corporal W. Dutton. Lance Corporal R. A. Armstrong's gun was also damaged. About 11 a.m. on the morning of the 28th, No. 3 Section appeared and relieved Callister and his Section. The relieving party was guided in by Private G. Pollock, who had shortly before taken out a report to Company headquarters.

Lieutenants A. N. Noall and D. McM. Lilley, the latter recently transferred from the 23rd Battalion, were in charge of the four teams of No. 3 Section. The journey in can best be described by one of the party. "It was about 11 o'clock on a bright, warm morning when the Section set out for the line. Leaving Bailiff Wood and passing the Chalk Pits, we were soon in the thick of it. Approaching the village, we passed dead Tommies, then 1st Australian Division men, and then saw numbers of our own Division lying around. The road was badly damaged, but the village! what a sight! It was just a heap of rubble and dust, shredded tree trunks, deep shell-holes, and upturned earth. A steady barrage was falling on the ruins in a pitilessly rhythmical way, and the shells threw up great quantities of dry earth and dust, to be followed by horrible gusts of air laden with the odour from dead bodies and the acrid smell from the explosives. At one point in Kay Trench, as we hurried along, I vividly remember passing a partially destroyed sector wherein a row of 24th Battalion men sat in 'funk' holes scooped out of the wall. Partly buried, they sat there, killed by concussion. One boy held, in the act of reading, a small book, but the fixed eyes that looked on its dusty pages saw not the printed words. Further on, a string of men with gas-masks on and blood-stained bandages from previous wounds, lay with their faces towards the rear. Gusts of shrapnel appeared to have caught them as they were moving out. Hurrying on, trying to dodge the bursting shells, conscious that we could be seen from the higher ground in front, gasping for breath, we finally fell into a very shallow trench where some of the leaders were resting. 'Where is the front line?' we asked. 'You are in it,' came the reply. Presently the party was divided; some were sent to the dug-out in Rail Trench, while the others were posted on the guns. No. 1 Section departed very cheerfully for the reserve positions at Bailiff Wood and the Chalk Pits."

No. 3 Section continued in the positions vacated by No. 1, which they improved by further digging. The shelling of the village and approaches continued steadily through the day, but the teams, owing chiefly to their advanced position, were not unduly disturbed. During the day it was learned that the Brigade, in conjunction with the 7th and 5th Brigades on the right, was to attack the ridge in front during the night, so everyone became keyed up. The Brigade's share in the assault was allotted to the 23rd Battalion, whose role was to secure the left flank of the joint operation.

The Company teams were not required to take part in the advance, but were to hold themselves in readiness to move forward if the attack was successful. Zero time was fixed for 12.15 a.m. on the morning of the 29th. The 23rd Battalion attacked with confidence, and despite considerable opposition and loss, gained its objective—the Orvillers-Courcelette road—as the left flank of the Division's attack. On the right, however, the 7th Brigade—mainly owing to meeting uncut wire—had to fall back, and their failure in turn obliged the 23rd Battalion to relinquish most of the ground gained. To the anxiously watching teams it was soon apparent that things had gone amiss. A tremendous volume of rifle and machine-gun fire was coming from the ridge, and enemy flares appeared to be rising in scores, while wounded men were coming back in large numbers. Soon after, unwounded men began streaming back past the gun positions. "Where are you going?" said the gunners. "Back to Sausage Valley to reorganise," came the reply. To the gunners it was a weird sight—the streaming infantry disgusted with the turn of events, the numerous flares throwing a brilliant illumination from the ridge, the incessant small-arms fire. It subsequently transpired that the 7th Brigade had fallen back in accordance with orders, and that the 6th did likewise, owing to their flank becoming exposed.

Later, the excitement died down, and a rather heavy ground mist accompanied the dawn. It was a fortunate circumstance, as it enabled the line to be re-organised, and the hard-working and heroic stretcher-bearers to bring in many badly wounded men from No Man's Land. Those devoted men worked well into the morning, risking the enemy's fire, which, in fairness it should be stated, was generally withheld. After daylight, it was reported that wounded men were still lying out in front, and some of the bearers and infantry went out to their aid. Their example was followed by two members of the Section—Privates F. V. W. Duncan and H. L. Heyne—both of whom were awarded the Military Medal for their action. Major M. Mackay of the 22nd took a prominent part in the re-organisation of the line. The extension of the Brigade's flank by the 23rd Battalion on the left, necessitated a change in the gun positions; accordingly one gun and team were detached from the Cemetery position and placed near the junction of Cemetery and Orvillers-Courcelette roads.

After the turmoil of the night, the day was comparatively quiet; it was but the calm that oft precedes the storm. The night that followed beggars description. Soon after sundown the German bombardment commenced to fall and by 10 o'clock had reached great intensity. A pitiless, devastating and continuous hail of shells fell on the wretched ruins and vicinity until it seemed impossible for any living thing to exist. The period of great intensity lasted for about an hour, eased somewhat, but continued until an hour before dawn, when it reached an even greater degree of intensity. The roadway, the bank, and surroundings were pitted by large and small shell-bursts. No words can convey the agony of that night. The teams on the guns huddled together in their little shelters, covered themselves with spare equipment, petrol tins, and odds and ends, and just shivered from minute to minute in that hellish storm, awaiting annihilation, for nothing else seemed possible. Two guns were blown to pieces, all the petrol tins were perforated in many places, and the web equipment ripped and torn; but only two men were wounded —Privates H. G. Black and E. Comerford. At dawn the storm subsided to a complete calm, when the shivering and well-nigh demented teams surveyed their surroundings. It was miraculous that men should have emerged from that shell-torn spot. While gazing at the wreckage around them, relieving teams arrived. How poised and normal the newcomers appeared! The latter's appreciation was revealed in their faces, and they asked few questions.

The outgoing teams then walked or tottered to Bailiff Wood. "Reaching the comparative quiet of this reserve position," said Private W. S. Clayton, "some of the gunners broke down completely. The tremendous strain of the past two days brought a curious reaction upon some, now that they were out and away from the terrors of those awful bombardments. None of us could sleep, although not a single one had slept a wink for over fifty hours. Some cried, others laughed and cried together, and one or two were merely moody and nerve-stricken. However, after a few hours everybody came back to normal and no harm appeared to have been done." But two members did not. Corporal W. H. Butterworth, shocked on the day of entry, was evacuated and discharged from active service with broken nerves. Private E. Comerford returned to the Company after his wound had healed, but his shattered nerves precluded him from line work, and he was allotted to the Transport Section and died after discharge.

The relieving party was composed of two teams under Lieutenant R. F. Bennett and Sergeant C. F. Murrell. Some of No. 2 Section, three drivers from the Transport Section, and three "attached" infantry men made up the party. The drivers had volunteered for line duty when it was represented to them that gunners were needed for reliefs. Sergeant Murrell took over one gun at the Cemetery and the drivers the gun on the left. Murrell's team set to work to dig a new gun position, but before it was completed a shell landed close by and Private J. W. Findlay was stunned by the force of the explosion. While Murrell was bending over, attending to Findlay, another shell burst and killed him outright. Findlay was taken out with a five-inch cut in his steel helmet, and evacuated; but recovered in a few days. It was a bad start for the new party. Sergeant Murrell was a respected and capable non-commissioned officer, and appeared destined for commissioned rank had he lived. About midday, Driver E. W. Barnett was wounded in the groin by a shell splinter and evacuated. No counter-attack was made by the enemy, but the enemy shelling continued. On the way out after the relief of the party on the 2nd August, Driver E. J. Nash was wounded.

Lieutenant J. D. Campbell was in charge of the incoming relief. Included in the two teams were a few drivers from the Transport Section who had volunteered for line work. The two guns were maintained in readiness for action, but no counter-attack developed, and no loss was sustained, although the shelling continued at intervals. On the evening of the 4th August, teams to take part in the second attack of the 2nd Division arrived, and Campbell and party retired to positions at Bailiff Wood and the Chalk Pits.

The experiences of the teams at the Orchard position will now be told. After the relief of the 2nd Company teams on the morning of the 27th, as previously noted, the surplus men were sent out, and the remainder set about improving their scanty shelter. The shelling became very severe at times, and during the day a 5.9 shell burst almost at Corporal H. A. Robinson's feet, wounding him and also Private R. O. H. Wood, who was close by. Robinson subsequently rejoined the Company, although his sight was impaired by the shell-burst—but Wood died of his wounds on the following day. The shelling continued at intervals, although no further loss was sustained. On the night of the 28th the teams witnessed the launching of the unsuccessful attack by the 7th Brigade, which has been previously alluded to. Early next morning they were relieved, but the shells pursued them as they hurried out, causing the loss of two men. Private G. A. Littler was severely wounded and was afterwards discharged from active service. Private A. G. Elliott sustained the loss of his right eye, and, after being boarded in England, served with the Army Medical Corps in England until the Armistice. Corporal Robinson and Private Elliott had stuck determinedly to their gun during the bombardment, and both received the award of the Military Medal.

Lieutenant F. J. Blenkarn, with Sergeant F. W. H. Matthews, had charge of the relieving teams from No. 4 Section. They had the usual severe shell-fire to endure, and some men were badly shaken and had to be sent out for a rest, although no evacuations took place. One gun position had to be re-dug. Sergeant Matthews saw to it, and then personally built a "block" in an adjacent infantry trench which was being enfiladed. His gallantry under fire and subsequent good work on the left flank brought him the award of the Distinguished Conduct Medal—the first of that coveted decoration to come to the Company.

After two days and nights, teams from No. 1 Section provided relief. Lieutenant Drummond was in charge. Again it is a story of inaction, but severe shelling to contend with. "At the Orchard," said Drummond, "I passed two of the worst days of the war for me. The shelling was terrific and almost without a break. We simply had to lie at the bottom of the trench with one man on watch." On the morning of the 3rd August, Lance

Corporal W. Dutton was seriously wounded by a shell-burst. His case was urgent, and although the shelling continued, he was at once carried out by Privates A. St.G. Tuohy and J. H. Hodge, who volunteered for the task. "They carried him through all that fire, anxiously watched by the remainder of us," said Drummond, "until they miraculously passed over the horizon in safety. How I admired those chaps with my whole heart and soul." Although Dutton had sustained a pitiable gash in the thigh, he displayed splendid courage. More than once he asked the bearers to rest themselves, assuring them that he was all right. However, his wound was mortal and he died the following day. Tuohy received the Military Medal for his action, but Hodge, for some unaccountable reason, was not rewarded.

While the teams in the line were engaged in the task of refusing to be blown out of their positions, and holding on in case of enemy counter-attacks, those in the rear were not idle. About the 30th July, indirect fire was commenced on enemy roads, tracks, and trenches opposite the Brigade front, sometimes by day, but generally by night. Most of the firing was supervised by Lieutenant Callister. A German prisoner captured at this time stated that transport waggons in rear of the enemy trenches had been hit by the fire. That the shooting was generally more effective than at the time supposed, may be judged from the following reference appearing in enemy records. The translation, kindly supplied by the Official Historian, has been taken from the history of the 86th Reserve Infantry, a Schleswig-Holstein Regiment, which was opposed to the 6th Australian Infantry Brigade at the end of July and beginning of August. Page 145:—

> "During the night the artillery fire on the front line lulls. Instead of it there falls light bombs, softly slipping through the air down upon our fragments of trench and craters. The 'English' also have built in covered machine guns, which graze the edges of our trenches with indirect fire. Our men press themselves against the trench walls and let the spluttering bullets strike into the mud only a hand's breadth away from themselves. Many a one is caught, mostly shot through the head or throat. In vain we wait the ration party. The men support themselves on what they can find on the bodies of the 'English' dead, and that is not much. . . ."

During the whole of the operations Company headquarters were maintained in Sausage Valley near Brigade headquarters. Early in the proceedings the attempt to maintain telephone wires to the line was abandoned, when it was seen that the terrific shelling rendered it impossible. Instead, the signallers were utilised to carry messages to Bailiff Wood and Chalk Pits positions, and were sometimes asked to accompany Captain Hore on his visits to the teams in the line. This was not regarded as a desirable job, because the Captain did not appear to be unduly impressed by the inevitable risks. On one occasion, the pair sheltered awhile at Gibraltar block-house. After a brief halt, the Captain looked out and said casually, "I think we will go on, the shower seems to be over" — a conclusion with which his companion by no means agreed. Signaller D. C. Howard has related an experience while accompanying his officer on a trip to the forward positions. Leaving the aforesaid block-house, the pair came to a freshly-made shell-hole, from which smoke was ascending, and wherein the Captain espied a small animal. Turning it over with his stick, he said, "By Jove! Howard, I believe it is a toad." Totally oblivious to some "black shrapnel" bursting almost overhead, the examination continued. "A toad, all right," said he excitedly, and, pointing to a luminous spot on the creature's forehead, continued, "You know what Shakespeare said of the toad, Howard," and then proceeded to quote:—

"Sweet are the uses of adversity;
  Which, like the toad, ugly and venomous,
  Wears yet a precious jewel in his head:
  And this our life, exempt from public haunt,
  Finds tongues in trees, books in the running brooks,
  Sermons in stones, and good in everything. . . . "

"Possibly the only occasion," said Howard, "when the Immortal Bard was quoted at Pozieres. For myself, I was also engaged in fervent quoting, but it wasn't Shakespeare." The incident serves to justify the opinion of one observer that "with all the Captain's enthusiasm and keenness to quickly prosecute the war to a successful conclusion, there were few less militaristic minds engaged as combatants."

Other rear activities included the cooking of meals in Sausage Valley by "Bill" Wormald and "Joe" Purchase, and the work of the Transport Section in bringing supplies to Company headquarters.

The dug-outs at the Chalk Pits, which sheltered most of the reserve teams, were steadily shelled, chiefly by field guns, but only two casualties were sustained, when Private W. H. Wilson was wounded on the 31st July, and Private G. A. Jeffery on the following day. While deep dug-outs afforded good shelter, their continuous use by troops during persistent and prolonged shelling had a most injurious effect on their morale. It was noticed, particularly at this time, that while individuals felt safe inside, they had to endure having to listen to the sound of every shell-burst, both near and far, which was curiously amplified and distorted by passage down the dug-out stairways. Imaginations ran riot and the effect was demoralising. Lieutenant Callister noted, "No. 1 Section left the Cemetery for Bailiff Wood, where they bivouaced in the open for two days. Went to Chalk Pits dug-outs in good fettle, but several men, much shaken at the Cemetery, were obviously again affected after living in the dug-outs. Those in the open on the indirect-fire guns were always plainly less affected at the end of a shift than at the beginning. Staunch men had to be urged to leave the dug-outs. Sergeant Hopper and a team on a gun located in a narrow trench off the road between the two Chalk Pits, and subjected to many shells and some phosgene gas, was light-hearted by comparison with those in the safety of the dug-outs. I noticed its effect on myself, though, because as I was in and out day and night it was perhaps less marked than with the teams in the dug-outs."

Since the failure of the attack made by the 2nd Division on the night of 28th-29th July, preparations had been carried forward, mainly by the long-suffering infantry, for another assault on the German lines on the ridge. The enemy wire had been steadily shelled with the object of rendering it passable, and a "jumping-off" trench had been dug some distance in front of the existing front line, so that the attacking infantry would not be called on to traverse the full width of "No Man's Land" once the attack had commenced. Ultimately the operation was planned for the night of the 4th August, zero time being fixed for 9.15 p.m. As on the first occasion, the three brigades of the Division were involved—the 6th on the left, the 7th in the centre, and the 5th on the right. The part allotted to the 6th Brigade—with which this narrative is mainly concerned—was to take about 400 yards of the enemy's first and second lines on the ridge, designated O.G.1 and O.G.2 respectively, as well as securing the Orvillers Courcelette road with the object of making it the left flank of the general operation. To the 22nd Battalion was given the task of seizing the Brigade's section of the O.G. lines, with the 24th Battalion in close support. The 23rd Battalion was to secure and hold the left flank.

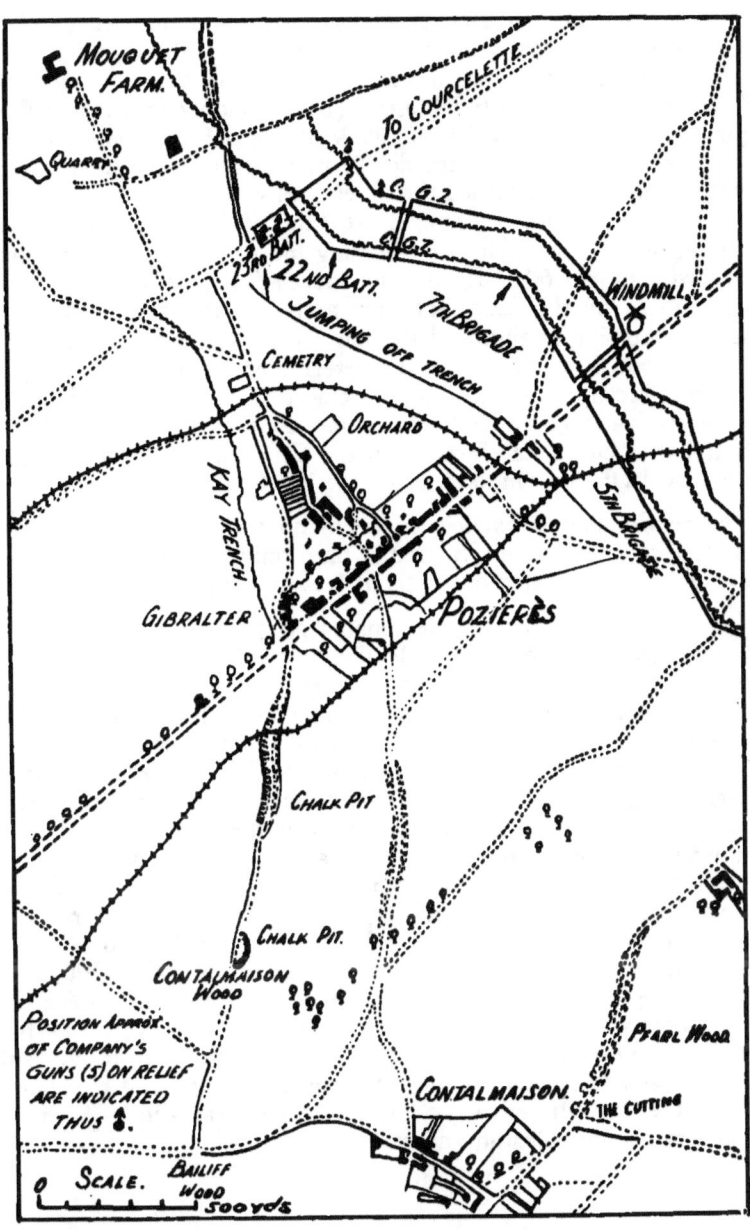

Attack by 2nd Division on Pozieres Ridge, 4th August, 1916.

The Company's orders were: (a) To provide indirect fire on the second objective from two guns at the Chalk Pits for two minutes after zero, and then switch to a line covering the left flank of the attack for two hours. (b) To supply four teams and guns—two to move to the left flank of the objective and two to the right flank. They were not to move until 40 minutes after zero, when it was assumed the objectives would have been taken.

In contrast with the first effort, the 2nd Division achieved a notable success in seizing and holding the ridge at Pozieres. On the front of the 6th Brigade, the successful issue was seriously jeopardised by the 22nd Battalion arriving late at the assembly positions, owing to another battalion using its avenue of approach to the front line. However, the determined leadership of Major M. N. Mackay was equal to the emergency, and the Brigade's objective was secured, and held against counter-attack. The 22nd Battalion secured its objective in the O.G. lines as ordered, and the 23rd Battalion did likewise on the left flank.

The Company's participation will now be noted. As to the modest indirect-fire programme, it need only be said that the task laid down was carried out without loss or unusual incident.

No. 3 Section, under Lieutenants A. J. Noall and D. McM. Lilley, was detailed to provide the teams for the attack. The intimation was withheld from the men until the evening of the 4th. When it was announced, it came as a disagreeable shock to them at the rear Chalk Pit dug-outs where they had been gathered meanwhile. Having been in the line, prepared to move during the first attack, they concluded that others would be called on for the second operation, although it must be admitted that they had been out of the line for six days. The news was received differently, according to the temperament of the individual. Some seemed stunned, while others expressed themselves in very forcible language. After Private "Tod" Nicholson had so relieved himself, he suddenly turned to his neighbour and said, "Bill, you have a copy of 'The Last Fight,' from Browning's 'Prospice' in your notebook; let me read it." It was handed over, and for some minutes, as his comrades pondered over the grim task ahead and the steady enemy shelling of Pozieres boomed and re-echoed down the dug-out stairways, he read and re-read—to his obvious comfort—those splendid and stirring lines:—

POZIERES.

> "I was ever a fighter, so—one fight more,
>   The best and the last!
> I would hate that death bandaged my eyes and forbore,
>   And bade me creep past.
> No! let me taste the whole of it, fare like my peers,
>   The heroes of old.
> Bear the brunt, in a minute pay glad life's arrears
>   Of pain, darkness, and cold."

It was early dusk when the Section moved up to the village. The attacking infantry had been moving some time previously, and enemy shells were steadily falling on the village and approaches. Making use of Centre Way, the teams soon joined the 22nd Battalion at the southern end of the village. Owing to some mischance, the 26th Battalion of the 7th Brigade were using the same avenue to the assembly positions, and acute congestion followed. The trenches were crowded with equipped infantry, trying, with little success, to get forward, and stretcher-bearers with badly wounded cases struggling to get out. The enemy had placed a heavy barrage on the south of the village, and a maddening time followed with shells bursting around the struggling impotent men, whose organisation was in danger, and who saw that they might be late for the attack. During the turmoil, the gunners were ordered to climb out of the trench and make their way overland to their destination. They did so, and a wild scramble through the heavily shelled village followed. Private W. S. Clayton has recorded: "The village was being liberally plastered with shells, and we had an exceedingly hectic time rushing, crouching, falling, and stumbling to our objective. We became separated from one another in the rushes, but we all eventually reached the position we had been allotted with our gear intact. I particularly recollect poor old Toddy Nicholson tearing through the village carrying two boxes of ammunition, hanging on to them like grim death, looking terribly angry, grunting, snorting, and swearing roundly, and every here and there throwing himself full length on the ground to escape the shells. He cursed the war, the Germans, the Kaiser, Billy Hughes, and everybody he could think of or remember. I grinned at his capers once and he thoroughly cursed me too and wanted to know if I was enjoying the 'picture show' very much. Toddy was fond of tinned 'petit pois' and he had a tin in his haversack, and I noticed that he would often feel to see if it was still there. He would never eat anything else as long as he had a tin of peas."

In spite of the shelling, Lieutenant Lilley and his two teams—who were directed to the left flank — reached the Cemetery position unscathed. There they remained while the attacking infantry assembled and went forward at zero when the British artillery opened. Shortly after 10 o'clock, the teams moved forward to the left flank while gusts of machine-gun fire swept by, most of it just over their heads. Stumbling over dead and wounded infantry, they came on the 23rd Battalion digging furiously along the Orvillers-Courcelette road, while German flares fell around them. Falling back a short distance to be out of the way of the diggers, the guns were mounted in defensive positions, and the night passed with the infantry digging and bombing, but without any opportunity for the guns coming into action. The morning found the line a little short of the objective, an enemy strong-post having held back the attackers who suffered severely in the vicinity. In the early morning, guns of the Brigade Trench Mortar Battery blew up the post by some accurate shooting, the teams watching with much interest the remarkably efficient work of the Stokes gunners. Except for some shelling, the day passed without incident. One diarist in the party noted: "Merciless bombardment of our communications all day, and again at night till dawn." Early in the morning of the 6th, Lieutenant F. J. Blenkarn brought in two relieving teams from No. 4 Section, who carried on till relief by teams from the 4th Machine Gun Company during the following day (7th) in accordance with the change by which the 4th Australian Division took over the line from the 2nd. None of the Company's guns in this sector came into action. Since the night of the 4th, both sides appeared to be uncertain as to the actual position on this flank, which probably explains the comparative inaction in this quarter.

Lieutenant A. J. Noall, with his two teams, reached the Orchard position without mishap. Shortly after 10 p.m., the party moved forward. One team appeared to have become lost in the darkness and confusion, and did not reach their objective; but the other team, under Sergeant J. W. Taylor, got into their allotted position before midnight, and established their gun on the right flank of the Brigade in O.G.2 at a point about midway between the Orvillers road on the left and the Elbow on the right. Before midnight, Private F. M. Graue was wounded and got out safely. The remainder of the team—Lance Corporal J. T. Milnes, Privates F. Wigmore and J. E. Smith—proceeded to prepare for the expected counter-attack next day. Shrapnel and shells were enfilading the trench from the left, and the assistance of

Lieut. F. J. Blenkarn, M.C.

Lieut. R. C. Callister, M.C.,

some of the 6th Company Engineers, who were constructing a communication trench back from O.G.2, was obtained to make a sand-bag "block" on the left of the gun. Near the gun position an old sap entered O.G.2 from the enemy's direction and required constant watching. During the night, two German parties, each of two stretcher-bearers, entered and were taken prisoners by the team. Afterwards about seven German infantry also entered and were taken by members of the 22nd Battalion. Dawn brought the expected counter-attack. Straggling lines of Germans were seen coming up the valley from the direction of Courcelette, and moving somewhat obliquely across the front. Lance Corporal Milnes opened fire on them. The advance had also been observed by the 22nd Battalion, and under the combined fire the attack soon withered away. About half an hour later it was renewed rather half-heartedly, and met the same fate. While sitting at his gun, Milnes was badly wounded by shrapnel. His mates carried him to a neighbouring dug-out, where he died soon afterwards. He was a keen and capable gunner, whose upright character was much liked by his comrades. Later in the morning, Wigmore went out to report the position, and on the way escorted about ten Germans who had surrendered during the counter-attack. Corporal A. Payton took in a team from No. 2 Section in relief of Taylor and Smith. They endured a good deal of shelling without loss, and were relieved during the night of the 6th-7th by a party from the 4th Machine Gun Company. Private G. T. Guinea conducted the relief and remained with the newcomers till the following morning. That morning the enemy chose to launch a serious counter-attack, which covered most of the 2nd Division's newly-won ground on the ridge; its right edge falling on the right of the 15th Battalion, who had relieved the 22nd. Guinea immediately picked up a Lewis gun, and, with close-range fire, helped to drive off the invaders. Later the attack was renewed, but this time Guinea used the Vickers gun of the 4th Company, and helped to break the stronger attack. Many were killed in the vicinity by Guinea's fire, and thirty of the survivors surrendered and were taken prisoner. For this very spirited action Guinea received the Military Medal.

When it became known that only one of the Company's guns was established in O.G.2, Lieutenant R. Bennett was hurried off with two of No. 4 Section's teams and guns. They were eventually mounted in O.G.2 to the left of Taylor's position before dawn on the morning of the 5th. They were not involved in the action against the counter-attack, but nearly 2000 yards away a

German field battery could be observed firing. Bennett pushed his guns some distance forward, "whence we directly engaged the German battery," said he, "firing three or four belts at varying ranges in an endeavour to 'bracket' the battery. Whether we were successful or not is not known, but within ten minutes of our opening fire the battery limbered up and retired." Feeling somewhat jubilant, Bennett returned to the front line, where, to his surprise, he was censured by the senior infantry officer "for endangering the safety of his guns." Finally one gun was mounted on the left flank on the Courcelette road, and the other at the junction of O.G.2 with the Courcelette road. About the morning of the 6th, Lieutenant Clive M. Williams, Sergeant F. W. H. Matthews, and two teams, relieved Bennett and party. The former carried on till the 7th. The incoming party from the 4th Machine Gun Company was incomplete, so Lieutenant Williams decided, after consultation with his Sergeant, to remain in the line. Consequently it was about 3 p.m. before they finally handed over their positions; the last of the Company, and probably of the Division, to leave the ridge. During the early morning they witnessed, away on their right, some of the fighting attendant on the penetration of the O.G. lines by enemy parties, and their rout, in which Captain A. Jacka, V.C., of the 14th Battalion, took an outstanding part.

Before the foregoing events took place, the reserve teams at the Chalk Pits had been relieved by the incoming 4th Company. A start was made at 6.30 p.m., and during the evening the teams retired to Tara Hill, where part of the outgoing 6th Brigade was located. Practically no cover was available, so the men slept on the open ground. Before daylight, the sleepers were disturbed by heavy shelling, which caused loss. A few yards from the Company's location, a shell landed in an old gun pit and wounded Lieutenant-Colonel Watson of the 24th Battalion, and killed four of his officers. Without waiting for orders, Captain Hore hurried his men away from the shelled area. Early in the morning, the Company marched to Warloy and billeted. Late in the afternoon, Lieutenant Williams and party reported, and then a re-assembled Company was able to count the cost and then proceed to enjoy much-needed rest away from the immediate sounds of incessant artillery explosions. How deep and sweet was that first sleep! Afterwards, it became possible to review recent events in something like perspective. For the moment it was enough to congratulate each other on survival, and to reflect that though the experience had been a terrible one, the losses had been relatively light. In the sober words of the Official Historian, the Division had passed through "the severest ordeal ever suffered by the A.I.F." With that conclusion—as far as their subsequent experience entitles them to speak—Company members are in hearty agreement. They were to suffer more disastrous shelling, but never again did it approach the long drawn-out agony of the prolonged concentrations of the days and nights at Pozieres.

In the circumstances, and in comparison with the tragic losses of the battalions of the Brigade (61 officers and 1814 other ranks), the Company figures—two officers wounded, five other ranks killed or died of wounds, 20 other ranks wounded, and one evacuated sick—were light. In addition to those mentioned, Private A. Matthews was wounded on the 5th August in circumstances which have not been recorded, and a number of men suffered such impairment of their nervous systems as to disqualify them from future line work. In some cases they were given useful but less exacting duties in the Transport Section. When the Company losses became known, a good deal of comment arose in the battalions of the Brigade; the underlying idea being that the Company was not used aggressively enough. There were, however, several factors which contributed to minimise loss, and they may be stated: (a) Prior to the attack on the 4th August, the line guns were sited at the most advanced points of the line, and consequently escaped a good deal of the hostile shelling directed at the forward areas. (b) The relatively small number of a gun-team unit made possible internal reliefs at short notice and with speed and celerity far in excess of, say, an infantry company. In this connection it should be mentioned that very early in the proceedings Lieutenant J. D. Campbell, of the Transport Section, drew Captain Hore's attention to the presence of a ground mist, which usually prevailed after dawn, and which was accompanied by almost total cessation of shelling. The traffic routes were usually also free of congestion and delay, so Captain Hore directed that reliefs be made in the early morning instead of by night. As a consequence, loss under this heading almost ceased. (c) In accordance with Brigade orders, the "attacking" teams did not accompany the assaulting infantry, but moved forward after the objectives had been gained. This was a wise policy in the circumstances, as both attacks were made at night and the guns would have been useless in infantry melees. Lives were certainly saved by withholding the teams until the objectives had been gained and the guns were available to deal with enemy counter-attacks in daylight. (d) The ingoing teams invariably carried two days' rations with them, thus dispensing with ration parties who would have to traverse the shelled areas twice on each trip. It is pleasing to note that in his report on the final attack, General Gellibrand stated that the Company was successful in performing the duties laid down for it in Brigade orders.

In addition to the award of one Distinguished Conduct Medal and eight Military Medals already recorded, two Military Crosses came to the Company. For his active and fearless handling of his charge, Captain Hore received the Military Cross and Lieutenant Callister was similarly rewarded. Following his courageous work in the line, he supervised most of the indirect fire from the rear guns as previously stated.

CHAPTER VII.

Respite and Return to Pozieres: Mouquet Farm.

7th-27th August, 1916.

Three days were spent at Warloy. The guns and gear were overhauled and cleaned, and promotions were made to fill the gaps caused by recent casualties. No drill was imposed with the express purpose of resting everybody as far as possible. The weather continued warm, and away from the sound of gun-fire and in green and pleasant country, undamaged by war, the Company personnel, after a few listless days, began to recover something of its wonted spirits. Experiences were compared, and each section became more familiar with the members of the others. A common experience had, in a few days, welded individuals into relationships approximating to those of a family with a common viewpoint. The old references by battalions were discontinued, and sections became known by their numerical designations. The action of the transport drivers, in volunteering for line duty, gave rise to much favourable comment in the gun-sections, and ensured their inclusion in the family circle. Overnight it seemed the Company had shed its mental divisions, and become a unit indeed.

Certain changes were made in the commissioned ranks. Owing to the heavy casualties sustained in the infantry battalions of the Brigade, Lieutenant A. J. Noall was permanently transferred to the 23rd Battalion on the 12th August. Eleven days later Lieutenant A. N. McLennan was transferred to the 22nd Battalion. In the latter case, the Company was very pleased to welcome Captain McLennan back later in the year. Captain Hore was promoted to Major, and Lieutenant Drummond received his captaincy; both promotions receiving the hearty endorsement of the whole of the Company. Company Sergeant Major G. Woodburgess was transferred to the 21st Battalion, and Sergeant E. J. Bice was promoted to the vacant position. Company Sergeant Major Bice held the rank for 16 days, and then received his commission when the Company was in the line. Sergeant H. L. Wilhelm became the fourth Company Sergeant Major.

The movement backward from the line into the "rest" area was continued at 2 p.m. on the 10th August. A march of about 12 miles brought the Company to La Vicogne at 8.30 p.m. An entry in the Brigade diary stated that "the troops marched well." The country traversed was open, undulating, and covered with ripening wheat crops. While en route, the Brigade was drawn up on one side of the road near Vadencourt while His Majesty King George slowly motored past and reviewed the troops. His obvious interest in his oversea members of the Empire appealed strongly to those present, who were greatly interested in their first view of His Majesty.

Only one night was spent at La Vicogne. The remainder of the Brigade went into bivouacs, but the Company was the only unit to secure billets. When the Transport Section reached theirs, one of the drivers "accidentally" killed a large duck, and what a hubbub ensued! Madam was soon on the spot, and the drivers quailed before her high pitched and eloquent eulogy of what was said to have been a drake of ancient lineage, and her scathing condemnation of his slayers. Madam insisted on a settlement, which was made; but the reverberations from Madam's tongue apparently reached Brigade headquarters because General Gellibrand, at a Company reunion, held years afterwards, mentioned the incident in his references to the Company's "achievements."

Leaving La Vicogne, and Madame, about midday on the 11th August, march was made to the furthest point from the line, and the Brigade and Company settled down at Berteaucourt for seven days. The village was reached at 5 p.m., after a nine mile march, and one diarist noted that the journey was very trying in the moist heat. Some relief was afforded by swimming in the adjacent Nievre River. The week at Berteaucourt passed pleasantly indeed. Daily drill and training were resumed, but neither was irksome, and reasonably comfortable billets in undamaged and rural France helped all ranks in recovering from the effects of their recent sad gruelling. A diarist, writing on Sunday, 13th August, noted: "As I write, from a high ridge, I can look along a long deep valley filled with trees and villages. The ridge is covered with ripening

RETURN TO POZIERES. 101

corn—a world to ourselves, quietly beautiful. Church bells are ringing, but apart from our boys moving about the streets of the village, there is little movement . . . warm day."

A notable event at this time was a convivial evening spent by No. 3 Section in a billet, which housed the whole of the Section. The occasion was the birthday of Sergeant J. W. Taylor, which coincided with a long run of good luck at "two-up." His winnings were devoted to the entertainment primarily of the Section, by the purchase of 48 bottles of champagne. It was a merry night. From an improvised table, Company Sergeant Major Wilhelm dispensed hospitality with fine impartiality and military precision to all comers, while the host looked on with quiet satisfaction. Corporal G. B. Crerar, ever mindful of order and arrangement, explained to visitors and others that "those fellows on the other side of the billet think they are over here, but they are not where they think they are, they are over there."

Quite naturally the tourist spirit reasserted itself, and the surrounding district was fully explored; little regard, as usual, being paid to the sacred demarkations of districts as laid down by the military authorities. But all ventures abroad were completely eclipsed by the exploit of Signaller D. C. Howard and Private H. F. ("Tod") Nicholson. Paris leave at this stage of the campaign was quite unknown, but these two worthies planned to give themselves literally "French leave," and included nothing less than a trip to gay Paree itself. The venture affords an instance of the initiative both in conception and execution of the Australian abroad, and that sturdy individualism which carried many past the barriers of custom, military restriction, and other obstacles. The exploit, which left many of the more venturesome ones green with envy, can best be described in the words of Howard himself:—

"Wild rumours are afloat that our 'rest' is to be curtailed, and we are to return to the struggles and trials of Pozieres almost immediately. We seek out Bob Watt (Company clerk), ever a mine of reliable information, and to our very ill content, he confirms the rumour and pronounces it fact. This is a blow of the worst order, for our plans had been steadily maturing for a visit to gay Paree, before resuming anything in the way of serious duties, or hostilities. We had mapped out our itinerary, and on our various expeditions to Abbeville and Amiens, had collected a lot of valuable data in regard to the best method of evading the guardians of the Paris Express. Two things stood in our favour: The O.C., in his goodness, and I might add, greatness, was not a disciple of strict discipline after the gruelling the Company had received in the recent attack. Secondly, the 'roll' was in a very healthy condition, thanks to the dividends from our little business of Crown and Anchor! This was a great factor, as we could see unlimited 'backsheesh' would have to be distributed before success could be hoped for.

"Tod was for immediate departure for Abbeville, where we decided the express was more accessible, but after considerable argument, we decided to leave it until the following day, which would give us more time to arrange reliable agents to 'double' for us in such trifling matters as parades, roll calls, etc.

"The morrow dawned fair, which pleased us mightily, considering the twenty kilos to Abbeville were to be negotiated by chance lifts and shank's ponies. After first parade, we sneaked off, the matter a dead secret of course, only the trusted agents knowing our destination, and even they prophesied our end would be the 'clink.'

"I think a word on Tod's 'going away' costume should be said at this stage. Never a dressy line as a soldier, he realised the importance of a visit to the French capital, and had invested in a pair of slacks, canary yellow—no less, but, as he explained, a perfect fit. These were supported by a rifle pull-through round the waist, with the metal weight dangling in front; one German and one Australian boot; regulation hat, and tunic, but not worn quite in accordance with the best military traditions.

"After sundry adventures and misadventures, Abbeville was reached, and we found we had an hour to wait for the express. We had previously reconnoitred the station, so proceeded to fortify our innards with food and stimulants; also secured a bottle of cognac which was to be used as backsheesh as occasion demanded. Now came the ticklish part. The train was in when we arrived at the station, and we counted no less than four English M.P.'s on the platform. To purchase tickets was out of the question, but five francs to the French railway official secured our entry to the station. A casual study of the Tommy Jacks decided us to operate against the one nearest the guard's van, Toddy saying he appeared the stupidest looking, and further wanted to bet he had been a village policeman in peace time. However, the ex-constable eyed us with not a little suspicion, but we approached the guard's van boldly, and proceeded to stow some valises, etc., much to the delight of the Monsieurs. Toddy, once in the guard's van managed to oil the palm of a gorgeous looking official, explaining we were returning to Amiens. The gorgeous one lapsed into a perfect torrent of French, which we feared meant the end of our adventure; but no, he hurried us out of the van, down the platform under the nose and stomach of P.C. 49, who watched proceedings very doubtfully, and with a most elaborate bow, opened a carriage for our accommodation. A few minutes of dreadful suspense, then we were on the move, and breathed more freely. Our travelling companions were two French soldiers, two women of doubtful age, and one fat boy busily consuming a sticky mass of pastry.

"The run to Amiens was without incident, and we took the opportunity to locate the lavatory, where we intended to secrete ourselves during the stop at that station. This we accomplished, but on our return to our carriage, we sensed we had aroused the suspicions of our friends. Toddy's display of a large map heightened this, and his knowledge of the 'lingo,' as he termed it, confirmed the worst. The two women were certain we were spies, and were doing their best to persuade the two soldiers to have us seized at the next stop. The situation called for extreme tact, and Tod, in his best French, explained the harrowing circumstances, how our wicked Captain would not give us permission to see the most beautiful city in the world, where we had sundry uncles, cousins, etc., just pining to see us. We produced our pay books, which were gravely scrutinised by Jules and Emil, the soldats. Then the bottle was brought to light, and we all drank "bon voyage," including the ladies. Even the fat boy looked up longingly from his pastry. From potential enemies we now had four definite allies, who promised to help us at the next stop which, they said, would be the last that the Gendarmes Anglais would inspect. Emil, who could speak a little English, having been a dock worker, became my special protector, and Jules did the same for Todd. Our hats were hidden under the seat, and with our protectors' greatcoats on, we looked passable Froggies, much to the delight of the Mesdames. At the station, the Cops duly arrived, and I feared our benefactors would be our undoing—the guilty looks of the ladies and the steady stare of the fat boy, as we crouched in our corner, were most disconcerting. No village cop was the M.P. who stood at the carriage door, but a living example of what Hawkshaw, the Detective, should be. However, his gimlet eyes saw nothing but four French soldats apparently suffering from a convivial journey. The rest of the journey was plain sailing, the numerous Gendarmes who gave us the 'once over,' being highly susceptible to the bottle, which had been replenished. In some instances, five francs was the backsheesh; this, Emil explained, was far too much. Emil evidently priced Gendarmes Francais at about 50 centimes per.

"We had taken leave of our lady friends some time before, and at Longchamps, Emil and Jules departed. With many good wishes, and a few francs for their valuable assistance, they left us, after advising us to alight at St. Denis, a suburb of Paris, to avoid any unpleasantness at the Gare du Nord. It was well after midnight when we eventually arrived at St. Denis, and had no difficulty in getting off the station. Our next move was to locate a cafe, or something of the kind, and we had not proceeded far when we were accosted by a sentry in front of a big building. More explanations and backsheesh. We learn the building is a hospital, and are escorted within. A great commotion ensues when some one discovers the magic word, 'Australian' on our shoulders. We are presented with hot coffee, biscuits, and cheese, and an orderly who can speak English, is dragged from his bed to interpret; Tod's linguistic powers having failed somewhat under the battery of dialects. By this time, M. le Capitan, has arrived, a gentleman with a huge black beard who, with the aid of the orderly, apologises for his sentry's mistake in dubbing us Italianos. Beds were placed at our disposal, and M'sieur promised that our English speaking friend would be given the day off to show us the sights of the city, and incidentally to see us safely on our train for the North.

"In the morning, it seemed the whole hospital came to see us at breakfast, not the usual French breakfast, but numberless small fish fried—a special treat, no doubt. Our guide to be was the envy of the hospital, and distributed our stock of cigarettes Anglais to all and sundry to appease somewhat the unsuccessful candidates for the job. M'sieur was anxious that we come back to the hospital, and he would arrange a pass, if possible, but although we promised, we had other plans. Eventually we got away, and boarded a tram for the city. At the gates of the old city wall, there was a guard, but our guide was evidently well known, and some shouted remarks sufficed a safe passage.

"The city at last—v⸱' ⸱t more beautiful sight than the Place de la Concord on a fine morning? Louis, that is our guide, shows us the Madeline, the Opera, the Arc de Triomphe, but seems more intent on showing us to the public. His delight is to enter a cafe, and over a convivial glass explain who we are and how we arrived to all and sundry. After luncheon, which was a sumptuous affair, quite staggering Louis, it was apparent that the good fellow was going to become a burden, being then about 'three sheets in the wind,' so, having suitably rewarded him, and promising to return to St. Denis, we left him in a cafe, but not until he had insisted on kissing us both.

"We had already purchased a guide book, and decided to visit Notre Dame that afternoon. The streets were infested with small red taxi cabs which seemed to rush hither and thither without any regard for traffic rules. We hailed one of these contraptions, which seemed even smaller than usual, the biggest part of it being the driver, who was huge, with a moustache to match, and a face like a comic opera brigand. Toddy said it was a great pity Jack Myers could not see the brigand's 'mouthweed' he would be consumed with envy. However, after a hectic dash, the brigand doing his best to imitate a 9.2 shell, we arrived at Notre Dame, and duly took in the wonders of France's greatest Cathedral.

"That evening we dined with an American Doctor who was in a Paris hospital—a Swiss by birth. He was greatly interested in us, and freely admitted that he was under the impression that the Australian troops were mostly coloured. After dinner, we decided to visit Montmarte, and had hardly hit the pavement when we were accosted in right friendly fashion by the brigand himself. Upon learning our requirements, the brigand hastened to assure us that in all Paris, there was no one more fitted to show us Montmarte than he. After explaining that la guerre had considerably dimmed the gaiety of le quartier, our friend proceeded to do his best, and, believe me, that boy knew his onions. Two a.m. found the two weariest men in Paris safe in a pension, the whereabouts I know not. We were awakened early by Madame, who said a visitor awaited us. Our faithful brigand, of course, who had contracted to take us to the tomb of Napoleon at some unearthly hour. The day was spent sightseeing, and imbibing all the good things the city had to offer.

One outstanding incident being a visit to the Bank de France to cash a large bundle of 'shrapnel' notes, which Toddy had kept concealed next his skin. The cashier handled them with implements like chop sticks, and after endless counting and sorting, handed over some brand new 'blankets.' Despite the festive day, we had made up our minds to entrain for the North that night, for we realised full well the consequences of being absent if the Company had to return to the line. We had by this time accumulated a large circle of friends, but I think we owe catching the train to two French officers, who marshalled us en masse into a taxi for the station. We often wondered afterwards were these gentlemen on duty, perhaps so, for they seemed to have the way considerably smoothed.

"Burdened with parcels of wine and food, we took leave of Paris, and settled down to a most tedious journey. The train stopped at every little hamlet, and in the early dawn we reached Longpre, the nearest station to Berteaucourt. Footsore and weary, we eventually arrived at Berteaucourt, only to find the Company gone, but our trusted agents had done well, and Madame a la Estaminet had a message for us, giving us the new location.

"By midday, we had caught up with the Company, and were glad to partake of that well-known delicacy, 'Wormald's Stew.' Conscious of rectitude, we waited and speculated upon our ultimate punishment, which happily did not eventuate into worse than a good 'talking to' by the Major himself."

The welcome spell at Berteaucourt ended on the 18th August when the return journey to the line was commenced. Four day's marching brought the Brigade and Company to the outskirts of the now familiar Albert. The route followed—a night being spent in each village—was La Vicogne-Toutencourt-Vadencourt-Albert. A Brigade church parade was held at Vadencourt, which General Birdwood attended, made a speech and presented ribbons to officers and men of their decorations won at Pozieres. The Company recipients were: Major Hore (Military Cross), Sergeant F. W. H. Matthews (Distinguished Conduct Medal), Privates G. T. Guinea, H. L. Heyne, F. V. W. Duncan, A. St.G. Tuohy, B. H. Johnson (Military Medals).

As the Company approached Albert, everyone felt that it was a case of being involved in the "Push" once again. Heavy artillery discharges and the distant and hollow sounds of the shell-bursts smote the ear, while the all too-familiar spectacle of spurting earth came before the eye. Late in the afternoon, a party of "Tommies" doing pack drill—as part of Field Punishment No. 1, under a very active and regimental lance corporal—were passed, and presented, to Australian eyes, a curious phase of Army life, within sight and sound of the guns.

It was a somewhat subdued Company which passed the night in the remnants of a wheat field close to Albert. Next day it was learned that the 2nd Division was relieving the 1st, and as part of the "change over," the 6th Brigade was to relieve the 3rd Brigade, and a battalion of the 1st. During the night of the 22nd-23rd August, the change took place, and morning found the 24th Battalion opposite Mouquet Farm, with the 21st in the centre and the 23rd on the right of the Brigade front. The 22nd was allotted to carrying duties. The Brigade's right neighbour was again the 5th, while on the left was the 143rd Brigade of the British Army. During the 2nd Division's absence from the front, the line had been pushed forward in small advances until a pronounced salient existed north of Pozieres, with its left edge close to Mouquet Farm. The 6th Brigade was directed to attack the Farm, and to enable the assault to be delivered on its left side, the attacking 21st Battalion changed places with the 24th on the afternoon of the 24th August. The Farm, with its tunnels and dug-outs, successfully resisted the attack of the 21st Battalion (and a number of subsequent assaults by other units), and after a tour of five days and nights in the line, the Brigade was withdrawn, and its place taken by the 4th Brigade of the 4th Australian Division.

Profiting by its sad experience during its first tenure at Pozieres, the Division did not man its front line so heavily, and that policy doubtless affected the disposition of the Company. When the inter-Brigade relief was completed, two guns of No. 4 Section had been placed in shell-holes on the right of the Brigade front, and two others near the Cemetery. No. 1 Section took over positions in Rail Trench, No. 2 were located near Gibralter, and No. 3 in the Centerway. Next day the two line guns were found to be too exposed, and they were withdrawn to Rail Trench and one of No. 1 Section was moved forward to the right of Kay trench to cover the sloping ground towards Mouquet Farm. It was an emergency position in case of counter attack. While moving in to relieve the 3rd Company, Private A. J. Skelly, of No. 4 Section, was wounded by a sniper, and died soon afterwards. An "attached" man, Private T. J. Ryan, from the 24th Battalion, was also killed by a sniper during the relief by No. 4 Section. As during the former tenure, the reserves were quartered at Bailiff Wood and the Chalk Pits. Company headquarters were established in Gibralter blockhouse.

It is not proposed to again describe the line conditions except to say that the artillery fire was raging as before, and pounding the grassless earth with the same results. Men fought and lived and died, trenches were dug, and destroyed as fast as they were completed, and many of their diggers with them. Flies were much in evidence, and a warm summer sun looked down on that throbbing inferno, while the Brigade prepared to attack the Farm. "Shelled continuously from going in till dawn with 4.2 and 5.9 H.E.," records Lieutenant Callister's diary. "Kay Trench," said the same officer, "was a gruesome place, and was demolished and re-dug at least twice while I was in the vicinity."

On the second day of occupancy, all guns except the emergency gun and three in reserve at Rail and Ration Trenches commenced a daily and nightly programme of indirect fire. Roads and communication trenches opposite the Brigade were kept under fire, especially those in the vicinity of the Farm, 55,000 rounds being fired. Although most of the teams were located in the heavily-shelled area, only one casualty was sustained up to the day of the attack, when Sergeant R. D. Desmond received a shell fragment in the left eye. He walked out and was evacuated.

At this time an incident occurred which brought the Company prominently before the notice of the Battalions. At a conference of Brigade officers, the question arose as to the disposal of a German machine-gun reported to fire from a dug-out on the south side of the Farm. Its capture was not considered possible by the 21st Battalion, and General Gellibrand referred the question to Major Hore. The upshot was that, on the suggestion of Major Hore, Private F. Wigmore (the "souvenir" king of the Company), of No. 3 Section reconnoitred the position about midday on the 24th. The following morning he went forward again, this time taking with him Privates L. G. Byrnes and J. E. Smith, from his Section. About 4 a.m. they located the dug-out, but no gun was to be seen. While on the way back they saw what appeared to be an enemy observation post in a shell-hole. Three Germans were using instruments like range-finders, while a fourth had a telephone

RETURN TO POZIERES.

in use. Wigmore borrowed a rifle from some adjacent infantry and, creeping back alone, shot three occupants of the post; the other managed to escape. For his enterprise, he was awarded the Military Medal. "The incident had another result," said the Official Historian, "unintended by the Brigadier. Some of the 21st appear to have held that his suggestion should have been taken up, and, when later they went into action, their determination to prove that the 21st was not faint-hearted caused needless impetuosity."

The Brigade's attack against the Farm was entrusted to the 21st Battalion, to whom a company of the 22nd Battalion was attached for the special duty of guarding the left flank of the 21st's attack, while the 24th were to co-operate on the right of the Farm with bombing parties. Zero time was fixed for 4.45 a.m. on the morning of the 26th August. The orders for the Company were to establish by indirect fire, a curtain in rear of the line to be attacked, as soon as the artillery opened. After firing for one minute, the curtain was to be lifted 300 yards. Special attention was to be given to possible counter-attacks up the valley from the direction of Thiepval, lying north-westerly. The Company preparations were well in hand at the opening of the attack, and the programme as laid down was carried out. For the first half-hour after Zero, fire was "rapid," then a normal rate was maintained for 3¼ hours, 44,000 rounds being fired. In spite of the strenuous and heroic work of the attackers, but little ground was gained, the Farm remained unconquered, and the Company shared in the keen disappointment felt throughout the Brigade. At noon, two teams and guns were pushed forward to the Quarry, close to the Farm and facing its S.W. corner. One gun and a team from No. 2 Section was under Corporal A. Payton, and a team from No. 1 Section under Sergeant J. E. Hopper comprised the other. At a quarter to one o'clock enemy movement was observed in the communication trench leading to Thiepval. Germans were observed coming forward, presumably to re-inforce the garrison of the Farm and a post on the left of the 22nd Battalion. The trench in question was damaged, and as it could be enfiladed, it afforded a good target. Lieutenant A. N. McLennan was in charge of a Company of the 22nd Battalion holding a line of shell-holes on the left flank of the Brigade, and close to the German post referred to. He directed fire from Hopper's gun on to the communication trench, and for a time, said he, "we were having good shooting, until German snipers and field guns made it too hot for us." There was no doubt about the effectiveness of the fire because red-cross stretcher-bearers were busily engaged afterwards, and bodies of the enemy were seen thrown up on the parapet. The Brigade Stokes Mortar Battery had one or two guns in the vicinity, and they joined in the shooting. The target was kept under observation and "bursts" were fired from the gun from time to time. Evidence of the effectiveness of the fire has been found in German records. The following translation, supplied by the Official Historian, has been made from the history of the 5th Guard Grenadier Regiment (4th Guard Division), which was opposed to the left of the 6th Brigade at Mouquet Farm:—

"On the morning of the 27th, an 'English' machine-gun south of Mouquet Farm makes itself unpleasantly felt by those who have to pass through the Schwaben Trench."

Subsequent to the attack, enemy shelling was at times very heavy indeed, and accurate too. Private C. A. Davies, who was with Corporal Payton's team, declared that "it was the neatest I had seen, and it appeared as if Fritz had chalk lines to direct his artillery." Despite its severity, no Company losses were sustained till about 9.30 a.m., when disaster befell a party which was going in to relieve Corporal Payton's team. Signaller N. S. Swindon was guiding them in, and as the approaches appeared to be more heavily shelled they decided to move across country. When near Gibralter blockhouse, a shell-burst on the edge of the barrage killed two men "attached" from the 22nd Battalion, Privates J. B. and E. R. Smith (not related), and Private A. Griffiths sustained a compound fracture of the right knee. Swindon and another, Private S. H. Deakin, escaped scathless. Griffiths never returned to the Company; after refusing amputation, he endured many operations and was left with a shortened leg and dropped foot. On the way to Australia he was operated on for appendicitis the night after leaving Durban.

About 1.30 p.m., the teams in the Quarry sustained their only casualty, when Private W. E. Marshall was wounded in the hand and evacuated. At 4 p.m., after Lieutenant F. J. Blenkarn had taken in two teams to relieve a like number under Lieutenant E. J. Bice, No. 4 Section suffered loss. The outgoing men had just passed Gibralter block-house when a big shrapnel shell burst close by and wounded three. Private H. M. Rollinson had an artery severed when a shrapnel fragment pierced his leg, and sustained numerous small wounds.

First Company billets in France: Rincq, March, 1916.

German machine-gun instruction. Riencourt, June, 1917.

The Company Cooker (Field Kitchen). The Cook at work.
(Transport limber in foreground.)

RETURN TO POZIERES.

He rejoined after an absence of twelve months. Private S. Borland ("attached" from 24th Battalion) was badly hit. In addition to face wounds, his arm and leg were badly broken, but with those injuries he scrambled off the roadway into a shellhole, and out of it into another. Private W. B. Russell bled freely from a number of small cuts and was evacuated to field ambulance, but prevailed on the doctor to allow him to rejoin the Company, which he did on the following day. "I admired the way Lieutenant Bice patched us up and got us away at great risk to himself," said Rollinson, "he had thoughtfully watched us from headquarters blockhouse (where he had gone to report) to see us safely through."

During the night of the 26th, the fine weather broke, and rain fell, turning the dust of the battlefield into mud, but no noteworthy incidents were recorded. Early in the evening of the following day (27th) the preliminary moves took place in connection with relief of the Company by the 4th Machine Gun Company of the 4th Division. By 9 p.m., the change was reported complete, and the Company moved out to the Brickfields near Albert, and thence to billets in Albert, where the night was spent. "Marched out in steady rain," noted one diarist.

During the tenure of five days and nights, the Company losses were three other ranks killed and seven wounded. It must be admitted that they were extremely light; so light as to again arouse comment in the battalions of the Brigade; some of it being of a pointed nature. The Brigade's own heavy casualties (896 out of a fighting strength of about 2,500), and lack of knowledge of the Company's dispositions and work doubtless gave rise to the remarks. It does not appear necessary to add to the comments recorded in the previous chapter except to say that in the present instance there were fewer opportunities for Vicker's guns in the front line. Furthermore, it should be remembered that the Brigade conferences prior to an engagement invariably dealt with the action expected from Vickers Machine Guns. The allotment and siting of the guns was decided after the Battalion Commanders and the Machine Gun Company Commander had given their views. Cause had to be shown for any departure from the orders issued. Major Hore was well aware of the Brigade views that machine-gun casualties could not be immediately replaced, and that he was held personally responsible for the most careful selection of his gun positions, and the movements of the teams.

From their location at the Brickfields, the Transport Section kept their comrades supplied with necessary supplies. One limber made a daily trip to the Chalk Pit and another to Bailiff Wood, where the cooking was done. The water-cart and its 100 gallons of water journeyed to both places daily. With its oddly assorted pair of horses (the clumsy but powerful "Hippo" and his pole mate "The Little Mare"), the turn-out often called forth humourous comment from friends and strangers alike, but the water supply never failed. It is believed that its driver (H. F. Carne) and team, alone of all the water-carts in the Brigade, escaped scatheless while traversing the much-shelled road to the Chalk Pits*. The Signallers performed similar duties to those described in the previous chapter. At first an attempt was made to maintain a line between Brigade and Company headquarters, but although it was laid, first through trenches and then overland, the difficulties of maintenance caused it to be abandoned.

Compared with the former tour in the line at Pozieres, the five days and nights did not impose the same terrific strain, nevertheless all ranks were profoundly thankful to reach the shelter of billets in Albert, and enjoy their first untroubled sleep. The line work added materially to the experience of the Company, in that the indirect-fire barrage fired on the morning of the attack was the heaviest undertaken to date, and various points were noted for future occasions. The demoralising effect on the nerves of men occupying deep dug-outs was again observed.

Private Wigmore's Military Medal was the only decoration to come to the Company.

* See Appendix for an extended reference to the horses and mules of the Transport Section.

CHAPTER VIII.

YPRES, 1916.

28th August-27th October, 1916.

When the 2nd Division was withdrawn after its second visit to the shambles of Pozieres, it must have been apparent to the higher powers that breaking point had been reached, and the first essential was a measure of respite for the sorely-tried remnants of the battle-shattered units of the Division. Accordingly, after a few days spent in moving backwards through "rest" areas, the battalions and associated formations marched to various entraining points and journeyed northwards. The destination was the oft-disputed ground close to and east of the ancient and much battered town of Ypres, whereon the original British Expeditionary Force, in the epic struggles of the first Autumn and Spring of the war, had been well-nigh obliterated in the herculean task of keeping possession of the Channel ports against the massed German attacks thrown against them. At this time (August, 1916), the Ypres salient and vicinity, owing to the German attacks at Verdun and the Somme offensive, had become a very quiet sector of the Western Front, and both sides followed the practice of transferring to that locality their broken Divisions in order to rest them from active operations. As the 1st Anzac Corps moved north, it passed the Canadian Corps moving south to make its first entry into the Somme offensive.

As part of the first stage of the transfer, the Company—conforming to the moves of the Brigade—left billets in Albert on the morning of 28th August, and reached Warloy about midday and billeted. Heavy showers of rain fell during the march, and the Company, feeling the reaction of its recent experiences and disliking the rain, did not present an impressive spectacle. Some of the men wore sandbags round their putties, some wore coats, others waterproof sheets. Generally speaking, there was a lack of uniformity and sprightliness which must have been very obvious to observers, more particularly if they were unaware of the nerve shattering experiences from which the rain-sodden Company had just emerged. No doubt the Company looked at its very worst. In this condition, it passed a Canadian Scottish battalion, immaculate, disciplined, indifferent to the weather, and looking and obviously feeling first rate. As they swung past, their comments were both forcible and audible: "Thank God we have a navy," "Wait till this crowd gets to the Salient, they'll learn a thing or two," "If this crowd took Pozieres, we'll take all France," and so forth. For once, members of the Company had little to say in reply; they knew only too well what the confident commentators had to pass through, and could even feel a degree of pity. A little time later they learned with much interest that the self-same battalion had lost some hundreds of men by shell-fire alone while in the vicinity of Mouquet Farm.

Warloy was left behind the following day, and via Herrisart (two days), Bonneville (three days), Gezaincourt (two days), the Company proceeded by easy marches to its entraining point at Doullens. During this stage some reorganisation was attended to, and the guns and gear brought to their usual efficient state. At Bonneville a Brigade parade was held, at which General Birdwood delivered an address and presented medals and ribbons. Away from the Somme battlefield in undamaged and pleasant country, the men, after the inevitable reaction arising out of their experiences in the line, began to recover a degree of their usual health and spirits. The weather continued warm but showery.

By rising very early on the morning of the 5th September, the Company was able to leave Gezaincourt at 3 a.m. March was made to Doullens, where entrainment took place at 7.30 a.m. The train journeyed northward to Proven, in Belgium, from whence the Company moved to Erie Camp, some distance forward of Poperinghe. The tramp of eight miles in the moist heat, after such an early reveille, was very trying. Rain fell during most of the journey from Doullens, but the men found much to interest them in the interesting country traversed. One diarist wrote: "Left Gezaincourt at 3 a.m. Wet most of the way; journey up through good country—miles of stooked corn. The first touch of Autumn gives a 'riper' look to the landscape. . . . Marched to Erie Camp. This is Flanders. Country grey, flat, and less interesting."

The Company now found itself in country quite different from the Somme. Instead of undulating terrain given up largely to the cultivation of wheat, flatness impressed the beholder. Wheat had, in large measure, given place to hops and root crops. The soil assumed a leaden colour, and imparted a greyness to the landscape, helped no doubt by the advent of Autumn. All ranks were keenly interested in the entry to an area which the early fighting of the war had immortalised. At the moment little evidence of former struggles was observable. Forward of Poperinghe, the country was almost deserted, and save for occasional rumblings from the direction of the Ypres Salient, a sullen peace seemed to rest over everything.

The first move of the 2nd Division was to relieve the 11th (British) Brigade with the 5th Brigade. As a consequence, the Company spent eight days in Erie Camp before being called on for line duty. The time passed pleasantly. Mild Autumn weather was experienced, and the camp possessed baths, duckboards, and reasonable comforts, a commodious Y.M.C.A. hut being a feature. Poperinghe was within easy walking distance, and as it was but slightly damaged and contained much of its civilian population, shops and restaurants were available. A brisk business was done in postcards, photographs of the famous Cloth Hall at Ypres, and Flemish lace. The inhabitants of the district were not so likeable as the French; their permanent grouchiness did not seem justified, even though their tall hop poles did tend to fade away. Some Canadian units were in the vicinity, and it was in refuting advocates of their great deeds that Driver George O'Gorman became involved in an estaminet fight. O'Gorman proved the better man with his fists, so carried off the honours.

On the 13th September, eight teams went into the Salient and relieved a similar number of the 5th Machine Gun Company. No front line positions were taken over, but the guns were distributed in supporting posts between the Ypres-Menin road and the Ypres-Menin railway. Manor Farm, Gordon House, Half-way House, Yeomanry Post, and Moated Grange were included in the positions taken over. Half of each team went to the posts, and the remainder stayed at the large railway dug-outs near Ypres, constituting a local reserve. Owing to the acute salient and the possession of the higher ground on the right (including the famous Hill 60), the enemy had, except for certain folds in the ground, complete observation behind the British lines. As a consequence, all movement had to be conducted at night. During the day, the teams slept, but at dusk restraint was cast off and out of their cramped quarters they emerged for work and exercise. Indirect fire from eight guns became the nightly routine. Each team saw to it that its gun was covered by a hessian screen to cover as far as possible the bright tongue of flame which showed up conspicuously in the darkness. The screen was held in position by sticks across the front and on both sides of the barrel, the bullets cutting a passage through the hessian. It may be assumed that the precautions taken against discovery were effective, because during five weeks' firing in the salient, no gun was molested by the enemy. Nearly all the firing was done at night, but evidently thinking the salient activities could be controlled by observation, the enemy commenced a good deal of movement behind his lines, especially along a road behind Hooge. To counter it, Corporal E. Moffat's gun (No. 1 Section) was placed in position and fired on the road by day as well as by night. With eight guns firing nightly, the laying, checking, and controlling brought numerous problems, the solutions thereof being permanently absorbed in the accumulated experience of the Company. The remedying of mechanical defects became matters of routine. "Blown" or "bulged" barrels were in evidence at this time. Certain differences in the brands of ammunition were noticed, and they were classified accordingly—the British brands showing up well in the comparison. The disturbing effect on the infantry in the Brigade had also to be considered. It must be confessed that some nervousness still existed at this juncture. When Moffat's gun opened during the daytime, Lance Corporal F. Nixon had a gun in a trench some 200 yards in front of Moffat. In the trench was a company of the 22nd Battalion, comprised mainly of reinforcements. Nixon was amazed to see the infantry huddled on the trench floor, wondering why the Germans were firing at them, although the bullets were at least 100 feet above them and rising sharply from the rear. At night, infantry parties, as they traversed paths close to the positions, were badly startled when an unsuspected gun opened fire.

In some positions the gun teams slept in tiny cellars of houses that had long since ceased to exist. Most of them were infested with rats and mice, which scampered backwards and forwards over the occupants and ate holes through the men's haversacks in their quest for food. It was a difficult matter keeping the men confined to those cramped quarters all day. In a couple of places a certain amount of movement was possible by day. Here enterprising ones gathered together old Ross rifles and ammunition lying around, and after various experiments with the latter, some excellent rat shooting was enjoyed. Sergeant Hopper and Private G. Pollock found, if after removing the bullet from the cartridge, only seven pieces of cordite were returned, the bullet stuck in the barrel, but by replacing eight the bullet carried 25 yards with little report. Corporal Stapleton's party was stationed right against Zillebeke Lake, and fished with improvised lines. In more than one instance, teams shot and cooked pheasant; relics of other and peaceful days when the adjacent Chateaux were happy homes instead of the deserted ruins to be seen in every direction. Later, blackberries ripened, and were added to the list of "extras." One day, Private Arthur Anders delighted some of No. 3 Section when he served roast pheasant and stewed blackberries with tinned milk.

The journeys to and from the line were made through the battered town of Ypres, and everyone became familiar with its pathetic ruins. Though but a fragment of its former self, the famous Cloth Hall retained traces of its exquisite beauty; a tribute to its builders, and a reproach to the ruthless invaders who had despoiled it. One member wrote: "The first trip through the ruined city was an experience to remember. The Section marched along its little-damaged paved streets to no sound save the clatter of their feet on the stones, and the occasional whining of a shell overhead, followed by its hollow-sounding crash among the tumbled houses. Sometimes, a sentry would challenge at a narrow passageway, but no other indication of life was observed. When the moon broke through the masses of cloud and illumined the gaunt ruins and tottering towers, the sensation was theatrical and awesome in the extreme. It seemed certain that the spirits of dead battalions haunted that "abomination of desolation."

After weekly spells, the half-Company in the Salient exchanged places with teams from Erie Camp. To the former, it was a welcome break to return to the comparative comfort and freedom of the camp. A daily programme of training kept everyone occupied, and some very fast gun-drill times were established. After the conclusion of the afternoon parade, the men were free till next morning, although they were expected to be in camp by "lights out." Poperinghe and the adjacent villages received much attention. One evening in the officers' mess, discussion arose regarding the difficulty of marching four abreast on the duckboards, and along some of the narrow field paths. The next morning, the parade was startled upon receiving, from Lieutenant Blenkarn, the order, "Parade, number! Form threes, right!" The threes, however, did not materialise. A puzzled parade shuffled into fours and moved off, muttering audibly.

On the 10th September, General Birdwood attended the Brigade Church Parade and distributed medals. Eleven days later, the Commander of the Second Army, General Plumer, on a slippery parade ground, inspected the 21st and 24th Battalions and the half-Company then in camp. About this time, Lieutenant R. F. Bennett was transferred to 21st Battalion, and Lieutenant C. M. Williams returned to the 23rd Battalion. Sergeant F. W. H. Matthews and Corporal E. N. S. Lawrence were promoted to commissioned rank.

Early in September, a new gas protector appeared, in the shape of a box respirator. It was a great improvement on the old P.H.G. helmet that it displaced. It combined a face mask with a metal container holding a filter designed to absorb the gas from the inward-breathed air. A nose clip ensured mouth breathing when adjusted. The new device called for much detailed instruction in its use, and Lieutenant Callister, as Company Gas Officer, again conscientiously and thoroughly inflicted much gas drill on an unwilling Company. Some time later, the small box respirator, a lineal but reduced descendant, was issued, and remained in use till the end of hostilities.

The turmoil arising out of the submission of the first conscription referendum in Australia re-echoed in the Company at this time. The subject became one for daily discussion, each side having warm supporters. One outcome of these controversies was the staging of a properly arranged debate between members of the 6th Brigade on the night of the 12th October. Chaplain A. P. Bladen presided over a large gathering in the Y.M.C.A. hut. Privates W. S. Clayton and W. A. Carne of the Company took part on the affirmative side. The chairman had at times a difficult task to perform in restraining the more ardent spirits in the audience, whose feelings led them to take part in the proceedings. After a spirited encounter, the "Yes" team secured the adjudicator's verdict by 75 points to 56. Long after the men had returned to their huts the debate was continued—unofficially and without chairmen. Amid the turmoil, the voice of Private Herbert Heyne rose above all others. After an impassioned address, in which he described in detail the black horrors awaiting Australia in the event of a "Yes" verdict, he declared the country would be drained of its men, and as a final catastrophe that the male babes "would be torn from their mothers' breasts"—a conclusion which brought down the house and put all parties in the best of tempers and ended all discussion for that night. The members of the Company subsequently recorded their votes without any untoward incident.

YPRES, 1916.

On the night of the 14th-15th October, the 6th Brigade extended its front to the right, taking over the sector held by the 2nd Brigade. In conformity therewith, the Company relieved eight gun teams of the 2nd Machine Gun Company, and as a result of the change the whole of the Company's guns were disposed in the Salient—eleven north of the Ypres-Menin railway and five south of it. Indirect fire at night by all guns was undertaken during the three following nights. The programme was then cut short by a Divisional relief, the 42nd (British) Division relieving the 2nd Australian Division. On the night, 19th-20th October, the 145th Machine Gun Company took over the Company positions, completing the exchange by midnight. Members were not impressed by the very noisy newcomers, who talked and smoked at great length. Taking advantage of the confusion, one of No. 2 Section appropriated a jar containing the "Tommies'" rum issue, but, after carrying it some distance and remembering the miserable post he was leaving, he relented, and with a "poor b——s, they will want it more than I do," he returned the jar to the rightful owners. Well after midnight, the tired men entrained at a point close to the rear of Ypres, duly appreciating the close proximity of rail transport and the methods adopted by the train crew to avoid noise and sparks. It was probably the only noiseless entrainment the Company ever made. At Godewaersvelde the train discharged its human freight, and the Company marched, via Steenvoorde, to billets in Oudezeele. An eight mile tramp did not improve the spirits of the men, who had passed a sleepless night, but when the pre-arranged plan to have breakfast ready was found to have miscarried, their tempers rose to boiling point, and the cook and his assistants were presented, in their absence, with some highly illuminated addresses. However, sleep remained, and by midday a refreshed party awoke to find a hot meal awaiting it. The addresses tendered partook more of the quality of thankfulness than of a warlike spirit.

At this time, Sergeant A. L. Newland was promoted to commissioned rank. Another change related to the war establishment of the Company. Other ranks were increased by 33 to 175, horses (light draft) by two to 47, and G.S. limbered wagons by one to 13. To bring the personnel up to strength, the "attached" men remaining with the Company since the Pozieres operations were absorbed and others were obtained, as usual, by calling for volunteers from the infantry battalions in the Brigade. The volunteers, following the usual practice, were subject to return to their units should they prove unsatisfactory. The extra limbered wagon (and horses) was supplied in response to requests for additional transport to accommodate the gear of the Brigade Light Trench Mortar Battery.

Two days were spent at Oudezeele. No drill was imposed, but everyone indulged in a needful personal "clean up," and the guns and gear were cleaned and adjusted. The country was green, picturesque and undamaged, and in such circumstances the Company soon shook off the cramping effects of its sojourn in the Salient. It was good to walk about the pleasant earth free from the view of enemy observers. The five weeks at Ypres were not unpleasant. No casualties or regrettable happenings disturbed the recovery from the effects of the dreadful days at Pozieres. Officers and men soon regained their mental and physical powers as healthy youth recovers from a sharp and severe illness. In a few cases men remained, owing to broken nerves. unfit for line work; they were transferred to the Transport Section, where they could perform useful but less exacting duties. By this time, the Company had finally come to itself as an actual fact and experience. The former battalion designations dropped out of use, sections looked at each other without the old imaginary lines, and the unit became the joint and several possession of all. From this time, the "family" spirit grew rapidly.

During this period one officer (Lieutenant Blenkarn) and 13 other ranks were evacuated "sick." Under the heading of sickness are embraced injuries and septic sores, as well as bodily ailments. Scabies made its first appearance at this time.

While at Oudezeele, the tourist spirit reasserted itself, and everyone explored the surrounding country. Many visited the quaint and elevated village of Cassell. From the summit, a splendid panorama was obtainable—on a fine day the view extended even unto Dunkirk on the English Channel. The weather became appreciably colder, with a touch of frost in the mornings, followed by beautiful Autumn days. Nobody gave the change a second thought. It was, however, the foretaste of the bitterest Winter many were to experience. Sergeant J. E. Hopper left at this time for a cadet school in England.

Oudezeele was left behind on the morning of the 22nd October, and an easy and pleasant march brought the Company to La Menequat and billets. A diarist wrote, "Country very beautiful. Fields, hedges, windmills, and woods made an idyllic picture. Blackberry hedges in full ripe fruit. Why should man war? Every prospect pleases and only man is vile. Beautiful day. Air keen." Next day, march was resumed to Eperlecques. The same diarist wrote, "Beautiful day; air fresh and clear;

everything serene and everybody enjoying the Autumn sun. Arrived Eperlecques at 5 p.m. A long march—14 miles; five longer than it need have been. Feet very tired."

On the 24th October, the Company left Eperlecques and marched to St. Omer, where it entrained and began the return journey to the Somme. The fine weather broke and much rain fell. A wet Company arrived at the station before the appointed entraining time, and in an endeavour to get the party into the train and out of the wet, Lieutenant Callister went to the office of the Railway Transport Officer. He was very promptly chased out by the Major himself. Undaunted by this expulsion, Lieutenant Campbell entered the office under a non-committal greatcoat which covered his badges of rank, his cap on the back of his head, and with his breezy, debonair manner he bluffed the Major, who was not certain with whom or what he was dealing. The Company entrained at once.

Departing at 4 p.m., the train moved slowly southwards through the night, and arrived at Longpre at 2 a.m. on the following morning. It was a very sleepy Company that detrained at the latter place and marched seven miles through the mud to Brucamps. The next day, the Transport Section moved off by road for the Somme area in showery weather. Each limber was accompanied by a man whose duty it was to apply the brakes when descending hills. At first sight it appeared that the men so detailed would have an easy time, riding on the limbers, but they found the unsprung vehicles gave such uneasy seats that they traversed most of the distance on foot. After a day at Brucamps, the Company, minus its Transport, marched to Mouflers, from whence it was taken by French omnibuses, via Amiens and Corbie to Buire, arriving at 5 p.m. The men were impressed by the sturdy French drivers, likewise their skill in handling their heavily laden vehicles, and very appreciative of the different means of transport provided. Tramping along French roads in showery weather in marching order, burdened with packs and rifles, did not commend itself to anyone. On the way, French Sengalese troops were observed; also German prisoners working on the Amiens-Albert road. The Transport Section rejoined the Company at Buire, where a few days were spent before resuming line duty in conditions of unprecedented severity.

CHAPTER IX.

THE FIRST WINTER IN FRANCE: FLERS.

28th October-22nd November, 1916.

A week was spent at Buire, where billets were cold and cheerless. The yards and approaches thereto, and the so-called parade grounds, were deep in mud. Cold and showery weather was experienced, with rapidly shortening days. Winter was advancing rapidly, and the roads were showing the effects of the weather and heavy traffic. The village was packed with troops, mostly of the 6th Brigade. In such conditions, training was persevered with, but it was a weariness of the flesh. Route marches provided some variety and stimulated the circulation of the blood. Speaking of this time, one member said: "I doubt whether from now on till May, 1917, I ever had warm feet or felt they were dry except while doing marches or some similar hard exercise." Sheepskin vests were issued at this time.

On the 3rd November, the Company left Buire and marched, via Dernancourt, to Mametz Wood, and occupied Nissen huts for the night. On the way it was noticed that the Guards' Division, who were quartered in and around Meaulte, were "spick and span" as usual; units of the famous 29th Division were also in the vicinity. The Company had now re-entered the extensive area over which the battles of the Somme had been fought during the previous Summer and Autumn, and made its first acquaintance with the terrible mud of those battlefields. For miles the surface of that undulating country had been blasted by high explosives till little remained but upturned soil; villages that were largely heaps of brick and rubble; and woods that could only be identified as such by scarred and blackened trunks and stumps. In Summer, the sight had been depressing in the extreme, but after the Winter rains had set in; a picture of utter misery presented itself. Practically all drainage was interrupted, so every shell-hole became a miniature reservoir and the ground a sticky morass. To render movement possible, duckboard tracks had been laid away from the roads in the rear areas, but in the forward sectors it was soon learned that they did not exist. Away from the duckboards, movement by heavily laden men was most exhausting. Men became bogged and were unable to extricate themselves unaided; the rescuers oftimes in turn having to be rescued. In this sea of desolation hutted camps had been erected, and into these refuges incoming and outgoing troops squeezed themselves (and there were always more troops than the huts could accommodate) for warmth and shelter. Fuel was very scarce, and the wooden lining of the huts was often requisitioned to make up for the deficiency. Much statistical ingenuity was devised to prove to the authorities that prior inhabitants were responsible for the depleted lining. Such was the Slough of Despond into which the Company now entered, to all of which must be added the incidence of a Winter of extraordinary severity, with its wind, rain, frost, and snow.

The 2nd Division was directed to relieve the 5th Australian Division, and in conformity therewith the 6th Brigade was to relieve the 8th Brigade, and the Company to take over from the 8th Machine Gun Company in the line to the left of Gueudecourt and one and a half miles north of the much-battered village of Flers.

In pursuance of the "change-over," the Company was astir at 5 a.m. on the 4th November, and after a hurried breakfast moved forward. No. 1 Section, under Lieutenant R. C. Callister, with four guns and teams of four men, was directed to take over the front line positions of the Brigade front opposite Bayonet Trench, which was in enemy hands. They were guided in by a Sergeant of the 8th Company, and reached their objective about 1.30 p.m. The other Sections went to positions corresponding to support and reserve. No. 2 occupied old enemy dug-outs near Factory Corner; No. 3, old enemy artillery dug-outs close to the northern edge of Flers; and No. 4, in ruined houses and cellars in Flers. The spare numbers of No. 1 and Company Headquarters and Signallers were also quartered in Flers.

Although the distance traversed by No. 1 Section was but eight kilometres (five miles), some of the men were crying with exhaustion when they reached their destination, after traversing the last 200 yards through a communication trench knee-deep in sticky mud and slush. No criticism is imputed by this statement. Only those who have passed through such an experience can realise what a heart-breaking ordeal it was.

By mutual arrangement, the heavy tripods and belted ammunition were left at the transport lines and handed over to the 8th Company, and their tripods and ammunition in the line were taken over in exchange. This was done to relieve, in some measure, the overladen ingoing teams, who carried their own guns, spare parts, rations, and water for 48 hours. The 8th Company gunners were unfeignedly glad to escape, and, as one narrator put it, "faded at high speed."

It should be explained that a front line existed in name only. Whatever trench system had existed had been mostly destroyed by the combined effects of shell-fire and the elements. Here and there in fragments of a water-logged trench, infantry posts had been established; sometimes in shell-holes linked together. In such conditions the guns were mounted and the teams settled down to make the best of a bad business.

The men soon discovered that the maintenance of themselves and their weapons, in the front "line," was a task of extraordinary difficulty. Enemy shelling, while not heavy, was persistent. On the evening of the 5th, fragments of a 4.2 shell pierced the barrel casing of Lance Corporal H. G. Oldham's gun, wounded Private V. G. Esmond and shocked Private J. J. O'Gorman, who was sent out to the transport lines to recover. Esmond was a heavy man, and getting him out on a stretcher was a severe task for four men. Captain Drummond, while inspecting the forward guns, happened to come along and assisted the bearers in getting the wounded man to Factory Corner. Lance Corporal W. J. W. Clarke's team on the left had a harrowing time. Three times in 24 hours the gun was buried by shell-fire, and had to be rescued, with its gear, from the muddy debris of the tumbled walls. The teams had many narrow escapes. The all-pervading mud had one beneficial effect, in so far as it neutralised, to some extent, the effects of shell-bursts, otherwise casualties would have been greater. Some diversion was afforded by sniping at odd Germans at ranges from 300 to 1200 yards, a practice which caused Private A. D. G. Bone to remark, "It seems very different when aiming a rifle at a man." Small parties of Germans were seen moving about under a white flag, apparently removing wounded men. In view of the severe conditions, the front line teams were relieved after a spell of 48 hours, and their places taken by the men in support and reserve positions.

On the morning following its entry, the 5th November, the Company was called on to assist in an attack by the 7th Brigade (in conjunction with the 50th (Northumbrian) Division on their left), on Bayonet Trench and "The Maze." The 7th Brigade held the frontage immediately on the left of the 6th, and the Company's co-operation consisted of indirect fire from its rear on Bayonet Trench from two guns, while four guns fired on Lime Trench. In all, 7000 rounds were expended. Owing to the lie of the ground, the front line teams saw little or nothing of the attack, and were not involved in any way. Some of the rear teams caught glimpses of the very gallant but unsuccessful advance by the sister Brigade, and shared in its keen disappointment.

Indirect fire by the rear teams on enemy roads and communications became a daily and nightly task, and kept them fully occupied with carting ammunition, filling belts, and cleaning and repairing guns and mechanism. Regular shifts were worked to spread the tasks and to give the spare numbers and newer men experience in firing by night as by day. Rations and water had to be carried daily from a dump in rear near Montauban, where they had been deposited by the Company's transport. At first, ten guns were employed on indirect fire, firing approximately 2000 rounds per gun each 24 hours. That number was subsequently reduced to eight. Guns were also mounted for use against hostile aircraft. In the latter case, the usual practice was to place the tripod on a small mound of earth and mount the gun backwards as it were. This arrangement gave the gunner a high angle of fire and enabled him to traverse and elevate at will without resorting to the elevating wheel. One difficulty remained, in that the high angle and free swinging of the gun resulted in imperfect feeding of the belt unless the No. 2 gunner was watchful. From this time on, the Company was called on to have in readiness, in and out of the line, guns specially set apart for use against aircraft. Even in districts known as "rest areas," precautions were taken owing to the steadily widening areas over which aircraft operated.

A few days after taking over the front, a new contribution to the casualty lists appeared, viz., "trench feet." This complaint was the result of conditions existing in the front line, where men had to endure hours of inaction during intense cold, with little or no hot food. Blood circulation was so diminished that frost-bite affected the feet. In bad cases, men had to be carried out of the line, and in extreme cases amputation was resorted to. In the Company, the menace never assumed the serious proportions manifested in the infantry battalions; nevertheless, one evacuation was recorded during this tour. Steps were taken to meet the trouble by the issue of dry socks and the rubbing of the feet with whale oil. It must be admitted that the purpose of the issue of oil was not at first perfectly understood. When it was explained to No. 1 Section, Private A. E. Noonan exclaimed: "For the feet, did you say? I drank mine!"

The front line and forward areas received a good deal of shelling, and were subjected to what were known as "five-minute madnesses," the enemy method being to concentrate heavily on selected positions. Unfortunately, one of these concentrations fell during the relief of No. 3 Section by No. 2, under Lieutenant A. L. Newland, on the 9th November. With Newland was Lieutenant F. W. H. Matthews, who had voluntarily gone into the line to make himself familiar with the ground. As the "change-over" was in progress, a shell fell right in the midst of the party, killing both officers, Sergeant J. W. Taylor, Private F. A. Anders and H. Buckley, and wounding Private E. Rhodda. This was a sad loss to the Company. Both officers were respected and trusted leaders, and had earned their commissions by their leadership and ability. No. 3 Section especially felt the loss of esteemed comrades. The death of Matthews was particularly distressing, in that he was the sole survivor of a team of five which was put out of action at Bois Grenier—a team which included his two brothers —to which previous reference has been made. Earlier in the day, Lieutenant D. McM. Lilley was evacuated with a wounded hand, and Privates H. L. Heyne and J. A. Smith were also wounded. Some months later, members of Nos. 2 and 3 Sections erected crosses over the joint grave of their comrades.

To fill the vacancies caused by the death of the officers mentioned, Lieutenants R. Douglas and E. S. Everett were attached, temporarily, from the 7th Machine Gun Company. Four days later they returned to their own Company, when Sergeants A. P. Earle and R. D. Desmond were granted commissions.

In spite of the weather and state of the ground, which should have precluded active operations, the Division again took the offensive on the morning of the 14th November, when battalions of the 5th and 7th Brigades (acting with the 5th Northumberland Fusiliers on their left), made a second attempt against "The Maze" and adjoining trenches. The Company co-operated again by indirect fire on enemy roads, communications and trenches. Between 6.45 a.m. (zero hour) and 8.45 a.m., 20,000 rounds were fired; thence till noon at a diminishing rate; in all, 40,000 rounds were expended. Thereafter the normal rate for day and night firing was resumed. This attack was also unsuccessful, and much sympathy was felt and expressed for the sister Brigades in the Division who were called on to attack in such circumstances.

Flers was regularly shelled, day and night, and locations held by the Sections in support and reserve received attention. While firing from No. 3 Section's position on the night of the 10th, a salvo of 77 m.m. shells fell, one of which burst at the feet of Lance Corporal M. Upton and Private A. W. Crisp, badly wounding both in the feet and legs. Although all of Upton's leg had been carried away except the bone, he hobbled to an adjacent dug-out and called for assistance in the mistaken belief that the other members of his team had been buried in their dug-out. Stretchers were obtained and eight men had a most strenuous and exhausting task in getting their wounded comrades across the deep mud to the forward dressing station. Both men bore their injuries with remarkable fortitude, and subsequently Upton had to endure amputation of the leg.

At night, gas shells occasionally fell in Flers. One night it was estimated that the ruined village received no less than 2000, when some members of the Company spent an appreciable part of the night in their gas masks. Parties carrying ammunition from the dump in the vicinity were usually shelled. While on this work on the afternoon of the 17th November, a 77 m.m. shrapnel shell killed Private W. H. George, and fatally wounded Private J. S. T. Dale, who died in hospital on the 24th November. On the 9th, Private J. Bone was wounded by a splinter of brick from a shell-burst in the village.

As the tour progressed, the weather got steadily worse. Rain was frequent and frost and snow appeared. During the night of the 16th, a heavy fall of snow turned the countryside white. To some members, it was their first experience, and called forth much comment on the beautiful effects produced. Their remarks were forcible, but not complimentary, when the melting stage was reached. "A thaw," said one man, "well, I have heard many beautiful descriptions of snow, but never one of this vile slush which you call a thaw." Fogs, especially at night, were frequently experienced. Their presence added materially to the difficulties encountered when reliefs took place. The blotting-out of landmarks rendered movement slow, difficult, and dangerous.

Some idea of front line conditions may be gleaned from the following narrative by a member of No. 3 Section. "I formed one of a gun team of three men and a Sergeant which went into an advanced post opposite Luisenhof Farm, on the evening of 14th November. The position (which was a little in advance of the infantry front line), was known as a 'strong post.' It was really a short shallow trench dug across a low mound and parallel to the enemy lines. In it were stationed two Lewis Gun teams, our Vickers gun, and some infantrymen. The Vickers gun was mounted a few yards out in front in an enlarged shell-hole, which was connected with the aforesaid trench by a still shallower one. The Post had a good field of fire, but was under observation from the enemy lines. During the night our gun was manned by two men—two hours on and two off—the Sergeant taking his turn. Except that the night was bitterly cold and a few shells fell around, nothing unusual was observed. The next day, though fine, was very cold, and proved very trying to the men in the exceedingly cramped conditions and the necessity of 'keeping low.' Except for a cup of tea at long intervals, no hot food was available. The tea was made with 'Tommy Cookers.' After sunset, the cold became intense, and, later, a misty moon looked down upon a world that was fast passing into the icy grip of King Frost. A waterproof sheet had been placed over the gun to protect it in some measure from dampness. As the night wore on, the sheet slowly whitened until it glistened with the hoar frost in the moonlight. The two shivering sentries, with loaded rifles and bombs beside them, watched. Indeed, but for an occasional shell, the contest had resolved itself into one with the elements. The routine of 'two hours on and two off' continued through the night. After each relief, my mate and I crawled back to the trench proper and huddled together in a hollow scooped out of the trench wall, and tried vainly to sleep. We had our overcoats buttoned over our sheepskin jackets. Some sensation of warmth was noticed, but it did not silence our chattering teeth or quivering limbs. One effect it had was to stir into activity the numerous lice with which we were infested. They crawled and crawled over our impotent bodies until we realised we were unutterably miserable and felt that the war was a great mistake. At the 'stand to' before dawn, the Sergeant gave out an issue of rum, which he had wisely conserved. It was greedily swallowed and gave some relief to our tortured bodies and racked spirits. The next day broke fine. I endeavoured to deepen the shallow cut that connected the gun position, but soon desisted when I came upon the head of an Australian a few inches underneath. On reporting the matter, I was informed that it was probably one of several who had been killed during the construction of the post. At dusk we were relieved. None too soon! Frost bite had affected both my feet, and next morning the Hun blew up the post, killing and wounding the garrison."

The blowing-up of the post referred to in the preceding narrative occurred on the 17th November. Lieutenant Callister had taken in two teams of No. 2 Section (seven men) on the previous evening, and placed one under Corporal S. Hall, just to the right of the Flers-Thilloy road, as previously described. He then took up a position some distance to the left of Hall with three men. An arrangement had been made for the 13th Machine Gun Company of the 4th Australian Division to take over Hall's gun position consequent on an impending change in the Brigade's front. Hall's instructions were that, even if relieved, he was not to retire till dusk, owing to the extreme risk of moving out in daylight. Early next morning, Callister heard brisk sniping, and a few minutes later Private E. A. Duncan appeared and reported having guided in the relieving team of the 13th Company. Duncan had calmly walked overland and escaped the eight shots which the German sniper directed at him. That unwise relief brought serious consequences. Some time later shelling by 4.2 shells was observed on the right, but Callister did not notice any special concentration in the vicinity of his other team. However, on visiting them at early dusk all he could find for a time were dead men and a few small parts of the gun gear. The whole place had been wrecked. Later, Privates A. E. Masters and J. N. Spittle were discovered, much shaken, and it was learned that Hall and Private A. S. Baudinette and the survivors of the 13th Company, team and infantry, had been evacuated. Both men returned to Australia and were discharged as a result of their injuries. A new position was chosen, and the undamaged gun placed in charge of Corporal A. Payton, Privates C. N. Price and L. Barrand, who worked all night and had the gun mounted by morning. During the night it was reported that a man was crawling about 50 yards in front of the left gun. The adjacent infantry post challenged twice without response, and then fired a shot. A man yelled, and when he was brought in it was discovered he was a member of the 21st Battalion who had been lost and shot through the calf of the leg.

At this time the ground became frozen hard, and digging made a ringing sound which brought shell-fire. Some improvement to positions was effected by digging forward "T" saps and roofing them over. The maintenance of the front line guns was a problem which tested the ingenuity of all ranks. To prevent freezing of the water in the barrel casing, a proportion of glycerine (up to 25 per cent.) was used. Waterproof sheets and blankets were wrapped round in such a way as to be readily removed. The recoiling portions were pulled back by hand at intervals, and at night, when possible, single shots and short bursts were fired to keep the gun in a state of readiness. The No. 1 of the team usually kept the spare lock (the vital part of the mechanism) on his person so that the bodily warmth would keep it in a state for immediate use. As the belted ammunition became frozen, the cartridges were withdrawn, cleaned, and replaced. Ammunition boxes were kept covered with waterproof sheets and as dry as possible. The teams derived a measure of grim amusement when they listened to their German gunner opponents firing single shots and short bursts; it was evident that they were in like case. The unprecedented conditions could not, of course, have been foreseen, and presented a double problem as to maintenance of men and guns. It is not suggested that the measures indicated were adopted at once; they were gradually evolved by constant endeavour. It was not until the second tour of line duty in that desolate area, that the Company fully learned to care for its guns and gear, both of which suffered at Flers.

On the 18th November, two teams of No. 4 Section took over gun positions from the 7th Machine Gun Company on the left of the Brigade front. They were sited near "The Maze," to which previous reference has been made. The teams reached their destination after a most exhausting journey through deep mud, during which Private W. Carrick, while carrying a tripod, sank up to his waist and had to be dragged out, but only after his would-be rescuers had first been rescued. Uncertain of their whereabouts, the teams spent a miserable night, shivering in the deep slush of a ruined trench. "One of the worst places the Section ever held in the line," declared one of the sufferers, Private F. L. Fitzpatrick.

Captain Drummond was unremitting in his labours to make the lot of his charges more endurable. One welcome innovation was the purchase of sufficient primus stoves to provide one per gun team. As one man put it, "they were veritable Godsends." By their aid, and some assistance from "Tommy cookers" (small tins of solidified alcohol), the men were able to obtain hot tea, coffee, or cocoa, day or night, the only hot nourishment partaken by many during the tour. The kerosene for the primus stoves was obtained ("wangled," in Army parlance), by indenting "for use in cleaning harness"—an astute move on the part of the

Company Quartermaster. The first use of a primus stove in No. 3 Section caused some consternation, when the too vigorous use of the pump by Private ("Tod") Nicholson brought about a violent explosion at the bottom of a dug-out. In the rush for the exit, three or four men jammed themselves in the narrow stairway. Fuel for fires was almost unobtainable; at times, cordite charges drawn from live artillery ammunition was used—a practice quite contrary to orders.

The Transport Section was quartered in the rear near Montauban. While free from line and forward area troubles, they had nevertheless a hard time. The activities of Lieutenant J. D. Campbell and Sergeant J. McGaffin had much to do with ameliorating their lots. Most of the drivers lived in holes cut into the bank of a roadway with sheets of iron (obtained in devious and unauthorised ways) for roofing, and straw for bedding. Some of the horses were quartered in an open shed, but others were fully exposed to the elements. The grooming of the horses—at times up to their girths in mud—was a never-ending job. Brushes were discarded in favour of scraps of hoop iron. Movement off the roads in the deep mud was almost an impossibility. Driver E. J. Nash has related how one morning eight horses were required to move the Company's water cart a short distance from the roadway; it was accomplished only after great exertions. In addition to the Company's requirements, those of the 6th Trench Mortar Battery had to be attended to. At this time, the roads were breaking under the strain imposed by enormous traffic and severe weather, consequently the movement of daily supplies meant many hours in the saddle. The difficulties of those days tested the mettle and skill of the drivers to the utmost. It is recorded that one driver found himself with a horse that refused to pull any weight of importance. He tried the experiment of wrapping barbed wire round the britching. The arrangement worked well until the ration dump was reached, which was situated on the forward slope of a hill. Here his steed refused to stop, but continued until the next slope was reached. It is to the credit of the Transport Section that it rose manfully to its tasks and on no occasion did the gun sections go short of their requirements. Campbell, in addition to his transport duties, supervised the Company details (Quartermaster's staff, cooks, etc.), in the rear, and thereby relieved Captain Drummond of any concern in that respect.

A word of praise should be accorded Company Quartermaster H. L. Smith and his assistant, Private A. H. ("Boss") Smith, who worked in close co-operation with Company cook "Bill" Wormald and his assistant "Joe" Purchase. The cooking was done at the transport lines, where "Bill" and "Joe" struggled in the mud and rain to prepare the cooked food. Owing to the Company not being up to the numerical strength of an Infantry Company, no army cooker could be obtained, although Captain Hore applied for one several times. The cooking had, perforce, to be done in dixies over an open fire—no easy matter in the circumstances. No "food containers" were available, so the cooked meat was sent forward in sandbags. How the Company obtained a cooker unofficially will be told later.

On the 7th November, Major Hore left the Company and proceeded to the Machine Gun School of Instruction at Grantham, England, and subsequently to higher commands, to which previous reference has been made. He carried with him regrets and best wishes of every member of the Company, who always retained happy memories of the Major's association with the unit in the early days of its existence. The departing Commanding Officer was succeeded by Captain J. H. Drummond, who continued in command—except for intervals due to wounds, sickness and detachments—for the remainder of the Company's existence.

At this time, Lieutenant F. Windsor rejoined from hospital, but in poor health, and his wounds, received at Pozieres, were hardly healed. Others to join were a small batch of trained gunners from the Machine Gun Depot at Grantham. These men had left Australia as machine-gun reinforcements, and had gone through a course of training in England. Up to this time all the Company's requirements had been met by calling on the battalions of the Brigade. The men so obtained were trained by the Company officers and N.C.Os., and, if satisfactory, were retained; if otherwise, they were returned to their battalions, in accordance with a standing arrangement with the Brigadier. From this time onwards, such trained reinforcements reached the Company at intervals, but the major portion of the Company's requirements were met as before, by drawing upon the infantry battalions in the 6th Brigade. The latter practice continued in force until March, 1918.

During the tour the Company Signallers were quartered in a cellar in Flers, where they maintained continuous communication between Company and Brigade Headquarters. Despite the continual shelling of the village, the lines were unusually free from breaks. One disadvantage was that the cellar was occupied by other denizens than signallers. Signaller Howard declared that the lice therein were the biggest encountered on the Western Front. On the other hand, vegetables were obtained from the remains of old gardens in the immediate vicinity—a food supply which was exploited by No. 1 Section as well. Close by lay two or three of the first tanks used in the war. Derelict and helpless, they were visited and inspected by practically all the troops in the vicinity.

On the night of the 21st November, the first stages of a welcome relief were carried through in conjunction with the 2nd Machine Gun Company of the British Expeditionary Force. Ten teams were withdrawn and retired to the transport lines for the night. The relief of the remaining six was marred by an unfortunate occurrence. Captain Drummond was specially anxious to have the relieving teams well forward, to be in readiness to slip in as the evening fog descended. The relieving Company, however, delayed its move to such an extent that the "change-over" occupied the greater part of the night, during which Privates T. H. Smith and G. Scott (name stated to be W. G. Parsonage), who acted as guides for the ingoing teams, were killed by shellfire. Apparently they had completed their duties and met their death on the way out. Their pay books were received by the Company some time later.

During this tour of duty the losses were:—Two officers and seven other ranks killed, one officer and nine other ranks wounded, eleven other ranks sick.

Such was the Company's first tour of duty in the Somme battlefield in winter-time. In spite of the unprecedented conditions, the men had stood up splendidly to the ordeal. But little outward complaint was heard; it had been a case of grin, bear, and make the best of an experience which called for all their powers of resistance and will. Horribly verminous, mud covered, and showing signs of strain, they emerged with a deep feeling of satisfaction that they had not been found wanting. In a few instances the strain had been too severe. Private H. Stebbing marched out obviously at breaking-point. A few days later he was evacuated very ill, and died of pneumonia on the 16th of January following, to the sorrow of his mates in No. 4 Section.

CHAPTER X.

The First Winter in France: Flesselles, Le Transloy, Ribemont.

22nd November, 1916-5th February, 1917.

Following the relief at Flers, the ten gun-teams marched to Quarry Siding on the morning of the 22nd November, and entrained for Meaulte. Arriving at the latter place at midday, march was made to billets in Dernancourt. The following day the six forward teams, who had been relieved the previous night, reported themselves after having spent the latter part of the night in shelters in Flers.

The first task was to overhaul and clean the guns and gear, while the Transport Section performed similar work with the horses, harness, and limbers. A certain amount of reorganisation was attended to, and a few promotions made. Everyone made serious attempts to remove the tenacious mud from their clothing and to "clean up." In some cases, individuals made special trips to Amiens, where the perfunctory wash at the Army baths could be supplemented by a real one at a large civilian establishment in that city. Meanwhile, Company training was resumed.

A Divisional Inspection by General Legge was announced for the 27th of November, and all ranks made a final attempt to remove the last traces of trench mud and be as presentable as possible. One exception was Private H. F. ("Tod") Nicholson, of No 3 Section. Inspections were one of his many aversions, and he looked on Divisional events with strong disfavour. When the Company was drawn up it was discovered that, in addition to certain other irregularities, he was armed with a German automatic revolver instead of the regulation Webley, and his putties were rolled from the top instead of from the bottom. It was too late to amend matters, so Captain Drummond had to content himself with certain words of censure.

THE FIRST WINTER IN FRANCE (II).

The tedium of the waiting ranks was greatly relieved when "Tod" muttered his illuminating comments on inspections in general and this one in particular, and concluded by declaring that he did not consider it a matter of NATIONAL importance how his putties were rolled.

On the day following General Legge's inspection, Captain Drummond left on English leave, and Captain A. N. McLennan —restored to the Company after serving with the 22nd Battalion since Pozieres' days—took charge of the Company. It is hardly necessary to mention that the temporary Commanding Officer received a cordial reception from his old comrades.

While at Dernancourt, one Section proceeded to Flesselles and relieved teams of the 1st Australian Machine Gun Company on anti-air craft duty near that village. Night flying operations by enemy airmen in "back areas" had made such precautions necessary.

The absence of a Field Kitchen, or cooker, was a continual grievance. That a body of between 150 and 200 men should be debarred from a necessity of this nature was incomprehensible. The official reply to all requests was that the Company's numerical strength did not entitle it to one, therefore it could not have one. The approach of winter brought the grievance to a head; something would have to be done in spite of higher authority. While at Dernancourt the problem was solved. The solution can best be described by inserting a diverting account by Signaller D. C. Howard.

"Winter, with all its severity, is upon us. More so than ever does the food question loom large upon the horizon, and the lack of a field cooker is commented upon at great lengths. The article in question had, of course, been requisitioned, but Officialdom, in its most Gilbertian attitude, decreed that the gallant Company was not entitled to the facility. Some obscure regulation was quoted in support of this contention; either we lacked the necessary number of men, or had too many horses. Other opinion, possibly a trifle biassed, had it that those on high had seen the illustrious Bill Wormald, and his genial assistant, Joe Purchase, at work, and considered the intricate working of the machine might, perhaps, interfere with the general excellence of their culinary efforts.

"The sight of these two worthies, on many occasions struggling against the elements to get a little heat under a row of dixies when the supply of whale oil or petrol was limited, not to mention the personal inconvenience, moved many a stout heart to pity and a resolve that, officialdom or not, things would be altered at the first opportunity. Several avenues were explored by trusty scouts, but without result. It was thought that maybe an English regiment would have a cooker 'to spare,' but, alas, no. Tommy Atkins, ever tenacious, was even more so when it came to the engine that kept his stomach supplied and his heart in the right place.

"A heartening 'furphy' at this stage was to the effect that a certain battery of Artillery would make us a present of the much needed stew factory, but, if history is correct, Driver "Mum" Lindsay who volunteered to accept delivery, hooked his team to the limber of an 18-pounder gun by mistake on a dark night, and, of course, negotiations were broken off somewhat hurriedly. However, nothing attempted, nothing done, sayeth the old proverb, and the next attempt was to be more successful. While in that doubtful state known as 'resting,' at the quaint village of Dernancourt, which nestles so pleasantly in the mud and slush of the valley of the Ancre, a most reliable scout reported a cooker seemingly abandoned on a dump near Buire, a few kilos away. That night, as they say in the pictures, when the agonised shrieks of Madame and Mademoiselle proclaimed that eight o'clock had arrived and the estaminet doors must close, a trusted few (which included Private B. H. Johnson) proceeded to investigate.

"Not abandoned as was thought, but labelled 'To the D.A.D.O.S.,' or some other dignitary, 'for minor repairs,' the contraption appeared to be in fair condition and, knowing full well the ability of Company Artificer Burtonclay, it seemed a pity to allow it to be consigned to Armentieres or the Swiss border as was probably the case. With due ceremony, the machine was 'taken on strength' and handed over to Wormald and his lieutenant, Purchase. Naturally, an official presentation was hardly in keeping with the circumstances of the transfer, but much ribald advice was tendered from all sides.

"After a thorough inspection, which consisted of peering doubtfully into the boilers and viciously shaking the wheels, Bill informed all and sundry that the b—— thing was no b—— good, not worth a nob of goat's feathers, or some such rare commodity, and flatly refused to have anything to do with the contraption. But later, when the labour saving possibilities became apparent to His Greasiness, it was quite a different matter. New boilers soon appeared through the medium of Quartermaster-Sergeant 'Horace' Smith and his disarming smile. The minor defects having succumbed to the artifices of Artificer Burtonclay, steam was got up, and from then on the faithful hash chariot did its duty nobly to the satisfaction of all. Indeed, some ironical spirits suggested that Bill should be graded somewhat higher on account of the technical nature of his duties.

"Napoleon is credited with saying that an army marches on its stomach, but it was the 6th Machine Gun Company who demonstrated that one of the most valuable instruments of warfare is a field kitchen."

It should be added that the unofficial acquisition was not displayed unnecessarily. At first, its retention appeared very doubtful, but it was hoped that the friendly relations with General Gellibrand would stand in good stead in an affair of this kind. When the General asked questions it is believed they were of a friendly nature, and it is evidence of his discriminating judgment that the matter was carried no further, and the Company was left in irregular but undisturbed possession of what the severe winter proved to be a necessity.

After nine days at Dernancourt, the Company moved to Edgehill on the 1st December, and entrained at the latter place for Vignacourt. From Vignacourt, march was made to Flesselles, where billets were provided. A diary record for the day reads: "Left Dernancourt, 10 a.m., arrived Vignancourt, 6.30 p.m. A tedious journey to go 20 odd miles. Marched to Flesselles, about 4 kilometres, and billeted. Cold intense, roads frozen." Next day, the water in the Company's water-cart was frozen. At this time, Lieutenant Lilley rejoined after recovering from a wound received at Flers.

Winter had now set in in earnest and gave a foretaste of what was to follow. The billets could not boast of any comforts. Usually rainproof, they were not wind-proof, and the cold blasts often entered in on one side and passed out through the other. Fires were the exception rather than the rule, and unless there were special reasons for remaining out, it was a case of "early to bed." A visitor to the billets about 8 p.m. would have observed the majority of men huddled together under their blankets, usually in pairs or small groups, candles fluttering, though protected from the draughts, by which some read, some talked, while the others brought primus stoves into action and provided a limited supply of hot coffee or cocoa, generally obtained from Comfort Funds issues. "Lights out" seldom required enforcement because the candle "issue"—cut into many pieces—was usually exhausted before the prescribed time. No diversions were provided, and life in the squalid billets in very cold weather was distinctly depressing. One consolation always remained in mind, that it was infinitely worse "in the line." That vague comfort was possibly one reason why little outward complaint was heard. In such circumstances, Company training was persevered with. It was a difficult and uninspiring business, but a serious attempt was made to carry out the pre-arranged syllabus. The many sunless days, added to the general depression in which the only variation was limited day leave to visit Amiens.

While the authorities provided but one form of relaxation, various enterprising spirits resorted to other means to combat the depressing conditions. One particular event took place late at night in a small billet occupied by Signaller D. C. Howard, Private W. A. Gornall, and two others. A supposed birthday party, in honour of Private J. N. Myers, was the initial cause of the event, but it was a well-known fact that the effort had little to do with the calendar, but depended on that worthy's ability to procure liquor. As a complimentary move, a hitherto undisturbed hen-roost was raided and six birds were obtained. Under the very active supervision of Private "Tod" Nicholson, feathers were soon flying in all directions, and other preparations were in hand, including the loan of "Bill" Wormald's dixies and such fat as could be surreptitiously obtained. Owing to a shortage of the latter article, "Tod" declared that the birds would have to be partially boiled before final roasting.

Naturally the cooking process was rather prolonged, and the patience of the "chef" wore thin. At that stage, the guest arrived, but as he was accompanied by two of his cronies from the 23rd Battalion, he was promptly told to go to hell, with an intimation that "we are not entertaining the whole of the A.I.F." The guest was not one whit disturbed, but in his quiet and confidential way explained that the difficulty had been foreseen. Then it was noticed that each of the three newcomers was clutching a fine black orpington, and that their pockets were literally bulging with bottles. Fowl feathers flew in greater clouds than ever, intermingled with drinks. In the glow of the fire, "Tod," with his swarthy skin and flashing eyes looked more like a demon or a marauding gipsy than anything else as he lifted fowl after fowl from the boiling dixies to roast them on the lids. As each was declared finished, it was literally hacked to pieces and consumed with slabs of French bread and liquor.

Soon all were finished and everyone was in a highly elated state, talking and singing at the top of their voices, with the exception of Gornall, who had crawled into his bunk, which was affixed to the wall near the roof. A few inches from his head a lighted candle was burning, and its flickering attracted the notice of Myers, who, in his usual quiet and confidential way, mentioned his prowess as a revolver shot. After sending a few bullets through the roof, he declared that he could put the candle out with a shot and, before anybody could interfere, he let drive, and out went the candle. His really startled mates fully expected to find Gornall minus his scalp, but the bullet had evidently passed between his head and the candle with less than an inch to spare. If the episode had any sobering effect on the party it was not noticeable. Other revolvers were drawn, and gun play became the order of the moment. The roof was riddled, and operations were then conducted outside. Anything that looked like a target received the close attention of the shooters. Happily the ammunition and the liquor petered out together, and towards morning all was peace. "No chicken Maryland or spiced capon can compare with the product of that obscure village," said one of the participants. "Perhaps it was the company that enhanced the flavour, but certainly it was interludes such as this that eased the burden of many a good digger compelled to live in such wretched circumstances of weather and habitation."

It was soon rumoured that an early return to the line was to be expected, in which case, the spending of Christmas—the second away from Australia—in the trenches, appeared certain. No. 2 Section, with admirable foresight, arranged and held their Christmas dinner in advance. A late night for the purpose was granted, and the dinner was voted a great success. Corporal F. L. Wright was mainly responsible for the successful arrangements.

After 15 days at Flesselles, the expected departure took place on Sunday morning, 17th December. An early start was made possible by rising in the dark at 5.30 a.m., and at 7.15 a.m. the Company marched out, after the customary cleaning of billets and the burning of the usual large quantity of discarded articles which always accumulated after a few days' occupation. Upon arriving at Flesselles, it was learned that no train was available, so a disgusted Company returned to the lately-forsaken quarters. Another attempt at 1 p.m. was quite successful. Detrainment took place at Buire, from which place march was made to Ribemont, where most of the Company found quarters in a large brick building. At this time, Lieutenant A. Palling rejoined from a cadet battalion in England, where he obtained his commission.

Diary entries make frequent reference to the weather, such as: "Woke this morning to find it snowing. A beautiful mantle of white over everything. Thawed, and rained all day; result, fearful slush." "Fine, a little sun; the first for many a day," pathetically adds one writer.

Much interest was aroused at this time by the formation of an additional machine-gun company for each division of the A.I.F. The new units were to be supplementary to the existing companies, and controlled from Divisional Headquarters. Their advent indicated the growing importance attached to machine-gunnery, and one of the means adopted to develop it. The 2nd Divisional Company was finally designated the 22nd, and was formed in England. As a preliminary step, the existing companies in the 2nd Division were directed to submit names of officers and non-commissioned officers for promotion and transfer to the new unit. Lieutenant A. N. McLennan was subsequently selected for the position of Commanding Officer (with rank of Captain), and Lieutenant D. McM. Lilley was also transferred. The Company nominated Sergeant J. W. Torrens and Corporal D. C. Chalmers, who later departed for England where the latter received his commission. The former was commissioned before leaving his old unit. Company Quartermaster-Sergeant H. L. Smith was transferred to act in a similar capacity. One result of these moves was a continuous, friendly and personal interest in the new Company. Its appearance early in the following year was noted with great interest. In due course, it was "blooded," and received as a brother unit in arms.

To fill the position of Quartermaster-Sergeant, Corporal R. W. Watt, who had discharged the duties of Company Clerk with tact and efficiency since Erquinghem days, was promoted to the vacancy. Corporal Watt was succeeded by Lance-

Corporal W. A. Carne. Private G. Doyle became assistant clerk.

After three days at Ribemont, the march to the line was resumed on the 20th December. Fricourt was reached in the afternoon, and the night was spent in the familiar Nissen huts. A diary entry for the day reads: "Passed a cemetery of nearly a thousand graves. Australians, New Zealanders, and Tommies sleep side by side. Countryside flecked with snow. Roads frozen."

From Fricourt, next day, the Company re-entered the desolate mud-covered Somme battlefield once more. After a long struggle in the mud, past bogged and abandoned transport vehicles, "E" Camp, Bernafay Wood was reached. Much uncertainty existed as to whether any shelter would be available for the night. However, a few huts, in a sea of deep mud, were made available, and into these the weary men squeezed themselves. The numerous occupants of one hut were decidedly unlucky. They had hardly settled themselves when the floor, which was elevated some distance from the ground, collapsed. The restoration of the sections of flooring in the dark called forth much labour and hearty profanity.

The 2nd Division was relieving the 5th Australian Division and, as part of the change, the 6th Brigade took over front and support positions from the 15th Brigade. The sector lay to the left of Les Boeufs, and opposite Finch Trench, and the ruins of Le Transloy, both of which were in enemy possession. On the left was the 5th Australian Brigade, and on the right the 60th (British) Brigade. The new location was a little to the right of the former position held in front of Flers. The Company's task was to relieve the 15th Machine Gun Company. The preliminaries had been well arranged, and the "change over" was conducted without a hitch. After the ingoing teams had been issued with gum boots—with tops which reached to the waist—No. 2 Section, under Lieutenant F. Windsor, took over, so called, front line positions: one in Gusty Trench, one in Spring Trench, and two in Zenith Trench. Eight guns were distributed in depth in reserve, three being mounted by day for anti air-craft purposes. The remaining four were with the details and Quartermaster's store at "C" Camp, Bernafay Wood. Company Headquarters were in an old German dugout in Needle Trench.

Enemy shelling, while not generally heavy, was persistent. Apparently the German gunners were unable to hit Zenith

Trench, but the area immediately behind was well pounded, the passing shells skimming over the heads of the occupants in Zenith Trench and causing many a gasp. Some distance out from Zenith Trench, in Spring Trench, a gun was mounted, from which position heads of the garrison in the former could be observed, but the enemy interfered but little.

After 48 hours in the front line, No. 2 Section was relieved by No. 3 Section, under Lieutenant D. Lilley, on the night of Christmas Eve. The major portion of the relief had been carried out, but the team relieving Lance-Corporal A. Robinson became lost, and spent a good deal of time searching for their objective. Meanwhile, some movements on the Brigade's right front, which was held by an English Division, brought enemy shelling which, in turn, drew sharp retaliation by the British artillery. Unfortunately, one of our own shells fell almost on Robinson's team, killing Robinson and severely wounding Lieutenant F. Windsor. Private L. J. Jury appears to have been wounded at this time. Although Windsor's left forearm was broken, he saw to the burial of Robinson before returning, on the point of collapse, to Company Headquarters in Needle Trench. At Needle Trench, Captain Drummond had spent an anxious evening awaiting the completion of the relief. Finally, becoming impatient over the delay, he went forward with 2nd Lieutenant E. N. S. Lawrence. Both were caught in the shelling and Lawrence was severely wounded. After recovering from his wounds, he received an appointment in England, and did not rejoin the Company. He spoke French with great fluency, and his services were often requisitioned in that respect.

As was expected, Christmas was spent in the line, but there was little to differentiate the day. The cold Army rations were supplemented by the issue of some "extras" and, assisted by the opportune arrival of home parcels, were helped down with hot tea, coffee or cocoa made with the aid of the invaluable primus stoves. At Company Headquarters, Private A. Chitty distinguished himself by providing a three-course meal with the aid of a primus stove. It must be recorded that the Army authorities, from their well-established and comfortable quarters, far in rear, did not assist with any spirit of good cheer. Evidently to ensure that no fraternising with the enemy should take place, two intense bombardments were arranged and fired during the forenoon, and brought the inevitable replies. The men in the line had ample opportunity to ponder grimly over the futility of cherishing happy Christmas sentiments and to reflect that two thousand years after Christ's Advent upon Earth, civilised nations who professed His Name had resorted to the barbarous and hellish expedient of War to settle their differences. The remainder of the day and night passed without unusual incident.

Conditions were much the same as were experienced in the Flers sector, but the weather was worse, and the whole area was water-logged. In fragments of trenches, half filled with deep slush, infantry posts were scattered. At one or two points less than a hundred yards separated the combatants who were in like case. Movement had, perforce, to be carried out at night. In the usual foggy atmosphere, deciding direction was an art; finding the way with but vague notions as to one's own and the enemy's positions was literally a nightmare. The guides, Infantry and Company, must have developed extraordinary powers of observation and sense of locality to enable them to traverse that labyrinth of mud, shell-holes, and ruined trenches. Among the Company guides who did good work were Privates V. E. Bliss, G. Malcolm, and R. C. G. Greig.

In spite of every factor which seemed to prohibit it, the ground was held. The mere holding of it with the incidentals of food supply, reliefs, and sending of reports, involved great labour and hardships, and produced many strange and unexpected happenings. Scouts going out on patrol must have had a nerve-racking time, if only from the danger of bombing or shooting by their own comrades; a very likely and almost unavoidable possibility in the circumstances. One night a member of the 21st Battalion was wounded in this way. He was a heavy man and, as one narrator put it, "he took some getting in." Later in the same night a patrol was bombed from one of our own posts, and one of the scouts wounded. One of No. 3 Section's teams was startled one dark night when a German was discovered a few yards from the gun position. A challenge did not stop him, so Private Harry Black fired his revolver point blank, but missed. The scared German threw up his hands very promptly and was taken prisoner. It transpired he had been sent out to obtain a dressing for a wounded officer and, upon returning, had found our lines instead of his own. During the remainder of the night, many other imaginary figures loomed up in the darkness, to be promptly challenged, but no further prisoners were taken. Another night, an infantry party arrived with supplies which were much damaged by the wet; the bread especially having suffered severely in transit. It was also noticed that one of the party was missing. Just as the Corporal was about to search for him, a voice lifted loudly in song penetrated the battlefield. The song continued, and soon the Corporal reported the missing man stuck waist deep in the mud of a communication trench, 200 yards away, with about half a jar of rum still in hand. Three men tried to get him out; two hours later they returned wet, infuriated, and exhausted. After immense labour they got the inebriate on to a stretcher, but their muddy hands were so slippery they could not carry him, and the stretcher lacked carrying straps. They left him on the stretcher, still singing. An hour later he was carried away, perfectly quiet, to die of alcoholic poisoning.

What little could be done to alleviate the dreadful conditions was carried out. Odd pieces of sheet iron were collected and helped to give some protection from wind and rain. Pieces of duckboard were used for flooring in the gun positions, but they tended always to sink further into the mud. "Trench feet" again made its appearance, but was countered by the regular changing of socks and the rubbing of feet with whale oil. The wet socks were dried over primus stoves. The difficulties in maintaining guns and gear, encountered at Flers, again presented themselves, but they had been foreseen and were dealt with on the lines previously described. Nevertheless, the difficulties were always very acute. Sergeant A. Payton has related how, during one cold spell, it was necessary to keep emptying and refilling the belts all night to prevent the cartridges from being frozen in the fabric belts. "It took one team all its time," he added, "to keep four belts in order in the front trench."

To the demands made upon them, officers and men, in almost every instance, responded manfully. The rate of sickness, of course, mounted sharply; during the tenure in the line, it totalled two officers (Lieutenants McLennan and Palling) and 31 other ranks. The latter figure, however, included three cases of "trench feet," a number suffering from septic sores, and one or two cases of injuries. On the other hand, much was endured with little or no complaint. Thus it was that Private R. H. Hamond's hands swelled and went black on the third day, but he refused to leave. Private H. G. Oldham lost his voice, and finally had to be evacuated with influenza. Private W. S. Wallin, during a relief, was observed to be depressed and inactive. On the way out his officer noticed that, when they passed through a sharp barrage, he merely grinned, but when "C" Camp was reached it was discovered that he was suffering from seven boils, and was on the point of collapse. Others suffered acutely from stomach troubles, but carried on. After two nights in Zenith Trench and five in succession in the line, Lieutenant Callister "was immensely relieved when Lieutenant R. D. Desmond arrived, as I had been anticipating the sixth night with some apprehension." Summing up as to the spirit of the men, one observer remarked: "Cold and miserable, but cheerful of speech; growling little, and showing consideration for one another."

The conditions called for more exacting duties on the part of officers, and are illustrated by the following extract from Lieutenant Callister's records. "On relief, with sodden overcoats of great weight, and men very fed up, the guide lost himself, but we soon got right. I called in at Needle Trench while the men went on over the duckboards to a prepared dug-out 1,500 yards in rear in the Flers Switch Line. After dumping my gear, I followed and overtook them. In the dug-out, got them out of their putties and boots, saw to their feet, rolled them in blankets, and gave them stew and tea and then a rum issue, and left them to it." After a tour of 48 hours in the front line, men came out with white, drawn faces and shaking as with ague, but attention to their physical needs soon brought about a recovery. Corporal F. L. Wright has recorded: "I left the trench feeling about 90 years old. Orders came that we could stop about half-way if we could not manage to get to "C" Camp, Bernafay Wood. I was one of those who availed myself of this privilege. Next day, I completed the journey. Strangely enough, within 24 hours, we were sprightly and gay, and taking long walks for the very joy of being alive." The inveterate tendency to make a joke of the worst conditions undoubtedly helped. Thus, one night during a relief by teams of No. 2 Section, Private J. T. Bates, who was near the head of the party, slipped off the duckboards into a deep, muddy shell-hole. His extraction called for much time and labour, and held the party up. From the rear came an enquiry as to the cause of the delay. Upon the reason being given, a resigned voice came through the darkness: "Ah! well, he's got very short legs, he'll soon drown."

The front line guns had occasional opportunities to come into action. On the 24th December, the gun in Spring Trench fired on a party of Germans moving out of Finch Trench, and claimed a dozen hits. Just after dark on the 3rd January, a party of about 50 Germans was seen coming toward Finch

Trench in close order, 60 yards away. A burst of 50 rounds was fired at them. Half an hour later another party, about 30 strong, left the same trench; a burst dispersed these. It was estimated that 25 casualties were inflicted. Just before daybreak on the morning of the 10th January, the same gun fired on a party of five. One fell, and the others jumped into Finch Trench. Other parties were fired on at night. Occasional sniping with rifles took place. Several observed hits were recorded.

The guns in rear positions fired indirectly by day and night on Le Transloy, enemy roads and communications, and on gaps in the enemy wire which were suspected of being used as traffic routes. Practically all the ammunition used was salvaged from the vicinity, thus avoiding cartage from the rear. Three guns were mounted by day for anti-air craft purposes, and more than once came into action against low-flying aeroplanes, but without known results. While inspecting the rear guns, a General Staff Officer found a spot of rust on Lance-Corporal L. Davies's tripod. The discovery led to a heated argument between the Staff Officer and Captain Drummond.

In an old German dugout in Needle Trench, close to Company Headquarters, the Signallers kept in touch with Brigade Headquarters. It was one of the worst positions occupied by them. Constant pumping was necessary to render it habitable, and the personnel suffered from "trench feet" and digestive troubles. The lines were often cut, and repairs were very difficult in the deep mud. About 2 a.m. on Boxing Day, a shellburst near the doorway released a great quantity of water, which rushed down the steps. A wild exit was made by the party (some were sleeping at the time) to escape the flood. They managed to save their instruments, but there were loud lamentations over the loss of the remnants of a Christmas pudding and a quantity of rum. It was a very bedraggled party who reported to Headquarters—sodden and homeless. New quarters were found and, after the instruments had been dried out, communication was re-established.

During the first week in January, the Brigade's front was extended to the right, and in conformity therewith, the Company relinquished three positions to the 5th Machine Gun Company and took over six from the 51st Machine Gun Company (B.E.F.). Three of the latter were placed in the front line; two in Zenith Trench, and one further south in Summer Trench, near the

Divisional boundary. One recorder mentions that "The Tommies in support were in sheepskin jackets, but without blankets; they brewed tea freely, and swore with unnecessary fluency."

"C" Camp was well back from the front line, but it was regularly shelled by a high velocity gun; the shell and noise of discharge arriving simultaneously. On Christmas night, Company Quartermaster-Sergeant R. W. Watt, and others, were playing poker when a shell landed very close without bursting. Some guesses were made as to its location and, upon investigation, Lieutenant A. P. Earle stepped out in the darkness into a hole at the doorway. It was then discovered that the shell had actually bored its way under the hut and out again. The twenty odd occupants of the hut were much interested in their narrow escape, and when the excitement had subsided, Watt collected 60 francs out of "kitty" for holding "four queens."

The Transport Section again lived up to its reputation for efficiency and hard work. The Drivers were fortunate enough to find quarters in a hut equipped with 16 bunks, as well as a fireplace. In comparative comfort they were enabled to dry their clothes for the first time that winter. In addition to Company requirements, Trench Mortar Battery Y.M.C.A., and Brigade supplies were carted. Drawing water sometimes meant waiting two hours for a "turn." During emergency periods, 16 hours were spent in the saddle. One cold night a driver took a fire pot with him while on picquet. While he was away attending a restless horse, a German airman, with unerring accuracy, dropped a bomb and blew the pot to pieces.

The 26 days' tour near Le Transloy came to a welcome end on January 17th, when the Company was relieved by the 8th Machine Gun Company, and retired to huts at "C" Camp, Bernafay Wood, for the night. The relief was well arranged and conducted, and was reported complete at 7 p.m. During the night preceding relief, a heavy fall of snow transformed the countryside into a picture of white, but the men had now definitely given up their notions as to the beauty of such an event. During normal conditions, movement over tracks and duckboards required the greatest care, but a heavy fall of snow obliterated them. Nevertheless, Section after Section reported at "C" Camp except No. 1. It was close on midnight when they appeared and explained how they had been relieved in a heavy snow-storm which covered all landmarks and left them with no option but to flounder straight ahead, sometimes into shell-holes five feet deep and snow-filled. The following day a pitiable spectacle was observed when many infantry of the Division toiled out, bootless, with swollen feet wrapped in sandbags, through the freezing snow.

Next day the Company marched to Quarry Siding and entrained for Mericourt. From the latter place it proceeded by road to Ribemont and billeted. It was a muddy, weary, and depressed Company that withdrew to the comparative comfort of miserable billets at Ribemont. In the verminous clothing they had worn for a month, everyone was in sore need of cleansing, sleep, and hot food. At this time, Sergeant J. L. Stapleton left to enter an officer cadet battalion in England. Upon receiving his commission he was posted to the 22nd Company, wherein he served till the end of hostilities.

The usual proceedings after a period of line duty were followed. Guns and gear were overhauled, clothing cleaned, and bathing requirements attended to. On the 23rd January, the Brigade was inspected by General Legge, Divisional Commander. With the General was Colonel Somerville, who roared at Lieutenant Callister and Privates B. H. Johnson and E. D. Saker, till the two latter veterans well-nigh cried aloud with vexation. The reasons for the outburst were that Johnson had shaved the night before instead of that morning, and Saker had some traces of trench mud on the handle of his entrenching tool. Meanwhile, the remainder of the Company stood at attention, shivering in the snow. Privates C. F. Skead and H. J. Cook got frost-bitten feet as a consequence.

The weather was now at its worst, with the temperature below freezing point, where it remained for four weeks. A biting east wind blew with great frequency, burning the skin and cutting to the bone. The strange spectacle of dust being blown along the frozen roads was witnessed. Men who had unwittingly washed their heads at the morning wash, found their hair frozen before they could return to billets to comb and brush it. The Company Clerk soon realised that his first daily task was to melt the ink. His initial effort was not quite successful, because the too frequent application of a candle resulted in the bottom falling out of the ink-well, to the serious detriment of certain official papers. Bread was oftimes frozen and required much strength and patience before it could be cut. The water-cart was frozen, and fatigue parties sent to "draw" water for cooking and drinking, went armed with bags, picks, and shovels. On reaching the water points, care had to be taken in moving across the wide, frozen bed with which the points were surrounded. The frozen roads presented a serious problem for the

Transport Section. To prevent slipping, horse-shoes were issued wherein threaded holes had been drilled for the reception of short spikes. Front shoes had three holes, and rear ones two. Each spike had four points which could be sharpened with a file after becoming blunt. The spikes were withdrawn or replaced as conditions required.

On the 27th January, the Company met 2nd Division Headquarters at football, but had to acknowledge defeat by four points, after a strenuous game. Foremost among the losers were Privates D. C. M. Parkhill and L. Barrand.

Soon after arrival at Ribemont, he Company took over two anti-air craft positions from the 7th Machine Gun Company. A few days later, two more were relieved at Buire. At the same time, three others of the 5th Company were relieved between Dernancourt and Meaulte, where a large dump existed. It was often bombed at night, but the teams escaped damage. While stationed there, they lived in bell tents, and suffered acutely from the weather. One advantage was the presence of many locomotives, the drivers of which were usually susceptible to diplomatic words, or the offer of a few francs, when it came to a modest request for a little coal.

At this time, a welcome innovation appeared in the shape of a Brigade canteen. It supplied a long-felt want. By its aid the men could obtain extras in the way of food, and the wherewithal to make hot coffee and cocoa at night; a necessity in the prevailing bitter weather. Organised concert parties first appeared, and supplied much needed recreation to men who had long since given up the amenities of civilian life.

During the period covered by this chapter, the losses were: one other rank killed in action and two died of illness; two officers and one other rank wounded; two officers and 42 other ranks evacuated sick. In addition to Private H. Stebbing, Private W. D. Watson died of illness in hospital.

After 11 days at Ribemont, the return journey to the line was commenced on the 29th January. A short march brought the Company to comfortable quarters in Becourt Camp, where it stayed for three days. Another easy stage to Shelter Wood Camp followed, where final preparations were made for re-entering the line. Diary entries made frequent references to the intense cold, the snow, and the slippery roads traversed. One diarist recorded: "Bread frozen. Day and night, the guns thunder forth over a white country—fire and snow—a strange contrast." Before the month was out, the enemy disturbed carefully laid plans by evacuating his line over a wide front.

CHAPTER XI.

The German Withdrawal to the Hindenburg Line, Le Sars to Bullecourt.

5th February-2nd May, 1917.

The teams on anti-air craft duty at Ribemont, Buire, and Dernancourt were relieved on the 5th February, and the same evening the Company—conforming to the relief of the 5th Brigade (right Brigade sector) by the 6th—took over front line, support and reserve positions (12), from the 5th Machine Gun Company, between Le Sars (left) and Eaucourt L'Abbaye (right), just to the right of the main Albert-Bapaume road. Four teams were kept in reserve at Pioneer Camp, and Company Headquarters were located in a deep dugout on the northern edge of the ruined village of Martinpuich. The following night, five guns from support positions fired indirectly on enemy roads and communications in and around Warlencourt, which lay opposite the Brigade front. This practice was followed nightly, from 10,000 to 15,000 rounds being expended. The only incident recorded relates to Captain Drummond being slightly wounded in the head by a shell splinter on the 9th. After a tenure of 10 days, the Company was relieved on the night of the 14-15th by the 7th Machine Gun Company, and assembled at Shelter Wood Camp. Four anti-aircraft positions in the Camp were manned at night to deal with frequent enemy visits; likewise two others at the Transport lines at La Boiselle.

The long continued "freeze" now came to an end, and a "thaw" set in, the bitter east wind giving way to rain and mist. As a result of the milder weather, the ice-bound country slowly reverted to a sea of deep mud. A diarist wrote on the 22nd: "Oh, this endless mud; miles of it as one looks across the country." About this time, 2nd Lieutenant A. Palling rejoined from hospital, and Sergeant F. V. W. Duncan and Driver H. DeB. Newcomen received their commissions. Owing to an injury, Company Artificer A. E. Burtonclay was evacuated and subsequently discharged. He was succeeded by Private G. E. Gamble.

THE GERMAN WITHDRAWAL.

Only three days' respite was allowed at Shelter Wood Camp. On the night of the 17-18th, the Company relieved the 5th Machine Gun Company in the left Brigade sector. Five teams went to the front line, seven in support, and four in reserve at Acid Drop Camp. The usual nightly routine of indirect fire was resumed and, in addition, firing was done during the misty parts of the day when it was assumed the enemy would be moving. Some direct firing was possible on Below Trench and Below Support Trench, where movement could be observed. At this time, the Company provided a quota of six to take part in a proposed raid on the enemy lines in front of the Butte de Warlencourt ("The Butte"). The members were Corporal F. L. Wright, Privates J. N. Spittle, F. Wigmore, H. G. ("Yank") Carthew, J. E. Smith, and another. With 30 men, under Lieutenant Foster, of the 21st Battalion, the whole of the raiders trained at Acid Drop Camp. The part allotted to the Company's quota was to dismantle and bring back German machine guns. On the afternoon of the 23rd, the plan was varied, and 12 only —including Spittle and Wigmore—moved up to Martinpuich to be in readiness for the operation. After waiting for some hours, the raid was called off, owing to the report that the enemy had vacated his front trenches.

After a week's tour of duty, the 7th Company provided a relief on the 24th, and the Company returned to its previous camp at Shelter Wood, and maintained the former air-craft precautions. Bathing parades were held, clothing issued, and general training resumed. The whole camp became greatly excited when the earlier rumours of a general enemy retirement were confirmed. Isolated from the world, in a hutted camp surrounded by a sea of mud, the news was a day-long topic of conversation, and provided a much-needed stimulant. The first signs of Spring, coinciding with an unheard of enemy retirement, gave new life and hope to everyone. The stagnation and depression arising out of this long and severe period began to melt away with the ice of Winter. In spite of the conditions, everyone insisted on being cheerful although it must be recorded they had little to help them. As the short days drew to a close and early darkness set in, the doors of the huts had to be kept closed and the windows carefully shaded so that no low-flying enemy airman should be guided thereto. Some huts were not provided with stoves, and the attempts to heat them by means of coal-filled braziers were only partially successful, while the inmates had to endure a heavy smoke-charged atmosphere. Some time previously, Chaplain Captain Durnford, M.C., had been instrumental in securing for the Company a portable organ. This was brought into use and, chiefly through the agency of Private E. D. Saker, songs and choruses were rendered by all ranks and voices who felt disposed to help. The singers often sang themselves hoarse and to sleep, leaving Saker to carry on till the sound of many snores disturbed the harmony from the organ.

A minor item of interest at this time was the issue of a new and greatly improved pay-book. Its advent rendered possible the solution of a long standing problem as to the individual's position in the matter of arrears of pay. Hitherto that question had remained (except to those skilled in figures) in a vague shadowland, with a large or small credit balance according to the particular individual's optimism. At this period, few of the Company had been on English leave, but those who had not, looked forward to the day when their turn would arrive, and each was anxious to have the necessary margin of £10 required by the Army authorities, standing to his credit.

After a spell of five days in Shelter Wood Camp, the Company moved forward, on the 1st March, and relieved the 5th Machine Gun Company in the line. During those five days, the German retirement had developed to such an extent that the new locations were about a mile forward of the former position. They were astride the Albert-Bapaume Road, with the village of Le Barque on the right. Indirect fire by day and night was resumed, 15,000 rounds per 24 hours being an average programme.

As the days went by, the enemy retirement gradually became more pronounced and necessitated much alteration and movement forward to conform to the Brigade's advance. The general direction was the line of the Albert-Bapaume Road, but by the second week in March the Brigade's advance took a northerly direction towards Grevillers. Teams were pushed forward in close support of the more quickly moving infantry, while rear guns harassed roads, trenches, and gaps in the enemy wire. Occasionally, parties of the enemy were fired on, but the targets were fleeting and small. The enemy bombardments were, at times, very severe in certain localities, the intention evidently being to dispose of ammunition supplies in that way rather than abandon them or remove them further back. During one of these outbursts, on the night of the 5-6th March, Private J. T. Bates was wounded in fifteen places by a shell burst. His team mates gave up their emergency dressings to help bind his

THE GERMAN WITHDRAWAL.

wounds. On the 12th, Private F. H. Lockwood was wounded by a shell from a high velocity gun. The next morning, Private J. W. Findlay was wounded by shell-fire. During the night of the following day, one of No. 2 Section's teams received a good deal of indirect machine-gun fire, during which Private A. E. Cameron was wounded.

Indirect firing was always a most uninspiring business, but at this time it called for much extra patience, labour, and endurance, and for a conscientious discharge of a monotonous and never-ending duty. Speaking of the period under review, Lieutenant Callister, who was responsible for much of it, said: "The weather conditions were bad. Fritz overlooked all our positions, yet all that firing in snow, fog, and rain and occasional sunshine, never gave a gun position away. Some days the men on the guns, always in shell holes and unprotected, had a very severe time, as even in snow and frost they had to sit low while visibility was good. Two men stayed with each gun. I had immense practice at laying Zero and other lines, and in maintaining accuracy. We lived in very poor shelters. I found, getting under cover about midnight, that if I scraped some of the slush off my boots and putties, put my feet into sandbags and then lay down on a duckboard, four inches above water level, with a waterproof sheet on the duckboard, and two of us under two blankets, that, when called at 5 a.m., I was warm, though steaming; whereas, if I left those sandbags off, I was stiff, and without feeling from the knees down. The dirt and discomfort were considerable. Fortunately, apart from the men on the guns and two sentries (for gas alarm), the teams were not unduly harassed. About twenty men were located a few yards from my shelter, in a much better one, where, by forbearance, they were dry and reasonably warm. But, while most of them had scabies, and others were very sick and covered with a rash, which transpired to be measles, nobody went sick, but we did have a time." The Company was, in truth, engaged in the double task of fighting the elements and harassing a retreating enemy. A certain amount of sickness was inevitable in the conditions. During this part of the tour, evacuations due to sickness averaged three per week. The primus stoves continued their useful and beneficent work.

The spectacle of the Army becoming "mobile" after many months of trench warfare was a welcome tonic. It presented many problems, however. Huge craters at road junctions were often encountered, and served the intended purpose of delaying wheeled traffic. Sometimes a "jam" on the Albert-Bapaume Road held up traffic for a mile or more on each side. The first complaints as to shortages of rations (extremely infrequent occurrences) were made during this period. As far as the Company was concerned, much strenuous work was involved in the manhandling of guns, gear, and ammunition forward. The Transport Section assisted as far as it could, but its activities were restricted to the roads because the sodden country would not carry wheeled traffic. In places, large dumps of enemy material were found; a pleasant discovery being a supply of briquettes, which were soon put to use by the enterprising ones by the aid of oil drums converted into braziers. While supplies lasted, some teams enjoyed fires such as they had not previously encountered in France. As the weather gradually became milder, snow fell at intervals, with the inevitable slush in its wake.

The advancing gun-teams were not the only discoverers of more or less welcome "finds." While Quartermaster-Sergeant Watt was attending to the drawing of rations, he noticed the Company cook standing in a very unmilitary attitude in the doorway of a hut recently taken over from a battalion of the 2nd Brigade. Just at that moment, a staff officer, attended by a numerous retinue, approached the hut and enquired of "Bill" as to what unit was in occupation. The reply was not clearly understood, and, becoming nettled, the officer demanded that Bill take his hands out of his pockets while addressing an officer. In a sudden effort to comply with the order, Bill overbalanced and fell backwards, and the disgusted officer passed on. On investigation, the Quartermaster-Sergeant discovered Bill jammed between some cases, with his feet projecting upwards. In the hut were no less than eight cases (sixteen jars) of rum which the outgoing battalion found they were unable to transport. This was indeed an Eldorado, as at the time rum was not on issue to the 2nd Division; oranges being supplied in lieu thereof. The question of hospitality had already been attended to by Bill, and it became necessary for Private H. E. A. Woods, of the Store Staff, to attend, temporarily, to the cooking arrangements. In a short space of time, the hut became the object of much pilgrimage from, it seemed, every unit in the district. The Quartermaster-Sergeant and his staff were highly amused by the greatly varying demeanour of the various pilgrims. Some, in all humility, enquired as to the health of the keepers of the shrine and, by judicious choice of language, turned the conversation to the state of their own health, and the necessity of keeping warm in the prevailing wintry weather.

THE GERMAN WITHDRAWAL.

When sundry hints appeared to fall on deaf ears, they finally named the desired warmth-provoking fluid. Others used shock tactics. Without possessing, or claiming any measure of finesse, they boldly asked straight out for a "drop." The Quartermaster-Sergeant saw to it that the Company requirements were fully attended to, but during the days following the discovery, he and his staff passed anxious hours in making a judicious distribution, and living in fear of premature discovery by an unsympathetic officer.

On the 12th day of March, the Brigade's advance took a northerly turn with the village of Grevillers directly ahead. On the 15th, a bright, sunny, but chilly day, Captain Drummond, Lieutenant Callister, and Private W. N. Riley reconnoitred Grevillers, which had just passed into the hands of the Brigade. Shelters were decided on in the eastern edge, and the party returned to Malt Trench, from whence Callister set out shortly after dusk with Nos. 1 and 3 Sections and some of No. 4 to assist in the carrying. The journey across the morass of mud and shell holes made by our heavy artillery fire was safely accomplished in the dark, Riley guiding the party unerringly through broken ground, damaged trenches, and masses of wire. On reaching the village, heavy shelling was in progress, so Callister coolly got his men into shelter and waited for it to ease. Moving into the village, the largest selected dugout was found to be full of infantry, so there was no option but to search in the darkness and ruins of the village for another. The search was not assisted by the fact that shells were still falling, one of which blew an adjacent gateway to pieces. At this stage, Privates W. Carrick, W. J. Morris, and J. Coleman were wounded by a shell burst. Ultimately the party were settled, but sat up all night in the crowded shelters where they were joined by Lieutenant Blenkarn and some of No. 4 Section. Coleman did not return to the Company, his injuries leading to his discharge later in the year.

Very early on the morning of the 17th, the forward guns hurried off after the more quickly moving infantry. The latter were in close pursuit of the departing enemy, who was relinquishing stretches of country at a faster rate than hitherto. As the laden teams, manhandling their guns and gear, toiled forward, low-flying enemy planes swooped over them; at times so quickly and suddenly that it was impossible to bring the guns into action against them. No casualties were suffered, however. Arriving at Avesnes-les-Bapaume, the teams came up to the 23rd

Battalion, then in close contact with the enemy. There were no orders for the teams, but later General Gellibrand and Major Plant arrived, and Lieutenant Callister was directed to silence German machine-guns in Monument Wood, to the north of Bapaume. A serious effort to carry out the order led to some interesting developments. Taking Private S. S. Smith with him, Callister went across to the road running north from Bapaume and skirting the west edge of the Wood. In doing so, they were well shot at, but escaped injury. Two Companies of the 23rd Battalion were lying along the edge of the road, held up by two machine-guns and two 77 m.m. field guns. The two machine-guns were located, one in the south edge of the wood, and the other some distance to the right. A way of advance for two teams was decided on, and Smith was sent back to bring them forward; no easy matter, for teams laden with guns and gear were a slowly moving and conspicuous target. Meanwhile, Callister, to get a better view, entered the upstairs portion of a semi-detached cottage facing the road. There was a gap in the roof, but, thinking the tiles on the rear side would make a good background, he stepped on to the ceiling. The spot was under direct observation. Hardly had he raised his glasses when two 77 m.m. shells arrived. Two others followed immediately and hit the cottage. Callister needed no further encouragement, but left hurriedly, just as two more shells cleared the roof and hit the ground in the rear. By this time the teams had arrived and, nothing daunted, the half-section did some good "crawling into action" behind a number of small manure heaps. Sergeant L. Davies' team (Lance-Corporal H. J. Cook as No. 1) undetected, got on to the enemy gun on the edge of Monument Wood—at a range of 700 yards—and silenced it; two German gunners being shot down as they attempted to run into Monument Wood. That gun did not open fire again. While the foregoing duel was taking place, Corporal C. M. Bowden's gun engaged the right hand opponent at a range of 900 yards. Observation in this case was not so good. Nevertheless, Bowden's party also silenced its opponent who kept quiet for the remainder of the day, although he became very active after dark. This had been foreseen, and Bowden's gun was kept laid on to his adversary, but, while the flash extinguisher was being adjusted (for night firing), the gun was deflected. No way of relaying in the darkness being possible, the German had the last word, but his fire proved harmless. While the duels were in progress, Captain McGregor and Lieutenant Gray, of the 6th Brigade Light Trench Mortar Battery, entered the damaged cottage.

THE GERMAN WITHDRAWAL.

Immediately their heads appeared on the upper floor, two 77 m.m. shells arrived. They merely laughed and swore, but when two more brought down a mass of tiles and dust on top of them they lost no time in departing. McGregor then sought to converse with the prone teams behind the manure heaps. It required some vigorous language to induce him to pass on and not give the positions away. He had hardly moved when Private W. N. Riley appeared, casually strolling up the road "festooned" with a supply of new boots for Davies' team; quite intent on delivering his goods and undisturbed by the matter in hand. He also required much emphatic language to divert him from a delicate situation. Soon after the duels had been decided, Callister, McGregor, and three officers of the 23rd Battalion were standing behind the cottage when the alert 77 m.m. Battery landed a shell at their feet. Someone said casually, "too close to be pleasant," and the party moved off. A few minutes later, a stretcher party was observed carrying away one of the 23rd officers who had been wounded in the abdomen by a fragment of the shell.

During the evening, the 23rd Battalion occupied the village of Favreuil, and later in the night, Captain Drummond and Lieutenant F. W. Duncan came up and occupied positions in the village. Captain Drummond selected a comfortable dugout which was reported to have been blown up shortly after he vacated it. The next day eight guns were established in Favreuil, four on its northern outskirts and four others in the vicinity of Bapaume. During the afternoon a German aeroplane flew over at a height of about 3,000 feet. Nine of the Company's guns opened harmlessly on the intruder. The din was considerable, and General Gellibrand had much adverse comment to offer. The General wanted to know what was wrong with markmanship which loosed such a large quantity of ammunition at a low-flying machine without effect; and further, were the Germans to fly about as they pleased? It was naturally disappointing to find that the visitor had escaped, but as a matter of fact, repeated efforts only served to show how very difficult it was to bring down aircraft with bullets. Not at any time during the Company's experience, could it definitely claim to have succeeded, although it had, since November, 1916, almost continuously, in and out of the line, guns specially set apart for the purpose. About a fortnight later, three machine-gun companies and many infantry fired on a low-flying aeroplane near Bullecourt, but it came to earth without a bullet mark upon it. The

Company was again concerned, and a further reference will be found later in this chapter.

The Company was now in country that was practically free from shell holes and barbed wire. It did the eyes good to look on a landscape which reflected the quiet beauty of the fields of France, and to get away from the inevitably depressing effect of living among blasted earth and ruined villages. From a distance, Bapaume, and the adjacent villages, had the appearance of being fairly intact, but a closer inspection revealed the fact that practically all the houses were unsafe, having been systematically rendered so by the destruction of the internal walls. Practically all the contents of the houses had been removed, so the souvenir hunters had a very lean time. No one expected that the retiring enemy would have left much of value, but it was noticed, with feelings of deep disgust, that German thoroughness had included the cutting down of all the dwarf fruit trees which were a feature of French gardens. Many of the dugouts had been mined, and it was not an uncommon sight to see tongues of flame shoot out of them when an explosion (brought about by a delayed action contrivance) took place. The area abounded with "booby traps"; innocent looking devices designed to kill or injure the unwary. Everyone felt nervous about making use of enemy dugouts, and it was only after a careful and minute examination that they were occupied. Articles left on tables or ledges were sometimes connected to bombs, which exploded when the article was removed. All wires were regarded with suspicion. Corporal F. Wright has related the finding of a number of wired traps. Sergeant R. Dodgshun disconnected them in a matter-of-fact way, "but," said he, "I wouldn't have touched them with a 40-foot pole." Smouldering fires were burning in Bapaume, and the villages of the district. At night, a lurid glare lit up the country for miles. Even wells came under suspicion of being poisoned, and warnings were issued accordingly. Some of No. 2 Section took a risk in one instance. Next day an English party arrived and took samples of the water for testing purposes. "We hoped it wasn't poisoned," said Corporal Wright, "because we had been drinking it for 36 hours."

By this time, the retreating Germans and their closely following opponents were well beyond the strongly fortified zones whereon the battles of the previous summer and autumn had been fought. Consequently, conditions approximating to "open warfare" were experienced. "It was strange," said one, "to be marching along a main highway with nothing to stop our progress."

Guns mounted for anti-aircraft duty:
  (Above)—Warlencourt. March, 1917.
  (Below)—Needle Trench. January, 1917.

THE GERMAN WITHDRAWAL.

The Field Artillery, like other arms, found itself disestablished from fixed positions, and well forward with the advanced guard. Out in the open, with no disguise, it was liable to attack from the air. As a precaution, ten of the Company's guns were attached to the 12th, 13th, 21st, and 23rd Batteries of Australian Field Artillery for a few days' action against enemy air-craft. Further assistance was given when two half-limbers, driven by Drivers E. J. Nash and J. Britt, each containing a mounted gun and three gunners accompanied them. The gunners had a particularly rough ride on the unsprung limbers across open country, but had the satisfaction of watching their artillery comrades get into action and scatter parties of German cavalry. During these open warfare movements, Lieutenant Blenkarn, mounted on his charger, was very active and covered much country. His activity was responsible for a diverting incident when he and his mount "turned turtle" in a large shell hole. The Company Transport Section was likewise very active at this time, and can claim to be the first of the Brigade's vehicles to reach Favreuil. Wheeled traffic was greatly hampered by the many trees which the retreating enemy had felled across the roads. A diary entry for the 18th March reads: "What a relief to look on country not shell torn. . . . Our forward guns and infantry have had some fighting of the real open-order variety. Yesterday, this house was a hot spot (on the Bapaume-Arras Road), to-day it is unnaturally quiet as we are eating our tinned rations and reading our mail. The roads here are perfect—further back, hundreds of men are rapidly putting the damaged parts to rights—circling the huge mined sections and clearing the railway."

By the 20th March the Brigade had reached the vicinity of the famous Hindenburg Line. The enemy was still holding an outpost line running north-west and south-east in front of the villages of Longatte, Noreuil, Lagnicourt. That morning, in bitterly cold weather, the Brigade attacked in co-operation with the troops on both flanks. The Brigade's effort was directed against the village of Noreuil, with the intention of occupying it if only small numbers were encountered, or to force the enemy to disclose his dispositions if his line was held in strength. On the Brigade front the attack was entrusted to the 21st Battalion (left), and the 23rd Battalion (right). The Company supplied three teams and guns to each of the Battalions; Lieutenant Bice with part of No. 3 Section on the left, and Lieutenant Blenkarn with part of No. 4 on the right. After some sharp fighting, the attack was called off when it was realised that the enemy line was strongly held. The Company's guns fired about 4,000 rounds on small targets, but no opportunities for effective work presented themselves. The two Battalions sustained regrettable casualties amounting to 13 officers and 318 other ranks, but the Company's teams came through scathless.

Next day the Company was relieved by the 7th Machine Gun Company, and marched back to Warlencourt, where it sheltered in cellars of the ruined houses of that village. Four teams still attached to the Australian Field Artillery, and three others on anti-aircraft duty passed, temporarily, to the command of the 7th Machine Gun Company. The "chats" (lice) at Warlencourt were described as "large, numerous, and very active." The day after arrival, the seven detached teams rejoined, and the re-united Company was directed to provide two teams for anti-aircraft duty at Bazentin railhead and Siege Loop. With the relief just recorded, the Company's participation in following up the German withdrawal came to an end. During the greater part of the retirement, the Company was actively engaged, and traversed with its parent Brigade a distance of over 12 miles of lately occupied enemy territory.

While at Warlencourt, the Company's Diary recorded: "Bathing parade" on two days. What it did not mention, however, was the fact that it was the first time for weeks that the great majority of officers and men had had all their clothes off. The baths were of the usual type encountered in the captured territory, and a short description will not be out of place. A small hut was erected for the purpose; about seven feet from the floor, a few rows of piping were fixed. In the piping, at short intervals, holes were bored under which a perforated tin was attached for the purpose of distributing a thin trickle of water. Beneath each tin, upon slippery duckboards, the shivering victims—usually two or more—jostled each other in their attempts to catch the descending trickle. The water invariably changed suddenly from very cold to scalding hot. The time allotted was generally one minute, when most frantic efforts were made to get lathered and flushed before the small boiler exhausted its limited supply. The boiler often finished first. In an outer room, underclothes were handed over, and a fresh supply received on emerging from the bath; but, on this occasion, as one narrator mildly put it, "the arrangements could have been better." Six-footers received outfits designed for short men, and vice versa; a situation which provoked much mirth for the fortunate ones. This was not the only criticism, how-

THE GERMAN WITHDRAWAL.

ever. The complaint made was justified that "the clothes I gave in were no dirtier than these, and at any rate, I was familiar with the live stock inhabitating them." On the way back to quarters, the "bathers" were caught in a heavy snow storm.

While at Warlencourt the Company—under the Captaincy of Private W. Sharp—met the 24th Battalion at football, but had to acknowledge defeat by the very strong Battalion team. After weeks of line work, the guns and gear stood in need of much overhauling and cleaning. This was attended to, and a portion of each day was devoted to salvaging war material. Some spare time was spent in exploring the enemy's lately vacated lines; Loupart Wood, on account of its height and commanding position, being visited by many. One diarist wrote: "Walked with George Jeffrey to Loupart Wood. Met General Gellibrand and Major Plant on a similar mission. It is the highest contour for miles around. What a landscape! Shell-torn earth, with the ruins of villages and stumps of trees standing out of a billowing sea of brown. Villages can be identified only with the aid of the map. Loupart Wood chewed up terribly by our artillery fire. The defence system adjacent heavily wired and well sited."

During the night of the 25th-26th March, watches were advanced one hour in accordance with "Summer time." Orders had been issued overnight to "fall in" at 7 a.m. on the morning following in order to move. Company Headquarters breakfasted hurriedly, but upon turning out to supervise the move, found no one stirring. Only the officers' watches, it transpired, had been altered. A very annoyed Company set off an hour and a half late for Mametz Camp, in the rear. A rainy, sloppy march did not help to shake off the effects of the bad start. The 13th Machine Gun Company took over the vacated quarters. After four days at Mametz Camp, an hour's march brought the Company to the more comfortable Becourt Camp.

On the 24th March, the new Divisional Machine Gun Company marched into Becourt Camp, and the day following, it officially joined the 2nd Division, and was designated the 22nd Company. Captain A. N. McLennan, late of the 6th Company, was in command. Unlike the other Companies in the Division, it did not come under the jurisdiction of any Brigade, but was controlled from Divisional Headquarters. Until the advent of the 2nd Machine Gun Battalion, a year later, it remained in the nature of an odd number. The new formation naturally aroused much interest, more particularly on account of the personal ties existing between the two units. A week after their arrival, the newcomers met the Company in a football match, the forerunner of a long and friendly rivalry. The older Company scored the honours in the first contest by a narrow margin of three points.

The following day being Sunday, a Brigade Church Parade was held, after which Lieutenant-General Birdwood inspected the parade. Sergeant R. Dodgshun left at this time to enter an officer cadet battalion in England.

While at Becourt Camp, many members visited and explored the battlefield of Pozieres. In sharp contrast to their previous visit, the whole area was strangely silent and overgrown with weeds. Gibraltar, The Orchard, and the Cemetery were examined at leisure, and finally the crest of the ridge that had been won at such cost in blood and valour, the evidence of which lay all too plentifully around. Some of No. 3 Section searched for, and found the remains of their young and respected comrade, Lance-Corporal J. T. Milnes, which were buried where he fell, and erected an inscribed cross to mark the spot. Others sought for the resting places of late friends in the battalions of the Brigade, and paid similar tributes.

The eight days spent in the comparative comfort of Becourt Camp passed quickly. The baths were a good deal better than those just described, and the Camp could boast of the presence of a large Y.M.C.A. hut; a welcome feature in such a place. To hear a piano played was like water to a parched tongue, and reminded the listener how very remote he was from friends and their refining influences of civilian life.

On the 8th day of April, the Company left Becourt Camp en route for the line. It was a beautiful day, but the long march was very exhausting. In a large, open field, free of shell holes, near the ruined village of Beugnatre, camp was pitched. That is to say as far as a couple of tents and a number of canvas sheets, known as "bivouacs," would allow. They were woefully inadequate, but the best use was made of them, and by night all ranks had contrived to squeeze under cover. From their cramped quarters, everyone was awakened early next morning by a strong wind and a heavy rain-squall. At the same time, sound of a terrific bombardment was heard away to the left. Much interest was aroused, and it was not long before the welcome tidings arrived reporting the successful storming of the Vimy Ridge by the First and Third Armies, and the capture of thousands of prisoners,

THE GERMAN WITHDRAWAL.

To relieve the congestion, Private B. H. Johnson and Driver G. Lindsay were sent off on a roving commission, and returned with several tents—obtained unofficially. They were erected immediately, and formed the nucleus of a tented camp. The presence of those tents was very difficult to explain to Brigade Headquarters when awkward questions were asked, but, somehow, possession was retained. The same afternoon a strange horse appeared at the Company horse lines, to be followed some hours later by a very, very irate English Artillery Captain. The meeting and almost wordless encounter between the visitor and Captain Drummond was extremely funny, but the English Captain took the horse away.

The 4th Australian Division was occupying the line in front of Bullecourt—a bastion in the Hindenburg Line—and the Company (with the 7th Machine Gun Company) in view of impending operations, was attached to that Division for duty. Captain Drummond, with his usual foresight, had taken the precaution during the day of arrival to ride forward and reconnoitre the ground. At 1.30 a.m. on the morning after arrival, the Company, without warning, was aroused and ordered to move forward for action. In the darkness, with a strong wind blowing and driving the falling sleet, it was a most disagreeable task to resume the habiliments of war: harness horses, issue rations, and march off in formation for action. Some very strong language, reflecting on the peculiar ways of the staff, helped to restore a semblance of good humour. By this time, the Company was under way, and snow was falling heavily. After passing Vaulx, Captain Drummond, who had ridden forward in advance, met the column and conducted it to and through Noreuil. Here the guns and gear were taken from limbers and carried forward. "There in the snow," related an observer, "I saw as silent and disciplined a collection of gear as could be desired. Nothing left or in wrong hands, and the limbers empty in two minutes.

The orders for the Company were to provide an indirect-fire barrage, in support of an attack by the 4th Division against the Hindenburg Line, on the right of, and close to, the village of Bullecourt. On the left of the 4th Division, the 62nd (British) Division was to give a measure of support. For this attack the usual "artillery preparation," i.e., the destruction of the enemy wire and defences, was dispensed with, and to twelve "tanks" was allotted the task of beating down the heavy belts of wire in front of the Hindenburg Line. The attacking infantry of the 4th

Division (4th and 12th Brigades) were in position before zero hour (4.45 a.m.). After their very hurried entry, in the darkness, to a new sector, the four Sections under Lieutenants Callister, Windsor, Duncan, and Bice, had some difficulty in finding their locations. However, before daybreak, Nos. 1 and 4 were established in the sunken road some 750 yards in rear of the railway cutting—virtually the British front line—and Nos. 2 and 3 some distance to the right in the railway cutting. All the guns were thus disposed in the right brigade sector of the Division. Gun positions were at once dug, and as soon as it was at all possible to read compasses in the dull light, the guns were laid and other preparations completed. Zero time came and passed, but no attack; it was cancelled almost at the last minute owing to the non-arrival of the tanks. Shortly after, the disgusted infantry of the two Brigades, showing signs of reaction after being keyed up all night, streamed back over the snow in hundreds, "like a football crowd after a big match," for, as one narrator put it, "all Germany to see." The withdrawal was, fortunately, unmolested. Some of the Company's guns opened their programme, but desisted as soon as it became clear that the attack had been called off. During the day, the teams dug in more effectively, endured some shelling without loss, and had a miserable time in the slight shelters they had contrived to make, but which gave little protection against bitter snow-squalls lasting all day.

Next morning, the attack was launched. The Company's sixteen guns fired their programme on enemy trenches and communications on the right flank of the Division's attack. For the first two hours, each gun fired at the rate of 1500 rounds per hour; thereafter, for six hours, at the rate of 1000 rounds per hour. When the programme had been completed, only visible targets were engaged. Several small parties on the right flank were seen and dispersed. At first, wounded, highly elated at the progress of events, came back, but it was not long before it became obvious that the attack was going badly. Most of the tanks had been put out of action, though a few were still firing. From the cutting on the right the teams had the mortifying experience of watching hundreds of Australians in the Hindenburg Line being surrounded and compelled to surrender. Their feelings were intensified by their inability to fire on their comrades' captors owing to the danger of hitting the former. Later, survivors of the thoroughly broken and disorganised attack drifted back, and the extent of the disaster became manifest. Many of the remnants became stretcher-bearers, and from No Man's Land

THE GERMAN WITHDRAWAL. 165

during the day it seemed that hundreds of wounded were carried in through the falling snow—the enemy, as a rule, not interfering unless parties entered his wire. The rescue work was carried on till darkness set in, by which time the rescuers and others had retired to the rear. This state of affairs left the Company holding a sector of the front line, about 1250 yards in width, practically the frontage of the right brigade. Thus for some hours the Company enjoyed the doubtful distinction of holding, alone and unsupported by any organised unit, an appreciable part of the Western Front. When it became obvious that the searchers in No Man's Land, mostly unarmed, were retiring through the front zone, No. 1 Section was moved up to the railway cutting on the left boundary of the Brigade. By this arrangement twelve guns were in the front line and No. 4 Section's four in support. It was hoped that the cross fire of No. 1 Section, with Nos. 2 and 3 on the right, would prevent any counter-attack from reaching the front line, especially as the mantle of snow showed up any movement. The teams prepared accordingly. The position on the right flank, however, caused a good deal of uneasiness, because the right-hand guns could not cover the falling ground towards Queant. Representations were made to the unit concerned, but it is understood that Captain Drummond received a rather frigid reception when he reported the state of affairs. As a measure of protection, Lieutenant Windsor, though far from well, pushed two of No. 2 Section's guns as far along the cutting as he dared, in spite of heavy shelling, and gave the flank a good deal of his attention. After the guns had been established, Sergeant A. Payton was wounded, and later Privates W. Compton and H. Wood were killed by different shells. That the fears were well-grounded was proved four days later (after the Company had been relieved), when a German counter-attack broke through to Lagnicourt. The 5th Machine Gun Company's right-hand section of four guns broke the flank of the counter-attack, but were themselves attacked and enveloped from the dead ground in the right rear. No counter-attack followed the attack of the 4th Division, but the railway cutting and vicinity were heavily shelled. After some hours as the lone guardian of the line, the Company was very glad to see a company of the 52nd Battalion arrive to share the responsibility. During the night three other Companies of that Battalion were disposed in the sector, thereby relieving an anxious situation.

Early in the morning, No. 3 Section suffered casualties, when a shell-burst wounded Lieutenant Duncan, Sergeant G. B. Crerar, Privates G. R. Turner, and L. G. Byrnes. With the exception of

Crerar, all recovered and returned to the Company. Crerar died in hospital on the 20th May as a result of his wounds. Some little time previously, his name had been sent to Brigade Headquarters with a recommendation to proceed to England for entry to an officer cadet battalion, but an unfortunate delay held up his transfer. By his death the Company lost a capable and conscientious non-commissioned officer, who had long since qualified for promotion by his sterling work. To a genial temperament was added a literary turn of mind, some evidence being discerned in the poem, "Up and Down the Duckboards," recorded in Chapter V. He was also a well-informed Shakespearian scholar.

On the night of the 12th-13th, the Company was relieved by the 7th Australian Machine Gun Company, and returned to its camp near Beugnatre. So ended a short but particularly strenuous and depressing tour of duty. The hurried call to action in falling snow was followed by 60 hours of front line work—allowing little or no sleep—in bitter weather. During that time a planned attack was postponed and launched twenty-four hours later. Then followed the depressing and mortifying spectacle of the splendid infantry battalions of the 4th and 12th Brigades, with little support, being broken to fragments in their valorous attempt to carry out an ill-conceived attack against the strong Hindenburg Line. The depression of the morning was followed by the task of guarding for some hours an appreciable sector of the line. In this the teams were not perturbed by their unexpected responsibility, being conscious of their considerable fire power, but a certain amount of anxiety in the circumstances was inevitable. It was a weary-eyed party, craving sleep, that arrived back at its scanty shelters. For his capable conduct of the Company operations, Captain Drummond was mentioned in despatches.

The next three days were spent overhauling guns and gear, and obtaining a measure of rest. Meanwhile, the 4th Division's sector had been taken over by the 2nd Australian Division, and the Company reverted to the command of the 6th Brigade. The camp was startled on the morning of the 15th, when reports of German retaliation came through. A determined thrust in the vicinity of Lagnicourt reached as far as the artillery lines, and some field guns fell, temporarily, into enemy hands, but prompt counter measures, mainly by the 5th Brigade, restored the situation. It was learned with much interest that the unsatisfactory position on the right of the ground, recently held by the Company's guns, had justified the fears felt at the time. In resisting the attack, the 5th Machine Gun Company lost one officer, 20 other ranks, and four guns—practically the whole of its right Section—though only after they had put up a good fight.

On the same night, the Company moved forward again. Four guns were placed in the railway cutting, with the remainder distributed in depth, most of them being placed in the Corps Line between Vaulx and Noreuil. The following night indirect fire, chiefly on enemy wire, was commenced. Enemy shell-fire was fairly heavy, and a number of men were buried at different times, but only one case of wounding was recorded—Corporal D. C. M. Parkhill, on the 16th. After four days, relief was provided by the 22nd Machine Gun Company. A sensation was caused on the Brigade front when Captain Drummond arrived on horseback to conduct the preliminary stages. It was the new Company's first experience of line work, and, by arrangement, the Nos. 1 of the Company remained for 24 hours with the new teams. The latter were duly "blooded." During the night, the team on the extreme left, in charge of Lance Corporal H. G. Black, suffered casualties. A shell burst close to the gun, blowing two of the crew to pieces. In a shelter almost under the gun (it was mounted on a bank) were Lieutenant Pritchard, his batman, and Black. All three were blown out, the two former suffering severely from shock and the latter less so. Black stayed on till the following night, when a fresh team was sent in. It so happened that the relief was in charge of Sergeant F. Hickey, who was one of the original members of the 6th Company. During its first 24 hours in the line, the 22nd Company lost four men killed.

At this time Lieutenant F. Windsor fell ill and was evacuated. He did not return to the Company, his broken health leading to his discharge early in the following year. By his departure the Company lost a sterling and trusted leader. Possessed of a will which would make himself go anywhere, he always believed in aggressive action, and there is little doubt that his energetic efforts—always in the direction of winning the war—led him to return to duty on two occasions before he was fit, and finally resulted in his death after discharge. On the 9th of April, he was mentioned in despatches, and in the following June was awarded the French decoration Croix de Chevalier, Legion of Honour.

The weather at times showed a tendency to improve, but was very unsettled. Thus diary entries read: "16th: Fine again, but rain set in at even. Boisterous night, tent very nearly blown down." "17th: Wet and sloppy; rain, hail, sleet, and wind."

Rumours had been afloat that another attempt was to be made against the Hindenburg Line, and very soon after the first reports were circulated, Lieutenant Colonel L. F. S. Hore, who was now 1st Anzac Corps Machine Gun Officer, informally visited Company Headquarters and announced a third attack in the vicinity of Bullecourt. The Company was very pleased to see its old Commanding Officer, but the same could not be said as to his tidings. On the 22nd April, the Brigade commenced rehearsals for the attack, in which the Company took part. Five days later, formal Brigade orders were issued, which stated, among other things, that: "The Brigade will attack the Hindenburg Line on a date to be fixed." The directions for the Company were to provide six teams and guns to accompany the attacking infantry, six to provide indirect fire in support of the attack, and the remainder, four, to be held in reserve. Officers were chosen for the different tasks, and they in turn selected the non-commissioned officers and men to compose the various teams. The parties selected to go over with the attackers took their place in the early morning rehearsals with the infantry battalions. Those rehearsals, near Biefvillers, were carried out at the hour it was proposed to attack, and over ground marked out to represent the German trenches. Success signals were fired and every detail that experience and thought could suggest was worked out. Meanwhile, those not included in the attacking parties underwent the usual Company training and daily Company routine. The 25th April was observed as a holiday for Anzac Day for those not on duty. Two days later, Corporal H. A. Robinson was promoted to 2nd Lieutenant.

Rehearsals for the attack were interrupted on the 24th, when the Company took over twelve guns in the Corps and Vaulx lines as part of the reserve defence plan. Two days later, to allow further rehearsals, the teams were relieved by the 1st Machine Gun Company. On the 27th the Company exchanged places with the 1st Machine Gun Company. The following day No. 3 Section had three men wounded by shell-fire—Corporal W. S. Clayton (head), Lance Corporal H. G. Black (cheek), and Private A. Campbell.

By this time the weather had definitely improved, but evacuations for "sickness" continued at about five per week. During the period covered by this chapter, losses totalled: Three other ranks killed in action or died of wounds, one officer and fourteen other ranks wounded, two officers (Lieutenants Windsor and Blenkarn) and 52 other ranks evacuated "sick." Scabies were prevalent (twelve cases being noted), while septic sores accounted for seven and mumps six.

On the 29th the Company again exchanged places with the 1st Machine Gun Company and reassembled at its camp. The same day polling for the Commonwealth elections was attended to. Another move was made on the early morning of the 1st May, when the Company relieved the 22nd Machine Gun Company in the line. At the same time, the "attacking" teams and details moved to a Brigade concentration camp further back near Bapaume. The guns in support positions fired nightly on enemy wire to prevent repairs being effected. The line and support positions were shelled with regularity, but no further casualties were sustained. Conditions seemed to indicate the calm before the storm. On the 1st May, Lieutenant Callister, from the front line, noticed, some 3000 yards away, a German limber and two men. He directed the attention of some 21st Battalion observers to it, but they complained (though it was 2 p.m. on a bright day) that the artillery were asleep and neglecting their opportunities. "Looking back," said he, "I could see about half of the 2nd Division strolling about, working, souveniring bits of aeroplane etc., and wondered what the German infantry thought." Next day, a German aeroplane appeared at about 3000 feet, and circled over the railway cutting. The roar from small arms was very great, and soon after the plane came to earth behind one of No. 1 Section's guns. It landed very neatly, but ran into a small trench and capsized. The observer, running back towards Noreuil, was shot by a Lewis gunner, but the pilot, aged about 19 years, on his first service flight, bore up well. Private W. J. Cotter, with many others, dashed up to the plane; but Cotter arrived first, conducted the pilot to the railway cutting, and secured the Parabellum air-cooled gun, which he carried for weeks, but which was ultimately claimed and kept by the 23rd Battalion. It is interesting to note that, while perhaps 25,000 rounds were fired at the plane by the 5th and 6th Brigades, and the 6th, 7th, and 22nd Machine Gun Companies, no mark of a bullet could be found—engine trouble had brought it down.

Meanwhile, preparations by the teams in the line were pushed ahead. Gun pits for indirect fire barrage were dug, ammunition carted, belts filled, gun charts and orders prepared. On the 1st May it was reported that General Gellibrand was anxious to have two forward German guns silenced just before the attack. Private J. N. Myers volunteered, and his offer was seconded by Private A. W. Birch. The scheme was to crawl up and attack the gunners with bombs. However, on the following night the volunteers were told that the Brigadier had cancelled the arrangements. To relieve feelings of disappointment, Myers was informed that an English leave pass awaited him at the Company office.

The 2nd Division's plans for the attack included special machine-gun arrangements. First Anzac Corps directed that the Corps Machine Gun Officer and the 8th and 14th Machine Gun Companies of the 5th Australian Division be attached to the 2nd Division, for the express purpose of giving flank protection during the operation. The three Brigades retained command of their respective Companies, but the 22nd Company was included in Divisional plans. The latter provided 22 guns for covering fire during the advance, 16 for action during counter-attack, four for anti-aircraft duty, and six in reserve. As the Company's plans included six guns for covering fire, 28 guns in all were to support the Division's attack. In this grouping of Companies (following the attachment of the 6th and 7th Companies to the 4th Division on the 9th April), will be observed the first co-ordination of the machine-gun fire of Corps. This co-ordination was to reach the fullest development in the following Autumn, during the Third Battle of Ypres, when Corps undertook direct command of the whole of its machine-gun resources and utilised them as an integral part of the Corps plan.

As the day of attack drew near, much speculation was indulged in as to the result. The very complete Brigade arrangements, which seemed to indicate that the errors of omission and commission in connection with the 4th Division's attack would be avoided, were hopeful signs; but it was realised that the proposition was a tough one. The feeling of the officers of the 21st and 23rd Battalions was twofold, i.e., that they would break through and hold at any rate a good portion of their objective, and also that few of them would be left after so doing. Their judgment proved very correct in both respects.

Brigade orders required twenty-five per cent. of the Company strength to remain out of the operation to ensure a nucleus of a new Company in case of heavy casualties. The men selected for the nucleus manned the guns in the line and carried out the preliminary preparations. On the night of the 2nd May they marched out to Brigade concentration camp near Bapaume, and their places were taken by teams who were to fire the indirect-fire barrage. The "attacking" teams also moved up to the railway cutting during the evening. By this arrangement, all those taking part

THE GERMAN WITHDRAWAL. 171

in the operations were thoroughly rested. During the night the "attacking" teams moved forward and were in their allotted positions on the "jumping-off" tape by 3.15 a.m. on the following morning. All preparations were well in hand, every detail had been arranged, and all that foresight and experience could suggest had been provided for. Nothing remained but to await the approach of zero hour and hope that the Fates would be kind.

CHAPTER XII.

BULLECOURT.

3rd-4th May, 1917.

Bullecourt has always remained in the memory of members of the Company as the shortest and sharpest fight in which they were involved. The carefully prepared and rehearsed plan of attack seemed to justify the hope of a successful issue, but within a short time of its launching that hope had to be abandoned. Faced by a resolute, well-prepared and expectant garrison, the attackers soon realised that they were involved in an undertaking from which but limited success could be achieved. As the day wore on, it became a life and death struggle to maintain a narrow footing in the front and support trenches of the enemy defence system. After a day of almost continuous and costly fighting, the 6th Brigade found itself—owing to failure on both flanks—isolated in a narrow and heavily beset salient. Against the fiercest opposition the Brigade stubbornly held its ground and lived up to its finest traditions that day. Its achievement in breaching, and holding on to, the Hindenburg Line must surely rank with the most splendid feats of the Australian Imperial Force.

The general attack was entrusted to two Divisions. The 185th and 186th Brigades of the 62nd Division, on the left, were to assault the village of Bullecourt, which stood out as a bastion in the Hindenburg system, and the 2nd Australian Division on the right. The frontage of the 2nd Division was divided between the 6th Brigade (left) and the 5th Brigade (right). The former's share embraced 650 yards of the Hindenburg front and support lines—designated O.G.1 and O.G.2 respectively—with a contemplated penetration of 2500 yards in a north-easterly direction and lying between the villages of Hedencourt (left) and Riencourt (right). The allotted ground was divided into three objectives—O.G.1 and O.G.2 being the first, the general line of the tram line some 500 yards in rear of O.G.2 was the second, and a line joining the north-eastern edges of the villages named was the third. The 5th Brigade was allotted 600 yards of O.G.1 and O.G.2, and its final objective included the capture of the village of Riencourt.

BULLECOURT.

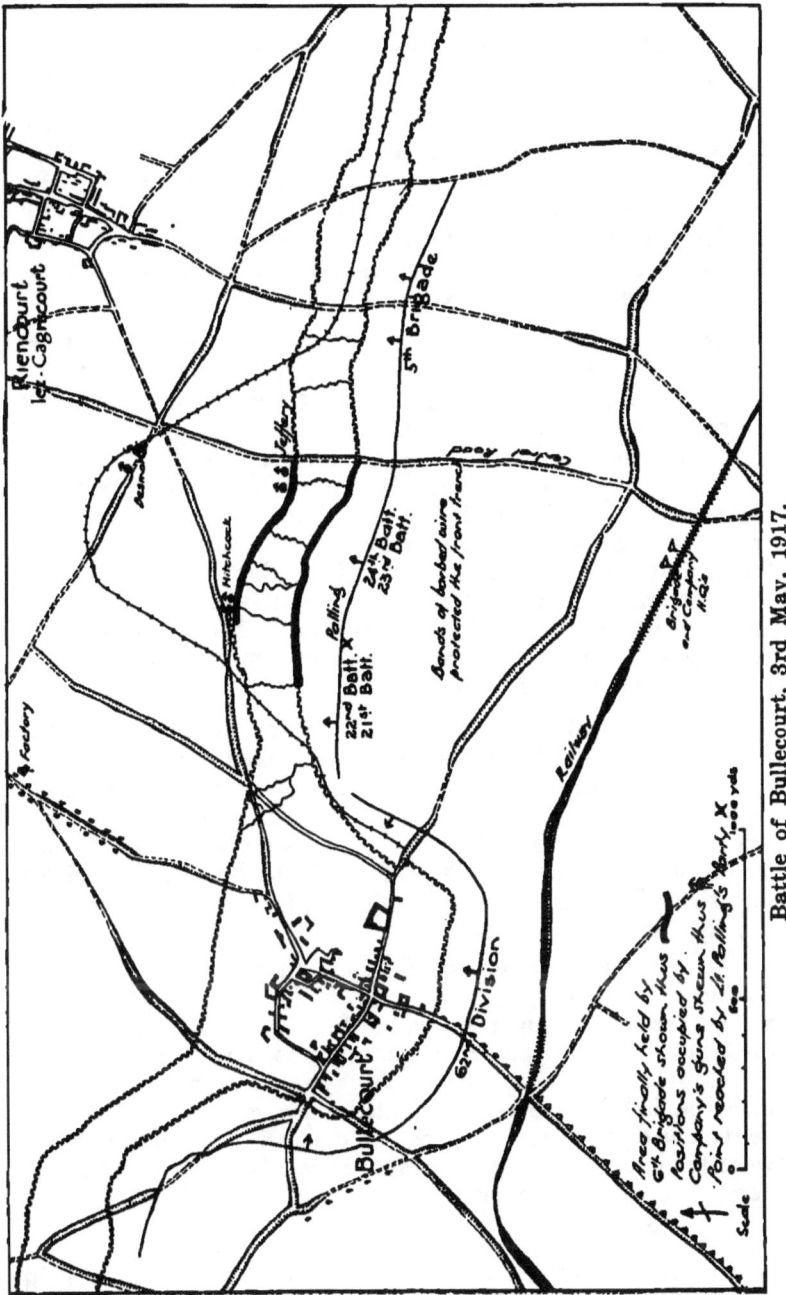

Battle of Bullecourt, 3rd May, 1917.

The boundary between the two Brigades was, for the greater portion, the sunken road running north, and was inclusive to the 5th Brigade.

The 6th Brigade planned to carry out its part "leap frog" fashion — that is to say, the 22nd Battalion (left) and 24th (right) were to carry the first and second objectives, after which the 21st (in rear of the 22nd) and the 23rd (in the rear of 24th) were to pass through their comrades and carry the third objective. The 7th Brigade was in reserve.

As part of the 6th Brigade's plan, the Company's tasks were to allot three half-sections (each of two teams and guns) to the two first assaulting battalions; six guns and teams to maintain indirect fire in support of the attack from the railway embankment; four guns and teams to be in reserve. The dispositions of the "attacking teams" were: Two from No. 2 Section under Lieutenant A. Palling with the left of the 22nd Battalion; two from No. 4 Section under Lieutenant A. P. Earle to the left of the 24th Battalion; two from No. 1 Section under Lieutenant R. D. Desmond to the right of the 24th Battalion. Brigade Headquarters directed that each of the two latter half-sections should be supplied with sixteen men from their respective Battalions to act as ammunition carriers.

Zero hour had been fixed at 3.45 a.m. on the morning of the 3rd May. By 3.40 a.m. the Brigade was in position on the "jumping-off" tape—in No Man's Land—in strict compliance with orders. Up till then the night had been very quiet, but a few minutes before zero the enemy placed a sharp, short barrage diagonally across the "jumping-off tape" and the men on it. Some disturbance and loss occurred on the left flank, where it fell most heavily, but it ceased before zero.

At zero the rear horizon lit up with a great flash, and a terrific roar broke upon a fine, calm morning. Heavy and light artillery opened instantaneously, but the first missiles to pass over the heads of the impatiently waiting troops were machine-gun bullets from the indirect-fire guns. The 18-pounders followed, then the heavier pieces contributed their quotas. No further secrecy was possible; the attack had opened. The eager infantry went forward, following the practice then developing of keeping very close to the advancing barrage.

On the Left:

Five minutes after zero the enemy replied with heavy and light

Warneton: February, 1918.

Some of No. 3 Section in Malt Trench Support, March, 1917. (Wearing German helmets and caps.)

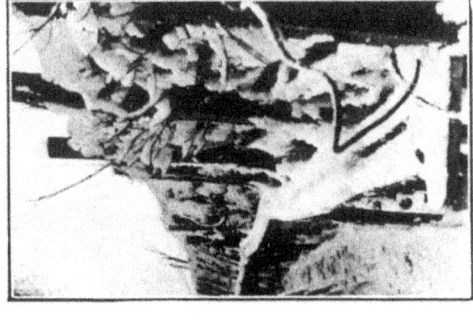

Zambuck Post: January, 1918.

artillery, minenwerfer, and machine-gun fire. The barrage on the left of the Brigade's attack appeared to be put down in the form of a cross, and fell heavily on the 22nd Battalion. Not only did it cause many casualties among the 22nd and the 21st in rear, but it practically split those units in half. The left portion of each Battalion naturally became somewhat disorganised, and failing to keep close up to the British barrage, came under heavy enfilade fire at close range from the defenders of the east side of Bullecourt and were pinned down in shell-holes. Isolated from the general advancing line, they were forced to fight a stiff musketry action with the alert and unshaken garrison. In the isolated sections were three of the Brigade's trench mortars under Lieutenant Gray, and two of the Company's guns under Lieutenant Palling. The enemy showed great enterprise in this sector, and attempted to counter-attack across the open to get possession of the trench mortars. Very few of the details succeeded in moving till dusk, and neither trench mortars nor machine-guns could be brought into action.

The right portion of the 22nd and 21st Battalions reached O.G.1 about 4 a.m., practically together and simultaneously with their comrades of the 24th Battalion on their right. Little opposition was encountered as the men followed the protective barrage closely. The captured trench was quickly "mopped up," and the success signal was fired by both Battalions at 4.10 a.m. The only real trouble experienced by the 22nd was on their left flank, which was strongly held; here they became involved in a bomb fight which lasted off and on throughout the day. No signs could be seen on the left of any progress by the 185th Brigade, but it was noticed that enemy flares appeared to be fired from their original places and his barrage was still on No Man's Land.

After reorganising in and near O.G.1, the 22nd and 21st followed the barrage closely and attacked and took O.G.2 on a little less than half of the allotted frontage. Considerably more opposition was experienced from the larger garrison, but as no time was given to man the parapet, resistance was soon at an end and the success signal was fired at 4.26 a.m., one minute after that of the 5th Brigade. Strong opposition again came from the left flank. Here a strong post was put in hand and supported by two of the Company's guns under Sergeant A. P. Hitchcock. From O.G.2 about 230 men of the 21st and 22nd Battalions pushed on to the second objective. Faced by stiff opposition from their front and left, they reached a point about 100 yards short of their destination and faced N.N.W., but were not in touch with the 24th on their right. The line was, however, held in sufficient strength to warrant the success signal being fired at 5.34 a.m. Soon after they became involved in a heavy bombing action. About noon the remnants were withdrawn to O.G.2.

On the left of the Brigade, events had gone badly. After its initial failure against Bullecourt, the 185th Brigade made repeated attempts against the village in daylight, but superiority of fire from the defenders cut short every attempt. About 8 a.m. the 27th Battalion (7th Brigade) attacked the S.E. corner of the village, but after the leading platoons had been wiped out the attempt was called off. During the afternoon a serious attempt was made by bombing to the left to secure the frontage originally allotted to the Brigade, preparatory to relief by the 1st Brigade. This was found to be impracticable. Though pressed with determination, the difficulty of supply of bombs and rifle grenades was too great. Each time the offensive was adopted, the increased expenditure brought the movement to a halt and the inevitable counter-attack forced abandonment of the captured ground. In the face of constant pressure no progress was possible. The lodgment made was, however, retained, and the precarious footing handed over to the 1st Brigade; relief being completed after delays from enemy shelling by 4 a.m. on the morning of the 4th. The Company's teams were, however, not relieved till the following night.

Turning to the Company's participation in this section, it will be recalled that Lieutenant Palling and two of No. 2 Section's teams and guns (each of one N.C.O. and four men) were allocated to the 22nd Battalion. The party took up its position on the left of the fourth wave, but while waiting for zero the preliminary enemy barrage descended heavily, so the teams (who were not directly concerned in the capture of O.G.1) moved back some little distance to the shelter of a sunken road. When the British barrage opened, the party moved forward amid a terrific roar of guns of all calibres. Two short halts were called, during which the German machine-guns could be heard distinctly through the pandemonium, and searchlights were turned on by the Germans. Lieutenant Palling looked in vain for the success signals—four white flares. As the party moved again it was daylight, and a hail of bullets smote them; shells also fell heavily. While carrying one of the guns, Private G. Malcolm was shot in the chest. He was hastily bandaged by Sergeant A. E. Masters and Private J. N. Spittle, and left in a shell-hole. Immediately after Palling was badly hit in the groin just as Spittle picked up Malcolm's gun. Spittle then attempted to drag Palling into a shell-hole, but a

BULLECOURT.

bullet struck him in the thigh, and at the same time part of his respirator was shot away. Masters succeeded in getting Palling into a shell-hole, but the other members of the party fared badly. Private J. German was shot through the head and died instantly. Private D. Smyth was struck in the foot, an injury which resulted in his subsequent discharge. At the outset, Corporal J. P. Adam and Private E. Daniel became detached during the turmoil; Daniel was wounded in the eye (subsequently removed), but Adam pushed on to the enemy lines and entered O.G.1. There he searched vainly for his comrades, but ultimately joined up with one of No. 4 Section's teams after sending word back as to his whereabouts. The five unwounded (Sergeant Masters, Privates P. J. Dinneen, J. C. Berriman, N. C. Hammon, and the runner, W. Roberts), assembled in one shell-hole and reviewed the situation. They were out of touch with the infantry and pinned down by close enfilade machine-gun fire; progress was clearly out of the question. Palling's condition was serious, so Dinneen and Roberts made a dash out—in spite of the danger of such a move—with the intention of returning with a stretcher. They reached Company Headquarters safely, but were ordered not to return in view of the extreme risk involved. For this plucky act, Roberts received the Military Medal. Every effort was made to stop the bleeding from Palling's wound, but he died about midday in the arms of Sergeant Masters. Spittle, running the risk from snipers, managed to hobble and crawl out with a stiffening leg during the day, and at night the remnants—the wounded being helped out by their comrades—returned to the railway cutting.

The centre half-section, under Lieutenant A. P. Earle, assembled with the left half of the second wave of the 24th Battalion. The party consisted of two teams from No. 4 Section, each of one N.C.O. and four men, and were assisted by sixteen carriers from the Battalion named. They were not unduly disturbed by the preliminary enemy barrage, and escaped much of the machine-gun fire and shelling which played such sad havoc with the left of the Brigade. At zero, the teams moved forward about 40 yards apart, Lieutenant Earle taking one and Sergeant A. P. Hitchcock the other. Approaching the enemy wire, Lieutenant Earle was wounded by a shell-burst, and one of his team, Private F. Braithwaite, received a bullet through the left leg. Sergeant Hitchcock's team sustained a casualty when a bullet passed through Private P. W. Dale's left wrist, breaking it. At this stage, it became apparent to Hitchcock that O.G.1 had not been taken on his immediate front, because of the continuous discharge of enemy flares. Reconnoitring forward, he came upon the other team at the entrance of a listening post sap, and his officer lying wounded in the head. Pushing forward, he discovered, in the sap, about a platoon of infantry of different battalions without an officer. These he led forward, and, with some assistance from his own men, cleared that part of O.G.1 after heavy bomb-fighting. In spite of his broken wrist, Dale assisted by carrying bombs, and while so doing a bullet struck the edge of his steel helmet, bending it flat against his face. After attending to Lieutenant Earle, and vainly trying to get him out, he finally came out with a message from Sergeant Hitchcock. For his devotion to duty he was subsequently awarded the Military Medal.

As soon as O.G.1 was cleared, the guns were taken into the captured trench and mounted, and at once came into action against enemy aircraft. Shortly after entering, Corporal J. Brandebura was wounded by a shrapnel pellet, apparently from an 18-pounder shell. Meanwhile O.G.2 had been taken, so the reduced party (Sergeant Hitchcock, Lance Corporal G. T. Guinea, Privates H. G. Carthew, S. Reed, and three others) moved into it. To obtain a better field of fire, the guns were eventually mounted in a trench just forward of the road running parallel to, and in rear of, O.G.2 near the Brigade's left flank. Much sniping came from the left along that road, and while a Lewis gun was set apart to deal with the snipers, Hitchcock engaged and scattered enemy parties marching along the road from Hendecourt to Bullecourt. It was estimated that about 30 casualties were inflicted. The position occupied by the party was strengthened by the attachment of a half-section of infantry. One serious counter-attack was driven off, during which Private Carthew coolly kept his gun in action throughout. Afterwards, he left the shelter of the trench and brought in wounded infantrymen. He was awarded the Military Medal for his work that day. The bomb fighting on the Brigade's left flank continued, off and on, through the day, but as it was confined to the trenches the guns had few opportunities of coming into action.

When the party was finally established, only six boxes of ammunition were available—the "carriers" and their burdens having been lost on the way. After much searching, eleven boxes and a good supply of S.A.A. were got together. During the afternoon, the half-section of infantry were withdrawn, leaving Hitchcock and his party in an exposed position about fifty yards in advance of the line proper. At night they could have been bombed from almost any angle, so Hitchcock wisely decided to fall back to the trench. This was done about nightfall. About midnight the teams were relieved by a party from No. 3 Section under Lieutenant E. J. Bice. No further losses were sustained. Unfortunately, Lieutenant Earle died in a London hospital on the 24th of July following, as a result of his wounds, and the Company was left to mourn the loss of a keen and promising officer, who had won his commission by his undoubted qualities of character and leadership. It is pleasing to record that Sergeant Hitchcock's spirited leadership was recognised by the award of the coveted Distinguished Conduct Medal, and subsequent promotion to commissioned rank.

The ingoing relief was composed of two teams from No. 3 Section under Lieutenant E. J. Bice. In the party were Privates R. C. Trevan, J. E. Smith, T. Millar, J. S. Campbell, E. J. Lyons, J. C. Muir, and W. H. Lucas. The newcomers were not heartened by the ghastly evidences of the day's bitter fighting; the trenches were littered with the dead and wounded of the very gallant Battalions of the Brigade. The left-hand gun took up a position near the left flank of the Brigade on O.G.2, where a sandbag "block" had been built. Shortly after arrival, a heavy bombing attack was launched against that flank. The attackers were headed by a "flamenwerfer," which directed a long flame of fire against the defenders. The latter, however, stood their ground, and as the carrier of the flame-thrower climbed over the barricade, the men, coolly waiting their opportunity, threw a few Mills grenades which sealed the fate of both carrier and weapon; the carrier was burnt to death by the flames of his own fire. The spare numbers of the gun-teams joined in the bomb-throwing, and the attack was beaten off, the gun taking part in the repulse. Attempts against the flank were repeated during the hours which followed, but ground was gained rather than lost, the defence receiving a fresh impulse from the newly-arrived 1st Brigade. The fighting was close and desperate. Private Trevan recorded in his diary: "The gun-team had a wonderful time sniping at the 'square-heads' who popped up everywhere at ranges of thirty to a hundred yards from the labyrinth of trenches. We used everything—bombs, revolvers, rifles and the Vickers. I had the pleasure of potting my first that morning at about ninety yards and with a German rifle. The net result was an extension of the trench. The bomb fighting was very fierce and desperate. The artillery also pasted the position relentlessly; hot fragments of shells were constantly falling on our clothes and tin hats. Shells were flying at a low trajectory and exploding everywhere around except on the right spot." The tense situation described by Trevan did not depress the nineteen-year-old Lucas, who was with the right-hand gun. When opportunity came for sniping, he was most active; when attention to wounded was needed he was most helpful. Shelling did not disturb him. When the shells fell close, his boyish treble was heard calling through the din—in imitation of a rabbit vendor—"They're woppers to-day, lady, they're woppers to-day." His obvious courage and high spirits were an inspiration to those around him, and attracted the particular attention of an English liaison officer in the trench. After watching Lucas for a time, the admiring officer asked, "Well, how do you feel now, lad?" "Feel?" said the confident youngster, "Good enough for ten of those bastards any time." "He was worth his weight in gold," said one of his mates, Private Lyons.

All day, under a hot sun, the men were without rations and water. It is hardly necessary to say that they were profoundly thankful when they were relieved at midnight by teams from the 1st Australian Machine Gun Company (1st Brigade). As soon as the "change-over" was completed, the parched men drank the dirty water from the barrel casings of their own guns. During the day, Lieutenant Bice visited Sergeant Jeffrey's teams in the Brigade's right sector, and while incautiously looking over the parapet was wounded in the neck by a watchful sniper. The wound was not serious, so he carried on till relief at night. No further casualties were sustained by the party, and in the circumstances it can be accounted extraordinarily fortunate.

On the Right:

The 24th Battalion, followed by the 23rd, experienced but little difficulty with the enemy wire, and practically no opposition was met in taking O.G.1, as the attackers kept close to the advancing barrage and gave the enemy no time to man his parapet. Touch was lost with the 5th Brigade on the right by the 24th Battalion, but the rear waves of the 23rd were in contact. The success signal was fired at 4.10 a.m. After reorganising in O.G.1, the 24th Battalion, followed by the 23rd, attacked and secured the allotted frontage in O.G.2. As on the left of the Brigade, stiffer opposition was shown by the larger garrison of the trench, but the close following of the barrage gave the attackers a distinct advantage, and the position was quickly secured and "mopped up." At 4.26 a.m. the success signal was fired, one minute after that of the 5th Brigade.

Although the success signal was fired by the 5th Brigade in both O.G.1 and O.G.2, it appears that only the left portion of the objective was occupied. With all the disadvantages of a flank unit in attack, serious difficulty was experienced in getting through the enemy wire, during which the Brigade lost heavily, especially in officers and non-commissioned officers. The disorganised attackers pushed on to the second objective, but of those who reached so far none returned. The remainder became involved in fierce bomb-fighting on their right flank, which, in turn, caused considerable anxiety as to the safety of the right of the 6th Brigade. Representations were made by the latter to both the 5th Brigade and Division Headquarters. The latter authorised the use of a Company of the 26th Battalion to stiffen a move to re-organise about 300 men of the 5th Brigade who were without officers, in an endeavour to extend that Brigade's foothold to the right. Captain W. R. Gilchrist, M.C., 6th Field Company Engineers (left) and Lieutenant D. N. Rentoul, M.C., 2nd Division Signal Company (centre), volunteered to lead the party, and were assisted by Lieutenant Gritten, liaison officer of the 5th Brigade, who took the right flank. This very gallant attack in daylight failed. Rentoul was wounded, and subsequently killed, while south of the wire. Gritten was held up in a line of shell-craters by heavy fire; Gilchrist (missing), with three men, succeeded in getting into O.G.1 about 200 yards east of the sunken road, which was the right boundary of the 6th Brigade. Viewing this advance from the railway cutting, Private F. L. Fitzpatrick said: "We witnessed one of the finest spectacles possible when some of the 7th Brigade, who had been in reserve, left our old front line and swept to the support of the hard-pressed 5th Brigade. The ground they had to traverse was a regular inferno of bursting shells, and swept by Fritz's machine-gun fire, but the magnificently steady and determined way in which those men moved through the welter to aid their comrades was something to remember. Our Brigade was Victorian, the 5th New South Wales, and the 7th was drawn from Queensland, South Australia, Western Australia, and Tasmania—but we were all Australians that day!"

Despite heavy fighting, the 5th Brigade's hold on its captured portion of O.G.1 and O.G.2 dwindled, and by evening its grip was reduced to a footing in the sunk road on the boundary of the 6th Brigade, thus leaving the latter completely isolated in its portion of the Hindenburg Line. At 9.15 p.m., 6th Brigade Headquarters repeated the S.O.S. call, and immediate action was taken by the artillery.

Meanwhile, the fourth wave of the 24th Battalion, under Captain G. L. Maxfield, M.C., advanced to the second objective (the tramline), with the 23rd in support. Two of the Company's guns under Lieutenant R. D. Desmond accompanied the advance, and were established about 150 yards west of the six star road junction. This point marked the furthest penetration of the Brigade, but in the nature of things it could not be held. Losses had been heavy, but a comparative handful of men settled down to hold their ground while other brave men pushed on, but to be immediately shot down. A defensive flank along the sunken road was formed, but pressure from the front and unsupported flanks compelled the ultimate retirement of the few survivors to O.G.2. The narrative will now turn to the experiences of the Company's teams in this advance.

Lieutenant R. D. Desmond, with two guns and teams, each of one N.C.O. and five men, accompanied by 16 "carriers" from the 24th Battalion, moved off at zero with the right-half of the fourth wave of the 24th Battalion. The preliminary enemy barrage fell mainly in rear, and free of flank complications, and despite the enemy barrage proper all went well till the wire was reached. While passing through, Corporal A. St.G. Tuohy was wounded in the leg and Lance Corporal A. D. G. Bone received an 18-pounder shrapnel pellet through the lung. In spite of his wound he struggled on and reached O.G.1, where he was ordered to retire. On the way he helped another wounded man some distance, and later came across Tuohy in a shell-hole bandaging his wounded leg. The pair, assisting each other, came out and were evacuated, but not before Tuohy was again wounded. Bone's plucky attempt to continue brought him the Military Medal. Hastily re-arranging their burdens, the reduced party made the crossing of O.G.1 with the foremost infantry. Indeed, as soon as Private W. N. Riley slid into the trench he was confronted by a German officer with revolver in hand. Riley got in first with his Webley, and the German's career was ended. As the party climbed out of the trench, Private A. McDonald's steel hat was knocked off his head by a bullet. In approaching daylight O.G.2, greatly damaged, was reached. At this point the general advance had lost much of its original weight and dash. Casualties in the Battalions had been heavy, and the fire from front and flank became accurate and sustained. The earlier waves of attackers had shrunk to a thin line; nevertheless they and the teams pushed on. While resting temporarily in a shell-hole, Private C. W. Dalitz was shot through the neck and died instantly. "It was broad daylight," said Private Riley, "and there was very little cover on the flat over which we were advancing. The rifle and machine-gun fire was dreadful, and each one of us was picked out and fired on every time we moved." The thinning line of men gallantly pushed on, reached the second objective—the loop of the tram line—and commenced to dig in. There, at the furthest penetration of the Brigade's advance, a handful of brave men, without support on either flank, settled down to the hopeless task of holding their ground. Captain Maxfield (24th Battalion) took charge, and by his active supervision and splendid example greatly heartened the defenders. Desmond, who had led his teams with great courage and determination, reconnoitred forward and mounted his left-hand gun about 150 yards from the six-star road junction on the edge of the tram line. The team (after losing Tuohy and Bone in the wire), suffered further loss when Privates R. O. L. Ey and W. J. Morris apparently became detached during the turmoil of the advance. Finally, Privates V. E. Bliss and H. Ford mounted their gun and gear, which were intact, and as some of the carriers got through most of the belted ammunition was available. The situation was precarious, but the unperturbed gunners got on to various enemy parties moving up to reinforce counter-attacks then developing. Several parties were scattered, and casualties inflicted, but before long the pair became engaged in duels with rival machine-gunners. Both men retained vivid memories of the accuracy of their opponents' fire. The end was inevitable, and it came about 10 o'clock, when a "burst" from half-right opened Bliss's left forearm and put the gun out of action. Ford, who was assisting, escaped. Leaving his useless weapon, he rejoined his comrades on the right-hand gun. Morris made his way back to O.G.2, where he found Hitchcock's party, and Ey subsequently located the right-hand team, from whence Lieutenant Desmond utilised him to take out a report. Bliss's injuries resulted in his subsequent discharge.

In the meantime, the right-hand team had come into action. Almost at the outset, misfortune attended the carriers. Six were known definitely to have moved off from the J.O.T., but on emerging from O.G.2 only two were present, and one of these was killed in the subsequent advance. The gun was mounted on the edge of the tram-line a little nearer to the six-star road junction, but only eight boxes of belted ammunition were available. Soon after position was taken up, the team had splendid targets. In the trenches on the outskirts of Riencourt (half-right) the enemy appeared to be in hundreds. "For a time," said Private Riley, "we played the very devil and made the Hun fly all roads." Regardless of risks, Corporal J. J. O'Gorman sat behind his gun, quite exposed, while bombs fell and bullets whistled by, firing as opportunity came. A German machine-gun team dashed forward, mounted, and came into action against troops on the right, but O'Gorman swung his gun round, and it is extremely unlikely that one escaped. Riley and Private W. J. Clark acted as No. 2 in turn, and they and Lieutenant Desmond begged for a turn as No. 1, but O'Gorman, full of fight, insisted on holding his place. The situation, however, began to grow desperate; the fighting became closer and bitter. Four infantrymen joined the team, and for a time their bomb-throwing helped to hold the attackers off; but only two boxes of ammunition were left. Heavily beset on both flanks and front, the unequal fight could have only one result. It came when a violent explosion behind the gun killed Desmond and two of the infantrymen, wounded Ford, Riley (severely), and Clark (badly). O'Gorman was blown from the gun, his clothing was in tatters, but blood-stained and undaunted he returned to his weapon. Soon after he was killed. So passed out one of the gamest spirits in the Company, unrewarded, except for the undying admiration of his comrades and this inadequate tribute. After O'Gorman was killed, Private A. McDonald took charge of the gun and found himself left with one unwounded comrade, Private M. G. Daffy, whom he sent out in charge of the badly-wounded Clark, and a message to Company Headquarters. Daffy got through, but Clark was killed by a bursting shell on the way. McDonald continued to fire the gun as opportunity offered, being helped by a member of the 24th Battalion who had some knowledge of the Vickers gun. Captain Maxfield drew his attention to columns of Germans moving towards Riencourt, presumably for counter-attacks. These were fired on at a range of 800 yards, and scattered. But the situation soon became desperate in the extreme. Captain Maxfield (badly wounded) and all the officers and non-commissioned officers were out of action, and a private of D Company, 24th Battalion, appeared to be in charge of the thirty-odd remnants of the 23rd and 24th Battalions. After McDonald had consulted with them, retirement was decided upon, and McDonald took his gun into the road running S.W. from the six-star junction so that he could engage an enemy gun firing from the front and another from half-right, and thereby cover the move. On the way, however, two bullets passed through the gun, rendering it useless. Previously the barrel-casing had been punctured by a bomb splinter, but the rent had been plugged with a handkerchief. Thereupon McDonald took the lock and spare parts, made his way out, and reported to Company Headquarters at 11.30 a.m., the last of the half-section of thirteen. Ford and Riley had previously got out safely, but not before the latter, while wandering about in a dazed condition, was fired upon by an infantryman in O.G.2 before his identity was discovered. McDonald was awarded the Military Medal for his part in the morning's work.

It is worthy of note that a reference to the effective work of the two gun-teams appears in German records. According to the historian of the 124th Infantry Regiment, which was concerned in the counter-attack, the movement of reinforcements against the east end of Bullecourt was much hampered by two hostile machine-guns near the Six Cross Roads. These were "continuously very troublesome."*

When it was decided that the Company would not be relieved during the night of the 3rd-4th, steps were taken to strengthen the Brigade's right sector. Accordingly, Sergeant G. A. Jeffery was sent in with two teams and guns from No. 4 Section, made up as follows:—Sergeant E. Mackley, Privates T. A. McKay, F. L. Fitzpatrick, W. E. Allen, S. A. Greaves, W. Sharp, T. Moran, H. H. Dunn, and A. V. Caldwell. Just before the party moved off, Private A. V. Caldwell was wounded by shell splinters, and when nearing the Hindenburg Line Sergeant E. Mackley was wounded in the left arm—an injury which resulted in subsequent amputation.

Jeffery was directed to mount his guns in O.G.2, but was to use his discretion in siting them. On arrival, he consulted the infantry officer in charge, and they agreed on a spot just forward of O.G.2, and close to the right boundary of the Brigade—the sunken road running north and south. When daylight appeared, it was found that the positions chosen in the darkness could not be bettered, so no change was made. Bombing went on during the remainder of the night and the morning of the 4th, when Stokes mortars came into action freely; but generally there was little work for the guns. The teams had, therefore, ample opportunities for observing the spirited work of the newly arrived 3rd Battalion. Private F. L. Fitzpatrick said: "The 3rd Battalion did splendid work in bombing parties out of a sap running from our line to theirs; also out of shell-hole strong posts. In this work a Lewis gunner ably seconded the bombers, the scheme being to bomb the post till it got too hot for the defenders. When the survivors endeavoured to run to the next hole, the waiting gunner, from a shell-hole in front of our parapet, laid them low. We (the gun team) did a lot of sniping, particularly on the

* See Official History of Australia in the War of 1914-18. Vol. IV, p. 466.

morning of the 4th. The Fritz front line was crowded, and, being shallow, we could see the tops of their helmets when they stood up. We scored numerous hits on them, success being signified by a "dong" and sometimes by a "tin hat" flying off its wearer. They also sniped at us from front and side, and got a number of 3rd Battalion men. They were only fifty or sixty yards from us."

As a result of the bitter and continuous fighting, the condition of the captured trenches was appalling. The dead, dying, and wounded of the 23rd, 24th, and 3rd Battalions, as well as the Germans, lay thickly, but the pre-occupied occupants had few opportunities to clear them. As the day wore on under a hot sun, the hard-pressed garrison suffered acutely from thirst; as much as £1 was offered for a drink. It was found necessary to keep a man constantly by the side of each gun to prevent the parched infantry from drinking the water in the barrel casing. During the day, a German machine-gun and five boxes of ammunition was salved, and mounted for action. Shelling from the British artillery added to the troubles, but it ceased soon after reports were sent back, much to the relief of the sufferers. In the evening, the enemy shelling increased to great intensity, and seemed to indicate an attack in force. During the day, one member discovered a German flare pistol and a supply of flares. These were used by Private W. E. Allen with great effect, being the only flares fired in that sector, and probably it was the only occasion that the Company ever used them. As soon as the attack developed, the teams fired steadily through the dust and smoke, making use of the German gun as well. Against the combined Vickers, Lewis-gun, and rifle fire, the attack melted away. "In the evening," recorded Jeffery, "Fritz increased his artillery fire to a terrific bombardment on our trenches. We surmised that he was about to counter-attack, because he had stopped firing his flares; so we made use of his flare pistol and flares—they were a Godsend. He counter-attacked, and, being alongside Battalion Headquarters, I knew exactly what was going on. Word came through: 'Enemy attacking on the right.' Then: 'Enemy attacking on left.' We opened up with our guns and had no trouble in knocking him back. The infantry took two prisoners; the remainder of the survivors were seen, by the aid of our flares, running back for their lives. We were a determined lot in our little corner, well prepared with plenty of ammunition." Soon after the bombardment, which had died down, was renewed, but no attack followed. A little after 11 p.m., the teams were relieved by members of the 1st Australian Machine Gun Company

(1st Brigade). Good fortune had indeed followed the party—after its initial losses no further casualties were suffered.

At the Railway Embankment:

The six teams allocated to the railway embankment carried out their programme of placing an indirect fire barrage in front of the area attacked by the Brigade. Lieutenant Bice supervised the three left-hand guns, and Lieutenant Callister the others. From zero to zero plus 1 hour 15 minutes, it fell in front of the second objective, then for 45 minutes just ahead of the first phase of the third objective; and, finally, for 20 minutes beyond its last phase. During the firing, No. 3 Section lost two men—Privates C. W. Franklin and W. Hayward—both killed by shells detonated by the new 106 fuse. This new device caused the shell to burst immediately it touched the ground, thus increasing the radius of effective action. They became known to the troops as "grass cutters" on account of the lateral spread of the shell-fragments. During the morning, Lieutenant Callister, Privates H. J. Cook and A. W. Dean were talking to Corporal Tuohy, who had shortly before reported himself wounded. Just as Callister moved away, a "pineapple" bomb burst right on the party. Dean was killed outright, while Tuohy received five additional wounds; Cook was unharmed and went on with his work. Three of the signallers' telephones were destroyed by the explosion. Recovering from his injuries, Tuohy received an appointment in London and did not return to the Company.

Prior to zero, Captain Drummond had established his headquarters in a prepared position about 500 yards behind the railway cutting, and was connected with Lieutenant Callister (second in command) at the cutting, but the line was repeatedly cut by shell-fire and finally abandoned, so Headquarters moved to the embankment close to General J. Gellibrand. The signallers were subsequently used as guides, and for carrying messages to Brigade Headquarters at Noreuil. They were utilised to carry Brigade messages as well, the Brigade line to the Noreuil headquarters having been destroyed. A "souvenired" bicycle was of great assistance in this connection.

The railway embankment was a scene of great activity that day, and consequently attracted a good deal of enemy shelling. The weather was hot, and the hard ground operated the 106 fuses very effectively. A number of British aeroplanes were shot down in the vicinity, and the enemy shelled every prostrate machine. Great disappointment was felt because the attack had fared so badly, and in the early morning a very depressing rumour went round indicating that a heavy counter-attack from the German lines was imminent. All available men "stood to arms" for an hour, prepared to deal with it. Near one of No. 1 Section's indirect-fire guns, a dressing station was located. The flow of wounded thereto was continuous. Rows of wounded were laid outside it, and shells and minenwerfer bombs landed from time to time and killed and re-wounded many of the waiting men. The weary but dauntless stretcher-bearers wore a path from that dressing-station to Noreuil, and were shelled and machine-gunned all day. A keen observer at the embankment (Lieutenant Callister) recorded his impressions: "I remember chiefly the fine weather, the hard ground, and first extensive use of the 106 (instantaneous) fuses, the heavy and continuous grenade fighting up in front, although none of the combatants was visible; the heavy shelling, the machine-gunning of the stretcher-bearers and wounded, the aircraft activities, the energy of the Pioneers, and the very fine way the men of the 1st and 3rd Battalions went in to relieve the men of the 6th Brigade. Passing back through Noreuil, I was again impressed by the cool, cheerful, though quiet way the 3rd Brigade units moved in to relieve the 5th Brigade."

The extremely heavy losses sustained by the Brigade were the price of its valour. Approximately 50 per cent. of those taking part became casualties. The figures were 66 officers and 1473 other ranks. As was almost invariably the case, the "attacking" gun teams shared in the fate of the assaulting infantry. The Company losses were: Killed, two officers and seven other ranks; wounded, one officer (subsequently died), and fourteen other ranks. To these figures must be added one other rank (Private F. Fraser) wounded on 5th May. Included in the 23rd Battalion casualties was Private H. F. ("Tod") Nicholson, who died of wounds. He was a foundation member of the Company, and one of its notable characters, but had transferred to the Battalion some weeks before his death.

Several official acts of recognition of the work of the Company's rank and file were announced. In addition to one Distinguished Conduct Medal and five Military Medals recorded, Captain Drummond, for his cool and capable conduct of affairs, received the Military Cross. Lieutenant Bice was similarly rewarded for his good work on the left flank.

Such was the Company's experience in its second major offensive. Disappointed at the result of the venture, and grieving for the loss of tried and trusted comrades, the weary and disjointed sections retired to reserve positions to sleep and to count the cost. Nevertheless, each one felt that he could hold his head high; had the Company not carried out, to the full extent of its ability, its allotted part in the splendid feat of the 6th Brigade?

CHAPTER XIII.

THE LONG REST.
5th May-28th July, 1917.

The 6th Brigade, in common with the remainder of the 2nd Division, had been promised a rest on a number of occasions. "A good long rest, boys," to quote General Birdwood. The promise had lost so much of its meaning by repetition that its fulfilment was looked on as a most unlikely contingency. "Blessed is he," misquoted one member, "that expected little, for he shall not be disappointed." However, for once, the unexpected came to pass, and for practically three months, in the Summer of 1917, the Company enjoyed a cessation from hostilities such as it had not previously experienced, and which did not fall to its lot again. "Rest," in the Army sense of the term, had its particular interpretation. As far as the Company was concerned, it meant that, except when interrupted by Brigade manoeuvres, daily Company training proceeded according to a pre-arranged syllabus, which provided for a half-holiday on Saturday, and Church Parade only on Sundays. The daily fatigues for drawing rations, preparation of meals, cleaning-up of quarters, etc., went on as usual. After the afternoon parade was completed, usually about 4.30 or 5 p.m., the men were free till the next morning. Day leave was given, to a limited extent, to visit adjacent towns, and passes to visit friends in other units in distant villages could be obtained.

After the relief at Bullecourt, described in the previous chapter, the Company marched out and went into "reserve." Eight guns were established in the Vaulx Line, and six in the Corps Line. Next day, four of the former were relieved by the 2nd Australian Machine Gun Company, and the six latter by the same Company. The remaining four in the Vaulx Line were relieved by the 1st Australian Machine Gun Company on the 8th May.

Meanwhile, the remainder of the Company had re-assembled in its bivouac camp near Beugnatre, and proceeded to "pull itself together" after its recent sharp experiences. Gun teams were re-arranged, promotions made where necessary, and the guns and

THE LONG REST.

gear were given a much-needed overhaul and cleaning. To fill the officer vacancies, Sergeant A. P. Hitchcock and Corporal F. L. Wright were (a few days later) promoted to Second Lieutenant. Lieutenant E. J. Hopper returned from a cadet battalion in England, where he received his commission.

On the morning of the 8th May, a move was made to Kookaburra Camp, near Le Sars, where the whole Company reassembled. "Rained all the way" is the bare and laconic entry in more than one diary. The recent events at Bullecourt were evidently still fresh in the writers' minds.

Next day's march brought the Company to Mametz Camp, on the edge of the Somme battlefield, to which previous reference has been made. Here eight days were spent, devoted mainly to light training. The inevitable innoculations recurred, and all hands were again subjected to the hypodermic needle. More acceptable items were the hot baths and the welcome and overdue changes of underclothing, and the advent of a "pay day." The weather improved and was mostly fine with alternating thunder storms.

Mametz Camp was left behind on the morning of the 17th May, and via Meaulte and Buire, past familiar scenes, the Company marched to Millencourt. Three days later, the march was resumed to Warloy, a pleasant little village where over three weeks were spent. Summer now appeared in all its glory, transforming the undamaged and undulating countryside into a thing of beauty; an acceptable tonic for eyes that had rested with great weariness on the desolate battlefield of the Somme during the long months of winter. Away from the war ravaged zones, all ranks settled down to enjoy their well-earned respite in very congenial surroundings. Company Headquarters and office were quartered in a commodious Chateau, and the majority of the men in the spare sheds of the village brewery, an arrangement much esteemed by the latter. The close proximity of beer in bulk soon set the inventive faculties of certain individuals to work. The first experiment was to join lengths of tubing (part of each gun's gear, to carry off steam from the barrel casing) together, which, attached to a long stick, was then passed through a 2-inch hole in the locked doorway leading to the cellar. After the end of the tubing had been pushed into a large vat, the desired fluid was syphoned off, rather to the mystification of the proprietor who, however, soon checkmated the proceedings. Defeat, however, only spurred the drinkers to greater effort, and the new move can best be described by the insertion of a humorous account written by Signaller D. C. Howard.

"The names of Pozieres, Bullecourt, Villers Bretonneux, are bywords with historians and those who read their more or less garbled accounts of the great deeds which have immortalised these places, but no history of the A.I.F. would be complete without a mention of that little Somme village, Warloy-Baillon, which sheltered many an Aussie unit in the trips to and from the line.

"Most of the 'Red Diamonds' will retain a pleasant recollection of Warloy, the reason, of course, being the substantial 'brasserie' which appeared to be the industry of the community. Contrary to the usual run of French beer, which has been on numerous occasions described as sour water by no less an authority than 'Bill' Wormald (Company Cook), the product of this establishment was 'tres bon,' being black, resembling a light stout, and carrying a fair kick. Just imagine a company of Diggers billeted in and around the precincts of a brewery. Of course, copious quantities were consumed throughout the day, but during the night, the sight of a 500 litre barrel of good ale separated only by a brick wall, was a great temptation. And so it came to pass, as they say in the Scriptures, that one evening at the hour when all good soldiers should have been getting their eight hours solid, one, 'Nobby' Pollock (Lance-Corporal George Pollock) was hoisted through the small window high up in the brick wall, a length of hose was inserted in a cask, the air withdrawn, and, hey presto, a cascade of beautiful beer. The operation was rendered quite simple by the fact that our bivouac was erected against the brewery walls, and Wormald's dixies were quite handy to accommodate the backsheesh. Needless to say, he of the dixies was usually on hand to taste and approve the brew.

"The carousals often lasted until the early hours, and it was during one of these lengthy sittings that Driver G. Lindsay immortalised himself by inventing the famous 'Hindenburg Shandy.' 'Mum,' to give him his 'nom de guerre,' soon found that a cook's dixie was not an ideal receptacle for liquor, as the grog was prone to become flat very quickly, so his ever active brain devised the scheme of reinforcing the brew with wine. One bottle of Vin Rouge and one of Vin Blanc were poured into a dixie of beer, the result being a purpleish looking liquid with more kick than a Spanish mule.

"On several occasions during the ensuing jollifications, our

THE LONG REST.

habitation was wrecked; it usually fell flat on the assembled company, and often remained so until reveille. Fred Nixon (Sergeant), who was training for the sports meeting, was frequently rubbed down with the Hindenburg mixture, as 'Mum' declared it was highly beneficial used externally, but only when no more could be taken internally. Harry Wilhelm (Company Sergeant-Major) called to gather some of his flock, and more often stayed to worship at the shrine of Bacchus and Hindenburg. Herb. Heyne ('The Swede') was another to instantly recognise the superlative quality of the shandy, and after a few pints, the life story of the Irish-Swede would pour forth, photographs and all. John Myers is credited with drinking the greatest quantity at one sitting, but this was strongly disputed by the Transport Section, who swore Jack McGaffin's (Sergeant) horse once drank four gallons. No reflection is cast at the good animal; with the example of A. P. Varney (Driver), Jim Bell (Lance-Corporal), Ernie Peacock (Lance-Corporal), to mention only a few; it's no wonder it developed a thirst.

"Only one case of actual aversion to this wonderful beverage is on record—Boss Smith (Assistant Quartermaster) whose opinion, without tasting it mark you, was to compare it with Red Head or Rot Gut, but possibly Boss, usually so tolerant and fair-minded, was a little biassed, as this description was given somewhat forcibly about 2 a.m., after being sounded for a drop of rum to liven up the last of a dixie full.

"But alas, even the best of friends must part, and the old 6th Machine Gun Company was soon heading for the line once more. Perhaps it was better so, for such little features usually had an unpleasant sequel, but whenever I think of Warloy it brings vividly to mind the one and only 'Hindenburg Shandy,' and instinctively I hold both sides of my head."

It should be added that the proprietor did not fail to lodge a claim for his lost beverage; a claim that was met by a levy which fell mainly on the soldier occupants of the brewery.

On the 19th May, the Company combined with the 6th Light Trench Mortar Battery in a football match against the 21st Battalion, but the combination had to acknowledge defeat by nine points to a better team. About this time, Captain Drummond returned from Paris leave, and the "Decca" gramaphone in the officers' mess commenced its long and overworked career. After Captain Drummond's return, Lieutenant Callister went on English leave, and during his sojourn in England was honoured by being invested, among other Australian officers, with the Military Cross by His Majesty the King. The decoration came as a well-deserved recognition for good work at Pozieres. A notable walking achievement was recorded by Corporal W. Carrick and Private F. L. Fitzpatrick, of No. 4 Section. Leaving Millencourt at 9 p.m., they walked to the outskirts of Amiens—about 28 kilometres—and slept in a haystack for the rest of the night. After walking about the City and visiting the grave of Jules Verne, some distance outside, they returned to billets at night, after traversing about 50 miles in 24 hours. Their fleeting reputation as walkers was not challenged by any member of the Company.

A Brigade sports meeting was held at Henencourt Wood on the 30th May, in which representatives of the Company took part. The only results available to the writer relate to the driving and harnessing competition, and the utility competition, in each of which the Company scored first place and prize money amounting to 55 and 40 francs respectively. Driver L. T. Carrick and his two horses (Darkie and Nigger) were responsible for the Company's success. The next Brigade event was a Brigade Parade, at which General Birdwood was present and distributed colours and medals awarded for the Bullecourt operations. Those members of the Company who were present received theirs from the hand of the General. Company training was varied by two visits to a rifle range at Thiepval, where the teams fired their guns in conditions which enabled them to observe the effects of their fire. At this time, Sergeant F. J. Nixon was promoted to commissioned rank.

While at Warloy, a number of men were detached—as part of the 6th Brigade quota—to enable them to spend 14 days at the 5th Army Rest Camp at St. Valery-sur-Somme. Men who had not received any furlough since leaving Australia were selected for the short vacation. While nominally a rest camp, light drill and camp routine were imposed. In green and picturesque surroundings—away from the sound of guns, and near the sea—the site was an ideal one. The town was a quaint old place, perched on the high banks of the estuary of the Somme, and contained the reputed prison in which Prince Harold was for a time detained. Cayeau-sur-Mer was within easy walking distance, and afforded some of the attractions of a seaside resort, and brought back memories of other and warmer beaches. The countryside held many historic spots, one of which was the site of the battlefield of Crecy; a circumstance which gave rise to debates as to the merits and demerits of the weapons used in that encounter.

It was generally agreed that bows and arrows were indeed light things when compared with modern machine-guns and high explosive shells.

Early in June, Privates H. H. Cook and E. Dight were "attached" from the 6th Army Medical Corps for the purpose of attending to minor complaints and injuries. Shortly after, the latter returned to his unit, and was succeeded by Private J. F. Pittendreigh who, with Cook, remained with the Company to the end.

The pleasant sojourn at Warloy came to an end on the 15th June, when the Company, with the Brigade, marched to Varennes and entrained for Bapaume. Detraining at the latter place, it marched to the adjacent village of Riencourt-les-Bapaume, and billeted in its scanty ruins. The Transport Section moved by road. The general round of Company training was resumed, but was varied by a considerable amount of open warfare practice in conjunction with the infantry Battalions of the Brigade. These exercises were designated "Tactical Training," and were conducted under the exceedingly personal supervision of General J. Gellibrand. At times, the limbers of the Transport Section assisted in the Company tasks. During these manoeuvres, all ranks became very familiar with the dilapidated villages of Villers-au-Flos and Le-Transloy, which were "taken" many times but without casualties, although some consternation was caused in one assault when a few "live" rounds mysteriously found their way into the blank ammunition used. Company training included a fair amount of firing on targets at close range to test aiming and "holding," i.e., holding the gun during firing, while the rectification of pre-arranged "stoppages" in actual firing received due attention. Revolver practice by all hands was carried out, and found to be very necessary. A regular item on the syllabus was training with the German machine-gun; a couple of captured enemy guns being retained for that purpose. In a short time, everyone was on the high road to efficiency in the various details of the growing requirements of machine-gunnery.

Up till now, English leave had been granted sparingly and at irregular intervals, with the result that a comparatively large number of men who had left Australia with the Brigade two years previously, had not received any furlough. General Gellibrand expressed great surprise when a list of names was brought under his notice, and gave instructions for an immediate increase in the allotment. In a few weeks, all the "originals" had received the usual "eight clear days" in the United Kingdom, and some of the later arrivals, who had left Australia in the latter months of 1915, also participated. After such a long period of absence from the ordinary associations and comforts of civilian life, those first visits to the Motherland were unforgettable events. To the uninitiated it would be difficult to describe the exhilaration felt on leaving behind, for a few brief days, the relentless routine and discipline of the Army life, and mingling with civilians of one's own blood. Such ordinary matters as eating from a table covered with a white cloth, using common table appointments, and sleeping in a bed between sheets, became matters of major importance. And how sweet was the sound of the English tongue to those who had not heard it spoken by an Englishwoman for two years or more. It may seem a strange experience to record, but it was, nevertheless, true. Private N. C. Hammon has related: "I left Australia with the Brigade on the 8th May, 1915, and got my first English leave in the middle of June, 1917, over two years later. During the intervening period, I never spoke to, nor heard an Englishwoman speak, nor had Bill Peters, who went on leave with me. It was like music to our ears when a Salvation Army lass spoke to us in a Salvation Army hut in Boulogne, where we went for something to eat. When we boarded the train at Folkestone, a newsboy poked his head in the carriage door and asked if we wanted a paper. Bill called him in and gave him sixpence just to sit and talk to us until the train started. It was a treat to hear that boy talk after two years of nothing else but Arabic and French from the youngsters we had come in contact with, not forgetting the coloured Australian which the Diggers had taught them." The "Old Country," with its venerable institutions, its developed civilisation, honoured customs and hospitable people, was a happy hunting ground for the visitors from the young country overseas, and was explored in such ways as the tastes of the individual demanded. Many looked up family connections, where they were received with high honour; others, without such inducements, went about in the truly casual Australian fashion, but with that extraordinary faculty which they possessed for finding their way into any place or circumstance which, to them, appeared worth while. London was the Mecca of all leave goers who, almost invariably, asked that their rail warrants be made out for Aberdeen or Douglas, in the Isle of Man, as a precautionary measure. It was noticed that all ranks returned with a temporary, but very decided disinclination for the ordinary duties of a soldier; likewise a marked increase in the out-going English mail. Later leaves sometimes led individuals to the scenes of their former visits, and in some cases, matrimonial alliances were formed.

THE LONG REST.

In pleasant summer weather much cricket was played. At first, the contests were restricted to inter-sectional games, but, as talent revealed itself, a Company team was formed, and games were played with the neighbouring 22nd Machine Gun Company, and other units who were quartered in the vicinity. Victory did not always rest with the Company team, but the matches were keenly fought out in a friendly spirit. In between whiles, the games of school days were revived by these "boys of older growth," and played in the same care-free spirit. Even "duck-stone" came in for its share. During one revival, as Private H. F. R. Lindsell ran to get his stone, a half-brick fired by another player struck him on the head. Lindsell rocked, sagged at the knees, and finally collapsed, exactly as a movie artist after much training has learned to do. Fortunately the injury was not serious, but required treatment at a neighbouring field hospital. Another minor injury was sustained by Private A. E. Cameron when a sharply rising cricket ball, delivered by Quartermaster-Sergeant R. W. Watt, struck him on the eye. Treatment in this instance was meted out by an American field hospital, and included an injection of anti-tetanus serum, rather to the wonderment of the recipient.

It was pleasing to note that the horses of the Transport Section showed a marked improvement in condition after emerging from the rigorous winter. Grass was abundant, and self-sown crops were available in addition to the ordinary rations. It must be admitted that the means adopted to replace unsatisfactory animals were not always in accordance with regular Army methods. Overnight, a new horse would sometimes appear in the horse lines, but the disposal of an undesirable one was not always an easy matter. On one occasion, when the Section was camped near Albert, the morning light disclosed a strange animal tethered in the prescribed way. Shortly after it transpired that the stranger belonged to a staff officer, so no time was lost in returning it before enquiries were instituted. Less doubtful means were employed when a party of drivers were sent to take delivery of a number of "reinforcements" for the Brigade. The party took care to see that the newcomers arrived at the Company lines first where selections and exchanges were made, after which Brigade received the correct number but not the same quality. The securing of a desirable steed usually called for initiative in securing and retaining, and the means adopted varied with the requirements of the particular case. Thus it was, on the morning of leaving the vicinity of Bullecourt, a fine animal disappeared from the lines of a British Wireless Unit. On the way out it was necessary to pass in full view and under the noses of the rightful owners, so the situation became rather delicate. However, the inventive faculties of one driver hit on the idea of removing one shoe to induce a limp, after which the horse was rugged in spite of the fact that the day was hot. The ruse was entirely successful. Sergeant Jack McGaffin's fine mount came from the Australian Army Service Corps, "but I think," said the narrator—in justification of that transfer—"we gave them one in exchange." The same driver went on to say: "The best bit of fun was trying to lose a horse called 'Harold.' I rode four miles from camp one day with him, cast him off, but he got back to the lines before I did. I took him out another day, when I had my name taken by a Tommy officer for trying to steal the beast, so I left it with him and got for my life." Before this time, the vehicles of the Transport Section had resumed their clean and efficient state in which Lieutenant J. D. Campbell, Sergeant J. McGaffin, Corporal C. Callaghan, Lance-Corporals J. J. Passeri, P. D. Bell, and the various drivers took such justifiable pride.

At this time, the opportunity was taken to test the accuracy of the methods of Indirect Fire. Captain Drummond and Lieutenant Callister set out in search of a suitable location which would include a range of about 2,000 yards, from gully to gully, and where a minimum safety clearance of about 50 feet could be obtained over the intervening hill. Finally a target was chosen on a road running into Ligny-Thilloy. The target was an eight-foot gateway in a piece of hedge, and marked on the map. Having decided on the exact spot, Lieutenant E. J. Bice was directed to mount the four guns of No. 3 Section at five yards intervals, just west of the Le Transloy-Bapaume Road, and to fire a "burst" of about 50 rounds from each gun on the receipt of a signal transmitted by a signaller with the two officers, who were in a position to observe the results. Lieutenant Bice emplaced his guns on the map reference given him, laid his guns by compass bearing on the map reference indicated, after calculating the distance (2200 yards), and corrected elevation by clinometer. The guns were not dug in or braced in any way, but mounted on the flat earth. The result of the test was highly satisfactory. No. 1 gun actually hit the target, and the result is indicated in the accompanying diagram. Some of the bullets were dug up from the track which ran through the gateway. After entering the ground, they had followed an upward direction. On two later occasions, and from other positions and targets, further confirmation was obtained, and the results were equally satisfactory. In one instance, it was found that an error of one degree in the calculations resulted in

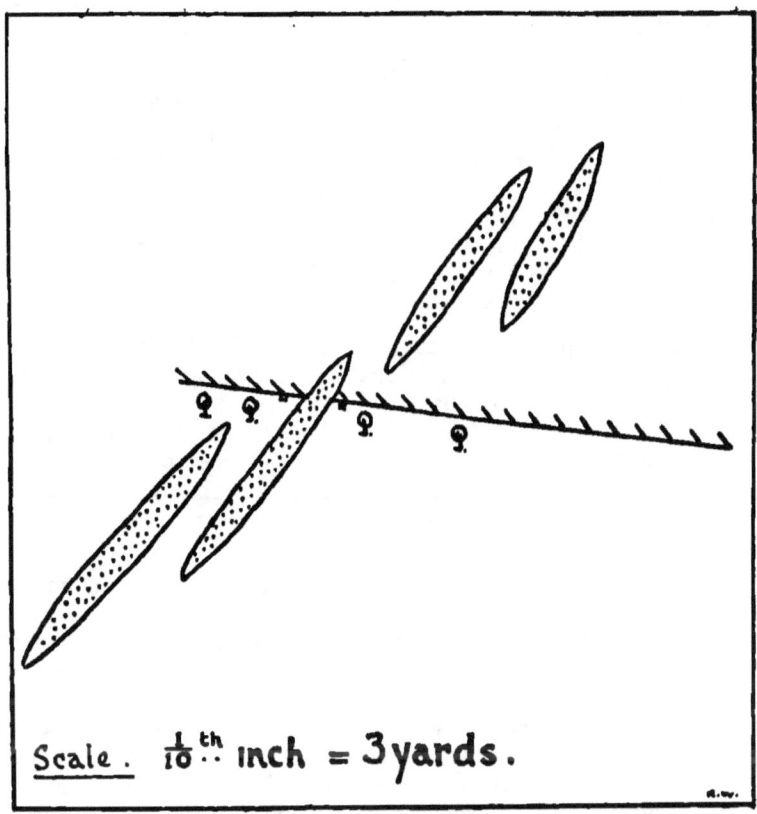

Diagram showing results of Indirect Fire from four guns on an eight feet gate-way. The effective "beaten zones," i.e., the portion containing 90 per cent. of the shots, shown thus: *0*. Guns were laid by means of map and compass. Range: 2,200 yards.

all bullets missing the target. During one of these firings, a Staff Major of the 2nd Division came along the Beaulencourt-Ligny-Thilloy Road safely under the cone of fire, but he complained because no red flags were shown, no sentries posted on the roads, and no notices sent to Division Headquarters. He departed quite unpacified by all the explanations offered. His risk, however, was trivial compared with that taken by the unconscious English infantry battalion encamped in tents near Riencourt.

The official criticism over firing methods just related was not the only one that cropped up. One afternoon, Captain Drummond was exercising the teams in firing operations against a four feet bank, with the aforesaid tented camp opposite, but some 450 yards away. A passing Town Major took strong objection to the practice. A heated exchange of opinions between the two officers followed, and the firing ceased. After the storm came a calm when Captain Drummond remarked: "Perhaps he was right, but it had been alright till now."

During this period, Company Artificer G. E. Gamble spent much time, trouble, and ingenuity in developing a flash extinguisher and silencer combined. He succeeded in perfecting a shutter which lifted to allow each bullet to pass and then closed to shut off the flash and report. It was found to be effective, but as no means were at hand to check its possible effects on trajectory, flight, and dispersion of the bullets, the development of the device was not carried further.

Flers and Le Transloy were within easy walking distance from Riencourt, and many men visited the scenes of their former trials during the winter of unhappy memory. Our own lines and those of the enemy were explored and examined in such a way as was not previously possible, and many interesting discussions took place. It was noted how deep and comfortable were the enemy dugouts and how well-stocked his trenches were with bombs, small arm amunition, and flares. The graves of fallen comrades were located and crosses, with legible inscriptions, were erected over the resting places of Second Lieutenants F. W. H. Matthews, A. L. Newland; Sergeant J. W. Taylor; Lance-Corporal A. Robinson; and Privates F. A. Anders, and H. Buckley.

The unexpected discovery of gold near the Company billets one morning, gave rise to some excitement. When an English unit was demolishing a ruined house, a quantity of gold coins were discovered in the old walls, evidently the "plant" of a miser. Although members of the Company were not present at the "find," they were soon on the track of the treasure, and succeeded in obtaining, by various trading methods and cash purchases on very favourable terms, a large share of the spoil. One of the first to hear of the discovery was the Company's "souvenir king," Private F. Wigmore, and he lived up to his reputation, both as to quantity and terms. It is worth recording that the original finders were punished for not handing over the treasure trove to the authorities, but the receivers were left in quiet possession of a number of apparently ancient French coins.

Early in June, Lieutenant D. F. Rae joined the Company as Second in Command. The newcomer was a member of, and had served his apprenticeship in the 5th Machine Gun Company (New South Wales). He was well qualified in machine-gunnery, and remained with the Company to the end, acting as Commanding Officer on a number of occasions when Captain Drummond was absent. At this time, the Company lost some of its best members by transference to the Machine Gun Depot in England for instruction purposes. Lieutenant R. C. Callister was selected by General Gellibrand to proceed to the depot at Grantham for six months on the instruction cadre. The six months were extended to twelve, during which time the Company was deprived of the services of one of its most efficient and trusted officers. Sergeant L. Davies, Corporals J. P. Adam and W. Carrick, and Private B. C. Georgeson departed for the same destination. At the end of May, Sergeant G. A. Jeffery left to enter an Officers' Cadet Battalion in England.

Some reference may be made here to the Depot from which the Company, from October, 1916, received almost all of its reinforcements. Belton Park, about three miles from Grantham (Lincolnshire), was organised in a series of "Lines," and all machine-gunners and reinforcements of the British Army, except the Canadians, were passed through to the units in the field. "E" Lines housed the Australians. Roughly, 1,100 officers, non-commissioned officers, and men were maintained in these quarters. The Schools of Instruction were in Camps at Harroby, about a mile from Grantham. Officers and non-commissioned officers went through these schools in as large numbers as possible, to be converted, as far as could be, into Instructors. The courses were thorough, and the instruction good. In "E" Lines, the Victorian Company ("B") was usually 250 strong. Reinforcements from Australia and from the infantry camps on Salisbury Plain underwent seven weeks' instruction—later, six—

before being drafted to France. Machine-gunners returning from hospital spent three weeks in the depot at Grantham before being placed on draft. The veterans disliked this training intensely, yet it was undoubtedly beneficial. Many non-commissioned officers and men, on arrival in the Depot, paraded at once, requesting an immediate return to France. During the early part of 1918, there was much organisation and reorganisation. About June, 1918, the Depot was transferred to Parkhouse. It was noticed that, when the Front was quiet, there were a lot of "absent without leave" cases, but when the Germans broke the Western Front in March, 1918, the men clamoured to be returned to France. There were always, comparatively, numerous 6th Company men in the Depot on Cadre, Training, and Draft. In a number of instances, particularly capable men were retained as instructors, to their ultimate disadvantage in the matter of promotion in the Company.

In France, machine-gunners were provided for by the machine-gun base at Etaples, and a few kilometers away, the school at Camieres (Dannes-Camieres). Officers and other ranks from England were passed through the base before being sent to their units in the field. The school at Camieres was reserved mainly for officers and non-commissioned officers from the Line. Both underwent a brief course of 14 days. It was in the nature of a holiday break as well as a brief refresher course, and an exchange house for latest ideas and practice from the Line to the training staffs, and vice versa. The training was supervised by a staff specially detailed, and assisted by ample, carefully selected, staff sergeants. Active service officers with a bent for instruction were "discovered," utilised, and, at times, passed on to Grantham. It was an isolated spot on the coast, and was also freely attended by Royal Air Force men.

On the 24th July, General J. Gellibrand relinquished command of the Brigade and departed to a command in England. He was succeeded by General J. Paton, C.B., V.D. An adequate appreciation of the departing General does not fall within the scope of this record. It is, however, not too much to say that every member of the Company deeply regretted the departure of a General who had won his sincere regard by his gentlemanly and soldierly qualities since his command of the Brigade, which dated from Gallipoli days. The relations of Brigade and Company had almost invariably been of a happy character. The Company was never oppressed with needless inspections or undue interference with its happy internal economy, nevertheless, the General knew the officers', the Company's doings—its successes and failures—very well. While allowing a free hand in minor matters, he criticised without mercy when occasion called for it, but always with the object of helping. The tendency of the Company to report accurately, without embellishment, and with a minimum of complaints, was evidently appreciated, and its striving to keep abreast of the times and to discharge its special functions, did not pass unnoticed. He looked for efficiency, and it may be observed, as far as machine-gun work was concerned, he got it. On the other hand, the General strove to give the Company adequate returns, especially in such matters as leave, decorations, and promotions. That he chose to ignore the unauthorised presence of a Company Cooker, and quite failed to notice the "unofficial" methods by which the Company Transport Section maintained its excellent standard of horseflesh and gear, was counted unto him for righteousness; but it was felt that any neglect of the same would incur his extreme displeasure. When the General's subsequent promotion to the command of the 3rd Division was announced, the Company unanimously agreed that the choice had fallen on a very worthy officer.

During this long "rest," a good deal of sickness manifested itself; no less than 43 cases being recorded. In some instances, "trench fever" was the diagnosis, a debilitating complaint which resulted, in a few instances, in return to Australia. Septic sores and scabies were also in evidence. Usually, however, the cases were not serious, but bad enough to warrant evacuation to hospital. No definite cause could be ascribed, except that the effects of the long and racking winter period were revealing themselves.

A greatly appreciated boon was the full-day leave given to visit Amiens. An Army motor van carried the visitors outwards, and a leave train to Bapaume brought them back. The outward journey passed through the wide battlefield of the Somme, now strangely quiet, and partially covered with weeds and grasses, among which grew millions of red poppies. It was noticed that usually where the heaviest fighting had taken place, the ground was covered with a blaze of red. Nature, it seemed, was indicating in her silent way the richer and costlier soil beneath.

The pleasant "rest" in the Somme area came to an end on the 24th July, when the Company, accompanying the Brigade, marched to Orviller Huts, near Aveluy, and close to the familiar town of Albert. So ended the easiest and longest period it had known or was to know. Many strenuous days and nights lay ahead, but the long absence from the line remained in the memory as a time not likely to be repeated. Mentally and physically, the Company had greatly benefited by the spell. The trials of the preceding winter were left behind as a horrible memory, and the easy times, leave and games, had secured a return of the gay and youthful spirits so characteristic of Australian troops. Technically, all ranks were thoroughly trained in the various phases of the "specialist" duties required of them; training to which the "open warfare" exercises with the Brigade had added the finishing touches. Internally, the Company's economy had assumed the form and substance of a large, happy family. Though the original men and infantry Battalion reinforcements always retained a very kindly feeling for their old units—a tie which held Brigade and Company in a strong bond—it was "The Company" which now held pride of place in the minds and outlook of its members. Each Section carefully preserved its particular memories and experiences of Egypt and Gallipoli days, but the significance of those times had faded somewhat during the past months. A certain amount of inter-section rivalry existed, but it was distinctly of a friendly nature, and served, by its competitive spirit, to ensure the health of the whole. To the individual, "The Company" was his home in a far country of alien speech and customs; a centre to which his thoughts turned when absent through wounds or sickness; an objective for which he fought, should the higher powers seek to divert him when the time came for his return. In the vast Army organisation, it provided him with a niche which he could regard as his own, wherein his service and energies could best express themselves. By this time, no illusions were cherished as to an early termination of the war, and the realisation that it was—as one of them expressed it—"a going concern," led them in the dreadful conflict to reach out for something to which they could pin their faith. In the association with comrades whose splendid qualities, like their failings, stood out naked and unmistakable, they found it. Out of this association grew a "team" spirit and co-operation which made possible an efficiency that became cold, grim, and businesslike. It is worthy of note that this "family" characteristic had a literal basis, in so far that no less than 17 instances of brothers (35 in all) serving with the Company have been recorded, as well as two of father and son; a large number for so small a unit. Particulars of these will be found in the Appendix.

THE LONG REST.

Four days were spent at Aveluy. The Army huts were reasonably comfortable, and the daily swimming in the River Ancre was a welcome diversion. Fishing with the aid of Mills grenades came under an official ban, but, in spite of pains and penalties, fish became, by the use of grenades, an acceptable variation of the distinctly monotonous Army rations. The deserted and overgrown heaps of rubble that were Pozieres and Mouquet Farm were again visited. Some men observed the anniversary of their entry into the inferno of Pozieres by wandering over the identical ground whereon the Brigade had endured its long drawn-out agony.

On the 28th July, the Brigade entrained at Aveluy at 9 a.m., and moved northward. At 5 p.m. it reached Arques, near St. Omer, and detrained. For the second time, the Company left the Somme area and made its third entry into the northern zone where it was to remain during the following autumn and winter. It was destined to return to the Somme for the third and last time in the early part of the following year—after the big German thrust had been stayed—and to hold line positions in the familiar ground of its former "rest" area.

CHAPTER XIV.

YPRES, 1917: THE BATTLE OF MENIN ROAD.
28th July-26th September, 1917.

Once more the Company found itself in an area made familiar by its previous visit to the Ypres Salient in the autumn of the preceding year. As previously mentioned, detrainment took place at Arques, about three miles distant from the old-world abbey town of St. Omer, in the late afternoon of 28th July. A march of three miles brought the Company to the village of Wardrecques at nightfall. Billets were found, and after a full day's travelling were very acceptable.

The stay at Wardrecques was prolonged to six weeks. Billets were fairly good, but, what was more important, the weather gradually improved, and mild autumn days were experienced. Company training in all its phases with which members were now thoroughly familiar proceeded steadily. English leave continued, and for a time, at all events, England seemed much closer by ties of sentiment and geographical situation than the Homeland in Australia. Each returning "leave" man had a different story to tell to which the older hands and novices alike listened with interest. The outward and inward mail now assumed considerable dimensions, and indicated probable alliances with the daughters of the very hospitable Motherland. Relations with the villagers were of a very friendly character, as shown by assistance tendered by members in getting in the wheat harvest. The pleasant undamaged countryside was thoroughly explored, and the estaminets visited daily. "Two Up" received the usual steady support, and the "Crown and Anchor" kings were well patronised. After the daily parades were over, and on Saturday and Sunday afternoons, leave was given freely to visit St. Omer, which offered the diversions of a large, undamaged town. On Sunday afternoons, British regimental bands played music in the civic gardens; an arrangement which provided a rallying point for the visitors, who mixed with the civilian populace, and were thus enabled, for a time all too brief, to share in some of the amenities of civilian life. The Infantry Battalions of the

No. 2 Section. Taken at Wardrecques. September, 1917.

6th Brigade were quartered in the adjacent villages, and the close ties of Brigade and Company were preserved by daily visits between members of both units. All things considered, the Company was nothing loth to accept the daily order of events, and make little reference to coming events near Ypres, which every one felt were not far distant. On the 30th July, Sergeant C. M. Bowden departed to enter an officer cadet battalion in England.

At this time, a new development in one phase of the Company training, i.e., "barrage drill," received a good deal of attention. Lectures for the officers and non-commissioned officers by Captain Rae, and drill for the teams, were features of the syllabus of training. The object of the new drill was to co-ordinate the action of a number of guns—organised as a battery—with a view to obtaining concerted fire, either on definite areas or targets, or in "creeping barrages" as part of a previously defined scheme. No departure from the established principles of indirect fire was involved, but the grouping of guns in batteries under a battery commander, and the delegation to non-commissioned officers of much of the responsibility for laying, elevating, traversing and firing to a programme or word of command, called for special training. Hitherto, the officer in charge of indirect fire guns exercised a close supervision over his teams which, with a certain measure of independence, fired tasks adapted to the immediate requirements of a Brigade area and from a Brigade point of view. The new plan sought, and obtained, a large volume of co-ordinated fire with much elasticity in conception, direction, and control. On the parade ground, the new practice took the form of laying all guns—usually a section of four—in line, on an aiming mark to a flank, or on zero lines, and at the word of command swinging all to a single target (which required slightly different angles for each gun), or swinging to similar angles, as given; searching and traversing were combined in practice. Other methods were the laying of all on a given line and elevating and firing to a "creeping barrage," or laying quickly on a given line and simulating at a high rate of fire, an S.O.S. protective barrage. The new method was evidently designed to meet new conditions and problems in attack and defence, all of which were revealed a few weeks later when the autumn offensives were launched East of Ypres. Meanwhile, the novelty engaged the close attention of all ranks.

Minor matters and incidents gave variety to the now very close "family" nature of the Company. A quartette party was formed which comprised Lieutenant F. L. Wright (baritone), Corporal W. A. Carne (bass), Privates B. H. Johnson (1st tenor) and E. D. Saker (2nd tenor). The portable organ was brought to light, with which the party rehearsed regularly (using music sheets kindly supplied by London publishers), and occasionally ventured into a formal concert in one of the large billets, in which other members assisted. Friendly rivalry with the 22nd Machine Gun Company took the form of a football match, from which the Company emerged victorious. A notable incident was the clash between two of No. 3 Section's ardent spirits, Privates H. L. Heyne ("The Swede") and J. A. Maloney. After "lights out" a slight misunderstanding led to an adjournment to the open air, where the two contestants faced each other in a ring of fluttering candles held aloft by the full strength of the Section. Each man decided on an immediate and vigorous offensive, which had the effect of neutralising that of the other, and resulted in the exhaustion of both parties as well as the illuminating candles. An unsatisfactory "draw" was recorded. Next morning each contestant found the other in a friendly mood, and peace was at once re-established. The incident did not end at that stage, however. At the morning parade, it was apparent that Captain Drummond was well aware of the contest. With a twinkle in his eye, he made use of the outward and visible scars to question both combatants, but the replies were perfectly non-committal. "Anyhow," said the Captain, with his characteristic tolerance, "next time you want to fight, let me know and I will arrange a proper ring."

The surrounding district was well tilled, and the fields teemed with various crops. The sight of luxuriant vegetables was a temptation to which Nos. 1 and 2 Sections yielded, in keeping the cook well supplied. One day an English cooking instructor from Hazebrouck visited the area, and in due course the Company's cooker was inspected. Looking into the well-filled stew-pans, the visitor asked of the cook where he obtained his supplies. "On issue, on issue," declared "Bill." "That's strange," said the inspector. "We have not had anything like this at our kitchens for months." But "Bill" was not to be lured into committing anybody, so stoutly reiterated "They are on issue here." In the face of such a statement, the visitor had to be content.

On the 23rd of August, General Birdwood, 1st Anzac Corps Commander, inspected the 2nd Division. The Company turned out in good order, including the Transport Section, which devoted the two days previous to much harness washing and the polishing of chains and other metal. The inspection took the

BATTLE OF MENIN ROAD.

form of a march past along the bank of the Canal de Neuf Fosse. Six days later, no less a personage than the Commander-in-Chief, Sir Douglas Haig, inspected the Division. All ranks were greatly interested in what was, to most of them, their first view of the leader of the British armies. All were impressed by his soldierly and dignified bearing, likewise his superb horsemanship. "I have never seen a man to better advantage on a horse," said one.

At the end of August, Captain Drummond was detached for a month's duty at Machine Gun School of Instruction, Camieres (France). During his absence, Captain Rae carried out the duties of Commanding Officer. Upon him devolved the direction of the Company during the operations recorded in this chapter. At the same time, Lieutenant E. J. Bice was notified that his application for transfer to the Australian Flying Corps had been granted, and he departed to qualify for his new duties in England. In due course he passed the prescribed tests, and was posted to a flying squadron. Before the end of September, Sergeant W. S. Clayton left to enter an Officers' Cadet Battalion in England, and Second Lieutenant R. Dodgshun rejoined upon receiving his commission in England.

On the 11th September, the Company said farewell to the friendly villagers of Wardrecques, and were carried forward by motor lorries to the vicinity of Belgian Chateau, close to the ruined city of Ypres. After the many miles covered in France and Belgium per foot, this method of transport was much appreciated. The Transport Section journeyed by road.

Approaching the Ypres section the older men were much impressed by the vast change which had come over the countryside since their previous occupancy. Then it was a grey, almost deserted landscape, many of its roads grass-grown, and a mournful air of desolation rested over everything. Battle-shattered Divisions from the inferno of the Somme were sent in the "quiet" line to obtain a measure of "rest." Now all was changed. Every familiar accompaniment of a vast offensive was observed, open and undisguised. There appeared to be miles of artillery batteries, anti-aircraft batteries, horse and waggon lines, supply dumps, stationary balloons and labour battalions (black and white). Overhead, squadrons of aeroplanes patrolled north and south, while numerous scouts, fighters, and others were active. The warm autumn sun shone down on a scene of restless activity, sinister and foreboding.

Although Belgian Chateau was a "back area," it was shelled

steadily night and day, by long distance shells, many of which fell close to the Company who were sheltered under pieces of canvas known as "bivouacs." The Company had a very uneasy first night listening to the occasional bursts. The nerves of the men, it seemed, had relaxed after such a long absence from the line in peaceful circumstances, and undue attention was given to the hostile sounds. During the whole period at Belgian Chateau the shelling continued, but the Company did not sustain a single casualty, although neighbouring units suffered. The 22nd Machine Gun Company nearby had the roof blown off the officers' mess hut, fortunately during the absence of its occupants. Horse lines suffered, and one shell found a recumbent balloon. On one occasion, shells fell so close to the Quartermaster's store that the staff judged it wise to leave very hurriedly, just as "Boss" Smith was grilling steak for the evening meal. From a safe distance he delivered much forcible and fluent speech, at which he was adjudged a past master, his chief concern being for the excellent steak slowly roasting to a cinder. His fears, however, were groundless; when it was deemed "all clear," the grill was done to a turn.

The highly congested countryside offered a tempting target for enemy bombers, who visited the area almost nightly. The first visit had some elements of novelty, and much of that first night was spent in getting up to observe the periodic visits of these bombers, and moving to an apparently safer spot when the line of dropping bombs appeared to be heading for the frail shelters of the Company. The novelty soon wore off and, except when the troublesome visitor appeared to be overhead, little further notice was taken.

The Company had hardly settled in its new quarters when it was visited, informally, by its old Commanding Officer, Lieutenant-Colonel L. F. S. Hore, as Corps Machine Gun Officer. After a happy exchange of greetings, the Colonel outlined the scheme of the operation about to be undertaken. That operation was destined to be the first of a series of autumn offensives undertaken by the British Army. By a big thrust east of Ypres, over ground upon which the early German advances had been brought to a definite standstill, it was hoped to force the Germans out of Belgium, and incidentally clear the Channel Ports, then in enemy hands. Launched in July, and rewarded by a limited measure of success, the thrust had been held up by heavy rains. It was about to be resumed.

The impending operation was designed on a big scale. The Second (General Plumer) and Fifth (General Gough) Armies were to take part on a frontage of about eight miles. The former involved the First Anzac Corps, which was allotted a sector of about 2,500 yards. The Corps then comprised the 1st, 2nd, 4th, and 5th Australian Divisions, and the attack was entrusted to the 1st Division on the right and the 2nd on the left; the 4th and 5th were in Corps Reserve. The 2nd Division, with which this narrative is concerned, in turn allotted its frontage to the 7th Brigade on the right, and the 5th Brigade on the left, the 6th being in Divisional Reserve. The objective given to the 2nd Division was approximately 1,200 yards wide, and the contemplated penetration into enemy territory extended over the same distance. Arrangements provided for the attack to be made in three stages, the limit of each being designated the Red, Blue and Green Lines respectively.

The operation referred to, and those following, were characterised by advances on wide frontages with definite and somewhat limited objectives, and a co-ordination of the activities of all arms that was unknown on the Somme. That co-ordination was reflected in the tactical handling and control of the Vickers Machine Gun. To show in perspective the part played by the Company, some reference to the means adopted to meet the requirements of the situation will now be made.

Since the piercing of the German lines on the Somme during the preceding summer and autumn, the enemy High Command had altered its method of defence. Instead of definite and continuous series of trenches, a fortified zone with troops "distributed in depth" was adopted. The area within the zone was defended mainly by parties in a series of mutually supporting concrete posts, known as "pill boxes," and constituted a problem to which the efforts of the British Army were now directed.

One of the new methods of attack evolved was the changed "artillery preparation." Instead of the previous concentration on the enemy front trench, to be followed by "lifts" to support and rear trenches, a "Creeping Barrage" was adopted, which fell first on the enemy front posts, then slowly moved forward, covering the whole area attacked, and providing a curtain of fire in front of the attacking infantry. The new plan influenced the employment of the Vickers Machine Gun; the fire of the indirect-fire guns was to conform to the artillery programme, both in attack and defence.

To carry out the new plan, the 16 Machine Gun Companies in the Corps were, as they arrived in the Ypres sector, detached from the control of their respective Brigades and Divisions, and came under direct administration of Corps Headquarters for operations, and were accordingly grouped in a Corps Machine Gun Camp near Belgian Chateau. This arrangement was adhered to during succeeding operations. In an admirable series of orders, the directions of Corps were made known to the Divisions concerned. In the first order, the role of the Vickers Gun was laid down as follows:—

(1) Harassing fire prior to the attack.
(2) Mobile guns for consolidation of ground won.
(3) Indirect creeping barrage.
(4) S.O.S. line barrage 400 yards in front of final objective.
(5) Fire on special targets.
(6) Reserves.

The responsibility for the preparation of positions and all preparatory arrangements as regards creeping barrage, S.O.S. barrage and special target guns in each Divisional sector, and their command in action devolved upon the respective Divisional Machine Gun Officers, under the direction of the Corps Commander, by whom authority was delegated to the Corps Machine Gun Officer. The guns designated as "mobile" (i.e., attacking guns) were placed at the disposal of the Divisional Commanders, and through them to the Brigadiers of the "attacking" Brigades; they were not dealt with in orders emanating from Corps. Corps also indicated the approximate Battery positions for the guns directed by it, on a map accompanying the preliminary order, and undertook the direction of "harassing fire" prior to the attack. By the allotment of 96 guns to indirect fire for attack and defence, which will be referred to later, the Corps front in the final objective was given a potential protection of one gun per 25 yards, in addition to the direct fire of the front-line guns attached to the assaulting Brigades.

To carry out its orders, Corps allotted its machine gun resources as follows:—

48 guns S.O.S. Barrage Group.	1st Aust. Division . 24 guns
	2nd Aust. Division 24 guns
48 guns Creeping Barrage Grp.	5th Aust. Division . 40 guns
	2nd Aust. Division 8 guns
20 guns Special Targets	1st Aust. Division . 8 guns
	2nd Aust. Division 4 guns
	4th Aust. Division . 8 guns

60 guns Mobile .. .. 1st Division .. .. 32 guns
                               2nd Division .. .. 28 guns
80 guns in Reserve .. .. 4th Division .. .. 56 guns
                               5th Division .. .. 24 guns

256   256

In conformity with Corps orders, the 2nd Division allotted its Vickers Gun strength (including the 14th Company "attached") as under. The Divisional Machine Gun Officer, Major H. Ordish, became responsible for supervision and control of the barrage groups and special target guns.

CREEPING BARRAGE GROUP (Captain D. F. Rae, 6th M.G. Co., Group Commander)—

Battery.	No. of Guns.	Company.	Commander and Company.
"E"	8	14th	Lieutenant Montague .. 14th
"F"	8	14th	Lieutenant Leslie 14th
"G"	8	6th	Lieutenant H. A. Robinson 6th
	24		

S.O.S. BARRAGE GROUP (Captain A. N. McLennan, 22nd M.G. Co., Group Commander)—

Battery.	No. of Guns.	Company.	Commander and Company.
"M"	8	6th	Lieutenant J. E. Hopper 6th
"N"	8	22nd	Lieutenant Field 22nd
"O"	8	22nd	Lieutenant Everett 22nd
	24		

SPECIAL TARGETS—

No. of Guns.	Company.	Commander and Company.
4	7th	Lieutenant Hargreaves . 7th

MOBILE GUNS (under G.O.C. respective Brigades)—
        16 .. 5th Brigade
        12 .. 7th Brigade

Grand Total 80 Guns

Turning to the machine-gun work of the 2nd Division in which the whole of the Company's guns were allotted to the Creeping Barrage and S.O.S. Groups, the situation developed on the following lines:—

On the 12th September, the Divisional Machine Gun Officer and Company Commanders of the 6th and 22nd Companies, accompanied by their Battery Commanders, reconnoitred the proposed Battery positions, and, after studying the lie of the ground, enemy shelling and the intelligence reports as to the latter, decided on the locations. The Creeping Barrage Group were sited on the Divisional (and Corps) Northern Boundary on the Bellewarde Ridge, about 500 yards behind and almost in rear of Westhoek. Group Headquarters were located in a large concrete emplacement among the ruins of Ziel House, and about 200 yards in rear of the Batteries. The S.O.S. Group were also sited on the Divisional Northern Boundary, in, and close to, the then front line held by the 47th (London) Division. A forward position was necessary to enable the protective barrage to be placed well in front of the furthest objective, as soon as it was taken, by Batteries already established and laid. Group Headquarters were some 200 yards in rear of the Batteries.

No time was lost in setting out to fill the ambitious programme laid down. During the night following the reconnaissance, a start was made by both Groups sending parties forward, who picked up shovels, picks, and sandbags at Birr Cross Roads, and commenced digging the 48 gun pits required. "E" and "F" Batteries almost completed theirs, but little was done by "G" owing to the teams losing their way in the darkness. Good work was done by the other Group. During the three following nights, the pits were completed, likewise positions for the spare numbers of the teams who would be busily employed in refilling belts as soon as firing commenced. Each gun pit was four feet deep and just large enough to accommodate the gun on a ledge and two gunners. The latter were below ground level as they sat at their weapons. It was the first time such pits were used, and they were evolved after experiment and discussion at Belgian Chateau while Major Ordish was present. Before the parties left their work in the early hours of the morning, ground sheets were placed over the night's work to cover it from enemy aeroplane observation. In view of the heavy and prolonged firing contemplated, the tripods were mounted on wooden T frames to ensure a stable and level platform. The nightly journey to the furthest Battery positions necessitated a tramp of over five miles each way. Sometimes the tired men would climb into Army waggons moving along the Ypres-Menin road, and so obtain a welcome lift along part of the journey. One night a party was returning in the way described when the engine

BATTLE OF MENIN ROAD.

stopped. After the driver had spent some time in a vain effort to re-start his engine, a casual enquiry was made as to their whereabouts. "Hell Fire Corner," just as casually replied the driver. The party fairly tumbled over itself in getting out of the waggon; no one had any desire to stay a moment longer in that very unhealthy spot.

At Lille Gate the Australian Comforts Fund had established a post, where hot coffee was handed to the men coming back from the forward areas. To the weary men returning from their nightly tasks it was a much appreciated boon, and many a heart-felt "Thank you" was tendered to the dispensers.

Meanwhile, the Transport Sections of the 6th, 14th and 22nd Companies had undertaken the heavy task allotted them in moving from Birr Cross Roads and Hell Fire Corner to the rear slope of Bellewarde Ridge the enormous quantities of S.A.A. indicated in the orders. The major portion was moved from Hell Fire Corner, a distance of two miles. Divisional Orders required a provision of 200,000 rounds for each Battery in the Creeping and S.O.S. Barrage Groups, plus 40,000 rounds for each Battery (three) engaged in harassing fire, or a grand total of 1,320,000 rounds. The task was completed in two nights, and its accomplishment reflects the highest credit on the Transport Sections concerned, who, needless to say, worked with a will. Pack horses only were used, each horse carrying four boxes hung on the hooks of the pack saddle.

Both Groups having completed their gun pits and belt filling emplacements, proceeded to carry the ammunition from the dump at Bellewarde Ridge to the Battery positions. Yukon packs were used, which enabled each man to carry one box per trip. Private A. J. Adams, of No. 2 Section, who was humorously referred to as "Tank" on account of his size and strength, calmly loaded himself with two boxes and was the envy and admiration of his mates, who found one box no inconsiderable burden. The S.O.S. Battery positions involved a carry of about a mile. It was feared that their supplies would not be forward in time, so the Transport Section of the Company came to their assistance with their horses, and delivered the boxes right at the gun positions, some of which were in the front line. Early one evening, Lieutenant J. E. Hopper, greatly daring, arrived with laden horses and teams, to the consternation of the English officer in charge of the sector. The latter implored Hopper to move off at once, but he, with his characteristic smiling nonchalance, calmly unloaded his burdens and sauntered away.

As soon as the Battery positions had been finally decided upon, Corps Headquarters—through Division—issued maps and instructions as to the definite tasks for each Group. Coincident with the work of preparation described, the necessary calculations were worked out and checked, and charts and orders for batteries and guns prepared. These details were carried through by the Company Headquarters allotted to each Group, in conjunction with the officers concerned.

By this time the major portion of the preparatory work was complete and the Signallers of the 6th and 22nd Companies proceeded to connect the Battery positions with their respective Group Headquarters by means of metallic circuits. Groups were then connected with a forward Brigade Signal Station, through which they were in touch with the Divisional Machine Gun Officer. Another preliminary step was the despatch of two officers and 25 other ranks to a Reinforcement Camp at Caestre, in accordance with the usual custom in the Brigade, of detaching 25 per cent, of a unit's strength before an engagement, so that, in the event of heavy casualties a nucleus would be available for subsequent re-organisation. To compensate for the absence of the "nucleus," twelve other ranks from the Battalions of the Brigade marched in and were temporarily "attached" to the Company.

Meanwhile, on the 16th, 17th, 18th and 19th of September, "harassing fire" in conjunction with the artillery had been carried out by 56 machine guns on the Corps front, by Companies in the Corps and the 47th (London) Division. These shoots were in the nature of practice barrages, and, apart from giving the enemy false alarms and inflicting damage, afforded experience for the larger scheme of the impending attack. During the evening of the 16th, the Company's "G" Battery and half of "E" Battery (14th Company), relieved teams of the 239th Machine Gun Company of the 47th Division, then in process of being relieved by the 2nd Australian Division. The former took over positions in Idiot Reserve Trench, and the latter near Ziel House. On the three days following, they fired barrages as previously referred to, as directed by Corps. In a letter written soon afterwards, Lieutenant H. A. Robinson has given a vivid account of what the records of those days merely described as "harassing fire."

BATTLE OF MENIN ROAD.

The following extract has been taken from Lieutenant Robinson's letter:—

"At last our orders came along. Move off 6 a.m., —/—/17, transport waggons will report at 5.30 a.m. No certainty yet as to our destination—of course we had ideas. Next morning we en-'bussed, and in the course of a few hours we arrived close to the scene of operations. Barrage work; I had charge of a battery of eight guns. The work to be done having been briefly outlined, and the positions of the different batteries approximately chosen, we sally forth, four of us (our second in command and three battery commanders) to make a reconnaissance —1 a.m. It is quite dark and we have to go through a much-shelled city (Ypres). This is about the busiest of the 24 hours for getting stuff up to the line. Motor transport, waggons galore, limbers, G.S. waggons, pack horses, mules, and occasionally a great slug of a thing goes crawling and rumbling along—a caterpillar tractor—drawing a huge gun up a little nearer to Fritz. All the time the booming of guns goes on. There is no rest for Fritz, and, as he cannot sleep, he spitefully sends back some hardware; some land where Fritz doesn't want them to land, and some where we least desire them. Four or five in quick succession landing close—dud, that is they either don't explode, or else make such a little noise that we are at once suspicious; they may be gas shells. We are very alert, sniff cautiously. Yes! that mustard-onion smell—gas! On go our masks and we have to almost feel our way through the busy traffic. All is dark, no lights being carried by the vehicles, of course. All the time the shelling goes on, not heavy but continuous. Fritz always endeavors to smother the dull explosion of gas shells by accompanying them with high explosives. Our guns have been firing intermittently, but now our 18-pounders commence firing more rapidly—this seems to be a signal—suddenly everywhere guns open, light guns in the front, medium guns a little farther back, well back our heavies all speak. Oh, the roar! Surely the gunners have gone mad? But no! If you could see them, working smartly, but not in the least excited. No single explosion can now be heard, but just a roar. Surely the lid has slipped off Hell.

"All this is just harassing fire. This pandemonium is brought about at any hour of the day or night, so that the chap living opposite will expect us to call on him; we don't go, however, and presently the din gradually lessens, and finally becomes once more the intermittent shelling which prevailed before the bombard-

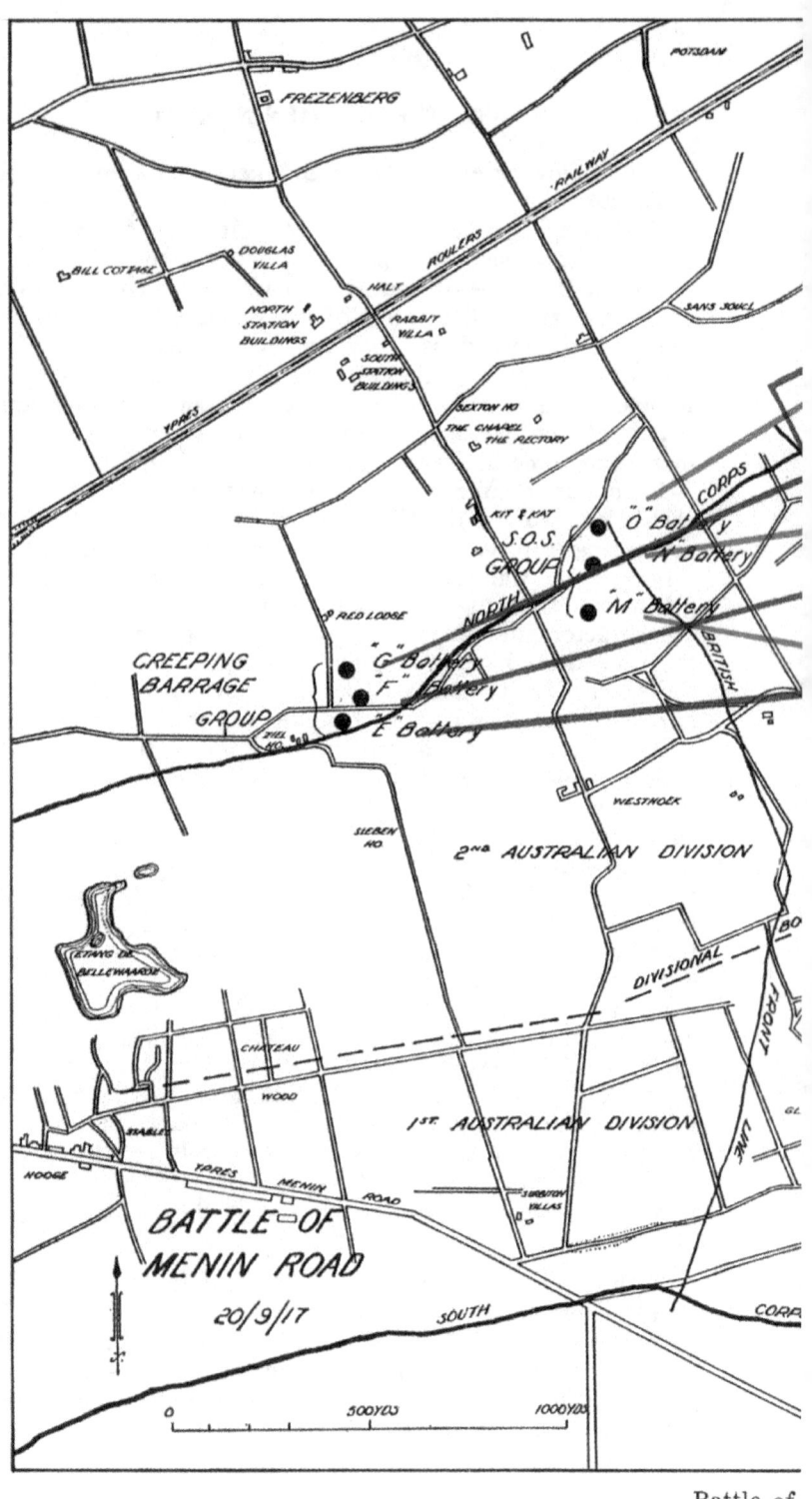

Battle of
The Creeping and S.O.S. Barr

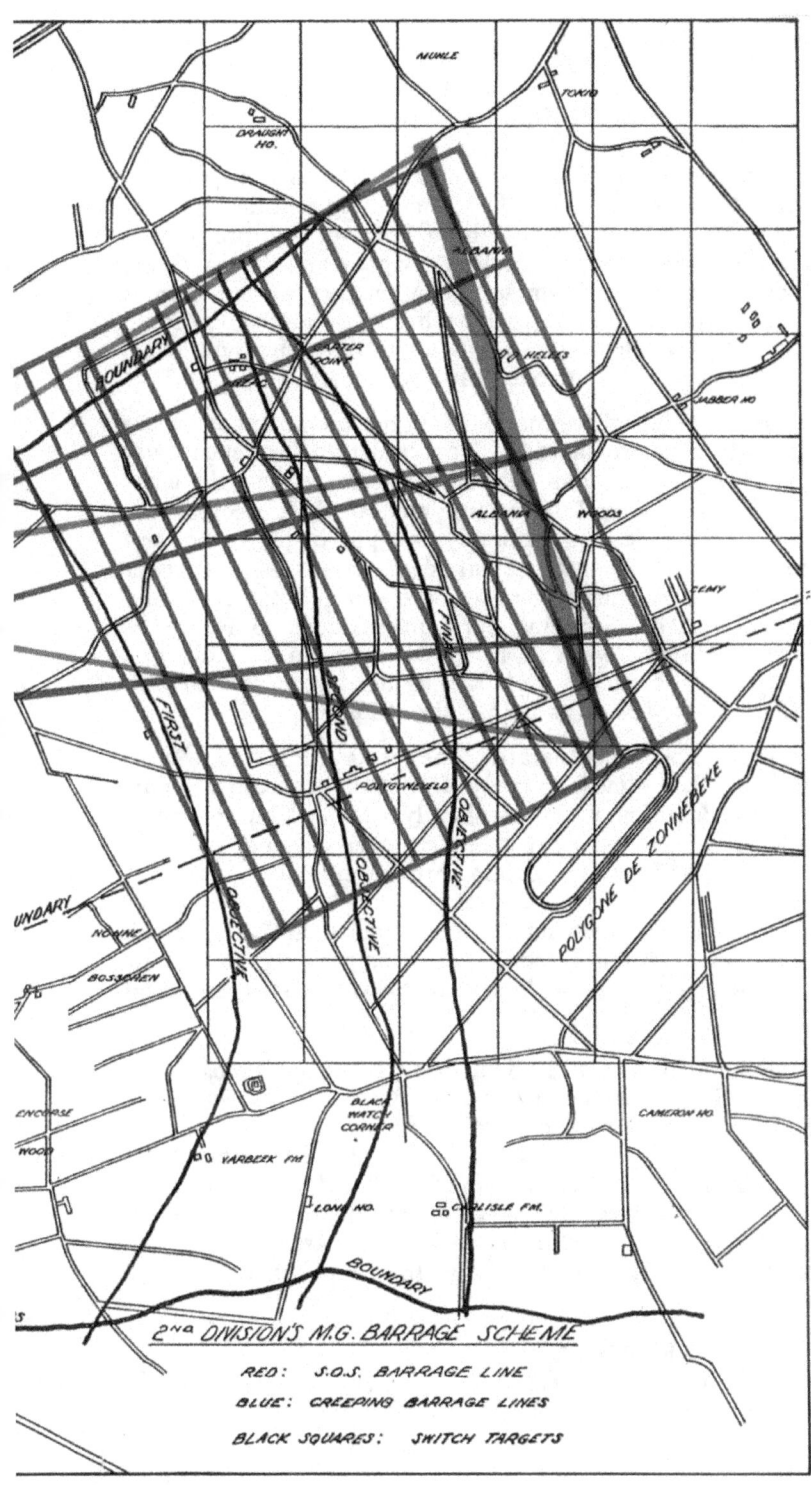

Menin Road.
age Schemes of the 2nd Division.

ment. In a few hours, this will happen again; Fritz expects us, once again we stay at home. The same thing will happen over and over again. By and by we will go, however, and probably as he has expected us so often and been disappointed, we may bring about some measure of surprise. This we aim at, but even if we do not surprise him, at least he has been forced to 'Stand to,' 'Stand to,' goodness knows how many times, for how long; what this means to him prisoners have told us.

"We arrive at the place marked roughly on our maps, where our guns are to be emplaced, and proceed to mark much more accurately the gun positions—for from these positions the bearings to our targets will be taken, and absolute accuracy is essential. Having decided definitely, we put in pegs, etc., and start for home. It is just peeping day, and as we are under observation here we must get away before it gets too light, and not run the risk of disclosing our gun positions to Fritz; it's unhealthy. To-night we will bring the men up and dig gun positions. Perhaps we will do harassing fire in conjunction with the artillery for a few days before the stunt."

During the work of preparation, the men in the Creeping Barrage Group were almost entirely free from casualties. One driver of the 6th Company was slightly wounded but remained on duty. The 14th Company had four wounded, but only one was evacuated. The S.O.S. Group parties were not so fortunate, as losses were sustained on four successive nights, when four men were killed, eleven wounded (one remained on duty), one injured, and one reported missing. The Company's good fortune did not desert it as all the losses were sustained by the 22nd Company.

The evening of the 19th September found all preparations complete, and the selected teams from both Groups with their guns and gear moved into their respective positions in readiness for the attack which had been planned for the following morning. "E" and "F" Batteries immediately laid on the existing S.O.S. lines covering the Divisional front line, in case of attack during the night. As different tasks were assigned to each Group, this narrative will follow the experience of each separately.

CREEPING BARRAGE GROUP.

The tasks laid down were:—

BATTLE OF MENIN ROAD.

(a) Creeping Barrage in conjunction with artillery to cover infantry advance.
(b) Protective Barrage for Second Objective.
(c) Switch Targets.

Each Battery was allotted a frontage of 400 yards (50 yards per gun), and they were so arranged to cover the frontage of the Division. The allotted area was then spaced in zones of 100 yards in depth and named alphabetically from the front, "A" to "N," or a total depth from the first fall of bullets of 1,400 yards. Target "A" was 1,400 yards from the Batteries, thus the total effective range of the gun (2,800 yards) was provided for. Rate of fire was laid down at one belt (250 rounds) per four minutes. The time-table set out the rate of "creeping" forward, in accordance with the artillery, which varied from four minutes per zone to 8 minutes and included a halt of 117 minutes on the Second Objective (Blue Line), during which time the Batteries were to "search" from "G" to "N" for 53 minutes. Fire was to commence on target "B," three minutes after Zero by "E" Battery, to be followed by the others till Zero plus 4 hours 13 minutes, when all guns were to stand on the furthest target and be prepared to resume barrage, or to fire on "Switch Targets" as per switch chart. The latter provided 60 targets (250 yard squares) covering the whole area across and in front of the final objective, and overlapped the objectives of the Divisions on right and left. The Chart enabled the Divisional Machine Gun Officer and Group Commander to tell at a glance if any given point was within range. In this case, the object was to engage hostile counter-attacking parties up to 600 yards in front of the final objective. For this purpose, the Group was required to have in readiness 2000 rounds per gun in belts after completing the barrage laid down.

The Group Headquarters was supplied by the Company, and consisted of Captain D. F. Rae (Commander), Lieutenant F. J. Blenkarn (Intelligence Officer), Company Clerk, 4 Signallers and runners. The Company's quota for the Group "G" Battery of 8 guns was provided by No. 2 and 4 Sections, under Lieutenant H. A. Robinson, who was assisted by 2nd Lieutenant R. Dodgshun.

During the night, drizzling rain fell, making the ground slippery and giving rise to fears as to the success of the operation; the rain, however, ceased before dawn. After getting into position, Headquarters and the Batteries tried, but not very successfully, to snatch a little sleep. All night the British artillery, now massed in tremendous strength, kept up a steady fire, "just like the continual splutter of bubble and squeak being fried," as one man put it. The German reply was likewise steady and persistent. At 12.27 a.m. on the 20th, a message was received from the Divisional Machine Gun Officer, giving Zero time as 5.40 a.m., also a watch showing the correct time. In the great attack to be launched, with its thousands of details all now arranged, the actual time of commencement was the last item to be completed.

Zero time came as a welcome relief. For some time the gun-numbers 1 and 2 had been sitting at their weapons. No. 1 with fingers on the safety catch and thumbs on the trigger; No. 2 ready to ensure correct feeding of the belt; officers with eyes on their synchronised watches, watching the minutes pass, oh, so slowly. At last it comes—the dreadful orchestra of light and heavy artillery breaks into a terrific roar, as if no shot had been fired for hours before. The darkness in rear is illuminated by a long wall of shuddering flashes; in front, in the dull, grey light, angry red explosions are quivering along the enemy front, while his multi-coloured flares immediately rise aloft; the white to illuminate No Man's Land and disclose the expected attackers; the coloured to send back S.O.S. and other messages. What a deafening pandemonium! Presently enemy shells are bursting around. In that din their explosions can hardly be heard, but their effect is revealed in the sudden spurting up of earth, and the sharp, acrid smell which impinges on the nostrils; fragments of steel and shrapnel pellets whistle past. Three minutes after Zero the barrage machine-guns join in; through all that noise can be heard their tat, tat. tat. as in a minor key. The teams are now busy, and pay little heed to their surroundings. The gunners and their assistants are fully occupied in firing to a definite time-table, slowly elevating their guns, and checking the elevations with the clinometer, and rectifying stoppages as they occur; the spare numbers, in the adjacent belt-filling positions, are refilling the emptied belts. Each man does his allotted part in the vast and comprehensive scheme necessary to launch such an attack.

Divisional orders required that a record be kept, in prescribed form, of all inward and outward messages and orders from 12 hours before Zero. Over 100 were noted, and from them and the Company's records, the following extracts have been made, and which will serve to indicate the work of the Group, and incidentally the Company's Battery.

BATTLE OF MENIN ROAD.

Just before Zero, one gun was put out of action by shell-burst. No casualties suffered

5.40 a.m.—Zero.
5.51 a.m.—Group opened fire, and fired in accordance with prescribed time table.
9.45 a.m.—Divisional Machine Gun Officer ordered "F" Battery to stand on "N" Barrage for S.O.S.
12.15 p.m.—Divisional Machine Gun Officer ordered "G" Battery to stand by on Switch Target No. 21 for S.O.S.
12 45 p.m.—Damaged gun replaced.
12.50 p.m.—Corporal W. E. Peters ("G" Battery) slightly wounded.
2.47 p.m.—Divisional Machine Gun Officer ordered "F" Battery to lift barrage 100 yards and open fire. Carried out.
3.5 p.m.—A message was intercepted from Forward Observation Officer, Heavy Artillery Group, reporting: Germans massing South of Zonnebeke. Batteries warned.
3.17 p.m.—A message was intercepted from Forward Observation Officer, Heavy Artillery Group, that Germans were advancing. "F" and "G" Batteries opened fire.
3.50 p.m.—Group Commander consulted Divisional Machine Gun Officer, who ordered "F" and "G" Batteries to cease fire and stand by.
6.27 p.m.—"S.O.S." call received from Brigade. Divisional Machine Gun Officer ordered "F" and "G" Batteries to open fire. Complied with.
7.17 p.m.—Request from Brigade to stand off S.O.S. Complied with.
7.24 p.m.—S.O.S. Signal noticed. "F" and "G" Batteries opened.
8.24 p.m.—Batteries ceased fire.

21/9/17:
4.50 a.m.—"F" and "G" Batteries opened at 50 rounds per minute for half an hour.
4.35 p.m.—"E" and "F" Batteries ordered to cut out and have gear ready to move.
"G" Battery ordered to cut out and rest as much as possible.
5. p.m.—"E" and "F" Batteries move back to Camp.

22/9/17:

2.20 p.m.—Divisional Machine Gun Officer ordered "G" Battery to return to Camp.

During the firing of the barrage, the Company's Signallers (D. C. Howard, C. Wood, N. S. Swindon, and C. A. Letson) had a busy time. One remained constantly at the improvised switchboard (constructed from salvaged gear), and the others stood by in readiness to mend breaks in the wires. After Zero, breaks were frequent, owing to the heavy enemy shelling. More than once, every line was cut at the point where they converged near Group Headquarters. It was subsequently found more expeditious to immediately run spare wires by different routes, and then mend the originals, which then became the spare lines. In this way, communication was maintained throughout. Owing to the limited number of Company signallers, the Sergeants in the gun-teams were instructed in the use of the telephone, and a simple code was improvised for the occasion. The metallic circuit used, gave improved reception and communication, but the two wires required, called for greater oversight, and added to the difficulties of repair. Signaller C. Wood repaired many breaks during the heavy shelling, for which he was subsequently awarded the Military Medal. The extensive wiring called for more material than the Company's compliment allowed, but the deficiency was made good by "borrowing" from Heavy Artillery Batteries, who used a superior material than that issued to the Company. During the repairs, a German prisoner "presented" a bag of long black cigars and a roll of insulating tape, to the repairers. "Evidently a brother in arms," remarked Signaller Howard, who shared in the gift. It is recorded that Private H. E. McHenry, who acted as runner during the operations, was unable to find Group Headquarters, but was guided thereto by the torrent of strong language emanating from the repairers. It so happened that McHenry brought a water bottle filled with rum, from the Quartermaster, which, when used in conjunction with the cigars, had, in the opinion of those who participated, much to do with the success of the operations.

To carry out the "Creeping Barrage" programme, the Group fired over 300,000 rounds, of which the Company's "G" Battery accounted for nearly 100,000 (from 7 guns). In addition, the Group fired some thousands of rounds on "Switch Targets" in response to S.O.S. calls. Casualties sustained were: three other ranks wounded, two in the 6th Company (one remained

No. 1 Section. Taken at Wardrecques. September, 1917.

on duty), and one in the 14th Company. One gun in "G" Battery was damaged by shell-fire. There is no doubt that the slight losses were due mainly to the deliberate siting of the battery positions away from habitually shelled areas, and the manner in which the personnel were protected by being dug in. The whole programme was carried out (except for one damaged gun) with precision, and on the lines laid down. All ranks in the Group worked loyally and well, for which Captain Rae expressed his appreciation, in which he included the members of the 14th Company.

THE S.O.S. GROUP.
Tasks laid down were:—
(a) S.O.S. Barrage.
(b) Switch Targets.

Each Battery was allotted a sector of the S.O.S. Barrage—50 yards per gun—to be laid down approximately 500 yards in front of the final objective (the Green Line). Rate of fire was prescribed at the rate of 300 rounds per gun per minute for the first ten minutes, then at the rate of 50 for 10 minutes, or as long as the occasion demanded. In addition, the Group was required to fire on "Switch Targets" to which previous reference has been made.

Group Headquarters were made up from the 22nd Company, under the command of Captain A. N. McLennan, who had as Intelligence Officer, Lieutenant Johnson, and that Company's signallers and runners. Lieutenants Field and Everett, also of the 22nd Company, were the Battery Commanders, who had with them teams from their own Company. The Company's "M" Battery was commanded by Lieutenant J. E. Hopper, who was assisted by Lieutenant H. de B. Newcomen, and the teams were provided by Nos. 1 and 3 Sections.

During the early stages of the attack the teams of the Group, unlike their comrades in the Creeping Barrage Group, had no tasks to perform. Consequently they had, from their front line positions, ample opportunity to watch the sweeping past of the waves of assaulting infantry in the Division. Private J. N. Myers, of No. 3 Section, has recorded: "The 28th Battalion attacked from Westhoek Ridge, about 100 yards in our rear. Evidently they were not aware that we were in position out in front of them, as they were inclined to give us a taste of the bayonet and bomb. Fortunately for us, they recognised us in the dim morning light and passed over us, full of fight and fury.

I shall never forget the determined look on the faces of those men. We opened fire (later), and word came back that we were finding our mark. Infantry men cheered us as they passed back near our Battery. Enemy planes tried hard to locate us, but had no luck. Enemy artillery searched the ground twenty yards in front and twenty in rear, but our positions escaped. Prisoners rushed back past us like wild cattle." Private E. D. Saker, of No. 1 Section (an ex-Imperial soldier), said: "I was struck by the cool manner of all ranks of the 7th Brigade in the 'hop over' at Zero hour. It seemed to me that there was nothing more important on than manoeuvres on Salisbury Plain or at Aldershot."

About .11 a.m. a heavy shell struck an old enemy concrete pill box in rear of "M" Battery, which was used for a store for ammunition. Unfortunately, two of No. 3 Section were in it at the time. In spite of the heavy shelling, Lieutenant Newcomen, Private J. N. Myers and others rescued the occupants, Privates W. H. Lucas and another, both of whom were wounded, and carried them to a forward dressing station close at hand. Although but a boy, Lucas displayed remarkable courage, his chief concern being his injured mate. He died soon after arrival at the dressing station, to the great grief of his comrades, with whom he was a great favourite on account of his singular cheerfulness and courage under fire.

About midnight, No. 1 Section sustained its first casualty, when Private A. W. Hamond was killed by an odd fragment of a shell. Hamond had served with the 23rd Battalion on Gallipoli (including the bombardment of Lone Pine). His brother, Private R. H. Hamond, exercised the elder brother's right to have the younger transferred to his unit, the 21st Battalion Machine Gun Section, which was arranged before the formation of the Company.

The following extracts from the records of the 22nd Machine Gun Company will serve to give the work of the Group, and incidentally that of the Company's "M" Battery.

20/9/17:
    5.40 a.m.—Zero Hour. Attacking formations successfully launched from jumping-off trenches. Enemy barrage which had been fairly constant through the night, now increased in intensity, and seemed to be aimed for the top of Westhoek Ridge, although quite a

BATTLE OF MENIN ROAD.

number of shells were falling short near the batteries. "O" Battery seemed to be suspected, for the old concrete gun-pits, where they were sheltering, were fairly heavily shelled.

8.30 a.m.—Message received from Division. Hostile counter-attack developing South of Zonnebeke.
8.35 a.m.—"O" Battery opened fire on its S.O.S. Lines.
9.00 a.m.—"O" Battery ceased fire. Counter-attack repulsed.
11.00 a.m.—"O" Battery reported one Sergeant killed, two other ranks wounded. All objectives reported taken.
1.30 p.m.—Congratulatory message from Corps Commander. Artillery barrage line now lifted 100 yards, our S.O.S. line raised in conformity.
2.25 p.m.—5th Australian Infantry Brigade reports counter-attack now being made near Helles. "N" and "O" Batteries opened on S.O.S. lines.
3.00 p.m.—Guns ceased fire.
3.10 p.m.—"M" Battery fired a special barrage at the order of General Officer commanding 7th Australian Infantry Brigade.
3.20 p.m.—"M" Battery ceased fire. Enemy counter-attack reported repulsed.
6.5 p.m.—S.O.S. signal went up from front line. All Batteries fired on S.O.S. lines.
6.35 p.m.—Batteries ceased fire. "N" Battery reported one gun out of action with split barrel casing.
7.22 p.m.—S.O.S. signal went up again from front line. All Batteries fired for half an hour, but no attack developed.

21/9/17:
4.50 a.m.—All Batteries fired on S.O.S. lines in conjunction with the artillery in a protective barrage.
1.10 p.m.—"O" Battery reported one officer (Lieutenant Connor) and two other ranks wounded.
6.00 p.m.—"N" Battery's Zero line shifted 3 degrees right.
6.45 p.m.—S.O.S. wire sent by 5th Australian Infantry Brigade. "N" and "O" Batteries commenced firing and fired for half an hour. Counter-attack reported repulsed. "M" Battery did not fire till later, as the message was delayed in transmission.
7.2 p.m.—"M" Battery opened fire and fired till 8.15 p.m.
9.00 p.m.—5th and 7th Australian Brigades relieved from the line by the 6th Australian Infantry Brigade. One

other rank in "N" Battery reported gassed by mustard gas.

22/9/17.—Orders received to relinquish gun positions and proceed to Camp.

As No. 3 Section was on its way out, Private A. Anders and another man were wounded by shell splinters, near Zillebeke Lake. Other casualties on same day were Privates A. Matthews and H. A. Hanley, wounded, as was Private A. Campbell, on 21st, and Driver R. J. V. Smith, on 20th.

The Group fired nearly 300,000 rounds on the 20th September in responses to S.O.S. calls, of which the Company's "M" Battery's share was 84,000 rounds. After taking up positions, and until retirement, the Group's casualties totalled three other ranks killed, one officer and nine other ranks wounded (one remained on duty), and one gassed; of which the Company sustained two killed and four wounded, one of whom subsequently died. One gun was damaged by firing, and had to be replaced. Except in one instance—due to a delayed message—the responses were promptly given. The work of the Group was well done.

The attack as a whole was a brilliant success. On the 2nd Division's front, to quote the official report, "It proceeded according to plan, all objectives being secured to time." About 300 prisoners belonging to the 7th, 15th, and 56th Regiments were taken. To members of the Company who had witnessed the strenuous efforts at Pozieres on narrow and restricted fronts, and the tragic losses sustained, it was a refreshing and hopeful experience to observe the altered methods of attack, which, attended with comparatively light casualties, were rewarded with such a full measure of success. A number 'of counter-attacks were attempted, and developed on the Divisional front, but, to again quote the official report, "the enemy troops were broken by the artillery barrage, assisted, no doubt, by the machine-gun barrage, and no counter-attack got home."

By the evening of the 22nd September, the Company had re-assembled in its camp at Belgian Chateau. Little rest, however, was possible, because the 2nd and 5th Armies were planning a fresh attack, involving the First Anzac Corps. The Corps attack was allotted to the 4th and 5th Australian Divisions, with the 1st and 2nd in Corps Reserve. The Machine-Gun activities were designed on similar lines to those previously described. The Company was called on for a measure of assistance. On the nights of the 24th and 25th September, 12 drivers and horses transported ammunition in conjunction with the Transport Sections of the 4th Division. On the evening of the 25th, Lieutenant Hopper, assisted by Lieutenant Newcomen, took in eight teams from Nos. 1 and 3 Sections, to the same positions occupied by them a few days earlier. The party formed "M" Battery of the Creeping Barrage Group of the 4th Division, and fired according to the time-table laid down in conjunction with the attack by that Division, on the morning of the 26th. After firing its programme without incident, the Battery stood by, but were not called on for further service. The 4th Machine Gun Company sustained casualties, and five teams of the Company, with their guns and gear, were retained during the day to replace them, but were dispensed with at night, when they returned to camp. The remaining three teams returned next morning. During the day, a shell-burst severely wounded Lieutenant Hopper in the thigh, and killed Sergeant E. A. Duncan. The latter had joined the Company about a year previously. Of more mature years than the average, he had won his stripes by conscientious and reliable work. In civilian life he had been a Labour representative in the Legislative Assembly of Victoria. Lance Corporal G. Pollock helped Hopper to the nearest aid post, while Private T. Ostle sought the officer's water bottle. At the aid post, while the doctor was attending to Hopper's wound and Ostle was giving him a drink of water, a splinter from a bursting shell entered just below Ostle's right eye, to finally lodge below the right ear.

During the period covered by this chapter, the Company's total losses were: killed and died of wounds, three other ranks; wounded, one officer and seven other ranks; evacuated sick, eighteen other ranks.

The artillery barrages on the morning of the attack on the 20th of September, and in response to the S.O.S. signals in the evening, were splendidly effective and awe inspiring. One infantry man in the assaulting waves facetiously remarked that it was so well defined and so dense that he "was able to lean up against it, but fell to the ground when it moved forward." Viewed from Ziel House, the responses in the evening were terrifying; a wall of quivering flame protected the new front. "If Fritz can get through that," said a bystander, "he is welcome to come at us." In the nature of things, the effect of the machine-gun contribution was difficult to judge. Evidence was, however, forthcoming as to some of its results. 2nd Division Headquarters (after referring to the artillery) stated: "The machine-gun barrage, not being apparent, cannot easily be judged, but infantry officers in the assaulting Companies and Platoons describe it as being most helpful to the men, and giving great confidence from the knowledge that the enemy was under heavy machine-gun fire."

The 5th Machine Gun Company, in reporting on the attack and the experience of its "mobile" guns which accompanied the assaulting infantry, said: "When the 20th Battalion was fairly well dug in, two guns moved forward at 6.55 a.m., and got into action close to Iron Cross Redoubt . . . opening fire on retreating enemy at 1,100 yards, our barrage (artillery) then obscured the enemy, but not before the excellent effect of machine-gun barrage put down by our Machine Gun Batteries had been observed." Testimony came from the infantry of the Division returning from the front. Slightly wounded men and runners complimented the teams on their accurate fire; some stated that the enemy could not get forward or go backwards; others, without stopping, cheered the teams; others, seeing the Batteries for the first time, explained what they had observed but not understood, viz., that parties of the enemy were seen to fall, as if shot, in areas where no shells were bursting, but which they now attributed to indirect machine-gun fire. German prisoners stated that they had suffered from machine-gun fire, and not from artillery. Others, passing the Batteries, pointed to their wounds and then to the guns, indicating the cause of their wounds.

The attacks launched by the First Anzac Corps on the 20th and 26th September, embraced the two greatest co-ordinated machine-gun efforts of the Australian Imperial Force.* The general tactical situation called for altered methods in attack, and that call included the Vickers gun. The steady improvement in methods and efficiency made such an effort possible; the association of the four Divisions in the Corps in attack—for the first time—rendered a Corps scheme possible. Much of the

* But one subsequent effort is comparable. On the 18th September, 1918 ,the 5th Machine Gun Battalion was attached to the 4th Division and the 3rd Machine Gun Battalion to the 1st Division for the purpose of providing a machine gun barrage in support of the Australian Corps attack on the Hindenburg Outpost line. Eight companies (128 guns) fired a supporting barrage which was planned by each Division independently, and which varied in design. The frontage attacked was greater but the allotment of guns (one to each 50 yards) remained the same. The total expenditure of ammunition was almost identical. No arrangements, however, were made for the elaborate scheme of S.O.S. fire as in the Ypres operations, nor was the Corps front treated as a whole.

credit for the successful planning is due to Lieutenant-Colonel L. F. S. Hore and, as to the 2nd Division's part, to the Divisional Machine Gun Officer, Major H. Ordish. Their endeavours were ably seconded by Captains McLennan and Rae, who carried out the elaborate arrangements and numerous details appertaining to their respective Groups. After the Ypres operations, the machine-gun companies returned to their respective brigades, but administration and control in major operations never again reverted to brigade command. In the following March, the divisional grouping of companies in machine-gun battalions was definitely established; an arrangement which served to administer and control the activities of the Vickers gun until the end of the war.

It is worthy of note that the gun-emplacements used (previously described) attracted the notice of General Headquarters. One result was the issue of an illustrated brochure which gave details of the emplacements for future guidance of machine-gunners in the Army.

As to the Company, it could feel well satisfied with its response to the requirements made upon it. Sufficient time had been allowed to execute the extensive programme laid down, in which the only real problem was the movement of such an immense quantity of ammunition. This was solved by the energetic work, during two nights, of the three Company Transport Sections, in which the Company's Section did a large share, and was materially assisted by the very active oversight of Lieutenant J. D. Campbell. Generally, all ranks worked with a will, but equally important factors were the efficient state of the Company's internal economy, and the definitely high standard of technical skill in its indirect fire methods. That was the outcome of steady and persistent effort on the part of all members during the previous months, in circumstances and difficulties which have been recorded. From the days of its first disturbing and faltering efforts at Fleurbaix, it now looked to the future with the confidence borne of the many and varied trials and difficulties successfully mastered.

CHAPTER XV.

YPRES, 1917: BROODSEINDE RIDGE.
26th September—5th October, 1917.

After the activities described in the preceding chapter, the Company re-assembled in its camp near Belgian Chateau, and devoted five days to overhauling its guns and gear, replenishing deficiencies, and cleaning up generally. On the 28th September, Captain Drummond rejoined the Company from School of Instruction at Camieres, and the same day, five men from each of the four Battalions in the Brigade marched in and were "attached"; those who were attached previous to the last operation having returned to their battalions. The new arrivals were at once placed under the Section Sergeants for training in the handling of the gun. It was obvious to everyone that further attacks were near at hand, and no surprise was expressed when some of the officers went forward on the 29th for the purpose of reconnaissance. The short but welcome spell came to an end on the evening of the 1st October.

In accordance with the relief of the 4th Australian Division by the 2nd, on the night of the 1-2nd October, the 6th Brigade relieved the 3rd and 9th Brigades on a frontage of 600 yards immediately south of Zonnebeke Lake. The Company took over positions from the 9th Machine Gun Company, and was disposed as follows:—

- 2 guns and teams in the front line.
- 2 guns and teams in support near Muhle.
- 4 guns and teams in reserve behind support lines near Anzac.
- 4 guns and teams on anti-aircraft duty near The Rectory.
- 4 guns and teams at Belgian Chateau, with 25 per cent. "nucleus."

Headquarters were established in Hennebeke Wood.

No. 1 Section, under Second-Lieutenant F. J. Nixon, supplied the two front line teams. Soon after leaving headquarters, heavy shelling was encountered, during which a shell-burst severely wounded Nixon and the guide who was conducting the party. Nixon was placed on a stretcher and carried to a forward dressing station by Private H. C. Reid and another. Meanwhile, Sergeant A. McDonald returned to headquarters and reported; the other members of the party waiting in shell holes. McDonald was directed to take the teams in. This he did, and after much wandering about in the darkness (without a guide) he located the front line and established his guns. During this time, Private R. Brown was wounded in the knee, but carried on till the following night when he was sent out. Two quiet days were spent, although the party was occasionally troubled by bombardments from trench mortars. On the evening of the 3rd, a shell from a trench mortar landed in the gun emplacement of No. 2 gun, and wounded Privates R. J. Saunders and H C. Reid. The former was injured in the mouth and wrist; the latter, in addition to a hip injury, lost two fingers and the thumb of his left hand, and was subsequently discharged from active service. The party remained in position till the morning of the 4th, at which point the narrative will be resumed later.

No mishaps befell the rear teams who carried forward ammunition, and made the usual preparations incidental to an attack. The weather continued fine and comparatively warm, with bright moonlight nights. Full advantage was taken of the favourable night conditions by enemy airmen, and Belgian Chateau and the rear areas were bombed nightly. "Fritz bombing all night," recorded one diarist in camp. As so often happened during the offensive east of Ypres in the summer and autumn of 1917, the weather broke. On the 3rd, rain fell in the morning and again at night, giving rise to misgivings as to the success of the attack which had been planned for the morning of the 4th.

The Second and Fifth Armies were about to resume their advance on a frontage of about seven miles. In conformity therewith, First Anzac Corps entrusted its share to the 1st Division (right) and the 2nd Division (left). On its left, the 2nd Division had, for its northern neighbour, the 3rd Australian Division as part of 2nd Anzac Corps—the first occasion on which three Australian Divisions attacked side by side. Corps again directed its machine-gun activities, and for its front provided 40 guns for each of the Creeping Barrage and S.O.S. Groups. Of these, 16 and 22 guns respectively were provided by and sited on the front of the 2nd Division. The attack of the 2nd Division was entrusted to the 7th Brigade on the left, and the 6th Brigade on the right; the 5th being in Divisional Reserve. The allotted frontage of the Division extended over 1,200 yards, and was divided equally between the brigades mentioned. The proposed penetration varied from 1,250 to 1,900 yards; for the 6th, it was from 1,250 to 1,550 yards, and embraced a section of the Broodseinde Ridge (including the village of that name) as part of the general objective for the day's attack. To the assaulting 6th and 7th Brigades was allotted the full strength of their respective machine-gun companies, with the proviso that four guns in each brigade were to be placed in the front line of the final objective, four to be set apart for anti-aircraft work, and the remainder distributed in depth. This arrangement conformed to the general infantry dispositions, and the method then in vogue of holding the line by "distribution in depth."

For the operation, the 6th Brigade—which embraced the whole of the Company's resources—disposed its forces as follows:—The capture of the Red Line (the first objective) was deputed to the 22nd Battalion, while the 21st (left) and the 24th (right) were to seize the Blue Line (the final objective). The latter extended over 650 yards—divided equally between the two battalions—and included the forward slope of the Broodseinde Ridge.

The Company's dispositions for the attack were:—

No. 1 Section, under Second-Lieutenant R. Dodgshun, to advance with the 22nd Battalion and assist in the consolidation of the Red Line.

No. 2 Section, under Lieutenants F. L. Wright (2 teams and guns with the 21st Battalion) and F. J. Blenkarn (2 teams and guns with the 24th Battalion), to take up positions in the Blue Line.

No. 3 Section, under Lieutenant H. deB. Newcomen, to occupy positions in the present front line, and engage low-flying enemy aircraft.

No. 4 Section, under Lieutenant A. P. Hitchcock, to move forward in rear of the 21st and 24th Battalions and take up positions on Broodseinde Ridge to (a) engage any targets in the valley east of it; (b) prevent field-guns in the valley from firing or being withdrawn; (c) engage low-flying aircraft.

The "jumping-off tapes" were so laid that each company in the attacking battalions had a tape on its front and one on

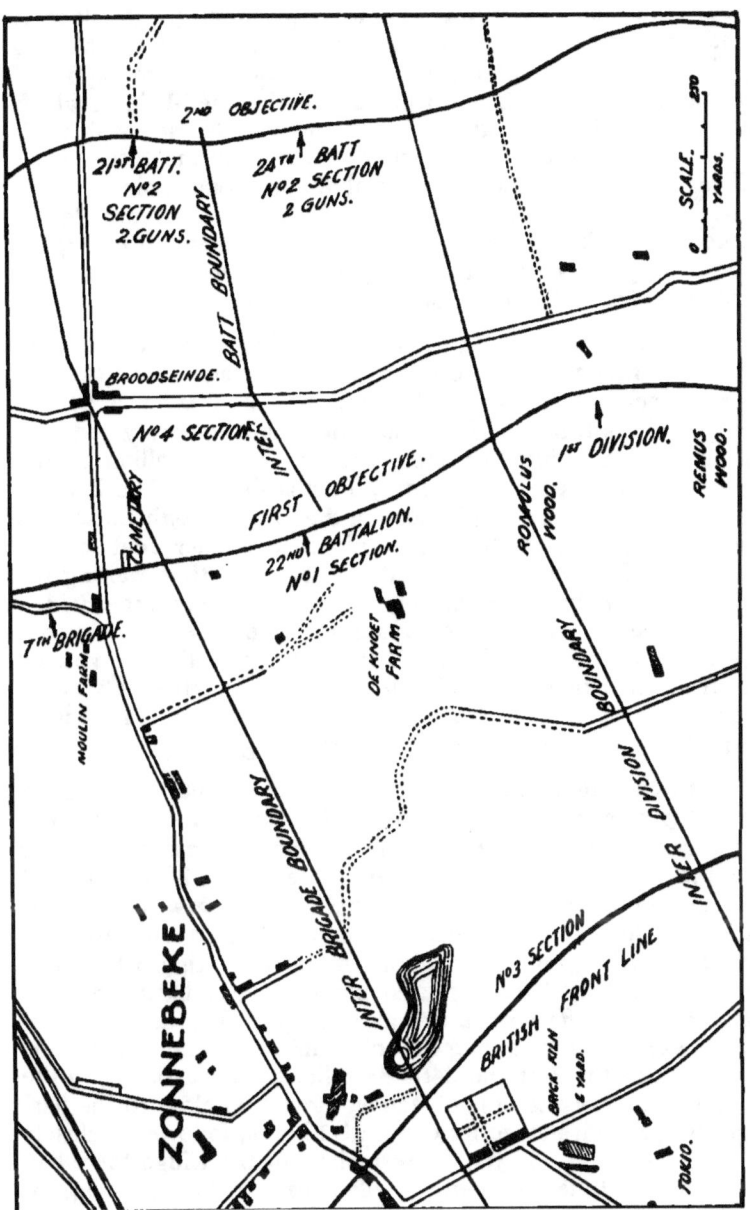

Broodseinde Ridge: 4th October, 1917.

each flank. The front tape was placed slightly in rear of the actual front line, as it was considered dangerous to place it right forward on account of the bright moonlight of the two previous nights. The night, however, was cloudy. It so happened that the front tape was laid right across the shell-hole in which one of No. 1 Section's guns was mounted. The rain which fell on the 3rd made the ground muddy and movement somewhat difficult, but the attackers assembled in good order despite occasional shelling. They could hardly have been more closely packed, three battalions being formed up in an area roughly 300 yards by 100 yards. The Company's 12 "mobile" teams were in position more than two hours before Zero.

Zero time was 6 a.m. on the morning of the 4th October. At 5.35 a.m. the enemy put down a heavy barrage of all calibres up to 8-inch, which extended as far back as 600 yards behind the "jumping-off tape." It so happened that the enemy had also chosen that morning to attack, and the heavy shelling of the forward area was his preliminary bombardment. The bulk of the shells fell on the rear platoons of the 21st and 24th Battalions causing casualties to the extent of 15 to 20 per cent. of the attackers. The waiting men had an agonising time waiting for Zero, but they stuck it admirably. Promptly at Zero, the British barrage opened with a tremendous roar, and its effect on that of the enemy was immediate. All accounts agree that its volume fell in a remarkable degree; one report stating that it was reduced to a few 5.9's. "No tribute to the artillery," said Lieutenant F. L. Wright, "could be too flattering."

Notwithstanding the gruelling received on the "jumping-off tape," the men in the Brigade went off in great heart. In their eagerness, some of the rear battalions reached the first objective with the leading 22nd. The leading waves of the 22nd almost at once encountered the enemy in force, advancing with bayonets fixed, but the issue was never in doubt. By 7.23 a.m. the 22nd Battalion had captured the whole of the Red Line, which was duly "mopped up," the captured including two battalion commanders and staffs with maps and papers. The artillery programme provided for a long halt of 71 minutes on the Red Line, during which the 21st and 24th Battalions, after assisting in the "mopping up" of the first objective, moved up close to the barrage, and when it moved forward at 8.10 a.m., followed it closely to the Blue Line. On the western slope of the Ridge there had been, till this time, no enemy shelling east of the "jumping-off line," but as the attackers moved over the crest, they came under heavy machine-gun fire and, within an hour, quite a respectable barrage had been placed about the Broodseinde-Noordenhoek road along the summit of the Ridge. A large amount of wine and cigars had been discovered in the German lines, and but few of the attackers went forward who were not smoking cigars and producing another smoke barrage that was not provided for in the orders of the day.

Consolidation of the Blue Line was proceeded with at once, and by evening both Battalions had a continuous front line trench. During the consolidation, many casualties were caused by enemy snipers and machine-guns in concealed positions and hedges within 300 to 400 yards of the new front, but during the afternoon the sniping died out, and there was comparative quiet. The enemy's arrangments for counter-attacks had, doubtless, been disturbed by the programme for his own attack, as no move was made against the newly-won positions, although some concentrations were reported during the day. About 350 prisoners were taken on the Brigade front, mainly from the 212th R.I.R. and the 5th Guards Grenadier Regiments.

The actions of the Company's teams were as follows:—No. 1 Section's party continued in the positions taken up on the night of the 1st, and had a trying time owing to the necessity of lying low and the difficulty as to hot food. A slender supply of "Tommy cookers" provided the only hot nourishment during the two days and three nights of occupancy. Sergeant McDonald continued in charge, and the casualties were replaced from reserve. During the night of the 3-4th, Second Lieutenant R. Dodgshun arrived and took charge. Shortly before Zero hour after making a final inspection of his gun, Lance-Corporal H. Ford was badly wounded in the right thigh by a shell splinter. Corporal B. H. Johnson stopped the profuse bleeding, arranged a splint for the fractured limb, and obtained stretcher-bearers for the sufferer. Ford was discharged from active service as a result of the injury. The teams endured the enemy bombardment without further loss, and moved forward at Zero with the infantry who, to quote Lieutenant Dodgshun, "rose from everywhere and moved up Broodseinde Ridge behind a heavy H.E. and smoke barrage." "We went, or rather dragged after them," said Private E. D. Saker, "what with the boggy ground underfoot and the loads upon our backs, we were about done when we arrived at a 'pill box' and were ordered to remain in reserve." The guns were mounted on "pill boxes," and came into action against the numerous enemy aircraft, but without any known results. About 11 a.m., Sergeant McDonald was badly wounded in the leg by a piece of shell which broke both bones. Saker (a veteran of the South African war) obtained two boards from the floor of a neighbouring pill box and bound the broken limb so effectively that the emergency first aid was untouched by the staff at casualty clearing stations, and was not removed till the operating table was reached. McDonald returned as a cot case to Australia, finally regained the use of his leg and was discharged from active service. Next day, relief teams were sent in, and the very tired men returned to camp at Belgian Chateau for much-needed sleep and rest.

The early arrival of No. 2 Section—in readiness to advance to the final objective—left them with over two hours to wait. Some of the men at once commenced to dig themselves cover, partly by way of employment, but as the action seemed a wise one, all were directed to work. Before long, the holes dug gave everyone appreciable cover. The precaution taken proved a wise move. Although the enemy barrage fell heavily, half-burying many, not a single man was injured. "I expected," said Lieutenant Wright, "to find that half my teams had been wiped out. We climbed out from the covering muck and shook ourselves. To my astonishment, every one of my men was O.K." "We had not advanced 50 yards," said Private A. E. Cameron, "before we met Germans coming in and giving themselves up." Our troops advanced so rapidly that we ran into our own artillery barrage on the ridge, and were called on to retire a little and await the time for it to lift. Ahead of us, on the ridge, were the infantry, and it seemed strange to see them standing on the skyline and taking pot shots at the fleeing German troops going down the other side, just as though they were rabbits. Ultimately, we dug-in on the Ridge beyond an old German trench. This point of going beyond the old enemy trench proved to our advantage. Later on when the enemy artillery again started firing, they ranged on to this old trench, and consequently their shells passed over our heads and burst behind us. Our position was rather exposed, but commanded an excellent field of fire in the event of a counter-attack, which did not develop during our spell in the front line. Everywhere ahead of us we could observe troops coming in from far behind the German lines, but beyond our range. We commanded a view of seven or eight miles, and every road seemed packed with transport going the other way."

On arrival at the Blue Line, the men of the 21st Battalion

were somewhat disorganised owing to heavy losses in officers. Lieutenant Wright stepped into the breach and coolly and cheerfully took charge of a sector of the consolidation, being helped in great style by a Lance-Corporal of the battalion. By night, only three officers were left in the Battalion's sector of the front line. Captain Sale directed operations, and placed Lieutenant Wright in charge of the S.O.S. Signal. It was the only time a member of the Company had it in his charge. "A nice responsibility for a new officer," said Wright, "I did not see anything to warrant putting it up, but somebody on our right flank did, and our artillery placed a perfect wall of flame and fire about 150 yards in front of us. It was magnificently precise, and nothing could have got through it. The Fritz stretcher-bearers were very busy next morning." During the day, two of the party were wounded, Privates T. W. Ivory and E. Williams, "attached" from the 22nd and 23rd Battalions respectively. Relief was provided during the following night (5th), when Lieutenant H. deB. Newcomen arrived with two fresh teams, but their leader was wounded on the way in. Wright, therefore, took the fresh men in exchange, sent Newcomen out, and carried on till relieved, as will be explained later. Shortly before the relieving party arrived, a "Whizz-bang" burst in the rear wall of the trench, just behind one of the guns. The explosion killed an infantryman who was sitting in an adjacent "funkhole" and severely wounded Lance-Corporal J. C. Berriman, who happened to be with Wright's party. Berriman received five wounds, and was taken out in a dazed condition by the outgoing teams.

Lieutenant Blenkarn, assisted by Sergeant A. E. Masters, with two teams from No. 2 Section, assembled with the 24th Battalion on the "jumping-off tape" with over two hours to spare. They also dug shelters like Lieutenant Wright's party. Here again the precaution taken undoubtedly prevented loss when the heavy German barrage fell. Some little time before, Blenkarn, after observing the strenuous labours of Captain Harriott in assembling his company, invited the Captain to share his shelter when the shelling commenced. Soon after, a 77 m.m. shrapnel shell burst over the two and wounded both officers. The Captain was severely injured, and Blenkarn was hit in the leg, but carried on. As soon as Zero hour arrived, the party moved off. In his anxiety to get away from the barrage, Lance-Corporal J. C. Berriman (accompanied by Privates D. Lazarus and E. R. Owen) hurried forward so quickly as to lose touch with the rest of the party. The three pushed on, and, just before reaching the crest of the ridge, Berriman mounted a "pill box" to observe his whereabouts. He noticed the methodical and effective way in which the infantry of the Brigade were "mopping up" the captured trenches and, facing south, observed a trench about 300 yards long with Germans strung out in it. The trench was on the front of the neighbouring division—the 1st Australian—and the defenders appeared to be holding that division's advance. Berriman mounted his gun on the top of the "pill box," and a couple of belts expended in "searching" fire up and down the trench soon put an end to the enemy's opposition in that quarter. Berriman received the Military Medal for his enterprise.

With half of one of his teams missing, Lieutenant Blenkarn pressed on. Moving up the ridge, the party came under fire from Germans on their right flank who were moving forward and firing at the men of the 6th Brigade. Private W. Roberts, immediately mounted his gun and opened on the advancing enemy. In a few minutes the opposition was silenced; as soon as Roberts commenced firing on his target, the Germans ceased theirs and came forward and surrendered. Continuing the advance, Berriman and his two mates were encountered, and the re-united party moved over the ridge and passed scathless through the shelling that was then falling on the high ground. The two guns were ultimately mounted in the Blue Line, but as no counter-attacks were made, they were not called on for further service. Captain Drummond visited the four front line guns on the morning of the 5th, and sent Blenkarn out. During the evening of the same day, teams from camp relieved the parties in this sector. The early detachment of Berriman's party and gun had caused much concern, and fearing that they had become casualties, Blenkarn sent Private H. Stevenson out to Company headquarters for another gun. Passing through the barrage, Stevenson delivered his message, and was back at 7 a.m. with the desired weapon. For this action and his valuable work as a runner, he was awarded the Military Medal.

No. 4 Section, under Lieutenant Hitchcock, took up its position in rear of the 21st and 24th Battalions. Like their comrades in front of them, they had to endure the half-hour's bombardment before Zero, which fell more heavily on the rear sections of the assembled battalions. Though they made the best use of cover fortune favoured them; no casualties were suffered, although the concentration in their quarter was particularly severe. "I have always considered," said Hitchcock, "that was my worst half-hour under fire." Moving over boggy ground to their allotted position on the crest of Broodseinde Ridge, the Section was surprised to notice, at that early hour, large numbers of prisoners coming towards them. While the advance was in progress, Private W. Ward also observed the resistance on the front of the 1st Australian Division. He boldly mounted his gun in an advanced position and helped to dispose of the trouble in that quarter. He also was rewarded with the Military Medal. On arrival at the crest of the ridge, the guns were mounted for anti-aircraft defence, but very soon after, the heavy shelling of the ridge disposed of about half of Hitchcock's party. Private J. S. Boland was killed, and the wounded comprised Corporals W. B. Sharp and W. E. Allen, Privates W. Ward, A. E. Coe, T. J. Frawley, W. H. Blackman, A. Napper J. V. Cullen, and T. J. Fennelly, the two last-named being "attached" from the 24th Battalion. Blackman was wounded as he was carrying out a report to Company headquarters as to the Section's losses. To avoid further loss, Hitchcock withdrew about 150 yards in rear. He also was wounded in the arm, but carried on till he had withdrawn his men, when his arm was dressed and he was evacuated. On the evening of the 5th, the survivors were withdrawn from the ridge. During the advance, the only Company losses were those sustained by Hitchcock's party.

No. 3 Section engaged enemy aircraft from its position in the old front line, but without noticeable results. It had some narrow escapes, but did not sustain any loss. During the day, two "attached" men were wounded in circumstances which have not been ascertained, Privates T. J. Dooley (21st) and D. Pearce (23rd).

With the evening of the 5th October, the operations for the capture of the Broodseinde Ridge may be said to have ended. No serious attempt for its recapture was made by the enemy, who contented himself with frequent shelling of the captured ground. During the day, Driver A. J. Letson and Privates S. S. Smith and W. E. Lavell ("attached" from 23rd Battalion) were wounded, bringing the Company's losses, since it entered the line on the 1st October, to twenty-eight. Details: four officers and twenty-one other ranks wounded; one other rank killed in action. It is significant that only two men were evacuated sick. The Company was able to return a clean sheet in regard to material lost, although each of the other three Companies in the Division reported gear lost and destroyed.

The loss of four officers reduced the compliment to six in all, including one on leave. When Lieutenant Newcomen was wounded on his way to relieve Lieutenant Wright, the position became acute. The latter pondered a good deal as to who would ultimately relieve him, but he was amazed when Lieutenant J. D. Campbell arrived, rosy-cheeked, debonair, and groomed as usual. Since the Company's formation, he had acted as Transport Officer, but when necessity arose at Pozieres, he took his place in the front line as a section officer. Again when the present difficulty occurred, he immediately offered his services, and, on acceptance, called on the quartermaster for a "tin hat," and demanded "rations for a dinkum soldier," with the explanation that "Frankie Wright had not been relieved for three days and there is no one to take his place." After nearly seventy-two hours in the front line, Wright was extremely glad to hand over to his successor, who carried on till the morning of the 9th, when he went forward in the next attack.

In addition to the awards of three Military Medals recorded, Lieutenants Blenkarn and Wright received the Military Cross for their leadership during the operations.

The general attack met with a very large measure of success, and the capture of the Broodseinde Ridge was—in spite of the weather and state of the ground—a notable achievement. The 2nd Australian Division reported that it "had gained all objectives except just in front of Daisy Wood, where our line, for about 250 yards, runs about 150 yards west of the original objective line." That area was on the left of the frontage of the 7th Brigade, and it fell to the lot of the 6th Brigade to attack it during a subsequent advance five days later, in which operation the Company was to receive its most disastrous and staggering blow.

CHAPTER XVI.

YPRES, 1917: DAISY WOOD.
5th to 10th October, 1917.

On the night of 5-6th October, the 6th Brigade was relieved by the 5th Brigade, which took over the whole of the Divisional front, but the Company maintained its line positions. Sections 1, 2, and 4 were withdawn, leaving No. 3 manning four guns in the front line and four in support, the former with fresh teams from the reserves in camp at Belgian Chateau. Needless to say, the outgoing men were greatly in need of hot food, sleep, and washing.

During the night of the 6-7th, the frontage of the Division was extended to the left as far as the Ypres-Roulers railway line, and certain changes in the locations of the brigades followed; one result being that the Company relinquished two gun positions in each of the front and support lines, and relieved the 7th Company—on the night of the 7-8th—in similar positions on the left of its holding. In effect, the change was a "side slip" northwards, bringing Daisy and Dairy Woods opposite the right brigade front. On the 7th, Private N. C. Hammon was wounded, and on the evening of the following day, Private C. Mitchelsen had two ribs broken as the result of a shell-burst.

The weather appeared to be definitely breaking. Heavy showers fell nearly every day—with lower temperatures—to the exceeding discomfort of the troops in the forward area. In spite of the conditions, preparations were commenced for another attack. It came as a very unwelcome announcement. "Another attack, I hear," said one diarist, "this is too much."

Since the British offensive had been resumed on the 20th September, it had been accompanied—in the main—by fine weather, and a large measure of success in the series of operations planned on wide frontages. But the weather, which had seriously interfered with the thrust launched on the 31st July, again intruded its disturbing influence. Where success had crowned the carefully conceived and co-ordinated schemes of the Second and Fifth Armies, partial success was to be the reward of the most valorous attempts to carry out the plans laid down. At this time, the Second Army was well astride the Broodseinde Ridge, and looked eastward to the lower lying country in front, but further north it was hoped, despite the approaching winter, to gain the north-eastern extension of the ridge—the heights of Passchendale—before the weather would bring to an end further plans for attack in 1917.

In furtherance of the obvious scheme to gain the final goal, both Armies resumed the offensive on the morning of the 9th October. The attack was restricted to a frontage of six miles and the southern end hinged on the frontage of the 1st Anzac Corps. The 1st and 2nd Divisions of the Corps were in the line, but the 1st, on the right, was not called on for any effort except "to take any opportunity to improve its tactical position locally." On the right of the 2nd Division the general attack actually hinged. From a point about 500 yards south-east of the village of Broodseinde, the objective for the day bore away in a north-easterly direction towards Passchendale, with a consequent gradually deepening area to be won. The 6th Brigade thus found itself allotted an area which, commencing at the "hinge" on its southern boundary, measured 1,100 yards to its northern neighbour, the 5th Brigade. The general objective was divided into two sections, the Red and Blue Lines, but the 6th Brigade, owing to its position on the "hinge," was concerned almost entirely with an area within the Red Line.

For the assault, the 6th Brigade assembled its four battalions in the line. The 23rd Battalion was on the left (northern) flank with a frontage of 175 yards and following the line south, the disposition was: 21st Battalion, 120 yards; 24th Battalion, 275 yards; 22nd Battalion, 550 yards. The northern battalions were compensated for the greater depth of their objectives by narrower fronts.

First Anzac Corps headquarters again directed its machine-gun activities, but on this occasion the Creeping Barrage and S.O.S. batteries were on a modified scale as compared with previous efforts. The attacking 5th and 6th Brigades were each directed to provide six guns for the Creeping Barrage batteries on their respective fronts, and the remaining ten as "attacking" and reserve guns.

Such, briefly, were the dispositions in the fourth large-scale attack, but what of the conditions and the state of the men in the Brigade and Company? After the capture of the Broodseinde Ridge, the infantry of the Brigade had been relieved on

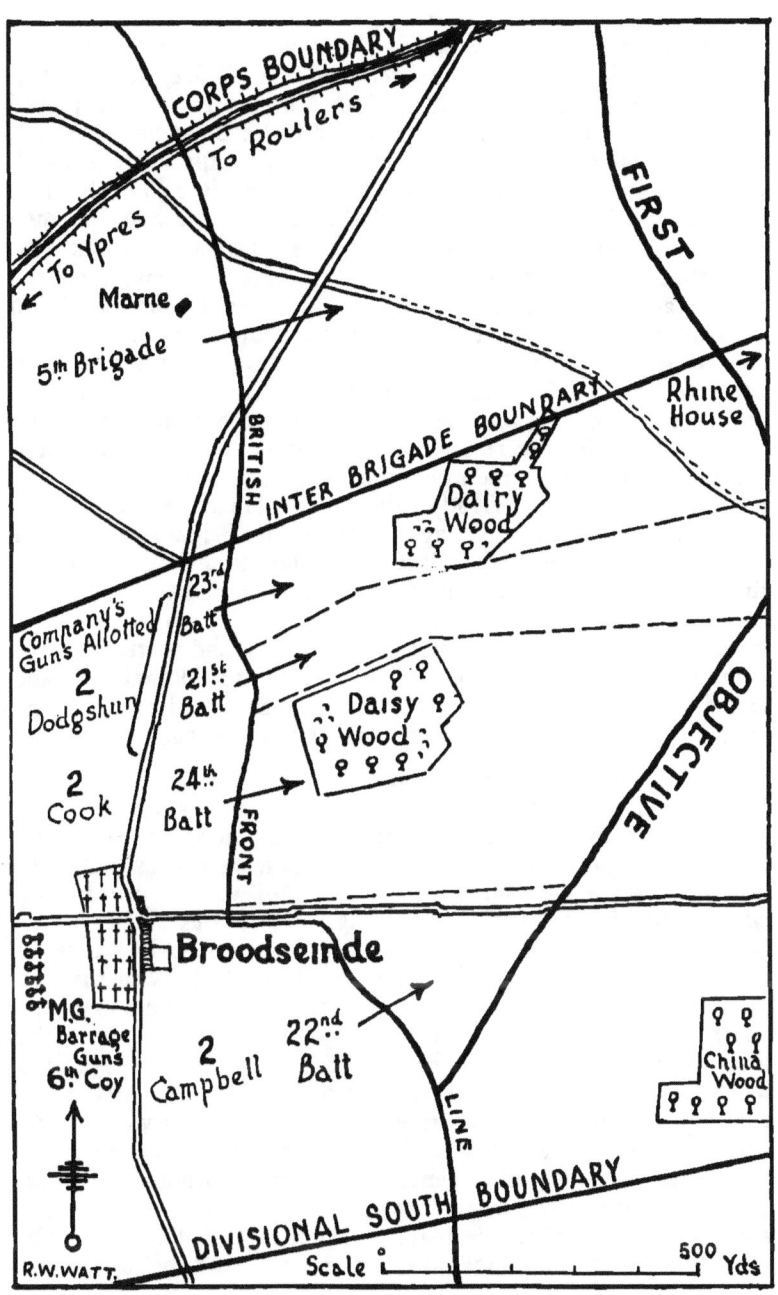

Daisy Wood: 9th October, 1917.

the night of 5-6th, as stated, and became the "reserve brigade" of the Division. They continued under shell-fire, and lived in such scanty shelter as could be found in the recently captured and much damaged area. To quote from the Brigadier-General's report: "On the 6th and 7th October, practically all men available in the Brigade were used in preparatory work for the next attack. Both days were exceedingly inclement, and the men became so fatigued and worn out through exposure and exhaustion that I had to represent to the Divisional Commander my doubts as to the advisability of putting men in this condition into an attack." To meet the situation, about 300 men from the reinforcement camp at Caestre were exchanged with men from the line on the 7th, but through some hitch in the arrangements, the incoming men were debussed at different points from which their guides were sent, and in consequence did not reach their units till after midnight, and were without rations. The same night, the 6th Brigade relieved the 5th in the line in the right brigade sector. To again quote the Brigadier: "Of the men of the 22nd and 23rd Battalions who started out to relieve the 5th Brigade, only about 80 per cent. reached the front line, the remainder fell by the wayside. Indeed, some were stretcher cases." The morning of the 8th was sunny and warm and the ground dried somewhat, but in the afternoon rain again fell and lasted till about 10 p.m., thereby spoiling the good effect of the morning sun. So much for the infantry battalions.

The Company did not share in the general relief of the Brigade on the night of 5-6th, as related, but maintained eight guns in the line. Internal reliefs gave a measure of respite from line conditions, and while the men were not called on to provide Brigade working parties, their own work of preparation was, in the circumstances, exceedingly labourious and exhausting. An extract from the records of Corporal A. E. Cameron will serve to indicate conditions in the line: "I took in the two gun-teams who relieved the 7th Company in the front line. . . . After getting my orders, we started on a long tramp into the line. It was a rotten trip in, mud and slush everywhere, and we had a hard job to find our positions. In one part of the communication trench, the mud was so deep that we got out and went along the top and chanced the gun fire which raked there every little while. Eventually we got in without casualties. We struck one of the worst 'possies' it would be possible to get anywhere. The other gun-team was just as bad, I believe. My team went to the left position of the two. Just before arrival a big shell landed right in the trench—our first greeting—and five or six diggers were lying dead in the trench. When mounted, our gun was in a trench running straight out towards the German lines, and under observation all day from a balloon which could see every movement. We were enfiladed by field artillery day and night, consequently were unable to move by daylight. Behind our position was a miniature lake, and whenever a big shell landed there we got covered with mud and water. The next day the boys had cleaned the gun up nicely and we had managed to scrape a bit of mud off ourselves and began to feel a little drier and happier, when a 5.9 shell landed in the mud and smothered us, gun and all. . . . About 40 yards in front of us was a German strong post, and thereby hangs a tale. It appears that the post was dug by the infantry in our trench, and after finishing it they decided not to occupy it till the next night. When they went to do so, they found the Hun in possession and could not shift him. This did not make us feel at all comfortable, and we had visions all night of being bombed from this post, but nothing developed. We were shelled quite enough, though, to satisfy anyone. We decided next day to shift our gun around to the left away from the enfiladed trench, and had spent the day cautiously working on the new position, intending to move at night, but just before dark a shell landed on the new position and smothered everything. On top of that, our existing position, owing to the heavy shelling, collapsed, and the parapet slipped into the bottom of the trench. One of the party 'sold out,' he reckoned he would not come out alive. While we were in this predicament, no gun position, and thinking about making a fresh one, to our great surprise and delight a guide arrived with a fresh team. We apologised for not having a position to hand over, but when the situation was explained they quite understood, so off we went."

Zero hour was fixed at 5.20 a.m. on the morning of the 9th October, and found the weary attackers assembled on the "jumping-off" positions which had been taped out by the 6th Field Company Engineers. In order to allow the artillery barrage to do its work on Daisy Wood and the well-known enemy strong positions near the front line, the "jumping-off" tapes were laid about 150 yards in rear of the Brigade's front line, which was evacuated at 4.50 a.m.—30 minutes before Zero. What followed is not to be taken as a criticism of the work of the artillery. The appalling conditions seriously interfered with their very necessary assistance, and explains why a feeble barrage was put down to support the attackers. To again quote the G.O.C.'s report: "It was inaccurate, ragged, and thin, and the percentage of 'shorts' on the right battalion sector, considerable. At no time was it sufficient to prevent sniping and machine-gun fire, and it is doubtful if it reduced its volume." With much to daunt them and little to help them but their own stout hearts, the shrunken but gallant battalions moved forward on their forlorn enterprise.

Following the advance from the northern end of the Brigade, it will be recalled that the 23rd Battalion was allotted to the flank. At Zero it moved off, 123 strong. Little frontal opposition was experienced, but heavy machine-gun fire came from their right, and inflicted casualties amounting to about 50 per cent. Dairy Wood, lying right across their sector was "mopped up," and despite the fact that their right flank was unsupported, the survivors pressed on and dug in on approximately the Blue Line near Rhine House, incorporating about 10 men of the 21st Battalion who were detached from their unit. Contact was made with the 5th Brigade on the left, and a defensive flank was formed S.E. from Rhine House.

Immediately on the right of the 23rd, the 21st Battalion met heavy trouble at the outset. Assembly had been made in good order, and the attack was launched punctually, but from Daisy Wood—lying on the right edge of their allotted area—came the heavy machine-gun fire which played havoc with the 23rd Battalion further north. All officers became casualties at the outset, and the formation of the attackers disorganised. Some elements reached their objective, and dug in near The Knoll with both flanks in the air; one party was absorbed in the 23rd Battalion, as described; others formed a rough line along the south edge of Dairy Wood.

It was with the two battalions mentioned that Lieutenant R. Dodgshun was detailed to go forward with two teams from No. 4 Section. He received his orders late in the evening of the 8th, and they directed him to advance with, and in rear of, the two battalions. On arriving near the assembly positions, he experienced a miserable time moving round over boggy ground in the darkness, looking for a suitable approach. While moving up, one of his party, Private W. ("Doc.") Porteus, an "attached" man from the 24th Battalion, was killed by a splinter from a shell which burst so far off that the other members of the team took no notice of it. Before going forward, Porteus informed the others that he had a decided premonition of his approaching death. Before Zero, Dodgshun had assembled his teams, and when the thin barrage heralding the opening of the attack fell, the party moved off; the teams about 75 yards apart. The left hand team was in charge of Sergeant G. T. Guinea, with Private S. A. Greaves as No. 1. As they moved off, terrific machine-gun fire came from Daisy Wood on their right flank, and the air "seemed to rain bullets." After going some little distance, Guinea halted his team, directed them to cover, and coolly remained standing while he surveyed his front and consulted a map. As he was being urged to take shelter he fell, shot through the chest. Greaves and another crawled out and got him into a shell-hole. It was obvious that he was dying, and that he knew it. Handing his map to Greaves, he said: "Never mind me, get forward with the gun." He was made as comfortable as possible, and the team made another dash forward. But that deadly machine-gun fire continued, killing Privates H. Jephcott and W. J. Richards, and the sole survivor, Private Greaves, was left to decide his own action. What he did can best be told in his own words: "Seeing a battalion runner going forward at the gallop, with dirt spurting up around him, I watched him go up the slope to my left and drop into a trench at the top. I made that trench my first objective and, carrying two boxes of ammunition, started on the liveliest 200 yard run—in short stages—that I have ever attempted, and at last, mud covered, breathless, and exhausted, fell into the shelter of the trench." This trench led directly to The Knoll which lay on the line of the 21st Battalion's objective. Moving along the trench in the hope of finding the other team, he came across some of the 21st Battalion. Failing to find any of his comrades, he attached himself to a Lewis gun team, who were exceedingly pleased to have his two boxes of ammunition, which they expended on excellent targets; Greaves joining in with a rifle. No trace could be discovered of Vickers gunners, so he decided to return to Company headquarters and report. While doing so, he fell in with Dodgshun and Private J. McMahon of the other team. It was agreed that the best course was to return to Company Headquarters. The area was dominated by enemy snipers, and while making the journey in short dashes, Greaves fell into a large shell-hole containing four artillery observation officers. "What they were observing, I don't know," said Greaves, "as our artillery had evidently decided not to take part in the fight. One of the officers, in a scornful voice, asked me what I was running for. I was too breathless to reply, and continued on my way. A few minutes later that officer was carried past me with four bullets through his thigh. He was too dignified to run, and eventually had to be carried."

Soon after moving from the "jumping-off" tape, Dodgshun lost touch with his left-hand team, but continued with the other. After going about 100 yards with the 21st Battalion, bursts of machine-gun fire were encountered from guns concealed in Daisy Wood, about 100 yards away on the right. Whilst carrying the tripod, Lance-Corporal J. B. R. Horne was shot dead. Lieutenant Dodgshun seized the tripod and directed the other three men to take shelter in a shell-hole. Before they could do so, a "burst" opened Private H. H. Dunn's forearm from wrist to elbow, killed Private W. J. Bell, and wounded an "attached" man (from 24th Battalion) in the head as he picked up the tripod. Fortunately his steel helmet saved him from anything worse than a groove in the skull. Dodgshun and the remaining man, Private J. McMahon, then worked away to the left, carrying ammunition, in the hope of joining forces with the left-hand team, but, on nearing the front line, fell in with Greaves, as related. While searching vainly for the lost guns, Dodgshun was wounded in the arm, thereupon the three survivors returned to Company Headquarters. McMahon bore a charmed life; no less than six bullet holes were discovered in his overcoat. Dunn's hand was amputated on arrival at hospital.

The 24th Battalion assembled in good time after losing two Lewis guns and about twelve men through shell-fire. The attack went well at the outset, but the well-established enemy machine-guns in Daisy Wood—in the left of the Battalion's area —appear to have broken up the attackers' formation, especially on the left, although a footing was gained in Daisy Wood. The right Company—reduced to 2 N.C.O.'s and 12 men—established a post about half-way to their objective.

With the 24th Battalion, two teams of No. 1 Section were directed to go forward in support. Owing to a shortage of officers, Sergeant H. J. Cook was placed in charge. The party got to the front line during the evening of the 8th, near the ruins of the village of Broodseinde, after traversing very deep mud. To quote Private E. D. Saker: "Conditions were 100 per cent. rotten." They saw few infantrymen, and during the night, a runner brought a message to the effect that the line was to fall back about 200 yards to escape the opening artillery barrage. "We decided," said Saker, "to stay where we were and take the risk of any of our shells falling short, and informed the runner to that effect. We did not relish the task of humping our guns and ammunition through the bogs and darkness in our weak state. At Zero, our artillery opened up a very half-hearted barrage. Hardly a shell fell our way. We saw Lieutenant Dodgshun and party, on our left, go forward with some straggling infantry, and were ready to go ourselves, but not a solitary man came our way, so Sergeant Cook decided to mount our guns and remain." After a reconnaissance, a more favourable spot was found, and the party, with the exception of Saker and Private T. H. Coote, moved into the new position. Heavy shells were falling, and Saker and Coote, considering it unwise for all to be grouped together, remained some little distance apart. It was not long before a heavy shell appeared to burst close to the larger party and, upon Saker and Coote going to investigate, they found that Cook, Privates J. Bone, C. P. Jeffery, C. F. Skead, and J. B. Wrigley had been killed outright. Private H. Cuthbert and another were rescued in a state of collapse. As Coote was suffering from shock (having been partially buried the night before), Saker decided—after covering the guns against the weather—to take his almost helpless party out. They reached Company Headquarters safely, and were sent back to Belgian Chateau.

The 22nd Battalion—on the right of the Brigade—was faced with the problem of a wide front (550 yards) and few men for the task. Its "C" Company was allotted to the "hinge" of the general attack, with a short advance to accomplish. For the main attack, two "strong post" parties were formed, and named No. 1 (right) and No. 2 (left). Lieutenant Campbell allotted one of his two teams and guns to each party. At Zero, "C" Company went forward and established its line without loss. No. 1 Party advanced under fire, and after some loss, constructed a post near its objective, but being isolated and almost surrounded at night, withdrew to avoid being cut off. With No. 1 Party was Lieutenant J. D. Campbell and a team and gun from No. 3 Section. Their instructions were to follow in rear of the infantry and take up a position with them. After the infantry had moved forward, the team attempted to follow, but, in the first rush, fire was opened on them from the front, coming, apparently, from a pill box a little to their left. The heavily laden team halted and took shelter, but, upon being urged by its leader, made another dash. Again bullets swished by, accompanied by hand grenades. Campbell fell, killed by a bullet, and the men went to earth. Privates A. Smith, H. H.

Penfold, and C. Taylor dived into one large shell-hole and were joined by two stretcher-bearers. Immediately after, a shell burst on top of them. The three Company members were wounded, Taylor receiving a serious head injury which led to a number of operations and his subsequent discharge. Early in the morning he had been wounded in the leg by shrapnel. The remnant of the team remained till night, then returned and reported to Company Headquarters. No. 2 Party—on the left of No. 1—had less success. After suffering loss from artillery "shorts," enemy machine-gun fire accounted for all except five men, who pushed on and dug in some distance in front of the original front line. The few survivors of the party returned to their own lines at night. With this party was a team from No. 3 Section under Corporal H. G. Carthew, with similar instructions to Campbell's team. A similar fate awaited them. In the first rush forward, heavy bursts of machine-gun fire smote them, coming, apparently, from the pill box already referred to. Lance Corporal E. J. Lyons was shot through the head as he ran with the tripod; some were wounded, and the gun badly damaged. Carthew found himself and one other man in a shell-hole where they had dived for shelter. After remaining in shell-holes all day, the survivors returned with the scanty remnant of the Battalion's party at night, Carthew bringing the lock of the useless gun with him.

During the afternoon arrangements were made to strengthen the disjointed front line by the despatch of four teams and guns which had been kept in reserve. No. 3 Section provided two, under Corporal F. Wigmore. They arrived at their destination about 4.30 p.m. after an exhausting experience getting through the enemy barrage which was falling on the ridge. The guns were mounted close to the spot where Sergeant Cook and his men met their end. Wigmore and Private R. C. Trevan found their ill-fated comrades sitting in a group just as the shell had caught them. After obtaining their paybooks and papers, the party buried them on the spot. Shortly after, the area was heavily shelled for three hours. Next day, Trevan penned a vivid account of the severity of the bombardment. "For over three hours last night," he wrote, "he gave it to us hot and strong, having the range of his old trench to a yard, placing the shells all along it and smashing it to pieces. We all fully expected every minute to be our last, as big shells were smashing in our trench all round us, in front and behind us as well. We felt so pessimistic that we started singing to keep up our courage. Soon after, between shell explosions, we could hear in the distance, Jack Fraser, of Corporal J. E. Smith's team, singing a certain ballad about Mademoiselle of Armentieres. Looking over the top now and again, I saw the men of the 24th Battalion who had crept out about fifty yards down the slope, digging for their lives, with shells bursting all around them—although the bulk were landing on the trench we occupied. This trench was choc-a-block with infantry of the 7th Brigade who had come in to relieve, and consequently there were two lots of troops in the trench at once. Men were falling everywhere, and the call, 'stretcher-bearers,' could be heard in a dozen places at once. It was a great sight to see the stretcher-bearers get out over the top in the thick of it all with their burdens, at a time when it was unsafe for the relieved garrison to leave, even by the saps. I particularly remember observing the faces of the officers and men in that trench, every one of whom was shaking like a jelly and as white as a sheet. I consider that bombardment was by far the worst in my experience of the war, putting Bullecourt in the shade." The teams were relieved the following evening about 7.30 p.m. by two teams from the 13th Machine Gun Company. The incoming men reported that they had "a hell of a time" getting in. The party got out without mishap. "Once more we have got away from that hell on earth, the Broodseinde Ridge," wrote Trevan, at 10 p.m., "and are congratulating ourselves and each other."

The other two reserve teams were made up from No. 2 Section, under Sergeant A. E. Cameron. It was dark when he was placed in charge and directed to take up positions in support of the 23rd Battalion. The available information was of the vaguest, and in the absence of guides, a compass bearing—over totally unfamiliar country—and a map location were all that could be given him. Taking one team and placing the other under Private L. Barrand, they had a wretched experience looking for their location in the darkness, amid tangled wire, deep mud, and shell-fire. It is not surprising that they became hopelessly lost. Towards morning their anxiety increased because it was necessary to "get in" before daylight. When there was light enough to see, Cameron went forward and discovered that he was in the area of the recent fighting, with all the evidences of bitter bomb-fighting; the corpse-strewn ground and dug-outs and pill boxes filled with dead. Low-flying enemy aeroplanes were numerous and attentive. Eventually, the 23rd Battalion was discovered and the guns mounted in a suitable position.

Except for heavy shelling in the morning, the day passed without unusual incident. In the evening, relieving teams from the 13th Machine Gun Company arrived and took over the positions. As no guides were available for the relief for Wigmore's party, Cameron—taking Private D. Lazarus with him—undertook the duties of guide. Being familiar with the locality, he found Wigmore's teams and carried out what was the final stage of the relief of the Company. "Then began," said he, "the long, long tramp back to Belgian Chateau, which we reached, footsore, weary, dirty, and badly in need of rest and sleep."

Owing to the depletion of the Company's resources, it was not possible to reinforce the frontage of the 22nd Battalion which was without effective machine-gun support. Consequently, Divisional Headquarters directed the 7th Company to send two teams and guns to that sector of the front line. This order was carried out in the afternoon of the 9th.

Turning to the experience of the teams set apart for indirect fire, an equally dismal and ineffective story must be told. Six teams and guns, under Lieutenant F. L. Wright, were allotted to indirect covering fire, and the positions were sited just behind the ruins of the village of Broodseinde. They formed the right battery of two provided by Divisional Headquarters in accordance with instructions from Corps. The 7th Company supplied six for the left Battery, and the 22nd Company eight for S.O.S. calls. Captain A. N. McLennan, of the latter Company, had charge of all three. The six gun pits for the Company's guns had been dug when Wright took the teams—made up from all four sections—in on the 8th October. He was told that 10,000 rounds were in the vicinity, and 80,000 were to be brought up by pack-mules at night. The pits had not been camouflaged, it was noticed, and at first the ammunition could not be found. Meanwhile, enemy aeroplanes were flying overhead, and soon after shelling of the ridge took place and continued without cessation for 24 hours. Later, the ammunition was discovered and made ready, but there was no appearance of the larger quantity because it was found impossible, owing to the deep mud, for the mules to bring it forward from the dumps in rear. What was beyond the strength of mules was manifestly too much for men. Indeed, in their weakened state, it took them all their time to drag themselves and their gear about in the wilderness of shell-holes, mud, and tangled wire. However, the available supplies were more than sufficient. The shelling increased in intensity, and most of the men were withdrawn to the shelter of a large "pill-box." What had been endured was but a foretaste of what was to follow. During the night, Corporal G. Pollock, Lance-Corporals H. L. Deslandes and R. C. G. Greig, M.M., and Privates W. J. Morris, W. H. Burns, and R. J. Selkrig were killed, Private N. C. Andrews and others were wounded. One heavy shell fell right in one gun-pit, killing the occupants. Two guns were destroyed, and two others put out of action. "By this time," said Wright, "we were all dazed and ducking involuntarily at every burst and shaking at every sound, waiting for our 'issue' with just a sheet of tissue paper—it seemed—between us and sheer lunacy. No one would give me authority to retire, yet it was senseless to stay there. One man jumped out of the trench and, on my challenging him, he just flung out his arms and, without a word, disappeared. In truth, I could but pity him. By morning all of us were on the verge of collapse. Needless to say, we never fired a shot; a barrage from the remaining two guns would not have been of much assistance, anyway. When word came to abandon the cursed spot, I had some difficulty in inducing the boys to stay long enough to bury their comrades." The remnants were withdrawn on the morning of the 10th October.

By 11 p.m. on the 10th, the relief of the Company by the 13th Company (13th Brigade) was reported complete, and all hands were clear of that ridge of unhappy memory. The worn out men returned to the comparative quiet of the camp near Belgian Chateau, and slept the sleep of utter exhaustion.

During the whole of the Ypres operations, the Transport Section remained at its lines near the camp, and kept their comrades supplied with their daily requirements. When the ground became too soft for wheeled traffic, supplies were carried by pack-horses; the practice being for each driver to ride one horse and lead one or two pack animals. They were necessarily often under shell-fire, but experience and careful watching of the barrage—and it must be added, some good luck—kept them almost free of casualties till the morning of the 11th, after the relief of the Company. Very early that morning, Drivers E. J. Nash and T.C.H. Britt, M.M., left Brigade Headquarters, each walking and leading a horse laden with gun and gear. While passing a party of artillerymen, two salvoes of heavy shells landed in the vicinity. One fell right in the group of men, killing eight and wounding six. Nash and Britt were badly wounded and both horses killed. Nash's horse received the full force of the explosion, which, doubtless, saved Nash's life. Britt died next day as the result of abdominal injuries; Nash escaped with the loss of a leg. The disastrous incident occurred about 6.30

a.m., and Nash's subsequent experience will be recorded as affording an illustration of the difficulties attending the evacuation of the badly wounded at that time and place. Shortly after the tragedy, both men were placed on stretchers, and bearers—four to each stretcher and two others to relieve them at intervals—set out for the Ypres-Menin road, about two miles distant, to await the ambulance. It was a most exhausting trip for the bearers who were, at times, knee-deep in mud. On arrival at a casualty clearing station near the railway station at Ypres, Nash was marked "urgent" and despatched to a hospital near Poperinghe, where he arrived about 5 o'clock in the afternoon. So much blood had been lost that an operation was deferred until about 9 o'clock, when he was placed on the operating table and a leg amputated, after which he knew no more for three days. Later he was moved to a hospital at Amiens, where he was the only Australian in the ward; a distinction which ensured special attention because there were two New Zealand nurses in the ward. Even at that distance he was not beyond enemy action. One night the hospital was bombed by aeroplanes, and the man in the next bed was killed. His good luck followed him to England. While in hospital in Birmingham, Captain Drummond (then at Grantham) sent him a substantial monetary gift which had been subscribed by the officers and men of the unit. The assistance rendered is an example of the very strong "family" spirit prevailing in the Company which reached out so far and stood by a distant member.

On the front of the 6th Brigade but partial success was attained. That any measure was achieved was due to the splendid spirit of the weary officers and men of the much depleted battalions. Officially, the reasons given for the result were—in order of importance—(a) Thinness of the barrage; (b) physical condition of the men; (c) insufficient numbers for the attack; (d) bad condition of the ground. In relation to the gains, the losses were tragic; a little more than half the attackers becoming casualties. The figures were: 24 officers and 392 other ranks. The Company losses were staggering, amounting to one officer and nineteen other ranks killed or died of wounds; one officer (remaining on duty) wounded as well as eleven other ranks. In addition to those whose names have been recorded, Privates A. W. Cumming and T. H. Cobatt were wounded in circumstances which have not been ascertained. They were "attached" from the 23rd and 24th Battalions respectively. It is significant that only

Horse lines at Warlencourt. March, 1917.

Company Headquarters. Hannebeke Wood. 4th October, 1917.

Company Officers. Watterdal, February, 1918.

one man was evacuated sick at this time. Material lost or destroyed was set down at two horses (killed), seven guns, six tripods, 90 belt-boxes and belts. Never before or after did the Company sustain such a blow, never did it emerge from an engagement so stricken to its soul. For the losses, there was no off-set; the extraordinary fact must be recorded that not a single shot was fired during the whole operation. The reasons are obvious. For the first time it was necessary to reinforce the Brigade front with men and guns from another Company. Since October 1st, losses had reduced the Company strength by five officers and 54 other ranks, leaving it at five officers (one on leave) and 147 other ranks. Days were to elapse before the personnel were able to shake off the stunning effect of the loss by death of such a large number of comrades whom they could ill afford to lose.

Where all died in the common cause, it seems invidious to single out individuals, but it may be said that no death caused such general sorrow as that of Lieutenant Campbell. He had endeared himself to the members of the Transport Section by his large-heartedness and personal example, and to the officers and men in the gun-teams only in a lesser degree. "It will be an empty Company," said Captain McLennan, of the 22nd Company, when he heard the sad news. It should be mentioned that shortly before the attack, Sergeant H. J. Cook and Lance-Corporal R. C. G. Greig returned from English leave, and orders directed them to the "nucleus" camp at Caestre, but the news that their comrades were in the line induced them to report to the Company instead. Handing their packs in at the quartermaster's store, and without waiting for orders, they immediately marched in and reported to Company Headquarters for duty, just in time to take their place in the attack. Brave boys! Private Hugh Wm. Burns was probably the youngest member of the Company to fall. He enlisted at the age of 16½ years, and was but 18 years and 5 months at the time of his death. He had served with the Company for four months.

In accordance with what appeared to be an Army practice of awarding few decorations for an unsuccessful operation and granting generously for a successful one, no official recognition for work done by the gun-teams was announced. The solitary Company mention was the award of the Meritorious Service Medal to Private A. H. ("Boss") Smith, assistant Quartermaster. Officially, the award was for services rendered during the series of operations recorded in the last three chapters, but actually it covered a record of eighteen months continuous service in impartial, fearless, and efficient distribution of clothing, equipment and rations. The men in the line were his first care. No genuine cases went empty-handed if it was in the power of "Boss" to supply their wants. Other applicants were not so successful.

CHAPTER XVII.

Ypres, 1917: Passchendale.

October 11th—November 12th, 1917.

After the withdrawal from the Broodseinde Ridge was completed, a weary, sad and depressed Company spent a day in the camp near Belgian Chateau. The day was fine, but members had little heart for the work in hand—the overhauling of guns and gear, listing shortages, making promotions, and re-arranging teams. The filling of the places of tried and trusted comrades and leaders was a dismal business, and a constant reminder of the ruthless ravages of warfare. Mental as well as material re-adjustments had to be made. What a shrunken Company it seemed! However, "carry on" was the watchword, and all ranks set themselves to the task, and to dispel the heavy cloud of depression.

After a showery night, the Company left next morning at 8 a.m. and proceeded with the Brigade to Ypres, where entrainment was made near the Asylum. After a short journey, Abeele was reached, from which march was made to billets near Steenvoorde; the Transport Section following by road. Here fourteen days were spent, chiefly in Company training. The "family" life was resumed, and proceeded uneventfully. Late autumn weather prevailed with occasional showers; "another typical autumn day," wrote a diarist on the 22nd October, when the Company again tried conclusions with the 22nd Machine Gun Company in a football contest, but lost by 2 goals. Not far distant was the old-fashioned abbey town of St. Omer, which was often visited, and which provided opportunities for the purchase of Flemish lace, post cards, and such articles as could be sent as Christmas presents to relatives and friends in Australia. The quartette party provided harmony in the evenings. During the stay, nine other ranks were evacuated sick. Corporal W. A. Carne departed to enter a cadet battalion in England, and was succeeded by Private Greg. Doyle, who was assisted by Private J. C. Ritson. Lieutenant H. DeB. Newcomen returned to duty after recovery from his wounds received on 5th October.

On the 26th October, the stay near Steenvoorde came to an end, and the Company set out for the line again. March was made to its old camp near Belgian Chateau, under Divisional command, the Brigade moving forward the following day. For eight days the Company was "in reserve," and was mainly employed in making preparations for line duty. Various kinds of sickness resulted in six men being evacuated.

The Brigade moved into "support" on the 2nd November, in relief of the 5th, and the Company did likewise on the following morning, when 20 teams relieved a like number of the 5th Machine Gun Company on S.O.S. lines near Abbania Wood, situated north of Polygonne de Zonnebeke. The relief was effected without unusual incident, but a fatal casualty marked the beginning of the tour of line duty. While some members of the Transport Section were carrying ammunition by means of pack-horses, Driver P. J. Mahoney was seriously wounded by shell-fire at Hell Fire Corner, and died two hours later. His horse was so badly injured that one of his mates, Driver W. B. Riley, had to destroy it. On the 4th, Privates G. H. Mayell, J. G. Anderson, C. R. Anderson, and F. Fraser were wounded.

The guns were grouped in four batteries, each with one gun set apart for anti-aircraft defence by day; provision being made for quick relaying in case of an S.O.S. call. The first use of "tracer" ammunition was made at this time by these guns, a number of the special phosphorescent coated bullets being spaced in each belt. All the batteries were connected by telephone with the forward Company Headquarters, and the signallers maintained connection and stood by for immediate repairs to breaks in the wires, usually brought about by shell fire.

The batteries remained in position without incident till the 5th, when orders were received for action the following morning. As it proved, the morning of the 6th November was to witness the last attack of the series of battles known as the Third Battle of Ypres. After weeks of tremendous efforts against the new German defence system, characterised by wide attacks and much success against a resolute enemy, rain, and mud, the great offensive of the British Army culminated in a last effort directed to gain the high ground, and village of Passchendaele, in which the Canadians achieved a remarkable victory. The day of the battle found the troops of the two great Dominions side by side, united in a common cause. On the right of the Canadian Corps was the First Anzac Corps, with its

1st Division, next the Canadians. The Australian co-operation was restricted to simulating an attack on the Droogenbroodhoek Spur by the use of artillery and machine-gun fire.

In accordance therewith, First Anzac Corps undertook to prolong the Canadian machine-gun barrage southwards and to direct "neutralising machine-gun fire" against hostile machine-guns firing from Eddy Heights. The 1st Division allocated 21 guns to the tasks, and the 2nd was ordered to provide eight to assist it. The choice fell to the Company whose contribution was to come under the command of the 3rd Machine Gun Company. The eight remaining Company guns with four of the 5th Company were to barrage the enemy outpost line on the front of the 2nd Division.

Lieutenant Wright was deputed to take charge of the guns attached to the 3rd Company. To carry out the orders, it was necessary to move to and construct fresh positions about a mile and a half distant, near the ruins of the village of Broodseinde, on the ridge of that name. The guns and gear had to be manhandled over waterlogged country pitted with shell-holes, and, as expected, it proved a heavy task. One member described the country as "a proper picture of desolation, with its dead horses and overturned transports." The battery was made up from Nos. 2 and 3 Sections, and Sergeant A. Payton assisted Wright and supervised the initial arrangements after a preliminary reconnaissance. While moving into positions, heavy shelling was experienced, so Payton wisely spread his men out and waited for the storm to cease. Meanwhile, he took refuge in a very large shell-hole with several of his men and two guns and tripods. For a few minutes he pondered on the apparently unlikely contingency of another shell falling in the same hole. Presently he felt a decided and unaccountable urge to move away, which he did, dividing his men still further. When he returned, he discovered that another shell had burst in the large hole and, although the tripods were visible, the guns were not, and a diligent search failed to locate them; apparently they had been buried by the shell-burst. While still searching, Major Ordish came along and, after hearing explanations, directed that two other guns be obtained from reserve. This was done. Later the two lost weapons were discovered; damaged in such a way as to put them out of action.

After a good deal of labour in the sodden ground, positions were built and arrangements completed in good time. At Zero time, 6 a.m., on the 6th, the battery opened fire and carried out its allotted programme without unusual incident, firing for two hours at the rate of 4,000 rounds per gun per hour. On completion, the battery stood by for S.O.S. calls. Lance Corporal J. W. Findlay recorded vith much satisfaction, that his gun carried out its heavy part without a single mechanical stoppage; a tribute alike to the gunner's care of his weapon and his skill in handling it. From their position, the teams had a good view of the great arc of quivering fire formed by the continuously bursting shells when the barrage opened in the semi-darkness; a very impressive sight—to those not involved in it. Later, when daylight appeared, parties of Canadians could be seen pressing forward in the infantry advance. For themselves, they were scarcely molested. In the evening, one S.O.S. call was responded to, the guns joining in a wonderful display given by the artillery in rear. The battery withdrew to its former positions on the 7th, without loss.

Meanwhile the batteries on the Divisional S.O.S. Lines also carried out their part, each gun firing for two minutes at 250 rounds per minute, thence 2,000 rounds per hour for 70 minutes. Three "lifts" were employed, and on completion, the batteries stood by on S.O.S. lines. No calls were made, and no loss was sustained.

On the afternoon of the 7th, the whole Company was relieved in its positions by the 7th, and proceeded to the front line and relieved the 5th. Locations were again on Broodseinde Ridge, east and south of the village that was Broodseinde. As before, on entering the line, losses were sustained. As No. 3 section went forward, they were accompanied by Captain Rae's batman, Private J. Williams, and while traversing a duckboard track, Williams was badly injured. He was carried to a forward dressing station by Private R. C. Trevan and another, but died the same day. Private S. S. Smith was guiding in a party of 34 of his mates, and, when more than a mile from his destination, was wounded in the leg. In spite of his injury, he took his party in, handed them over without loss, and refused assistance on his way to the dressing station, from which he was evacuated. This act of devotion to duty and his previous good record brought him the award of the Military Medal. Before the day was out, Lance Corporal H. G. Carthew was wounded.

After taking over the line positions from the 5th Company, three days passed with little to record except the wounding of Lance Corporal Fitzpatrick, on the 8th, after he had guided in a relief crew for one of the forward guns. Soon after, an enemy aeroplane flew very low, and the team opened fire against it with "tracer" ammunition, but with negative results. At the same time, shelling commenced in connection with a counter-attack against the Canadians, when an odd shell fell among the party. As a curious effect of shell fire, it is interesting to note that the gun was damaged, the ammunition blown up, Fitzpatrick had the hair on one side of his face and head burnt off, a cut in the face, and a shell splinter through his shoulder into his chest; his steel helmet was bent in various shapes without being dislodged from his head—while the man next him escaped with nothing but a fright. Since the entry into the line, the losses were: two other ranks killed or died of wounds, and seven wounded; no evacuations due to sickness were recorded.

A Divisional relief took place on the 11th November, the 49th (Imperial) Division relieving the 2nd Australian; the 146th Machine Gun Company taking over from the Company. The incoming teams were disgusted at the wretched shelters available, and, it should be added, Company members were in hearty agreement. Although it was not known at the time, the Company was making its final departure from the Broodseinde Ridge with its tragic experiences, and where all that was mortal of so many gallant comrades remained. So ended the last occupancy of the line positions for the year. Not till the new year did the Company again come into close contact with the enemy.

CHAPTER XVIII.

THE WINTER OF 1917-8: LOCRE—NEUVE EGLISE—WARNETON WATTERDAL.

12th November, 1917—2nd April, 1918.

After a night in camp at Belgian Chateau, the following day was spent in the customary cleaning of clothes, guns, and gear, and packing up for departure. The next morning, 12th November, the whole Company marched to billets near Steenvoorde, arriving in the early afternoon. General Birdwood viewed the Brigade as it marched to its new quarters. Two days later, the General was present at a Brigade church parade, and at its conclusion, presented medals and ribbons. The only Company recipient was Lieutenant F. L. Wright, who received the ribbon of the Military Cross for conspicuous work on Broodseinde Ridge. Six days passed without recorded incident, except for the evacuation of two cases of sickness. Captain Drummond returned from the investiture of the Military Cross in London by His Majesty the King.

On the 18th, the Company, with the Brigade, marched to Locre and occupied huts at Pasteur Camp. The same day, Captain Drummond departed to take up duty at the machine-gun school at Grantham, England. During his absence, Captain Rae assumed command of the Company. At Pasteur Camp, 27 days were spent training according to a pre-arranged syllabus. The morning session was of a general nature, while the afternoon was mainly devoted to games; football coming in for much attention. Winter was approaching apace, and members received a forcible reminder when the first snow fell on the 4th December. To the majority, the novelty of such an event had long since worn off, and those with memories of the previous winter spent in the mud and ice of the Somme region did not entertain pleasant anticipations. A football match with the old and frequent rival, the 22nd Machine Gun Company, was decided on the 22nd, the Company emerging victorious. A few days later, Sergeant A. E. Masters left to enter a cadet battalion in England. Unfortunately, his health broke down before completing the course, and after a spell, he was given camp duties in England before being returned to Australia. About this time, Lieutenant Duncan rejoined after recovering from wounds received at Bullecourt; likewise, Lieutenant Hitchcock, after recovery from wounds received on Broodseinde Ridge. On the day when the snow appeared, the Company held a sports meeting, and the events staged were in the nature of a "try-out" for the Brigade sports held four days later. A well assorted programme of events was carried through, but although Company entrants appeared in most of them, it was not until the last event of the day that the Company scored a victory in the "Tug of War," amid great excitement. After defeating in turn, teams from the 24th and 22nd Battalions, the strong combination from the 21st Battalion was disposed of. Much of the team's success must be ascribed to its captain, Private W. Roberts, and the earnest attention given to training. For about a fortnight, Roberts exercised his team daily, mainly by pulling against a tree, while he evolved a system of silent signals with which members became quite familiar. The members were: Privates H. H. T. Harris, A. E. D. Marsh, A. E. Forster, A. J. Adams, W. Howden, Cramp, and Paull. Each received an inscribed bronze medal.

Although in what was nominally a "rest area," precautions were taken to deal with enemy aeroplanes. Two guns were mounted on posts and manned at night. The men on duty had a dreary duty to perform in the occasional freezing weather. To meet the case, two men shared the two-hour shifts; one remained on post for a half-hour at a time (with his mate at short call indoors), during which he walked from gun to gun and repeatedly moved the recoiling part of the mechanism to prevent freezing. Another precaution taken was to build earthern walls around the huts to minimise the effects of enemy bombs.

English leave continued, and in spite of the winter season, each leave-goer managed to enjoy himself immensely in the Motherland, and sometimes en route. Lance Corporal E. D. Saker has related an incident at Le Harve, when returning from England. Leave from camp was granted only to warrant-officers; a rule which the English staff would not vary. However, Australian initiative was equal to the situation. Saker's first application was refused, but when he and another donned, temporarily, the badge of a warrant-officer (crown) they received passes. Next morning the Commandant called for a warrant-officer to take charge of the Australians who were returning to their units, but none appeared. The Commandant looked surprised, and said: "Where are all the warrant-officers? I signed 15 passes for them last night." However, he possessed a sense of humour, and joined in the general laugh which greeted his announcement. In the circumstances, it was a heart-breaking experience to leave the hospitable Motherland, its comfortable homes, fires, and beds, and re-enter the relentless routine of the Army again, and sleep on a wire bunk in a smoky hut, or the draughty barn of a squalid French village, or, worse still, renew acquaintance with the mud and horrors of the line. One member who was never suspected of being chicken-hearted, noted in his diary on the day of his return, that he was "broken-hearted."

Early in December, Second-Lieutenants W. B. Davies and W. Elliott joined the Company from cadet battalions where they had been granted commissions. They were nominees from the 6th and 4th Light Horse Regiments respectively. During the stay at Locre, one officer (Lieutenant Wright) and 19 other ranks were evacuated sick. "Sick," in the Army sense, included any ailment or injury which required medical attention away from the unit. In the present instance, eye trouble, ear trouble, swollen hand, helped to swell the list. Usually evacuations were much more numerous when "resting"; in active operations they fell away to a minimum. Lieutenant Wright returned to duty on 3rd December.

Voting in connection with the submission of the second Conscription Referendum was attended to on the 12th December, but it does not appear to have evoked the interest attaching to the first, over a year before.

An inter-divisional "change over" between the 2nd and 3rd Australian Divisions brought the Company's stay at Locre to an end on the 15th December, when it left Pasteur Camp and marched to Penzance Lines, near Neuve Eglise, and became the "reserve" company of the Division. The camp was a small one, somewhat isolated from the others. Strange to relate, the fuel supplies were actually sufficient, and when straw mattresses were issued, the camp was, in the Army sense of the word, "comfortable." At the outset, orders indicated that the duties of the reserve brigade were to "lay out and form the Corps line of defence"; a proceeding considered necessary owing to the defection of Russia from the Allied cause, and the consequent release of the German Armies on that frontier for action on the Western Front. Meanwhile, Company training was resumed, and preparations made for spending the third Christmas away from Australia. In vastly more comfortable circumstances than the preceding year, when the festive season was spent in the line near Le Transloy, more elaborate and fitting arrangements were possible. The day was decreed a holiday, and after the morning church parade, all hands took a share in the dinner preparations. The cooks—to mark the occasion—roasted the meat, and with an "issue" of plum pudding, the basis existed for a good meal. Gun-teams, and in some instances, Sections, clubbed together in the purchase of "extras," and the resultant feast was counted worthy by all hands. Even the rum issue was promoted on the occasion for a special function, when it was poured over the puddings and ignited. The timely arrival of "home" parcels and mail added the finishing touches.

Two days after Christmas, the Company commenced its contribution to the Corps line of Defence. After preliminary surveys by Captain Rae and Company officers, followed by inspection by the G.S.O.2, the Divisional Machine Gun Officer and Brigade Major, four four-gun battery positions were prepared at Hasted House, Dead Cow Farm, Fusilier Farm, and Le Bizet, on the northern outskirts of Ploegsteert Wood. In addition to the gun positions, splinter-proof quarters for 20 men were constructed at each battery position. Both were duly camouflaged. A further precaution was taken when alternative defensive positions in rear were selected and marked on prepared maps, which were handed over to the relieving unit when the Company afterwards left the area to enter the line. Some speculation was indulged in as to whether the Company was likely to use the positions in the event of a German thrust in that quarter. It so happened that the Germans did overrun the deliberately planned defensive zone a few days after the Division had left for the Somme area.

The Corps Line work having been completed, part of the afternoons were devoted to salvage work. Among the material gathered were rails, and a large quantity of artillery ammunition and equipment, including cordite charges. Nearly every man succeeded in storing away a few of the latter, and the subsequent nights were devoted to a series of glorious rat hunts, the charges being dropped into likely holes—to the consternation and rapid departure of the inmates. Corporal Wigmore eclipsed all other efforts by climbing on to the top of a Nissen hut and dropping a charge down the pipe which served as a chimney. A very hurried evacuation was made by the occupants —human in this case—fortunately without damage.

While at Neuve Eglise, a number of changes relating to personnel took place. About mid-December, Sergeant A. G. Stevens and Private G. E. Gamble (Company artificer) were successful in their applications for entry to the Flying Corps, and departed to qualify in England. The latter duly qualified, and after service in France as a flying officer, returned to Australia. Sergeant Stevens also was successful, but shortly after qualifying, an order was issued debarring those who had enlisted in 1915 from going to France. Instead, he received an appointment in England until the Armistice. Later in the month, Sergeant G. E. Rennie left to enter an officer cadet battalion in England, while Sergeant A. Payton and Corporal S. A. Greaves departed for a period of duty at the machine-gun base at Grantham, in England. Second-Lieutenant G. A. Jeffery returned from England, where he received his commission, and with him was Second-Lieutenant T. F. Turnbull, who had passed a similar course. The latter was a nominee of the 2nd Australian Casualty Clearing Station. Early in January, Lieutenant F. J. Nixon returned after a quick recovery from severe wounds received on Broodseinde Ridge in the previous October. Another to depart in January was Lieutenant Hitchcock, who left to report at A.I.F. Headquarters in London. Shortly before, the Army authorities called for volunteers for special duty, and those interested were certainly not led astray by false hopes. With others, Hitchcock was informed by the acting Brigadier that they would probably be called on for service in some foreign and distant land, might be in tight corners, possibly be hard pressed for food at times, and with only a forlorn hope of coming out alive. A week was given for reflection, and at the expiration of that time, Hitchcock decided on the venture. Thus it was he became a member of that small but highly efficient body known as the "Dunster Force." He survived the peculiar perils of that arduous campaign in Persia and Mesopotamia and afterwards returned to Australia.

Wintry conditions prevailed at this time, although not nearly so severe as a year previous. In the first week in January, records indicated: "Weather clear and cold"; "heavy snowstorm, approximately three inches"; "thaw commences." The casualty reports at Neuve Eglise showed eight other ranks evacuated "sick."

Before the end of the old year, a welcome innovation appeared in the shape of Paris leave. It is true the issue was a limited one, but none the less welcome. It opened another avenue of exploration and adventure, and much interest centred around the first leave-goers; to be intensified when they returned with tales of wonderful experiences. It need only be said in passing that the Australian was as much an irrepressible Australian in Paris as in London, or any other place; to the wonderment, and oftimes delight, of the residents. A full account of the adventures of one pair of Company members has been recorded in Chapter VII.

After 29 days at Penzance Lines, the Company, on 13th January, exchanged places with the 7th Machine Gun Company, which had been holding positions in the left Brigade front in the right divisional area of the First Anzac Corps. The 6th Brigade also entered the same sector. The location was about one and a half miles south-east of Messines, and opposite the large German-held village of Warneton. No actual front line positions were occupied, but fourteen guns were distributed "in depth" in the brigade area which extended over 1,750 yards of the low-lying ground at the confluence of the Rivers Lys and La Douve, the latter forming the northern boundary. The Company's dispositions were:— Forward Group (5 guns), Left Group (4), and Rear Group (5). A heavy snowstorm on the day following the Company's entry, and subsequent violent storms and heavy rain, converted the Douve from a mere trickle in summer to a stream 60 yards wide and consequent flooding of the locality. The trenches held 18 inches of water in places, and constant bailing was necessary to keep some dugouts dry. The familiar gum-boots of the previous winter were again brought into use, and were a necessity in the circumstances. Another necessity in that sodden area were "T" frames to ensure a stable mounting for the guns, especially those used in indirect fire. Enemy artillery fire was not particularly heavy, but the forward sector received a good deal of persistent minenwerfer fire and enemy machine-guns were equally attentive to approaches, and a light railway line used by the ration parties. Private A. V. Caldwell has recorded the effect of a large "minnie" shell which fell in a "bay" adjacent to his gun. One box of S.A.A. was demolished, while two were blown on to the parados and their wooden cases stripped, but otherwise undamaged. The trenches were overrun with rats, one member noting: "Rats in millions, and as large as cats." In accordance with the usual custom, the guns were manned by four men, while the remainder of the Company were located in Lark Camp. The Nissen huts occupied were in good order, and duck-boards helped to make the muddy conditions bearable. The men in camp were utilised in carrying forward ammunition and rations, as well as the general company fatigues.

The teams in the line at once commenced indirect fire by night, about 7,000 rounds being an average programme. Some of the teams had to be detailed for repair work owing to parapets collapsing as a result of wet weather, while much pumping was necessary to keep dugouts reasonably dry. A good deal of compass variation was noticed, due, doubtless, to the presence of large quantities of iron in the vicinity.

One evening, Lieutenant-Colonel Brazenor, commanding the 23rd Battalion, sent for Lieutenant Turnbull, and complained that bullets from the indirect-fire guns were falling short and harassing his men in the front trenches. A perusal of maps, fire charts, and an inspection of gun positions, guns and gear, only confirmed the confident feeling that the Company was not at fault. Nevertheless the same thing happened the following night while the Colonel and Turnbull were in the front line. It was a perplexing and disturbing business. On the third night, in an endeavour to locate the trouble, the suspected guns were fired according to a pre-arranged time table. At a time when none of the Company's guns were firing, a couple of bursts fell in practically the same locality. A search was then made, and revealed what Turnbull had, by that time, suspected, viz., that an enterprising Lewis gunner was the culprit. With a "borrowed" clinometer and improvised elevation and aiming sticks (?), he had been conducting a private hate, with the disturbing results described.

After a week in the line, the teams at Lark Camp changed places with their mates on the guns. The daily routine and nightly firing continued without unusual incident, except for the wounding of Private H. Jefferson, on the 28th January; the only casualty during the period in the line. After the snow and violent storms of the first few days, the weather improved somewhat. During this tour of duty, three other ranks were recorded "sick," and evacuated. On the 18th January, Second Lieutenant N. F. Wilkinson joined the Company from a cadet battalion in England, to which he had been nominated by the 2nd Australian Casualty Clearing Station.

A divisional relief on the 27th January, the 3rd relieving the 2nd, brought the 14 days' tour at Warneton to a close, the 10th Machine Gun Company relieving the Company. The formalities were completed shortly after 5 p.m., and the outgoing teams were very pleased when the limbers of the Transport Section met them at Hyde Park Corner and conveyed their guns and gear to Kent Camp, to which location, headquarters and the men at Lark Camp had moved in the morning. The entry to the new quarters was enlivened by a heated argument which arose between Private "Boss" Smith and an officer of another unit. The latter disputed the right of "Boss" and the Quartermaster Sergeant's staff to occupy a certain hut. As a wordy argument proceeded, "Boss" continued to place articles in the hut as the officer tossed them out. Growing exasperated, the officer declared: "I will bring you before my Colonel." "I don't care a hoot for your b—— Colonel," said "Boss." "He is not a b—— Colonel," countered the officer. "Then let me shake hands with you for having the only one in the Army who is not," responded "Boss." Such an adroit move fully quenched the high temperatures, and the matter was settled with "Boss" in possession and his reputation for never losing an argument quite untarnished.

Kent Camp was one and a half miles from Neuve Eglise, and three days were spent there, cleaning guns and gear, as well as a personal shedding of the mud and slush of the trenches. At this time, Company Sergeant-Major H. L. Wilhelm left to enter an officer cadet battalion in England. After some time spent in hospital, he completed the course, and received his commission as an infantry officer after the Armistice. Sergeant J. N. Myers was promoted to the vacant position, and became the Company's fifth Sergeant-Major.

On the 30th January, the 8th Machine Gun Company arrived at Kent Camp, and the Company moved out on its western journey, entrained at Drekenbek at 7 p.m., and detraining at Lottinghem shortly after midnight. The moon shone brilliantly during the 2½-hour march to billets at Watterdal, but the tired men's spirits were not improved by the peculiar Army methods which, on this occasion, required detrainment at a point five miles beyond the nearest station and necessitated a return journey over a road which contained at least two very steep hills. The Transport Section journeyed by road, and after spending three nights en route—at Strazeele, Renescure, and Lumbres—reported on the 1st February.

Watterdal was in the Lottinghem brigade sub-area, and no great distance from Boulogne on the coast. It was one of the poorest places in which the Company was ever quartered in France. Located off traffic routes, it was a veritable "sleepy hollow." Some of the inhabitants had never seen a train, and the patois of the children was so broad that the school teacher had some difficulty in understanding them. Nevertheless, the villagers were very kind, and did what they could to make the men comfortable. Among other things, they placed the local schoolroom at their disposal for reading and writing at night. Billeting regulations were relaxed somewhat, and some men were enabled to arrange for living quarters in civilian houses, and thus avoid the draughty barns which, in winter, were about the most cheerless places imaginable. The officers were well provided for in civilians' houses. Lieutenant N. F. Wilkinson has recorded how he and Lieutenant W. Elliott lived in comparative luxury with a single room each, and morning coffee served by a sweet French maid, whose parents saw that she attended to all the comforts of the bon Australian officers. "On returning one evening," continued the narrator, "I was greeted by the whole family in the kitchen with a half barrel in the middle of the floor and a cauldron of water on the stove, nice and hot. This water was straightaway put into the barrel, and I was informed that a nice hot bath was ready for me. I tendered my thanks, and prepared for the bath. On returning to the kitchen, I found the same family party still quartered round the stove. They made no move and I, embarrassed from head to foot, had to go through it, so hopped in. It was the first time I dressed myself after a bath, in the bath."

Company training was varied and comprehensive. It included squad drill, rifle exercises, musketry practice on a short range, gun and barrage drill, rectification of mechanical stoppages, mechanism, revolver practice, gas drill, map reading, and physical training. Three afternoons a week were devoted to "recreational training," in which football matches (Australian game) claimed a large share. Intersectional contests preserved the internal rivalry, but when a combined team met other units, the "family" spirit was predominant. In the latter games, defeat was suffered at the hands of the 6th Field Ambulance. On the other hand, the Company team emerged victorious when it tried conclusions with the 2nd Division headquarters, and the 2nd Australian General Hospital. To meet the last-named, Lieutenants Turnbull and Wilkinson took a good team to Boulogne, but as the opposing side was very weak, the game was concluded at an early stage and the players spent an hour or two in the town.

Winning Team (Tug-o-War), 6th Brigade Sports, Locre, 8th December, 1917.

In spite of the distractions of an undamaged centre, all hands were at the rendezvous on time, and a very merry party returned together. Limited Paris leave continued. Another welcome diversion was leave to visit Boulogne on the coast, motor lorries being provided for transport. A further much appreciated innovation was the advent of a Company canteen, which functioned under the direction of Lieutenant Wilkinson, assisted by Private W. Blackman. The capital was provided by a per capita contribution from all members, and the profits earned were held for the purpose of re-opening the canteen at a future date. On the 1st March, the Brigade held a horse show at Lottinghem, at which the Company secured two first places in the prize list. Lieutenant Newcomen won the bare-back Mule Steeplechase, while the Company's best turned out pair of pack horses secured the judges' verdict.

During the stay at Watterdal, further changes in the Company's personnel took place. On the 3rd February, Corporal R. H. E. Dixon proceeded to a signalling school in England for a tour of duty. Two days later, Lieutenants Blenkarn and Hopper rejoined after recovering from wounds received in the Ypres fighting. On the 9th, the whole Company was pleased when Captain Drummond returned from a period of duty at the machine-gun depot at Grantham, and resumed command of the Company. Early in March, Lieutenant F. L. Wright left to take up duty at the machine-gun base at Grantham, and was so engaged at the Armistice. The weather on the whole was fairly good for winter time; a vast improvement on the previous February when the country was veritably frozen for four weeks. In spite of the winter conditions, the 34 days at Watterdal, in the circumstances, passed happily. 14 men were evacuated "sick," but the remainder were rested and refreshed as a result of their sojourn.

On the 5th March, the Company reluctantly said farewell to the friendly villagers of Watterdal, and rose at 3 a.m. on the following morning in order to make an early start. Three-quarters of an hour later it moved out of billets and marched to Lottinghem, where entrainment was made at 7.30 a.m. After a slow journey lasting nearly four hours, Steenwerck was reached, whence march was made to Bulford Camp. It was a beautiful day, and the tedium of the journey was relieved at Steenwerck when a thrilling air duel was witnessed, about eight aeroplanes being engaged. Ultimately the enemy planes were chased back over their lines, and one was forced down. As before, the Transport Section journeyed by road, staying the three nights en route at Elnes, Renescure, and Strazeele.

In accordance with the relief of the 3rd Division in the Corps right divisional front, the 6th Brigade relieved the 9th in the same area it had previously occupied in the line on the 7th March. The Company relieved the 9th Company, and found itself in its former positions. Half the gun-team strength went to the gun positions, while the remainder of the Company—after two nights at Bulford Camp—moved to Lark Camp. The "change over" was effected without mishap during a very quiet night. During the latter days of the 3rd Division's occupancy it had not—owing to inclement weather—been able to do much repair work, and the night before the Company's entry, a "thaw" set in, with the result that the trenches were partly choked by masses of previously frozen earth which had collapsed. The first night was particularly uncomfortable and dismal. However, the whole 16 guns were disposed in three Groups, and after a night spent in repair work and erecting fire screens, the nightly indirect fire was resumed. The forward positions were again troubled with minenwerfer shells, and in an endeavour to curb their throwers, some of the guns fired in conjunction with the artillery according to a pre-arranged scheme by which fire could be directed on a given spot when the harassed infantry or gunners indicated that they required retaliation. The scheme was based on the known minenwerfer emplacements in and near Warneton, and the various locations were distinguished by the allotment to them of girls' names. Thus a request would come from an infantry battalion in the line to "tickle Mary," or some such name, "which was done with pleasure," noted Captain Rae. Occasionally Company guns fired, inadvertently, ammunition containing "tracer" bullets, designed for use against aeroplanes —with some interest to the teams concerned. The interest, however, was changed to apprehension when watchful enemy observers directed artillery fire against one gun position concerned. The shooting was accurate enough to cause the team to vacate its position for some time.

Two days after entering the line, Corporals J. P. Adam and W. Carrick rejoined the Company from the machine-gun base at Grantham, where they had been engaged in instructional work during the preceding nine months.

At this time, a purely "family affair" gave rise to much interest and amusement. Indeed, for the moment, it assumed major importance, being no less than the appearance of the Company cook in the line as a fighter. It all happened over a little matter of rice. Just then rice was "on issue," but just "plain boiled" it was not welcomed as a "dish," and much of the resultant dissatisfaction was directed at the cook who had to stand a lot of good-natured but very pointed abuse. Protests directed to the Company Sergeant-Major by the cook were of no avail; he insisted on Bill doing his duty. For the time it remained at that, but matters came to a head one afternoon after Bill returned from a friendly call on an old friend, Quartermaster Sergeant Smith, of the 22nd Machine Gun Company. The guest was well treated, and when the time for departure arrived, a kindly driver of the Transport Section saw to his safe return. All went well till the party arrived at the Company's billets, where a lot of interested spectators gathered and tendered many pleasantries to the occupant of the limber as he sat therein, feet dangling over the tail-board, the picture of happy confidence. Unfortunately, the appearance of the Sergeant-Major introduced a different note. Memories of rice! Strained relations! Definite orders! The happy cook seized the opportunity to address his superior officer—beginning with a sweeping gesture—"Look at him, look at him, the b—— rice king," followed by a string of jests. The bystanders were delighted. The Sergeant-Major's response came next day when Bill was detailed for "the line." By a strange and remarkable coincidence, the delinquent found himself allocated to a gun-team composed mainly of total abstainers, with the result that he was able to lawfully appropriate almost the whole of the team's rum issue. In the circumstances, the return from the line was awaited with much interest. The spectators were not disappointed. Displaying an unsuspected sense of the dramatic, Bill rose to the occasion. Striking himself on the chest, with great gusto he declared to all and sundry: "Ha! ha! you b—— cold-footers. Here's me, Bill Wormald, Daylight Sap Gallipoli, Plugstreet Wood. How's that for a dinkum soldier?" and proceeded to detail how his "holiday" was spent with appropriate emphasis as to the rum issue.

Meanwhile, the long-expected German thrust against the Western Front was taking shape. Allusion has already been made to the construction of a Corps Line of Defence. As far as the machine-gun preparations in it were concerned, they were completed in good time, likewise those in the front area of the Division. The 2nd Machine Gun Battalion, embracing the four companies in the 2nd Division—to which an extended reference appears in the following chapter—came into being in mid-March, and co-ordinated the machine-gun defence of the Division. S.O.S. barrage lines were arranged to be put down on the S.O.S. signal being observed, or at any time when an unusual amount of rifle fire was heard in the barrage area. Flank defence was provided for and maps and fire charts were prepared for alternative gun and battery positions already chosen. Ample ammunition was on hand, all belts were filled and carefully scrutinised, and there seemed little or nothing else that could be provided for. Among the men, a feeling of quiet confidence prevailed should the enemy attack in their sector. "I hope the b—— has a go here," was an expression heard at this time. "You keep her shooting, Vic., I'll fill the belts for you," Private B. Caligari was wont to say to Lance Corporal A. V. Caldwell. "We used to clean the gun after each nightly shooting," said Caldwell, "as if it were a new born babe." As the days wore on, the feeling became tenser, and the expression often heard was: "If the b—— is coming, I hope he attacks to-night." Meanwhile the enemy became more active daily, his shelling increased in intensity, and much mustard gas was used. On the night of the 21st March, about 3,000 gas shells fell, mainly on the 24th Battalion in support at Prowse Point, causing 178 evacuations but without loss in the Company. The following night, the frontage of the 21st Battalion in the line was raided, the enemy suffering some loss, but succeeding in taking a few prisoners. During the accompanying bombardment, Private E. Phillips was wounded in the head by a shell splinter while doing a lone watch on his gun. After rousing his mates, he lapsed into unconsciousness, from which he recovered in St. Alban's Military Hospital in England. Afterwards he was invalided to Australia and discharged.

Although the Company escaped loss in the heavy gas bombardment, it did not come through the tour of duty scathless. Evacuations due to gas were: Corporal H. L. Heyne (27th), Privates C. W. Lewis and T. Hartley (29th), J. Ford (2nd April). Other casualties were: Private W. Flintham, killed in action (17th March); wounded: Privates A. E. Yates (9th), T. Dolan (17th), and G. R. Turner (22nd). Private W. Flintham was a member of a gun-team with Lance Corporal F. L. Fitzpatrick, T. Dolan, and T. Healey. They went in on the 16th March. It was a very wet spot, and after spending the night dodging minenwerfer shells, the party had taken off their socks and putties and were drying them over their primus stove. While

THE WINTER OF 1917-8.

so doing, a 4.2 shell burst among them. Flintham—known as "Bluey"—was killed in the act of lighting a cigarette, and Dolan was wounded in thigh and left arm. The gun was damaged, but the other two escaped injury. Flintham had a strong premonition of his approaching end and, with tears in his eyes, informed his mates, who did their best to cheer him. Dolan, remarking that "surely nothing would happen to four Irishmen going into the line for St. Patrick's Day." During the tour of line duty, one officer and seven other ranks were evacuated "sick." The former was Lieutenant Nixon who, while playing football, re-opened an abdominal wound received on Broodseinde Ridge. After prolonged hospital treatment, he was returned to Australia and discharged. Another change in Company strength was the return of Second Lieutenant M. J. O'Brien from a cadet battalion in England, where he had obtained his commission. Nearly two years had elapsed since he had been evacuated—as a Lance Corporal—owing to wounds received in the 6th Brigade's raid at Bois Grenier. After recovering from his injuries, he had been allotted to duty in England, where he was nominated for a commission.

The 27 days at Warneton came to an end on the 2nd April, when the Company was relieved by "C" Company of the 25th Machine Gun Battalion of the 25th Division. The "change over" was part of the plan of relief of the 2nd Australian Division by the 19th and 25th Divisions of the British Army. By 9.30 p.m. the Company had finally quitted its position. The 25th Division had formed part of General Gough's Army in the south, where the great German blow had fallen, and it bore many evidences of its experiences in that encounter. The teams which came in to relieve the Company described themselves as "part of General Gough's Army re-constructed." They appeared to be composed mainly of recent and inexperienced drafts, very young, mere boys they seemed—and as some members said, "in a blue funk." Serious shortages existed in their gear, necessitating hurried arrangements being made by which part of the Company's guns, gear, and ammunition were handed over to the incoming teams. On leaving the area that was well-known and which they had helped to prepare for attack, the members of the Company were very depressed by the condition of the new arrivals. "God help them if Fritz attacks here," said more than one sympathetic commentator. Although it was not known, of course, at that time, the Company was finally quitting the northern area of the line in France to which it had journeyed on three occasions, and wherein it had spent much strenuous effort and given freely of its best members. The departure found the air full of rumours as to the state of affairs "down south" where, it was agreed, German attacks had made considerable progress and where, in fact, a critical condition existed. The stability of the Western Front was indeed trembling in the balance. But while members felt they were in for an exciting time, no thought of panic was entertained. The writer has searched the notes and records of this time, but without discovering a single pessimistic note. Maybe hard fighting lay ahead, and it might fall to their lot to retake well—or badly—remembered places and villages, but no question of their ability to do so was entertained. No doubt the possibility of leaving trench warfare behind and the prospect of something like open fighting was an incentive, but it is significant that at this time there was a marked quickening of interest and a general improvement in morale and outlook.

CHAPTER XIX.

FORMATION OF THE 2ND MACHINE GUN BATTALION

1st March, 1918.

When the Company was in the line at Warneton, an important variation was made in respect to the organisation of machine-gun companies in the A.I.F. The change brought the A.I.F. in line with the British Army, and as it marked the final development in the organisation and tactical control of the Vickers gun in the war and affected the Company in no small degree, an extended reference has been considered necessary.

A General Staff Circular from Australian Corps headquarters dated the 11th March, announced the scheme, as a part of which the four machine-gun companies in each division were to be amalgamated as a machine-gun battalion as divisional troops, and to function as such. By an odd coincidence, the new unit of the 2nd Division was deemed to have commenced its official existence on the 1st March, which was the official date of the Company's advent, two years before.

In accordance with the order, the 5th, 6th, 7th, and 22nd Companies were amalgamated to form the 2nd Machine Gun Battalion, and the new unit was allotted as its distinguishing colour patch, a black diamond with a yellow diamond inset, and the former yellow crossed guns below it. The General Staff Circular set out the Establishment, and directed that the officer commanding would be responsible, under the divisional commander, for discipline, administration, and training of the troops under his charge. Another provision was the increase in the Company Establishment from 175 other ranks to 205, and a reduction in horses from 54 to 51. The new Battalion commenced to function at Tahuna Camp on the 17th March. The previous day, 2nd Divisional headquarters announced the formation of the new unit, with certain provisional appointments for the headquarters staff. Lieutenant-Colonel A. W. Ralston,

C.M.G., D.S.O., late 20th Battalion, was appointed to command, with Major L. F. S. Hore, M.C., as second in command. The new C.O. was directed to at once take over the administration of the 22nd Company, and to arrange direct with Brigades as to taking over the other Companies in the Division.

The personnel of the Battalion headquarters staff was composed by calling on that of the Companies. The Company's quota was Lieutenant H. deB. Newcomen, transferred to become Battalion Transport Officer; Company Sergeant Major J. N. Myers, to become Regimental Sergeant Major; Quartermaster Sergeant R. W. Watt, to become Regimental Quartermaster Sergeant; and Corporal R. Dixon, to be Battalion Signalling Sergeant. The new Company establishment provided for eight privates per gun—exclusive of range-takers and scouts—with the intimation that sufficient men had been allowed for the manning of each gun and its ammunition supply, and that "the attachment of infantry to machine-gun companies as carrying parties is now no longer necessary, and will be discontinued." To complete the new provision, 26 men who had been "attached" from infantry battalions of the Brigade during and since the Ypres fighting of the previous autumn were taken on strength, as well as 17 other ranks from the same source.

The General Staff Circular was followed by a further one on the 20th April, which set out the "principles governing the employment of the machine-gun battalion." The important provisions were:—

(1) Mobile Warfare:
    Such units (Companies, half-companies) as are considered necessary will be placed under the command of the Infantry Brigadiers, who will be entirely responsible for their tactical employment.
    The Brigadier may allot sections or half-sections to Battalions if he considers it desirable.
    The remaining units of the machine-gun battalion will be kept in the hands of the divisional commander for special tasks.

(2) Trench Warfare:
    (a) In attack—
    Certain units may be allotted to Brigadiers as mobile guns to take part in or follow up the attack. The remainder will be under the command of the C.O. machine-gun battalion, who will employ them in accordance with

orders received from the divisional commander.

(b) Defence—

The machine-gun battalion commander will discuss with G.O.'sC. brigades in the line, their requirements for machine-gun defence and will submit proposals to the divisional commander as regard the number of guns required in each brigade sector. The necessary units will be allotted to each brigade and the brigade commanders will be responsible for tactical employment except that changes in disposition will be discussed with the machine gun battalion commander and referred to the divisional commander for approval before being carried out. The machine-gun battalion commander will supervise the work of his companies, and will act as advisor to the brigade commanders as well as to the divisional commander for their tactical employment.

Such units as are not allotted to brigade sectors will be kept under the command of the C.O. machine-gun battalion, who will dispose of them in accordance with orders of the divisional commander.

The machine-gun battalion commander will be responsible for the reliefs of all machine-gun units.

The completion of the new arrangements naturally took some time, and was somewhat hampered by the Division's line activities and the subsequent move to the Somme. However, as the weeks passed, the new unit settled down to itself, and its capacity to function. As it did so, certain advantages and disadvantages revealed themselves. The position from a divisional point of view was doubtless an improvement. The direct connection with the companies kept the divisional commander well informed, and placed him in a better controlling position as regards the companies, and enabled the divisional area to be treated—from a machine-gun point of view—as a tactical whole. In the process, the work and responsibility of the four companies was evened up, especially as regards the 22nd Company which, having no parent brigade, was in the nature of an odd number. These advantages became apparent in trench warfare, and when the Division was out of the line, although even in the former case, it was deemed necessary to modify the new arrangements as between companies and brigades. During the last stage of trench warfare—in the following June—the guns in the line were "grouped" under two "group" commanders, and a close liason arranged with the two brigades in the line.

On the other hand, during offensives and open warfare movements, it was necessary to continue the old method of attaching half and full sections to assaulting infantry units, and at that point, control by battalion vanished. The circumstances inevitably contributed to detachment. Before action, the Brigadier formulated his plans, incorporating his machine-gun attachments after consultation with the machine-gun commander or representative, and then in action—in which the situation often changed from hour to hour—direction had, perforce, to come from the infantry commander on the spot.

From a Company point of view, the change was unwelcome, and continued so. No doubt a natural conservatism had much to do with the Company outlook. It had—doubtless true in the case of the other brigade companies—grown up as an intimate unit of the parent brigade, and had been cared for by the Brigadier as "his" company. Both parties knew where they stood, and Company officers and men knew many of the officers and men in the infantry battalions, a factor which made for speedy and friendly working. Now, personal and long-standing connection was to be changed, and the Company was to go out in the wilderness, as it were, and be left to the mercy of a comparatively unknown Colonel and less sympathetic division headquarters. The Company did, of course, work with other brigades of the division, but the relative strangeness of both parties did not make for smooth working. The Battalion arrangement brought the machine-gunners of the Division into close contact, but at the expense of considerable intimacy with the infantry. Further, it was liable to, and in fact did, bring officers from their own companies over to other companies as O.C.'s, and, though it subsequently proved workable, the idea was objectionable. The esprit de corps towards the Company and Brigade also stood in the way of the new organisation. Some criticism was raised against the extra personnel (73) required for Battalion headquarters at a time when the shortage of man power had become a pressing problem.

A further and more personal grievance was the advent of the new Battalion colour patch. Among the newer men it did not raise any objection because they had not grown up with the Company traditions, but to the older ones it became a very sore point. In giving up something to which they were greatly attached, it emphasised the fear of loss of the Company's identity. Stubborn opposition was displayed. As late as July, some members were still wearing the red diamond, while others compromised by displaying both old and new patches. In the end, the erring ones had to be specifically and individually ordered to fall into line. Thus the red diamond, at first itself an unwelcome stranger and later a cherished emblem for two years, was given up very grudgingly for a new and unwelcome design. It is significant that members, ever after, almost invariably gave their unit by its Company designation, rather than by its battalion classification.

A table is appended which shows the various increases in the machine gun strength of the 2nd Division.

Table showing increases in Vickers Machine Gun strength of 2nd Division.

Date	Composition.		Commanded by
1915—	5th Brigade	8 guns	Section Officer
	6th Brigade	8 guns	(Lieutenant) under
	7th Brigade	8 guns	C.O. Battalion.
	(2 guns per Battalion)	24 guns	
1916—			
March 1	5th Machine Gun Co.	16 guns	Company Com-
	6th Machine Gun Co.	16 guns	mander (Major or
	7th Machine Gun Co.	16 guns	Captain) under
		48 guns	G.O.C. Brigade.
1917—			
March 1	5th Machine Gun Co.	16 guns	Company Com-
	6th Machine Gun Co.	16 guns	mander (Major or
	7th Machine Gun Co.	16 guns	Captain) under
	22nd Machine Gun Co.	16 guns	G.O.C. Brigade.
		64 guns	
1918—			
March 1	2nd Machine Gun Batt.	64 guns	Battalion Commander (Lieutenant-Colonel) under G.O.C. Division.

CHAPTER XX.

THE FINAL MOVE TO THE SOMME.

2nd April—10th May, 1918.

The day following the relief at Warneton, the Company left Lark Camp in the early afternoon and marched to Bulford Camp whence motor buses carried the personnel to Rouge Croix, where the night was spent. Next morning (4th April) march was made to Strazeele, where entrainment was effected at 5.30 p.m. Travelling through the night in the apparently haphazard fashion prevailing on the French railways, Hangest-sur-Somme was reached at 5 a.m. on the 5th. An eight hour march brought the Company to St. Sauveur in the early afternoon, and billets were found for the night. The original members recalled that it was at the self-same village in which they were quartered when on their way to Pozieres nearly two years before. Although the railway journey was of the usually tedious character, it did not appear so tiresome because of the prevailing excitement and the large number of "furphies" (rumours) passing from mouth to mouth. Truth to tell, there were many outward and visible signs of an unstable "front." Hitherto, Amiens had been well outside the war zone, and as it had retained a large proportion of its citizens and functioned as in peace time, it was a favourite rendezvous for troops in the district. Australians had specially favoured it. But now the blighting hand of war was very much in evidence. Tram lines had been torn up, and much damage had been done to the houses. It was well-nigh deserted, but a few plucky souls insisted on remaining in spite of the enemy shelling and bombing at night. Some of the adjacent villages, Ailly-sur-Somme in particular, seemed full of French refugees from the lately vacated countryside, the villagers having fled before the retreating British Army. Such was the state of affairs when the valley of the Somme was reached.

When the Company arrived at St. Sauveur—still under

THE FINAL MOVE TO THE SOMME.

Brigade orders—it expected to have a night of undisturbed rest, but at 8 p.m. orders arrived directing an early start in the following morning (6th April). Reveille was consequently fixed at 5.30 a.m. After breakfast, half of the gun team strength were carried away in motor trucks, in battle order, and carrying their guns and gear with them. Passing through pathetic looking Amiens, they were transported to the village of Baizeaux, where the transports left them, and where they rested till evening. Meanwhile the remainder of the Company had moved to Allonville. What a change, thought the forward teams. Close at hand was the well-remembered village of Warloy, where, nearly a year before, they had come back to "rest," and Albert itself was in enemy hands, likewise dearly-won Pozieres and the ridge beyond. In spite of it all, no pessimistic note has been found in diaries or notes relating to this time. As soon as darkness fell, the teams moved forward through Lavieville and relieved the 24th Machine Gun Company in the line, while the 6th Brigade relieved the 12th as part of the relief of the 4th Australian Division by the 2nd. The "change over" took place in miserable circumstances, the night was dark, and rain fell incessantly. The line consisted of hastily constructed trenches without duckboards or revetting. The 12th Australian Brigade was on the right and the 12th (British) Division on the left, but little was known of enemy dispositions. On the morning of the previous day (5th) the 4th Division had—in magnificent fashion—held at bay heavy attacks by four German divisions. Apparently all the fight had been taken out of the enemy, for the two succeeding nights were very quiet, and the relief of the hard-pressed 4th Division was not disturbed by attacks. When morning dawned, the familiar town of Albert was in front, with its conspicuous basilisk tower and leaning statue of the Virgin and Child. Continued rain made the new trenches very muddy and uncomfortable. Fourteen guns were established astride the Amiens-Albert road, in front of Lavieville. Two guns were kept in reserve at Company headquarters in Lavieville. The distribution was "in depth," as usual. On the first day in the line, an enemy shell demolished the building housing Company headquarters, wounding Captain Drummond (in the leg) and Privates J. Watson and T. Hartley. Watson succumbed to his wounds soon after. Both men were engaged as cooks at the time. Captain Rae (who was at rear Company headquarters and expecting a spell from line work) again assumed command of the Company.

To establish touch with the enemy on the Brigade front, the

22nd Battalion pushed out fighting patrols at night, and advanced their line, but while the gun-teams were on the alert, they were not called on for action. During the next few days, the forward guns fired on the junction of the Amiens Road at a point where it crossed the railway on the outskirts of Albert, where small enemy parties were observed. The weather continued, as it usually did in April, very changeable; a fine day breaking a sequence of bleak, windy days and occasional rain. Enemy shelling was heavy at times, but it fell mainly on the back areas. The forward positions were swept occasionally by machine-gun fire, and during one gust Lance Corporal J. N. Spittle was wounded on the night of 9-10th April.

After four days in the line, the teams were relieved by their mates, who had moved up with the Company from Allonville to Montigny. Meanwhile, consolidation of the new line proceeded, and the Company did its share by improving its gun positions and by the construction of dug-outs. The latter called for much labour. The heavy frames were constructed of stout timber and covered with galvanised iron by the Engineers and Pioneers, and were sufficiently large to accommodate five men. When complete, they were brought as close as possible to the line on G.S. waggons, and then carried shoulder high to the positions by eight men. After a deep excavation had been made in the fore part of the trench, they were emplaced therein and covered with earth. The job had, perforce, to be completed between dusk and dawn, so stout-hearted toil was necessary, but willing hands saw to their installation. They were said to be 4.2 proof, although doubts were raised. It is recorded, however, that on the night following the installation of one occupied by Lieutenant Turnbull, it sustained a direct hit by a shell of unknown calibre, while he was absent on his rounds. Although the occupants were rather stupified by the burst, they escaped injury; so the efficiency of the cover was held to be proved. While the work on dug-outs absorbed a good deal of the energy of the personnel, indirect fire on a reduced scale was maintained at night. At this time, the Army authorities were apprehensive of further attacks by the enemy, and sent repeated warnings to the line units. About this time, Captain Rae was mentioned in despatches for his capable direction of the Company during the absences of Captain Drummond.

On the 15th April occurred an unfortunate incident which, while it was derisively styled the "battle of the bath," resulted in eight men being evacuated, beside minor injuries to others;

THE FINAL MOVE TO THE SOMME.

at least three of the former being serious. In an old French chateau near Montigny, a bath for Army purposes had been installed. The upper floor was used as a changing room and contained a 200 gallon tank, while immediately below, on a concrete floor, was the wash room with the usual array of "jam tin showers." While about 25 men were disrobing in the upper room, the floor collapsed and precipitated them on to the concrete, the tank with them. During the subsequent confusion, the tank was emptied among the victims. Those evacuated were: Corporal H. G. Black, Lance Corporal A. V. Caldwell, Privates E. J. Burtonclay, G. Malcolm, A. E. Nicholson, C. J. Warner, W. Greening, and J. R. Palmer. The worst injuries were sustained by Black, broken pelvis; Burtonclay, bent spine, which left permanent effects; and Malcolm, who lost the sight of one eye. The two first mentioned were returned to Australia and discharged from active service. Caldwell sustained a split shoulder blade, but the shock did not cause him to forget the presence, in his trousers pocket, of about 200 francs, the result of a recent win at "two-up," when he called correctly 18 times. He saw to the recovery of the trousers before departing. Some artillerymen who were using the bath at the same time were also injured.

Other casualties about this time were: Privates W. R. McLennan, evacuated as a result of gas (slight) on 15th; and T. H. Coote, wounded while going for rations on 19th. Private A. F. Woodman was wounded on the 24th, but remained at duty.

As the respective lines became more defined, the shelling became more accurate, but the Company escaped with the few casualties recorded. On the afternoon of the 16th April, the line teams became interested in the shelling of the red brick church tower in Albert by 8 in. howitzers of the British artillery. "At 3.45," recorded Private H. Horner, "a big shell hit the tower fair in the middle, and we then saw it waver and slowly fall over on the right. The statue has now fallen, and we are wondering if the prophecy will be fulfilled." According to report —current when the Company first viewed it in July, 1916—the French peasantry believed that the end of the war would coincide with the fall of the precariously-held image. The same writer went on to remark: "How strange the scene now is with the tower no longer to be seen."

Enemy shelling was very heavy at times, and especially so on the morning of the 24th April, when the areas behind the forward system were heavily straffed for two hours. It was, apparently, part of a demonstration covering the enemy attack which successfully stormed the village of Villers Bretonneux on the right of the Brigade front. The following day (Anzac Day) members were thrilled by the announcement that the 5th Australian Division had, by a brilliant night operation, retaken that strategically important village.

The 1st May was a fine, sunny day, and heralded the advent of early summer. With its arrival was ended definitely the winter of 1917-8. Compared with its predecessor, it was not nearly so severe, and consequently more endurable. At no time did the prolonged severity of 1916-7 manifest itself. Another factor was the location of the Company away from the desolate mud area of the Somme battlefield. The Warneton sector was, at times, very wet, but an established trench system with duckboards minimised the sufferings of the gun teams, and the mud problem was kept within bounds.

When opportunity offered, the men, as usual, visited the neighbouring villages. The first to receive attention was the adjacent and familiar village of Warloy, now close to the line. Some of the original inhabitants were in residence, and friendships formed in the previous summer were renewed. The remnants of the former populace had much to tell concerning the consternation arising out of the retreat of the defenders, and the advance of the German Army. Private H. G. Merry has related how he visited some old friends. "They told me," said he, "of the retreat of the British, in great disorder. Most of the inhabitants had fled with the British, but as my friends had just finished packing and were ready to leave, the Australians marched into the village. The Diggers told them to unpack, as THEY would stop Fritz, and they would be safe. So my friends remained. They were full of praises for the Diggers, and though their food was scanty and there were shell-holes in the garden, they remained, cheerful and optimistic. My presents of bully-beef, etc., were received with gratitude."

Towards the end of April, the 2nd Division Artillery made itself very unpopular by installing an eighteen-pounder gun on the Amiens-Albert road in the forward area of the Brigade. The purpose was to obtain close shooting on the roads in rear of Dernancourt. "Fired both day and night," said one recorder, "but drew a lot of strafe on Battalion headquarters just along side." It is believed that its shooting was very effective, but enemy retaliation and strong protests from the 22nd Battalion headquarters brought about its removal, much to the relief of the troops in the vicinity, including the Company's teams adjacent, who at once appropriated the well-constructed dugouts used by the artillery men.

With the advent of finer weather, came relief from line work on the 1st May, when the Company was relieved by a Company of the 47th Machine Gun Battalion, as part of the relief of the 2nd Australian Division by the 47th Division. The "change over" was completed by 11.30 p.m., the outgoing teams marching to Henencourt, whence G.S. waggons conveyed them to Montigny, where the whole Company re-assembled. The tour of line duty extended over 25 days. The casualty list was as follows: Died of wounds, one other rank; wounded and/or gassed, one officer, five other ranks; injured, eight other ranks; sick, one officer and 21 other ranks. The latter included Lieutenant H. A. Robinson, whose evacuation was due to an affection of the eyes (cellulitis), developing as a result of injuries sustained at Pozieres. He did not return to the Company, as his disability led to his discharge from active service. Most of the "sick" ones returned after a short spell.

After a night at Montigny, the whole Company marched to Querrieu, less than two hours sufficing for the journey. The new location was a hamlet on the Hallue River, about three miles from its junction with the Somme. Tents were provided in the chateau grounds, and the Company at once settled down to what was probably the happiest camp during 1918. Beautifully situated among trees which were rapidly donning their summer dress, all ranks felt that they were on holiday. Ever responsive to sunshine and happy environment, everyone felt the joy of living, and the war and the things of war were cast aside. Swimming naturally became a daily event, and just as naturally, fishing, although the finer art of rod and line was discarded in favour of the Mills grenade. Borrowing the idea of the "box barrage," the method followed was to use two old punts arranged parallel and some little distance apart. A grenade dropped into the water from each end—with the pin out—completed the "box," and as the stunned fish came to the surface they were collected and carried off. "This lovely spot," noted Private R. C. Trevan in his diary, "camped in the chateau grounds by a lake full of fish; chaps are bombing them and living royally." Bombing for fish became a popular pastime until a boat was blown out of the water by Sergeant Wigmore—fortunately without injury to anybody—and then the prohibition of such "fishing" was more rigidly enforced. Most of the units in the neighbourhood had added some of the stray live-stock to their strength at this time. An unofficial addition to the Company was a goat which, however, was looked on by all hands as a fountain and consequently soon became dry.

While at Querrieu, an epidemic of influenza appeared in the area and, in common with other units, manifested itself in the Company. Attacking suddenly, it did not attain a serious form, but gradually affected a large number of the personnel. The sufferers usually recovered in a few days, during which they were accommodated in separate tents and were attended to by Privates H. H. Cook and J. F. Pittendreigh—attached from the 6th Field Ambulance—the Battalion Medical Officer making an occasional visit.

On Sunday, 6th May, General Birdwood attended the Brigade church parade, and after distributing ribbons, delivered the usual speech on the military situation.

The 8th May was the anniversary of the departure of the 6th Brigade from Australia, three years before. The older members of the Company celebrated the event in various informal ways, and in some cases joined with their old comrades in the battalions of the Brigade, where dinners had been arranged and "great evenings" spent. "At least it seemed so next morning," added one participant. Up to the present, the advent of the 2nd Machine Gun Battalion had not resulted in the Company being allocated to another Brigade for service in or out of the line, so the old ties between Brigade and Company had not suffered any unwelcome severance.

On the 10th May, the enjoyable "holiday" at Querrieu came to an end, and preparations were made for re-entering the line. During the stay, evacuations due to sickness totalled four.

CHAPTER XXI.

VILLE-SUR-ANCRE.

10th-21st May, 1918.

The months of March and April covered a very critical period for the Allies, particularly so for the British Army in France. On the 21st March, the long expected and much heralded blow had fallen on the southern end of the front, heavily involving the Third and Fifth Armies, especially the latter on the end of the line. Before an immense German flood, the front was broken, and the tide ran till the whole of the Somme battlefield —and more—was overrun. It was not stopped till Villers-Bretonneaux—within striking distance of Amiens—was reached. Meanwhile, Pozieres and other places, dearly bought with Australian blood, had passed to the possession of the invader. On the 9th April, the storm broke afresh, this time on the First Army, near Armentieres, and again the tide flowed westward: Fleurbaix, Armentieres, and surrounding districts, familiar to Australians, likewise passing to the invader. The Australian Divisions were not involved in the initial stages of that attack, but entered the battle line soon after. When they did, they showed in unmistakable fashion what efficient instruments they had become. Three years of campaigning and accumulated experience in close encounter with a highly organised enemy had welded them into skilful units with a high standard of battle discipline, the effects of which were about to be revealed. By the end of May, the German thrust had been definitely stayed on the British front—at tremendous cost—and both sides settled down to hold and strengthen their new lines and recover from the effects of their great exertions. Stagnation descended on the front; the only offensive actions being provided by the Australian Divisions. Those comparatively minor actions were to be but a prelude to, and to culminate in, the great drama in the following August, which led to the termination of the war. On the front of the 2nd Division it was not hard to find a point at which offensive action might be directed. The small salient held by the enemy at Ville-sur-Ancre naturally suggested itself. Its removal would straighten the line; deprive the enemy of a covered line of approach, and clear the way for an advance eastwards when the time arrived. Though the capture of Ville-sur-Ancre was described as a "minor operation," it constituted a local problem, in so far that it appeared necessary to attack the village from both sides of the river, the northern thrust involving the construction of bridges and the successful crossing of the river.

While these considerations were occupying the minds of the authorities, the Company vacated its happy camp at Querrieu in the early evening of 10th May, and proceeded to the line to relieve the 23rd Machine Gun Company in accordance with the relief of the 3rd Australian Division by the 2nd. By 11 p.m. the change was complete, and the 16 guns were disposed around the small salient formed by the enemy's possession of the village of Ville-sur-Ancre which lay in the valley of the Ancre, and adjoining the river. Company headquarters were established in Treux Chateau, adjacent. The new location was just south of its former line position. Meanwhile, the 6th Brigade had moved in and relieved the 10th Brigade in the left Divisional sector. The Brigade occupied a frontage of 3000 yards, and as the Company's guns were disposed "in depth" over that area, they were a good deal scattered. On the left was the 47th Division, and on the right the 5th Brigade. Astride the Amiens-Albert road and the Ancre river, the area was familiar ground. Close at hand was Buire, and in front—in enemy possession—was Dernancourt, where the Company was billeted in the early winter of 1916-7.

Meanwhile, the remainder of the Company moved up to Franvillers and billeted in the main street of the village. Indirect fire at night was resumed, the targets being mainly the exits to Ville-sur-Ancre. Enemy shelling of Buire and vicinity was heavy at times, including a liberal use of mustard gas shells. No casualties, however, were sustained till the 15th May, when an odd shell killed two respected members of the Company at the morning "stand to." Privates F. Lockwood and W. Sage were members of a gun-team situated in the sunken road near Treux. As they were leaning side by side against the wall of the gun position, the shell landed right between them, killing both outright Sage was 58 years of age at the time of his death, and easily the oldest member of the Company to fall. An extended reference to him will be found in the Appendix.

The Company had hardly settled down to its new positions when reports of expected enemy attacks were circulated. Precautionary measures were taken, but no developments took place. More interest was taken in rumours of offensive action against the enemy. As often happened, the latter brand of report was far more reliable. It came as a welcome change from the stagnation which was again settling down on the front, and gave the men a fresh interest in their work.

The rumours were confirmed on the 16th by the issue of orders for attack. Briefly stated, the main effort was to be made by the 22nd Battalion (four companies) pushing forward about three-quarters of a mile on a frontage of about the same distance to a line running due south from the S.E. outskirts of the village, and including the capture of "little caterpillar" and "big caterpillar," two sunken roads so named from their resemblance, on the map, to a caterpillar. Two companies of the 21st Battalion were to form a defensive flank on the south edge of the village, protecting the 22nd. To prevent the occupants of the village from devoting their attention to the 21st and 22nd, the 24th Battalion (two companies) was to attack from the north, and incidentally make the retreat of the garrison a difficult matter. Fire on the village was to cease at a specified time to enable the patrols to "mop up" the village in daylight, if found practicable. On the right of the 6th Brigade, the sister Brigade, the 5th, was to co-operate by swinging forward its left flank on a front of 500 yards. On the left (or north), the neighbouring 54th (British) Brigade was to carry out a raid and "Chinese attacks." In an endeavour to attain a measure of surprise, and to consolidate under cover of darkness, the unusually early hour of 2 a.m. (summer time) was chosen as Zero hour.

The newly formed 2nd Machine Gun Battalion undertook its first "offensive" in arranging the machine-gun activities. After the Brigadier—at a Brigade conference—had decided on the role of the "attacking" guns, the M.G. Battalion Commander arranged for the machine-gun barrage and co-operation of the remaining guns in the Division. The 7th Company was in reserve, but from the remainder, 29 guns were allotted to barrage work on enemy approaches and possible assembly places. The Company provided eight of the barrage guns, the four in the existing front line were to remain silent, but could engage any visible targets in daytime on the ridge north of Morlancourt, while the remaining four guns were allotted to the 22nd

Battalion; two to each flank as "attacking" guns. They were to move forward in rear of the attackers, assist in the consolidation, and especially to watch the exits of Ville-sur-Ancre.

The Machine Gun Battalion orders for the attack were issued on the 17th, but as the Company actually commenced its preparations the day before, three whole days were available for the preliminaries. The ample time available allowed a deliberate and cold-blooded preparation such as the accumulated experience of the Company suggested, and in conformity with the skilled staff work general in the A.I.F. The familiar duties attendant on firing a barrage need but a passing reference. Extra ammunition was moved to the gun positions, teams chosen, fire charts for each gun and battery were prepared, and telephone arrangements made such as have been described at length in Chapter XIV. For the four "attacking" teams, it was decided that Lieutenant G. A. Jeffery would take charge of two from No. 3 Section to the left flank of the 22nd Battalion, and that Lieutenant J. E. Hopper would take two from No. 1 Section to the right flank of the same Battalion. No Vickers guns were allotted to the 21st Battalion, or for the 24th engaged in the northern Sector of the attack. The Company was very pleased when it learned that it would be operating with its parent Brigade in the operation. While the plans were being discussed at Treux Chateau, the proceedings were enlivened by a telephone conversation which Lieutenant Blenkarn was conducting with Captain Rae, respecting certain calculations. The former disagreed with figures sent him, and to the delight of the listeners, indulged his propensity for uncommon words and phrases; a sample being: "It is obvious," said he through the telephone, "that you have made an erroneous computation."

In accordance with the deliberate and detailed preparations alluded to, some extracts taken from Lieutenant Jeffery's note book will indicate the lines followed. As soon as the orders for the Company had been studied and requirements noted, the teams were selected, and every man carefully instructed in his and other men's parts. Guns and gear were closely overhauled and belts filled. From an artillery observation post, the line of the proposed advance was studied by the aid of field glasses. Compass bearings from different points to the objective were taken for future use, when they could be used with the aid of a luminous compass in the darkness. The question of equipment was then studied, and decided as follows: "Fighting Order," with water-proof sheet rolled round overcoat and strapped to

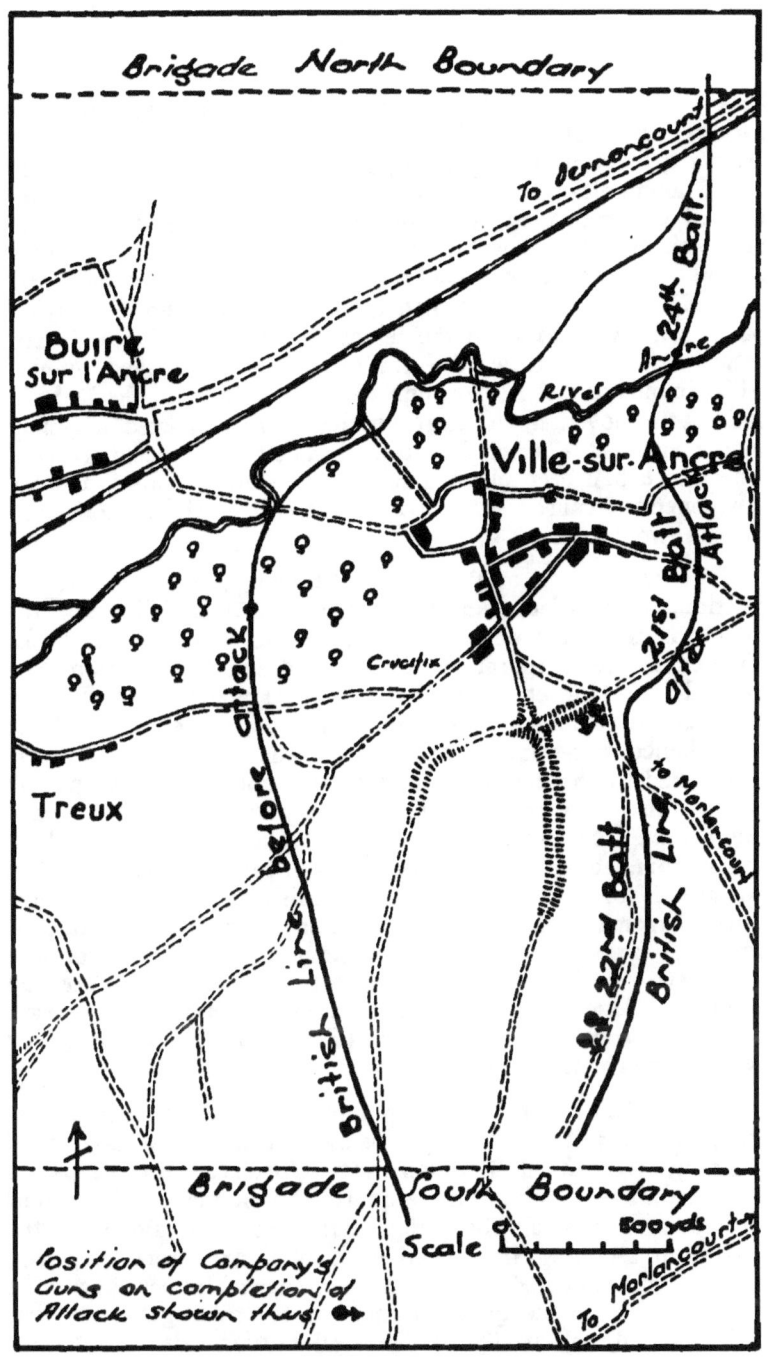

Ville-sur-Ancre. 19th. May 1918

back, water-bottle filled, 48 hours' rations in addition to "iron rations," 100 rounds of S.A.A. in bandoliers per man. Each team's gear comprised gun, tripod, spare part wallet, 14 boxes belted ammunition, condensor tube attached to gun, two petrol tins of water instead of condensor bags. Other items were: one pick and two shovels per team, 10 sand-bags, and success signals. To assist the relatively small teams (four men and N.C.O.) each half-section had attached to it a small carrying party, who were to assist the teams to their objective and then return and bring forward from previously established dumps, 4,000 rounds of S.A.A. per gun. During the night of the 18-19th, the teams moved up to their previously reconnoitred assembly places via routes which had been inspected and decided upon. The attack had been planned for the previous morning, and the postponement caused some re-arrangements in the personnel of one or two teams.

The experience of the two right-hand teams from No. 1 Section, under Lieutenant Hopper, will now be followed. Included in the party were Corporals W. N. Riley and A. Y. E. Turner, Lance Corporals V. G. Esmond and G. P. Nolan, Privates H. E. Horner, R. A. Bate, W. J. Hyland, A. McHowie. Although assembly had been made in good order and without disturbance, some natural nervousness was exhibited, and it was intensified by the action of enemy flare-shooters who crept forward to fire their brilliantly illuminating flares. "Look at those Very lights," said one excited member, "they are Fritz's and we are surrounded. The 6th Company has never lost prisoners, but we are in for it now." It was a ticklish moment, but it produced the man for the occasion. Thrusting his head forward into the group, Private Nolan remarked—with appropriate emphasis—"Eh! X——, you ought to join a b—— cheer up society." The effect was instantaneous. "I shall never forget it," said one of the new members (Private H. E. Horner), "my windiness vanished as if by magic."

Promptly at Zero, the 18-pounders opened almost as one gun, the "heavies" following closely; the eager, widely-spaced infantry of the 22nd Battalion moved forward, four companies on a frontage of about three-quarters of a mile. The teams' orders were to await the firing of the "success" signal on the Battalion attaining its objective. No signals were, however, seen at the expected time, and Lieutenant Hopper, becoming impatient at the delay, went forward to investigate, and was accompanied, voluntarily, by Corporal Turner. Before they had gone far they ran into trouble in the shape of an enemy machine-gun team which had not been "mopped up" by the attacking infantry. The Germans opened fire at 25 yards, but the pair rushed the gun and captured the crew. Meanwhile, the situation in front had cleared, and the two returned to the anxiously waiting teams and led them forward to their objective, a little forward of the sunken road known as the "big caperpillar," with the village of Morlancourt, half-right. As soon as the guns were mounted, Turner took the carriers to the rear and brought forward the 8,000 rounds of S.A.A. without mishap. Taking up his position with the right-hand gun, Hopper placed the other on his left, distant about 100 yards, under Corporal Riley. It was just daybreak when Riley and his team were established. The infantry were very pleased to see them, and gave a cheer. An infantry officer was reconnoitring out in front, and just then he ran back calling: "Look out, here they come." Riley picked up the gun and, running out a little distance, the team came into action against figures moving about in front. The firing of three belts dispersed them, and they were not seen again. Meanwhile, Hopper had engaged an enemy gun and put it out of action, and subsequently fired on two parties, one about 150 and another 200 strong, who were moving into Morlancourt from a southerly direction. They were quickly dispersed by the fire of the gun. The captured German gun was mounted for action in case of counter-attack. Thereafter, that sector of the front became comparatively quiet, and when the carriers had returned with the S.A.A., they took the places of the gun-team members, who retired through Mericourt and Ribemont, to Heilly, where a G.S. waggon took them to bivouacs near Behencourt. As the party moved out, they helped some of the wounded of the 22nd Battalion; one man being carried "fireman fashion," owing to a damaged hip. Moving out, Privates Horner and Bate came upon a party of four Germans huddled under a waterproof sheet in a gun position. Mere boys, they seemed. They were taken in hand and made to carry out the wounded infantryman. "We could have got many souvenirs," said one of the party regretfully, "only for having the wounded chap to attend to." The "captures" did not end with the incident recorded. The runner for the party was Private S. Watts. During one of his journeys he spied a German, apparently dead, but upon going through his pockets, the "dead" came suddenly and vigorously to life, and a fierce struggle ensued. Fortunately Watts was able to secure his opponent's rifle, whereupon he surrendered, and was duly handed over as a Company "capture."

The teams for the left flank were drawn from No. 3 Section, under Lieutenant Jeffery. The party reached their assembly position, well forward, about 1.40 a.m. An apparently long wait took place after the opening of the barrage, but at 2.50 a.m. the "success" signal—a succession of three green flares—was observed. The teams and carriers moved forward at once. "I hopped over the top," said Jeffery, "and the boys followed in grand style. I immediately took a bearing with my luminous compass, and marched on it to a certain point, took another compass bearing, and marched on it to my objective. We expected to do some scrapping here, but Fritz had gone. I ordered the men to dig in and make machine-gun emplacements, which they did. We fired on small parties of the enemy; I supervised operations, then when all was correct, my batman and I dug a small shelter." During the afternoon, a German machine-gun and ammunition were found and, both being in good order, were mounted for action. At dusk, Lieutenant Duncan came in and relieved Jeffery, but the teams carried on. No enemy counter-attack followed.

At 7.30 a.m., Battalion headquarters ordered two guns to be emplaced in front of Ville-sur-Ancre. Two teams and guns from No. 2 Section, under Lieutenant Wilkinson and Sergeant D. C. M. Parkhill, were accordingly sent forward. After a careful reconnaissance by the two officers, no suitable positions could be found, so the guns were mounted near The Crucifix, just south of the houses of the village, and to the left rear of Jeffery's party. Heavy enemy shelling was in progress, but the teams were established without loss, and clung to their positions on a road bank, while heavy shells skimmed the top and burst close in rear. During the afternoon, a large dug-out was discovered in the bank, and into it the spare men and infantry crowded for shelter. It was furnished as completely as a house, with two beds, stove, pots and pans, etc. Although exploding shells extinguished the lights, the fifteen feet of earth overhead gave protection to the inmates.

The 29 barrage guns of the Machine Gun Battalion (including 8 of the Company) were given rather an ambitious programme. There was no attempt to put down a barrage on the whole front, as the guns available were not numerous enough. To compensate, in some measure for the paucity of numbers, the tasks laid down provided for a rate of fire at 70 rounds per minute for 10 minutes, then 100 rounds per minute for 1 hour 50 minutes. This involved an expenditure of 11,700 rounds per gun, but in many cases teams failed to get through their programme in the time allowed. On the expiration of the appointed time—two hours after Zero—they stood by on S.O.S. lines. Early in the morning it was expected that the enemy would launch a counter-attack, so at 7.15 a.m. the barrage was resumed by artillery and machine-guns. No attack, however, developed, and Brigade headquarters ordered the cessation of firing. The Company's barrage guns fired 50,000 rounds during the proceedings. A number of German belts were used, and proved as satisfactory as our own. No S.O.S. calls were received by the batteries, and but three casualties were sustained, two of which related to Company members; Lance Corporal H. F. R. Lindsell and Private E. Daniel being slightly wounded about 3 a.m., the former with a shrapnel pellet in the temple, while the latter was struck in the knee.

The attack was a complete success. Many of the enemy machine-guns were over-run in the first rush, and did not come into action. The attackers on the north successfully crossed the river and established themselves as planned. The "mopping up" of the village was proceeded with in daylight, and although stiff resistance was met with, the attackers finally gained the whole of it by 7.30 a.m. During the attack the enemy's artillery retaliation was not severe, but late in the day the new positions were heavily shelled. Every unit in the Brigade reported having captured prisoners, the total being set down at 8 officers and 268 other ranks. 34 machine-guns were included in the material taken. The Company figured in the prisoners captured to the extent of five. Brigade headquarters, in noting the complete success achieved, ascribed the results to "the fine offensive spirit of the officers and men, the very careful preparations made, and the thorough co-operation between the infantry, the engineers, the machine-gunners, and trench mortars." Losses were reported at 16 officers and 251 other ranks. The Company was fortunate in suffering but two casualties; the two recorded in the barrage gun-teams. Company members were grieved to learn that the only officer killed in the 22nd Battalion was Second Lieutenant C. M. Bowden, who was a foundation member of the Company. Late in the preceding year, he had been sent as a Company nominee to a cadet school in England, but after completing the machine-gun course, had been posted to the 22nd Battalion a fortnight before his death. He had proved himself a sterling soldier, and was greatly respected for his manly qualities.

Resulting from the action, three decorations came to the

Company. Lieutenant Hopper received the Military Cross and Corporal Turner the Military Medal for their reconnaissance and capture of the machine-gun team already related. Private S. Watts received the Military Medal for his good work as runner. Several times he traversed the shelled areas, carrying messages, with courage and coolness, as well as guiding two teams to their positions without a casualty.

Previous allusions have been made to the "family" spirit prevailing in the Company. Shortly before the attack, an incident occurred which affords an illustration. Just after the "attacking" teams had been selected, Private G. Nolan, as a result of a blow received in an altercation at "two-up," was carried away to the nearest hospital, where the English doctor pronounced the case one of "trench fever," and one for transfer to base hospital. Before the transfer was arranged, Private G. D. Beanland visited the hospital to enquire about the sick man, and during a conversation with Nolan, informed him that his place in the "attacking" teams had been taken by Private T. Ostle, who was a mate of Nolan's. As soon as he heard the news, the patient hopped out of bed and made his way across country to the Company. He was just in time to take his place —which he insisted in doing—with the attackers. Later, when Ostle had an opportunity to question his impulsive mate and cast reflections on his sanity, the reply was: "When I knew that it was you who had taken my place, I felt I could never forgive myself if you had been killed in my place." "I thought it very fine, true comradeship," remarked Ostle afterwards.

Apart from some heavy shelling of the new positions, nothing noteworthy followed the taking of Ville-sur-Ancre. Enemy gas-shells in plenty added to the troubles of the forward areas. On the early morning of 21st May, a team of No. 1 Section was evacuated as a result of mustard gas. They were: Privates T. Ostle, W. S. J. Weight, J. A. Smith, and A. Robertson. The two latter returned after a brief stay at Divisional Rest Station, but Ostle and Weight were sent to England before rejoining the Company.

At this time, Second Lieutenant W. S. Clayton rejoined from a cadet battalion in England, where he passed the prescribed course, and was granted a commission.

During the evening of 21st May, the Company was relieved by one of its sister companies, the 7th, and its 15 days' tenure in the line at Ville-sur-Ancre came to an end. Losses sustained were: Killed in action, two other ranks; wounded, two other ranks; gassed, four other ranks; Sick, three other ranks.

CHAPTER XXII.

JUNE, 1918: FRANVILLERS—VILLE-SUR-ANCRE—QUERRIEU.

21st May—28th June.

Upon relief at Ville-sur-Ancre, the Company passed into divisional reserve, and became the "mobile reserve company." Its instructions stated that: "It will be prepared to form a defence on either flank or to operate on any position in the divisional sector." It was also directed to act under the orders of the G.O.C. reserve infantry brigade unless ordered otherwise by Division. The disposition was astride the Albert-Amiens road, with two Sections at Bonnay (on the Ancre), one on the Amiens road and one a little further north at Franvillers. As part of its "mobile" character, each Section was obliged to keep its "fighting" limbers close at hand, with guns and gear packed ready for action at short notice. For the first time while in reserve, the Company was dispersed over a wide area, Company headquarters some distance in rear of Franvillers, being over two miles from the two Sections guarding the bridgehead at Bonnay.

In pleasant weather and surroundings, everyone settled down to enjoy the respite from line work. It was, in the Army sense of the word, a rest, and with easy conditions. Company training, especially for the reinforcements which were taken on strength at the end of March, was at once reverted to. The increasing action of enemy aircraft in the way of bombing rear areas, brought about precautions to protect horse lines. Instead of the customary double row of animals tethered to a single line, they were grouped in small sections, and members of the gun teams were called on to help build earthern banks around them to provide shelter from bomb splinters. The usual precautions were taken to set aside a number of guns mounted for action against enemy aircraft. A more popular item was the revival of the Company canteen, which functioned under the control of Corporal J. W. Findlay. Cricket was also revived;

the inter-section rivalry finding a fresh outlet in games between sections. Sometimes a combined team tried conclusions with neighbouring units. The teams at Bonnay indulged in rowing and swimming in the River Ancre, and, of course, the fishing possibilities of the stream were exploited with Mills grenades, as previously described. The fine weather brought about great activity in the air by both sides, with the inevitable clashes. Private H. Horner recorded in his diary at this time: "When on guard this morning, I saw nineteen of our planes going over to visit Fritz, whilst twenty-two were returning, and two others were low down; forty-three in all; a grand sight." Other entries read: "Three Fritzs brought down to-day"; "our planes going over in great numbers to bomb Fritz." After relating the daring action of a German aeroplane in pursuing a British machine, he describes how, a little later, another enemy aeroplane came over and was fired on by Lewis gunners. The airman landed without molestation, got out, and walked up to a "Tommy" and said: "Give us a cigarette, Tommy, I'm fed up with this b—— business." It was a single-seater, quite new, and had only one mark upon it. The Company's anti-aircraft guns came into action at times, with the usual negative results, although Lieutenant Turnbull has recorded how "we had one exciting incident when an enemy plane flew low near the Albert road, and we put several belts from two guns into him, but did not appear to be very successful. He landed ten minutes later about four miles behind our positions, but we did not learn for what reason."

A notable change in leadership took place at the end of May, when General Sir William Birdwood left to take command of the Fifth Army, and Major-General J. Monash assumed command of the Australian Corps, then consising of the 2nd, 3rd, 4th and 5th Australian Divisions.

Thus passed quickly and happily the ten days in reserve. The spell practically came to an end on the 29th May, when a Battalion sports meeting was held, near the Company headquarters, for the two Companies out of the Line (5th and 6th). Next day, preparations were made for re-entering the line.

During the evening of the 31st May, the Company moved into the line and relieved the 7th Machine Gun Company, the "change over" being completed before midnight. The guns and teams were disposed in the area of the left Brigade, the 6th, who had relieved the 7th during the same evening. Six guns were located in and near the front line in its former positions, in front of and north and south of Ville-sur-Ancre. The remaining guns were distributed "in depth" in the Brigade area as usual. Company headquarters were established at Chateau Treux, in rear. The Company completed the move without mishap, but the 28th Battalion of the outgoing Brigade suffered sad loss. When its "B" Company arrived at La Houssoye Switch Trench, an enemy aeroplane appeared overhead and, guided it is said, by the glow of pipes and the lighting of cigarettes, dropped two bombs, which killed 27 men and wounded 40.

On re-entering the line, it was noted that much work had been done since the Company vacated the area on the 21st May, although a good deal still remained to be done. The line of posts then established had been linked into what was practically a continuous front line. Commenting on the situation, one writer said: "The front generally proved to be very quiet, and the enemy's attitude docile. Apparently he is desirous that we should leave him alone until he has properly established a new trench which air photographs show he is slowly developing close to our own." If such was his desire, he was to be grievously disappointed.

The night following the entry into the line, the never-ending indirect harassing fire from the rear guns was directed on enemy roads and communications, and continued nightly. After the lapse of five days, an internal relief was carried out, the front line teams exchanging places with their mates in the rear positions. Nothing noteworthy occurred till the 6th June, when a minenwerfer shell landed near one of No. 4 Section's guns, wounding Corporal W. B. Sharp (second occasion), who was carried out unconscious. He was subsequently returned to Australia and discharged. The same day a shell burst close to Company headquarters, wounding Private O'Brien in the left shoulder, and Lieutenant Hopper in the thigh, as he was playing croquet. It was Hopper's third wounding, and he did not return to the Company.

At 1 a.m. on the morning of the 8th, "Z" Special Company, Royal Engineers, fired 200 drums of gas into the village of Morlancourt from the Brigade front, using electrically operated projectors. Three of the Company's guns (co-operating with the 22nd Company on the right) fired in conjunction with the discharge.

Two nights later, the 10th, at 9.45 p.m., the enemy was again irritated, to great purpose, when the 7th Brigade—on the right of the 6th—pushed forward its front line between Sailly Laurette and Morlancourt, in conjunction with an advance of its southern neighbour, the 4th Australian Division. The 6th Brigade's contribution, presumably to keep the enemy occupied on its front, was a raid by the 22nd Battalion, and another by the 23rd. In the latter case, the 47th (English) Division on the left, provided the protective barrage. The machine-gun share in the combined-operation—on the front of the 2nd Division—was, in addition to sending "mobile" teams forward, to provide the raiders with covering fire from 34 guns. The Companys' quota was 10 guns, grouped in two batteries of four each ("F" and Treux Battery), and two single guns. The programme was duly carried out without unusual incident as far as the Company was concerned. At 2.30 a.m. on the following morning, "F" Battery fired for one hour, expending 12,000 rounds as a protective barrage. The whole operation was very successful, and over 300 prisoners were accounted for by the 2nd Division. In reporting on the night's work, Battalion headquarters said: "A prisoner of the 90th R.I.R. who was captured stated that his battalion was advancing to counter-attack from the direction of Morlancourt (probably up the valley, S.W. from that village), but was scattered by machine-gun fire. The counter-attack only reached our line in a few elements, and it is reasonable to suppose that the fire was most useful in dispersing the enemy. A prisoner of the 449th Regiment stated that his unit experienced severe discomfort, and had to give up the idea of counter-attacking because of our machine-gun fire." "F" Battery, under Lieutenant Blenkarn, was one of the batteries which fired across the valley referred to. During the night of the 11-12th, all guns kept up harassing fire, especially at sundown and before dawn, to deal with possible counter-attacks. The Company's part was a subsidiary one, but even such a limited share involved a good deal of labour in the preparation. For each gun, 20,000 rounds of ammunition had to be close at hand, all available belts had to be filled, battery and gun charts and programmes prepared, and guns and gear overhauled and adjusted.

During the evening of the 11th, an internal relief was carried out. While Private T. A. McKay was going out to guide the incoming teams, a 9.2 shell exploded two hunded yards away, and a fragment struck him on the temple, rendering him unconscious. McKay had previously been wounded in the neck at Pozieres while a member of the 24th Battalion.

Company Officers. Taken at Querrieu. June, 1918.
Australian War Memorial Photograph. Copyright.

JUNE, 1918.

The line activities naturally brought retaliation from the enemy. At times his shelling was very heavy, a good deal of gas-shell being used. That no further casualties were reported till the 14th is, to some extent, due to members' familiarity with the effects of shell-fire, the use of cover, and avoidance of habitually shelled areas. The spell of immunity was broken on the morning of the 14th, when a heavy concentration fell on part of the support line in Marrett Wood. One of the first results was to sever the telephone lines connecting the Section in the trench. Signallers W. J. Jarvis and C. Wood set out to repair the broken lines. Eight breaks were mended, and as the two reached Section headquarters, the shelling became intense, and the trench appeared to be filled with gas while they sought shelter. Jarvis got into a galvanised iron shelter used by Lieutenant Duncan as his headquarters, but a few minutes afterwards a shell burst on top, killing Jarvis and wounding Duncan and Private G. H. ("Pick") Mayell. Duncan returned to the Company a few weeks afterwards, but Mayell, a well-liked member of No. 3 Section, died of his injuries two days later. Prominent among the helpers who carried on in spite of the shelling, was Sergeant B. H. Johnson. Wood was badly shaken, but after summoning aid from the nearest gun-team and assisting with the wounded, completed his work by locating and mending two other breaks in the wires. His courage and disregard of danger deservedly brought him the award of a Bar to his Military Medal. Jarvis was a sterling, reliable signaller, whose death was deplored by many more than his signaller comrades.

The night of the 14-15th must have been a bad one for the enemy opposite the Brigade front. Two successful raids were carried out. Parties of about 50 men from the 24th and 21st Battalions brought back prisoners and machine-guns, besides accounting for a number of the enemy; the former raiding at 11.30 p.m., and the latter at 12.30 a.m. The Company's guns fired in conjunction with the artillery in placing a "box barrage" round the points attacked. For the 24th Battalion's effort, five guns fired for fifteen minutes at 50 rounds per minute, then 100 rounds per minute for the succeeding fifteen minutes, expending 11,000 rounds. Six guns fired in similar fashion in support of the 21st Battalion raiders. The well-laid plans and close co-operation of all the parties concerned ensured the success of both operations, and brought to a fitting close the Brigade's energetic tour of line duty.

Soon after the completion of the programme just related—at 2 a.m. on the 15th—the 8th and 15th Companies of the 5th Machine Gun Battalion moved into the line and commenced to relieve the Company. The formalities were reported complete by 4 a.m., and the guns and gear were loaded into the limbers of the Transport Section, which had been sent forward in anticipation. After the teams from the line had taken breakfast at rear Company headquarters, they marched to their former camp at Querrieu, where the whole unit reassembled. In spite of the line activities, the losses sustained were very light. They totalled two other ranks killed and died of wounds, two officers, and three other ranks wounded, one other rank evacuated sick.

The relief of the Company was part of an inter-divisional relief, the 5th taking over from the 2nd, and the latter passing into "Corps Reserve." For the Company it was in the nature of a "rest," always with the qualification as to the Army sense of the word. In very congenial surroundings—described in its former occupancy—all ranks set about enjoying the relaxation, in pleasant summer weather. The newer men were well drilled in gun drill and rectification of actual "stoppages" during firing, while the seniors went through a varied programme, including physical training, gas drill, moving forward in attack, barrage drill with limbers, concealment in attack and defence. Bathing parades were held, and some afternoons in each week were given up to "recreational training," when sports and contests between Sections took place, chief of which was cricket. Many inter-sectional matches were played, and occasionally a combined eleven tried conclusions with adjoining units, when the friendly section rivalry disappeared in a common cause. With all four Companies of the Battalion "resting," a Battalion sports meeting was possible, and a programme of events was drawn up, and decided at Petit Camon, near Amiens, on the 22nd of June. The programme was too lengthy to be completed, but judged by the results of the events held, it was found that the Company was victorious, and had won the Battalion shield. From the ascertainable results, it will be seen that Private R. C. Trevan was materially responsible for the Company's success. Details of Company members' successes are:—

Event	Name	Place	Pts.
100 Yards	Captain Rae	1st	3
220 Yards	Private R. C. Trevan	3rd	1
220 Yards	Captain Rae	2nd	2
220 Yards	Sergeant J. McGaffin	1st	3

440 Yards	Private R. C. Trevan	1st	3
Half-Mile	Driver J. McManus	1st	3
Half-Mile	Lance Corporal A. V. Caldwell	3rd	1
120 Yards Hurdles	Private R. C. Trevan	2nd	2
High Jump	Private A. Chitty	2nd	2
Long Jump	Private A. Chitty	1st	3
Hop, Step & Jump	Private R. C. Trevan	1st	3
Gun team into action	6th Company Team (including Private Trevan)	2nd	2
Not ascertainable			4
		Total	32

The epidemic of influenza continued to affect members, although not in a serious form, a few days' rest generally being sufficient to enable the sufferers to throw off its hold. Private H. Horner noted in his diary, under 19th June: "Laid up with the so-called 'dog's disease' or 'flu; had to stay in bed; about 12 of our Section affected." Among a few who were evacuated at this time was Corporal J. J. Riley, of No. 3 Section. Influenza was followed by pneumonia, and he died at the First Canadian General Hospital at Taplow (Bucks.) on 12th July, four days after his arrival in England. Interment was made in the beautiful Italian garden of Major Aster's Cleveden Estate, which had been converted into a cemetery for soldiers. No. 3 Section subscribed funds for an inscribed headstone, which was duly placed on the grave of their old and respected comrade. Riley was an efficient non-commissioned officer, and one who seemed destined for commissioned rank had he lived.

As was the usual custom, officers received and repaid visits from their friends in neighbouring units. An old friend of Lieutenant Wilkinson, Lieutenant Preston, of the 13th Australian Light Horse Regiment, was a frequent visitor, and as one said: "Was always talking horses." One evening, Wilkinson managed to get his friend to challenge Lieutenant Newcomen (Battalion Transport Officer) to a horse race; the visitor to ride his mare against anything that Newcomen could produce. The challenge was immediately accepted, with 100 francs as the stake. The race took place a few evenings later, along the canal bank. Members of the Company—true to the "family" spirit—backed their one-time officer, and had the satisfaction of collecting from the friends and supporters of the visitor when Newcomen won the contest.

Before the end of June, the Company received, as reinforcements, a draft of thirteen men from the 2nd Pioneer Battalion, to be followed by four from the Army Service Corps. Apparently the authorities were determined to keep machine-gun battalions up to strength, although the infantry battalions were carrying on with sadly depleted numbers. The regrettable, but necessary expedient of reducing the brigade complement from four to three battalions—in accordance with the existing plan in the British Army—was being deferred at this time, although it became an accomplished fact before the Armistice.

The thirteen happy days at Querrieu soon came to an end. Just before the close, the Official Photographer attended, and photographed the officers and non-commissioned officers. The results became part of the official records of the A.I.F., and reproductions will be found in this volume. At this time, Sergeant A. D. G. Bone left to enter an officer cadet battalion in England to qualify for a commission. Seven evacuations due to sickness were recorded, also one case of injury, during this period.

In the early afternoon of 28th June, half the gun-team strength and Transport Section marched to Lamotte, while the remainder moved into the line and manned 16 guns. Lamotte was situated on the bank of the Somme, some six miles west of Villers Bretonneux. Officers and men were agreeably located in the grounds and against the walls of a small chateau, past one corner of which the Somme flowed. The weather continued warm and pleasant, and the occupants of the camp, as well as other units in the vicinity, made full use of the acquatic facilities. A swim before breakfast was a rare privilege, and the opportunity was seized in true Australian fashion. At any time of the day, Australians could be seen sporting in the steadily flowing stream, while at times they appeared to be present in hundreds. It was a case of being literally "on the Somme."

CHAPTER XXIII.

HAMEL AND ITS AFTERMATH.

28th June—28th July, 1918.

While one half of the gun teams and the Transport Section were settling down in their new quarters at Lamotte, sixteen teams moved into the line and relieved the 11th Machine Gun Company (3rd Machine Gun Battalion), in accordance with the relief of the 3rd Australian Division by the 2nd. The relief of the 11th Company was reported complete by 8 p.m. on the 28th June. When the divisional "change over" was complete, the 7th Brigade was disposed in the right sector, and the 5th in the left. While two brigades were holding the Divisional front, the Machine Gun Battalion allotted three of its companies to the same area, the Company holding the central position. In accordance with Divisional orders, the companies were organised in two "groups," each under a "group commander" who, with an intelligence officer, was located at or near their respective brigade headquarters. This arrangement brought the machine-gun resources of the brigade areas in close contact with the respective brigadiers, with the obvious advantages of such close association.

When the Company settled down, it found itself in and near the partly ruined village of Villers Bretonneux, which had been taken from German hands in a brilliant night operation on 24-25th April by the 13th and 15th Australian Brigades. The village lay on the western edge of a plateau, which sloped northwards and southwards, and was, by reason of its position, a point of great strategical importance. Situated on the main Amiens-St. Quentin road, it gave a commanding view westward, even to Amiens, and was within striking distance of that city, and its highly important rail and road communications. The possession of the village by the enemy would have enabled him to menace Amiens, the most important centre in Picardy, possibly separate the British and French Armies, and destroy the railway system on which so much depended. Australians were by no means displeased when such a key position was captured by them, and remained in their custody. For a comparatively new "front," the area was in good condition, that is to say, the front line was continuous, fairly deep and wide, and the communication trenches good, although in most cases too narrow to permit the passage of a stretcher. Two guns were placed in the front line, on the eastern edge of the village, six in the rear outskirts, and the remainder distributed, as usual, "in depth." Company headquarters was established at a point where the railway crossed the Amiens-St. Quentin road.

The rear guns were sited in defensive positions, and in some cases underground shelters for the teams were dug, under the supervision of sappers from the 6th Field Company Engineers, the teams assisting in the excavation by raising the white chalky rock. The method followed was to fill sand bags with the broken rock and then, by lifting on to successive platforms, the bags were brought to the surface, and by means of salvaged wheelbarrows, dumped in the surrounding wheat crops. The dumps were then camouflaged by the Engineers to prevent detection by enemy aircraft. Subsequent aeroplane photographs showed that this had been successfully carried out. The shelters so constructed were practically shell proof, and were probably the strongest the Company ever constructed.

Owing to the hurried evacuation of Villers Bretonneux by its inhabitants, much of the furniture and effects had, perforce, to be left in the houses. One result was that some teams found themselves quartered in odd places with strange articles for company. Private R. C. Trevan recorded that his team took up a position close to the railway. The members not on duty at the gun, lived at an estaminet which had a shell-proof cellar in addition to complete furnishings, crockery, and a "penny-in-the-slot" piano. "It was a very comfortable front line pozzy indeed," added Trevan. Sergeant A. E. Cameron, of No. 2 Section, had charge of the teams (2), and his records mention, in addition to the foregoing list, the possession of an oven and a coffee grinder. "This was no pleasant place," he wrote, "as we caught plenty of shelling, but we lived pretty well. We used the coffee grinder when short of bread to grind wheat, of which there was any quantity in the village. With flour obtained by this method, we made rough (very rough) biscuits and jam tarts, Bob Trevan being head cook. Between times, we had foraging expeditions through the village for souvenirs, which were there galore. The best find I had was a big parcel of sugar and cakes of chocolate. We used the wheat until we struck some that had been impregnated with gas, and that finished us, as it made most of us sick."

The first task was to arrange for the usual nightly indirect harassing fire on enemy roads and communications. Rumours of an attack were confirmed on the 1st July by the issue of orders which indicated that the 6th Brigade acting in conjunction with the 4th Australian Division on its left, would attack the enemy line on the 4th July. When the plans were examined, it was found that the projected operations covered a front of 7,000 yards, and included the capture of the village of Hamel, and Hamel and Vaire Woods. For the first time since their ill-fated venture at Bullecourt, tanks were to take part with Australians; they were, however, a greatly improved weapon. An interesting item was the inclusion of American infantry with the assaulting infantry. It was evident from the issued orders that a close co-ordination of all arms had been worked out, with nothing left to chance. Furthermore, it was to be the first offensive enterprise of appreciable dimensions on the Western Front since the close of the Passchendaele fighting in the previous autumn.

While the attack was to be arranged and carried out by the 4th Australian Division, units of the adjoining 2nd and 3rd Divisions were placed at the disposal of the 4th Division. On its right or southern flank, the 6th Brigade, as previously mentioned, was incorporated in the scheme, as well as part of the artillery and machine-gun resources of the 2nd Division. The function of the latter arms was to barrage the front of the 2nd Division's sector of the attack and to prolong on the south, the barrage of the main operation. The right flank of the attack rested on a point close to the Amiens-St. Quentin road, near Villers Bretonneux, and bore away in a north-easterly direction to the Somme River.

In conformity with its allotted part, the 2nd Machine Gun Battalion set apart four guns of the 22nd Company to accompany the 6th Brigade, and 35 for barrage work. The 4th Division laid down the conditions that the fire would be directed from guns disposed for defence of the forward zone, and must not be of such nature as to prevent their use for the defence of the present defensive organisation. In short, they were to co-operate without disturbing the existing defensive arrangements of their own division. In accordance with orders, the 2nd Machine Gun Battalion arranged for a fixed barrage on the front of the 1,000 yards of the southern end of the attack, and for its continuance 1,500 yards in a south-westerly direction in front of the existing front line; the obvious intention being to give ample flank protection on the right "hinge" of the advance.

To carry out the foregoing, the Battalion organised its existing formation as under:—

Left Group.		"Y" Sub-group .. .. 5 guns
"A" Battery .. .. .. 4 guns		(Two of 6th Coy.)
(5th Coy.)		
"B" Battery .. .. .. 4 guns		"W" Sub-group .. .. 9 guns
(6th Coy.)		"D" Battery ..
"C" Battery .. .. .. 4 guns		(6th Coy.) .. 5 guns
(22nd Coy.)		"E" Battery .. .. 4 guns
"Z" Sub-group .. .. 2 guns		—
"X" Sub-group .. .. 7 guns		9 guns

In all, 35 guns were employed of which the Company's contribution was eleven. It will be noted that the newly initiated "group" system was maintained. Major Ordish (5th Company) was in charge of the left group, and Captain M. Burrell (7th Company), of the right. Lieutenant R. Dodgshun had charge of "D" Battery, and "Y" sub-group was under Lieutenant T. Turnbull.

As soon as the plans were known, preparations were put in hand on 1st July. Orders required that, for each barrage gun, 20,000 rounds of bulk ammunition and 4,500 rounds in belts had to be at the gun positions. For this work, men from the reserves at Lamotte were sent forward to do the necessary carrying at night, after the Transport Section had delivered their loads as far forward as practicable. Each delivery was carefully camouflaged to prevent detection by enemy aircraft. The actual firing positions for the attack were sited some distance to a flank from the defensive locations, so that the latter might not be endangered by possible detection while firing. At Lamotte, the usual battery and gun charts and fire orders were prepared. Meanwhile, the nightly harassing fire was continued, a heavier programme than usual being completed. Three days and nights were available for the preparatory work, which was carried out without interruption, the only noteworthy incident being the wounding of Private L. J. P. McNamara on the 3rd. Presumably, to accustom the enemy to aeroplane activity at night, aeroplanes patrolled over the lines so that it would not be an unusual event on the night before the attack, when the droning noise from the engines would cover the final sinister preparations. On the 3rd, Lieutenant Turnbull noted (referring to the cartage of ammunition), "plane activity of previous nights had the effect of keeping enemy well under cover, and we got ammunition into position without a mishap of any kind. Enemy machine-gun searching fire was fairly heavy, but overhead; unusual good fortune."

By the evening of the 3rd, when the signallers had connected the batteries, all preparations were complete, and the barrage teams did their best to sleep during the remaining hours of the night. Towards morning, British aeroplanes patrolled the front, and by their droning noise, masked the noise of the tanks as they moved to their positions with the assaulting infantry on the "jumping-off tape."

Zero hour was fixed at 3.10 a.m. on the 4th July. Punctually the artillery opened, the barrage machine-guns adding their quota to the deafening clamour. Firing at the rate of 50 rounds per minute for 45 minutes, the Company's guns, as part of the machine-gun barrage, completed their programme without unusual incident or loss, although the other teams sustained a few casualties. On completion of their programme, the teams stood by on S.O.S. lines. No counter-attacks were made by the enemy, but "X," "Y," and "W" Sub-groups answered an S.O.S. call at 4.40 a.m. In its report dealing with the operation, the 6th Brigade reported that the "machine-gun barrage put down was satisfactory." Prior to the attack, arrangements had been made with the Flying Corps to drop ammunition from aeroplanes on receipt of a ground signal from the troops. A quantity was dropped close to "D" battery. In its report dealing with the operation, the 2nd Machine Gun Battalion said that "several prisoners of the 3rd Battalion, 137 Infantry Regiment, captured by our right brigade during the operations of 4th July, stated that their casualties during the time they had been in the line had been heavy, and that they were very largely due to machine-gun fire at night."

With the completion of its minor part in the attack, and the receipt of reports of its complete success, interest of Company members faded. Indeed, at least two decided to interest themselves in other matters. They were the two inveterate souvenir hunters of No. 3 Section, Sergeant F. Wigmore and Private R.

C. Trevan. What followed can best be told in Trevan's own words. "What I clearly remember," said he, "in connection with the aftermath of the fight, was the souveniring trip to the newly-won trench system made by Wigmore and myself. We set out soon after finishing our barrage task, Wigmore being arrayed in a topper and frock coat, and I in a suit of dungaree overalls, souvenired in the Villers Bretonneux ruins. Arriving at the new front line by devious routes, rendered necessary on account of enemy strafing, we followed the trench along to a dead-end, or barricade of sandbags, which, the infantry informed us, divided our trench from Fritz's, and also that they were forbidden to pass. As we considered ourselves outside their jurisdiction, we climbed the barricade and went off down the trench, each with two automatics well to the front. After proceeding fully 150 yards along the trench, we came on a wounded officer and his servant. While I mounted guard over them, Wigmore went back and brought a stretcher, and we all got over the top with the officer on the stretcher, and took him and the private soldier back to a first aid post, and handed them over. We then went back, and, proceeding about 100 yards further along the trench, we saw an enemy post with half a dozen square helmets showing over a bend in the trench about 25 yards from us. We spent about 20 minutes sniping at them, and finally went back to the infantry and gave all information to the officer in charge, who proceeded to occupy the trench."

The attack was a complete success, being an object lesson in conception and execution. Ninety-three minutes sufficed to complete the whole operation, which yielded 1,500 prisoners and 171 machine-guns, at a total cost of less than 800 casualties. Remarkable as the results were, General Monash has declared that the moral results to both sides were far more important than the material gains. Apart from the battle's effect on the Corps side, "its effects on the enemy were even more startling. His whole front from the Ancre to Villers Bretonneux had become unstable, and was reeling from the blow." To follow up the success, the line troops were enjoined to institute vigourous offensive patrolling along the whole Corps front on the afternoon of the battle. Such tactics appealed strongly to the enterprise of the Australian soldier, and the response to the order, combined with the remarkable results achieved, would provide pages of striking narrative of individual enterprise and daring adventure. "Divisions, Brigades, and Battalions vied with each other in predatory expeditions, even in broad daylight, into the enemy's ground, and a steady stream of prisoners and machine-guns flowed in." Almost nightly, slices of territory were taken from the enemy, the effects of which further elevated the high spirits of the Australians as they correspondingly depressed those of the enemy. Usually these enterprises were designated "peaceful penetration" by the troops, although the vigorous and daring methods employed were far from peaceful. In these enterprises, members of the Company were, in the circumstances, debarred from participation, and had to content themselves with the knowledge that they were performing less exciting but necessary duties in maintaining the machine-gun defence of the Divisional front. Although the front line was steadily moving eastwards, the system of defence had, nevertheless, to be maintained, and its maintenance required much changing of gun positions to conform to the new alignment with corresponding alterations to S.O.S. lines, and cartage of gear and ammunition. The Company appeared to be doing a lot of work without any definite results.

On the night following the capture of Hamel, the usual harassing fire was maintained, and on the morning of the 5th a protective barrage was put down as a precautionary measure. The same provision had been arranged for the evening, but owing to the activity of the enemy artillery, and the fact that the S.O.S. signal had been observed on the left flank, the guns of the Left Group and "Y" Sub-group of the Right Group opened fire at the request of the left brigade. 250 rounds per minute were fired for 10 minutes, then 50 per minute till ordered to cease. During the night, the teams in the line were relieved from the reserves at Lamotte, to which the outgoing members retired.

Following the "peaceful penetration" activities of the front line units, changes in the barrage lines became necessary on the 7th, and in addition, arrangements were made for firing in conjunction with a discharge of gas cylinders on the same night, which, however, did not take place owing to the wind being unfavourable. More penetration into enemy territory required further alterations in Company arrangements on the 8th, while preparations were made to cover a small night attack near Monument Wood, by the right brigade (7th) during that night. The enemy was completely demoralised, and the objective taken with trifling loss. One of the Company's guns was moved into the captured area, and mounted in Stamboul Trench. During the night, Lieutenant W. Elliott was wounded and evacuated.

Continued progress eastwards required further alterations in dispositions. During the night of the 11th, inter-company changes with the 22nd Company brought the Company under the control of the Right Group Commander, with fresh night targets and S.O.S. lines. Three nights later, the enemy was dispossessed of Monument Wood by the 7th Brigade, who again took the offensive on the night of the 17th, and further extended its gains. On the latter occasion, artillery support was given, and eight of the Company's guns also co-operated, firing 33,000 rounds. New targets were again arranged, aeroplane photographs being used in selecting points where evidence of movement was recorded.

Following the thrust of the 7th Brigade, enemy retaliation came on the evening of the 18th. About 6.30 p.m. bodies of men estimated at fifteen hundred, were seen advancing, and reported by the 7th Brigade. Artillery fire was directed on to them, but the S.O.S. was reported from the front line of the 5th Brigade shortly after 9 p.m. In response, the Company's guns fired 43,000 rounds. It transpired that three front line posts were attacked, but the attackers were driven off by the combined rifle, machine-gun, and artillery fire. In this connection, Sergeant A. E. Cameron, who was concerned in the firing, said: "In the evening the Huns attacked, but were everywhere repulsed, and in this our guns fired some thousands of rounds. I remember we received special mention from Brigade headquarters, and thereby hangs a tale not known to the Brigade 'heads.' Infantry who were in the front line during this attack, told us afterwards that our bullets just skimmed the front line and caught the advancing waves fairly, causing casualties. This should not have been, as our targets were lines of communication behind the German lines, but owing to our barrels having become very worn, our bullets dropped several hundred yards short, luckily to good purpose. I remember that one of our officers came up and saw that new barrels went into our guns, as that shooting was cutting it a bit too fine to be safe for our infantry."

During the night of the 21st-22nd July, the Company exchanged positions with the 22nd Machine Gun Company, and passed from the centre sector to the right sector of the Divisional front. This rearrangement brought the Company into the area of the right brigade—the 6th—and as a consequence, its weapons became the extreme right—or southerly—Vickers guns of the British Army in France. Adjoining the Australians was the 31st Corps of the French Army, with its Algerian Tirailleurs and Zouaves. At the junction of the two armies, "international posts" were formed, comprising Australians, Frenchmen, and their coloured allies, which naturally produced some interesting situations. To ensure a good overlapping junction, two of the Company's guns and teams were established some distance in French territory. The close proximity of the Company's guns were, however, "a constant source of worry and wonder to the Algerians," said Lieutenant Callister, "the French did no indirect fire, and the steady use of the Company's guns frightened them. After some days' firing, they could not credit that the Germans had not located them, and that they had not been shelled. They kept their trenches very deep, narrow, and clean. Our indifference to these things, and our free movement made them very fidgety. Captain Rae and I strolled overland one day, and a little French sub-lieutenant (they were officered by Frenchmen) was appalled at the risk to us, and afraid we would bring shells on him. They had few officers, and believed in lying pretty low unless attacking." Corporal F. L. Fitzpatrick, who was in charge of the teams in French territory, said: "On the high ground where we were, a good view was to be had over Monument Wood on our left, where the daylight operations of our infantry were greatly admired by the French officers, who told me they had never seen such daring daylight tactics, and thought they evidenced high-class infantry. The men were most friendly, offering us part of their rations. The Zouaves received a wine ration, and the rate of exchange was one Australian clasp knife to one petrol tin of vin rouge. Until the clasp knives gave out, a constant watch had to be kept to ensure reasonable sobriety in No. 4 Section. They repaired their trenches, carefully camouflaged all machine-gun and trench mortar positions, and generally set a high standard in regard to trench maintenance; much higher than our own."

As part of the re-arrangement mentioned in the previous paragraph, two of the Company's guns were placed in the front line a little to the left of the junction of Stamboul and Syria trenches, which marked the right boundary of the 6th Brigade. These guns—for the time being—the two extreme right-hand guns of the British Army, were manned by teams from No. 2 Section, under Corporal R. L. M. Cox and Lance Corporal N. C. Hammon. Following the prevailing policy, the front line was thinly held; so much so that the whole of the slender garrison in the sector stood to arms through the night, and after breakfast would retire to dug-outs to sleep, while two snipers, specially sent up from the rear for day duty, would keep watch. In response to representations made by the infantry officer in charge, a number of French troops were sent in on the night of 23rd-24th, to strengthen the defenders. They departed the next morning, and were not specially careful to keep down while moving out through the shallow trenches. Some time after, two English artillery officers in peaked caps arrived with a telephone and observed for their battery from the front line, exposing themselves meanwhile. About 10 o'clock, Corporal Cox discovered that the snipers had not arrived—it was learned afterwards that they had been detained to guide an infantry relief in that night, and noticed how peaceful and quiet the sector was. Looking through one of the sniper's loopholes, he saw a German intently gazing at the British front, with head and shoulders well above the parapet. Obtaining a rifle, Cox fired one shot; the German disappeared, and was presently carried away by two others; Cox, firing another shot wide to hasten them on. No doubt, the presence of Australian, French, and English troops in the same sector had roused the enemy's curiosity. At all events, from about 2 p.m. in the afternoon (24th) the enemy steadily shelled the vicinity of the trench junction where the 23rd Battalion maintained a platoon of infantry, with two Lewis guns, supporting a small bombing post about 70 yards in front, in Craft trench. Shortly before eight o'clock enemy shelling became intense, and five minutes later a bombing attack was launched against the advanced post, while about 20 men were seen advancing along the western side of Craft trench. The bombing post of five men fell back on their supports, and a brisk but local fight ensued. "The shelling ceased like magic," said Corporal Cox, "I jumped on to the firing post to see what was doing, and saw the Germans jump from their trench carrying their rifles at the high port. I ran to the dugout and shouted down the stairs: 'they are coming over,' and heard someone below repeat to the others, 'they are coming over.' Those below were wearing their equipment loosely about them, and in the rush to get up jammed themselves in the stairway. Just as the Germans left their trench, a carefully aimed shell burst on a block in the trench, and covered the Lewis gunners with dirt. A few shells continued to fall near the Company's guns, and while Private E. B. Rolls—of Corporal Hammon's team—was feeding in the belt, one burst close by, blowing the gun into the air, damaging the barrel casing, and wounding Rolls in the arm. By this time, a lively bombing and sniping fight was in progress, but it was difficult, owing to the dust raised by the exploding bombs, to see clearly what was taking place; moreover, some traverses in the trench hampered fire from Cox's gun as he watched for an opportunity. The infantry put up a spirited defence, and the attackers pressed, each side giving bomb for bomb, until the German officer in charge was killed, whereupon his men, shouting to one another, retreated. The eager infantry and a Lewis gunner followed hard after them, one man carrying his steel helmet filled with bombs, as he ran along the top. In their hurry, some of the Germans ran across country, and the watchful Cox had his opportunity at last when a few bunched together as they ran. Some fell in response to a burst from his gun, but the actual number is not known. One wounded German was captured, while the infantry lost one man killed, and three wounded. While it was a purely local affair, it was very exciting to those involved in it. The artillery was called on, but the fight was over when their response was made.

Enemy retaliation on the night of 22nd-23rd July took the form of an intense bombardment with gas shells of Villers Bretonneux and vicinity. It commenced at 10.5 p.m., slackened at 11 p.m., and still further at 11.30 p.m. At 11.45 p.m. it reached its greatest intensity, slackened at 1 a.m., and ceased at 4 a.m. It was estimated that 8000 green and yellow cross shells were used, containing mustard gas. The night was dark, and favourable from the enemy's point of view. The 6th Brigade reported over 300 casualties, and the 5th Brigade adjoining, nearly 100. The chief sufferers were those men who had cause to move about while attending to their duties. The great majority of cases were slightly affected, but the fighting strength of the 6th Brigade was seriously diminished owing to the evacuations. At the time, Lieutenants Dodgshun and Jeffery were sharing a cellar of a big house in the western part of the village. They donned their respirators, but while Dodgshun was unaffected, Jeffery had trouble with his respirator and became ill early in the morning. He was taken to an advanced aid post by Dodgshun, and evacuated. The latter set out to report his colleague's departure, and while passing through a wheat crop (wearing the nose clip of his respirator, but with his eyes exposed) his eyes became affected to the extent of painful blindness. He was also evacuated, but recovered after treatment, which necessitated his eyes being bandaged for three weeks, during which he never saw daylight. He rejoined the Company after the Armistice, but Jeffery was returned to Australia and discharged. In addition to the two officers, six other ranks were evacuated. They were: Privates E. R. Blake, E. Blair, W. A. Birch, J. R. Palmer, A. Lean, and T. Bull. All through the night, while they remained in their respirators and in the cellars and dug-outs, they were unaffected, but when they moved out the following morning, the delayed action effect of the pervading gas caused them to go blind.

For some months previously, the continuous arrival of American troops in France was common knowledge, and some detachments, as previously mentioned, had taken part, in association with Australian infantry, in the capure of Hamel. But it was not till the 11th July, when six men of the 131st Machine Gun Company, American, were attached for experience in night firing, that the Company came in close contact with them. They were followed by a larger contingent on the 26th, when five teams of the 129th Machine Gun Company were allotted to the Company for general experience in line duty. They were accordingly allocated to various teams in the line and forward positions, the officers and men sharing quarters with Company members respectively. The association was naturally a very interesting experience for both parties. What follows is not intended as a criticism of the qualities of a welcome ally, but it was inevitable that the impact of raw and inexperienced troops with Australians who combined in a high degree their natural enterprise and the sharp lessons of over three years of active campaigning, should produce some sharp distinctions. At the very outset, the newcomers made no secret of their admiration of the Australians. Indeed, their outspoken regard for the "diggers" was almost embarrasing. On the other hand, the "diggers" were well disposed towards such a friendly lot of men, and the two parties got on splendidly together. But when it came to the business in hand, Company members were appalled at their ignorance and want of perception. "The officer attached to me," said Lieutenant Turnbull, "was a particularly charming fellow, and used to ply me with so many and such pointed questions that I used to wonder at times if he had mistaken me for Sir Douglas Haig. His general idea was to mount a gun in the clock tower in Villers Bretonneux, and from that vantage point proceed to clean up the opposing regiment. A few enemy retaliatory shellings for our indirect fire showed him that the idea was, if enterprising, not sound in actual practice." "As individuals," said Lieutenant Callister, "they were of fine

Company N.C.O.'s. Taken at Querrieu. June, 1918.
Australian War Memorial Photograph. Copyright.

physique, clean and well kept, though their gear was rather shoddy, but as troops, they were entirely raw and inexperienced. They were cheerful and willing enough, but not very curious about things, not too enterprising; their interests were essentially in U.S.A. Their administration was top-heavy, and they ran a paper war at least three times ours. The coming in of their five teams nearly gave me heart disease from the manner of their arrival, bunching dispositions, dilatoriness, and general neglect of the precautions set out in the relief programme. Once our guides took charge of them, it was much better." Their comments were very interesting and novel to the casual and deeply experienced Australians. One of their sentries enquired: "What are those?"—"those" being hostile bullets arriving in his close vicinity. Another commented: "I never thought to see so many shells. I didn't know they fired so many. There are more shells flying about than I thought there were bullets." In spite of their extreme rawness, Company officers agreed that they would prove very staunch in action if well led, and would have welcomed them as reinforcements. The wide difference between the two parties made thoughtful Company members realise how very far they themselves had travelled since Gallipoli days, and what a vast amount of experience they took for granted, and looked for, in troops in France.

The Battalion "group" scheme of tactical control of guns and teams—to which previous reference has been made—necessitated a good deal of shuffling of senior officers in the battalion. Each Group Headquarters required a captain to direct it, also the service of an intelligence officer. For some time, Captain Rae acted as Right Group commander, and in the latter stages, controlled both 6th and 22nd Companies when they constituted the Right Group. The temporary detachment of Captains from their companies brought temporary rank of Captain to Lieutenants Callister and Blenkarn. The former held the appointment for a month, and directed the Company, except for four days, when Captain R. C. Webb, M.C., of the 5th Company, assumed command; the only occasion when an "outside" officer was in charge. Lieutenant Blenkarn held the appointment for three weeks, and he took command of the 7th Company.

During the month, Lieutenant G. A. Williams was transferred to the Company from the 7th Company, and Second-Lieutenants F. G. Hamilton, M.M. and Bar, and W. A. Carne reported from cadet battalions in England, where they had gained commissions. The former was a nominee from the 7th Field Ambulance.

Before leaving the line, three other casualties were sustained, Privates B. Barrass and A. Campbell being wounded, and evacuated on the 23rd and 26th respectively; the latter by a shell-splinter as he was coming out of the line. On the 24th, Captain Callister was proceeding to gun positions near Monument Wood when he was struck by a small fragment of a 4.2 shell, which went through and out of the triceps muscle of his left arm. The medical officer of the 23rd Battalion injected anti-tetanus serum, and its effects were worse than those of the shell-splinter. As on a previous occasion, when wounded at Pozieres, Captain Callister carried on and made little reference to his injury. All things considered, the casualty list for the 30 days of line duty may be adjudged light. It showed two officers (one remaining at duty) and four other ranks wounded: two officers and six other ranks gassed, while there were five other ranks evacuated sick; a total of 19.

During the night of 28th July, the Company was relieved by the 5th Machine Gun Company, although it was 1.20 a.m. on the following morning before the "change over" was reported complete. The outgoing teams greatly appreciated the presence, well forward, of the Company limbers to carry the guns, gear, and some of the personnel back to camp at Lamotte, some five or six miles distant. Some of the men made use of a returning G.S. wagon, and their presence on it led to a diverting incident after daylight. Some days previous to the relief, a brigadier was inspecting the forward positions, and while near one of No. 2 Section's guns, a sharp enemy barrage caused the brigadier and his small party to beat a hurried retreat, during which the former lost his red-banded and gold-edged cap. It was "salved" by Private A. F. Woodman, and treasured for the time. While sitting with the party on the G.S. waggon he bethought himself of the cap, and thereupon placed it on his head. His tired mates took but mild interest in the pseudo general officer, but when some passing English units were encountered, they "sat up and took notice." The subalterns in charge of several small parties manifestly could not understand the spectacle of a doubtful looking brigadier-general sitting on a crowded waggon among a party of diggers, but—there was the cap. However, succeeding officers gravely gave the command, "eyes left," tendering the salute meanwhile. Woodman just as gravely returned the courtesy, to the suppressed merriment of his companions,

So came to an end a tenure of line duty which was full of incident and movement. While the battalions were involved in almost daily personal contact with the enemy, and carrying out remarkable individual and collective enterprises, Company members could point to but one encounter, which has been recorded. They had to be content with hearing of the infantry activities while they moved their guns and gear forward from time to time, carried ammunition, and re-arranged their harassing fire charts and S.O.S. lines. To feel that the machine-gun defence was well maintained seemed poor recompense for absence from the exciting episodes being enacted by their infantry comrades. Nevertheless, there is evidence that their work was not in vain. The diarist of the 2nd Machine Gun Battalion under the date, 18th July, noted: "Prisoners captured in last night's advance state the greater number of their casualties were caused by our barrage, and few by artillery. This is the third occasion in the past two months that a similar statement has been made by prisoners."

Although it was not known at the time, events on the Western Front were hastening to the Armistice. In mid-July, the Germans launched an offensive in the south against the French, and, for the second time, reached the Marne River; but, a counter-stroke by the French, aided by Americans, threw them back with the loss of no less than 15,000 prisoners in one day. It was a heartening success for the Allies. No doubt the Allied leaders considered the time ripe for a general counter-offensive because, early in the following month, it was launched. Before passing to a record of the three months which ultimately led to the Armistice, it is appropriate that some reference be made to the state of the men of the A.I.F., who were to take a strikingly successful part, and who provided, in the initial stages, the spear-head of the Allied attack. The moment found four of the five Australian Divisions working harmoniously together—shortly to be joined by the remaining one—highly efficient, deeply experienced, and directed by a Corps Commander and staff who, in a remarkable degree, combined the lessons of over four years' campaigning with a clear outlook on the problems ahead, and a firm confidence in their ability to deal with them. Some said at the time that the morale of the A.I.F. had never been higher. Without making a pronouncement on the point, it is certain that the "peaceful penetration" tactics of all five Divisions, combined with the obviously declining German morale, had raised the spirits of the men to a very high pitch. That confidence joined to their accumulated experience and efficiency, certainly equipped them for any undertaking which was humanly possible of achievement. Not every man could be classed in that category—there were instances to the contrary—but the dour, dependable back-bone of each unit carried on to the end, and, knowing their superiority, undertook all tasks set them with a fair amount of serenity. With all of this, it should be remembered that months and years of severance from home and country, the divorce from comforts and relaxation of civilian life, and the horrors of modern warfare, had produced an inevitable war-weariness and its various reactions. To go forward confidently in an attack with such a background, must surely be one of the high-water marks in the achievements of human nature.

Turning to the Company, it may be said that the foregoing applied in generous measure. The writer cannot forebear from penning a personal testimony at this stage. He has always carried in mind the uplift he received—after he returned from the safety and relative comfort of a sojourn in England—when he undertook his share of the disagreeable duty of censoring the correspondence of members of the unit. Remembering that some of the writers had been campaigning for over three years,[*] he was deeply impressed by the cheerful tone and almost total absence of complaint in the home letters. "Fritz has been getting a bad time of late," seemed to sum up their modest references to recent events, and while no forecasts of an early conclusion were indicated, there was a spiritual and deep-seated conviction of the justness of their cause, and the certainty of final triumph. At no time did the possibility of defeat disturb their minds; now their faith in ultimate victory flamed higher.

[*] A remarkable instance of continuous service is that of Corporal R. L. M. Cox, particulars of which will be found in the Appendix.

CHAPTER XXIV.

The Beginning of the End: 8th, 9th and 11th August, 1918.

(28th July—17th August.)

It has oftimes been noted that a calm precedes a storm. The old adage was to receive striking confirmation on the British front in the month of August. Apart from certain activities of the Australian Divisions, stagnation was the order of the day. The enemy might well have imagined that the British Army was a spent force. If he did, he was to be sadly disillusioned. Unseen and unsuspected forces were gathering for his overthrow, although it would appear that neither side realised how a splendidly conceived and executed blow would stagger, by virtue of its absolute surprise and weight, and lead to a dramatic and almost total collapse of the German Western Front. The closing days of July did not give any indication of violent changes. The "peaceful penetration" activities of the 2nd Division continued, and while they furnished encouraging evidence of the complete ascendancy of the Australians over their opponents, the results—in relation to the remainder of the front —did not warrant or suggest the hope of an early end of the conflict. It may be doubted if a single individual—excepting the higher placed officers—had any conception of the proximity and dimensions of the approaching storm.

The last four days of July found the Company "resting" in congenial circumstances of weather and location. Upon relief, as described in the preceding chapter, it returned to its tented camp near Lamotte, and settled down to the daily routine when out of the line. The weather continued warm, and gave added zest to daily and frequent bathing in the adjacent Somme. A diarist noted at this time: "Company resting in this restful glade alongside the Somme." Members were quite content to accept —with the soldier's comforting fatalism—what appeared to be the natural order of events, and did not pay undue attention to vague rumours of another attack. The usual Company training and overhauling of gear went on pleasantly, and the long days gave ample opportunity for relaxation. Games were played, the chief activity being cricket. On the 29th, Captain Drummond relinquished his appointment as Left Group Commander in the line, and resumed command of the Company. Three other ranks were evacuated: 2 sick and 1 (Private R. A. Bate) slightly gassed and wounded before the recent relief from line duty.

On the night of 4th August, arrived the first orders of an impending offensive, and the following morning the first steps were taken to give effect to the instructions. A study of the plans and maps revealed a strikingly ambitious scheme. For the Australian share in the attack, the whole five Divisions were to be brought together for the first time to act under their own Corps Commander. Two Divisions, the 3rd (left) and 2nd (right), were to attack side by side, and, assuming the attainment of their objectives, the 4th and 5th were to pass through, or in Army parlance, "leapfrog," and carry the advance a stage further. The second stage of the advance, involving a "double leapfrog" carried out simultaneously by two separate pairs of Divisions operating side by side, was a manoeuvre unique in the history of war. The proposed Corps front extended over four miles, and the contemplated penetration provided for a depth of practically four miles, sufficient to over-run the whole of the enemy artillery dispositions; the scheme, in effect, aimed at "biting out" by destruction and capture, the whole of the enemy defensive organisation opposite the Corps front. Complete surprise and a close co-ordination of all arms and services, aided by the new tanks, were the factors upon which the scheme was based; together with the loyal, active, and intelligent co-operation of officers and men.

Extensive as were the plans for the Corps sector, it was found that they were but a part of a larger scheme. On the immediate right, the fine Canadian Corps was to take its allotted place next the Australians, and further south, a Corps of the First French Army was to provide necessary flank protection for the Canadians. On the left, or north, of the Australian Corps lay the Somme River, and on its northern bank, the Third British Corps was to arrange the defensive flank in that quarter. The whole attack was planned over a frontage of 15 miles, with the men from the two major sections of the Empire holding the pride of place in the centre, and supplying the spear-head of the great blow.

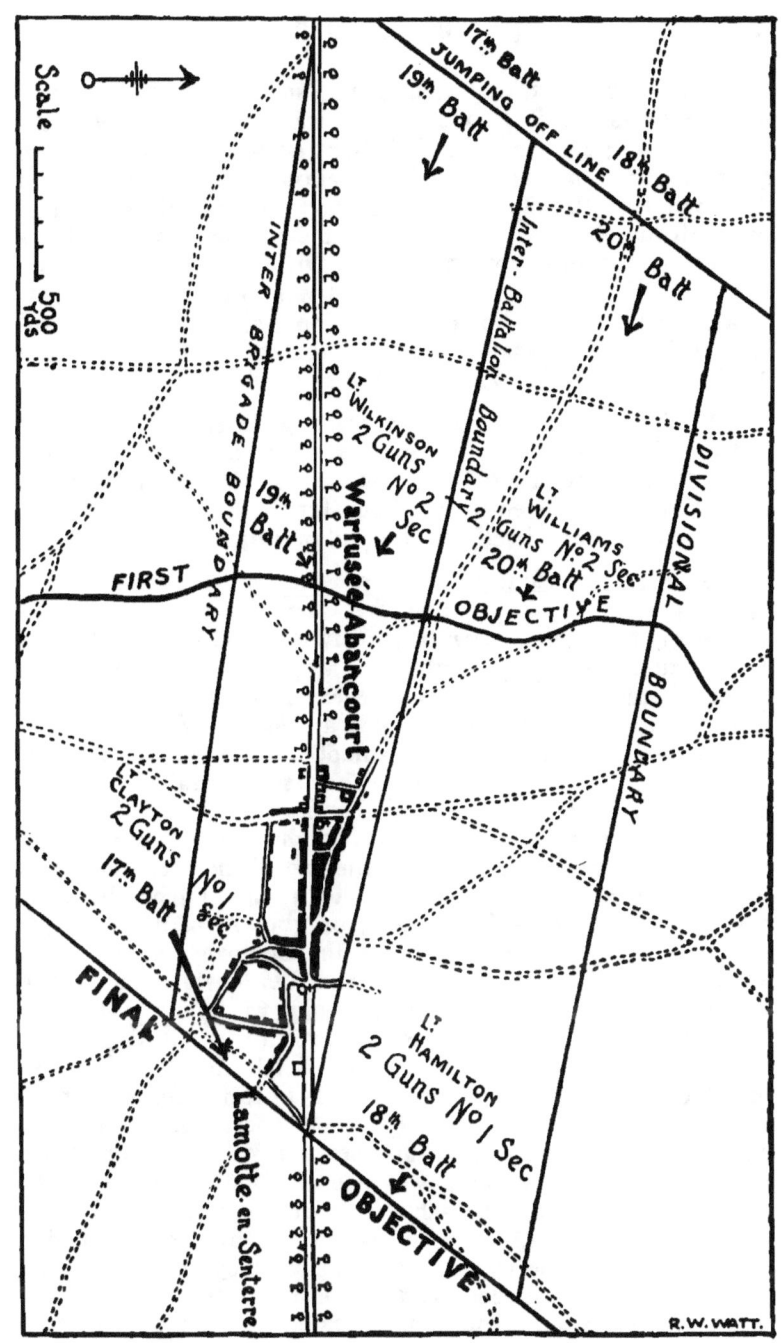

Attack of 8th August, 1918.

Turning to the task allotted to the 2nd Division, it was found that the Divisional front of two miles was allotted equally to the 5th Brigade (left) and 7th Brigade (right), with the 6th in reserve. In turn, the 5th Brigade allotted the 20th Battalion (left) and 19th Battalion (right), to take the first objective, and the 18th and 17th to pass through their comrades and attack the second and final objective of the Division. The right flank of the 5th Brigade rested on the east-west Villers Bretonneux-Amiens road, and the line of advance bore slightly to the south-east until the road marked the inter-battalion boundary. The depth of the objective was just over two miles.

The Divisional machine-gun plans were simple. The 5th and 7th Companies were given creeping barrage tasks, and the 6th and 22nd were allotted to the attacking 5th and 7th Brigades respectively, in their entirety. Thus, for the first time in attack, the Company found itself attached to an unfamiliar brigade.

As events proved, three full days were available for the Company's preparatory work, and the time was ample. Officers and teams were selected with deliberation, and guns, gear, and ammunition thoroughly overhauled. Maps and aeroplane photographs were closely studied, and every detail which experience and forethought could suggest was arranged. Meanwhile, the general preparations proceeded smoothly, and without display; secrecy being the watchword. The 1st Australian Division arrived in the area, and a large contingent of "fighting" and "carrying" tanks—under cover of night—were grouped and hidden in adjacent woods. With the end of the preparations in sight, everyone became keyed up to a high pitch; the chief question being, "does Fritz know or guess?" Apparently he did not. Every officer and man in the Company shared in the prevailing high spirits and enthusiasm with which the attack was viewed. It was felt that the grouping of the five Australian Divisions in one unit enormously increased their striking power and stimulated intense pride which all felt in the A.I.F. In the officers' mess, bets were freely made as to the actual number of prisoners that would be taken in the operations of the day. Never did the Company enter an operation with such confidence and assurance. If anything was needed to stimulate all ranks still further, General Monash's final message to his troops—read to the assembled Company before it moved off—provided it. With a fine understanding of the psychology of his men, he disclosed the general scope and magnitude of the attack on the morrow. Its graphic and concise statements and note of sup-

THE BEGINNING OF THE END. 327

reme confidence made a direct and irresistible appeal. Nothing more, it seemed, required to be said. As one member commented: "Surely great deeds would be done on the morrow. War weary as many were, small was his spirit who felt no thrill of pride, nor splendid confidence in the tremendous attacking power of the whole five Divisions of Australian Infantry; 20 Brigades—60 Battalions of them." The text of the message is as follows:—

Corps Headquarters, August 7th, 1918.

TO THE SOLDIERS OF THE AUSTRALIAN ARMY CORPS.

For the first time in the history of this Corps, all five Australian Divisions will, to-morrow, engage in the largest and most important battle operation ever undertaken by the Corps.

They will be supported by an exceptionally powerful Artillery, and by Tanks and Aeroplanes on a scale never previously attempted. The full resources of our sister Dominion, the Canadian Corps, will also operate on our right, while two British Divisions will guard our left flank.

The many successful offensives which the Brigades and Battalions of this Corps have so brilliantly executed during the past four months have been but the prelude to, and the preparation for this greatest and culminating effort.

Because of the completeness of our plans and dispositions, of the magnitude of the operations, of the number of troops employed, and the depth to which we intend to over-run the enemy's positions, this battle will be one of the most memorable of the whole war; and there can be no doubt that, by capturing our objectives, we shall inflict blows on the enemy which will make him stagger, and will bring the end appreciably nearer.

I entertain no sort of doubt that every Australian soldier will worthily rise to so great an occasion, and that every man, imbued with the spirit of victory, will, in spite of every difficulty that may confront him, be animated by no other resolve than grim determination to see through to a clean finish, whatever his task may be.

The work to be done to-morrow will, perhaps, make heavy demands upon the endurance and staying powers of many of you; but I am confident that, in spite of excitement, fatigue, and physical strain, every man will carry on to the utmost of his powers until his goal is won; for the sake of AUSTRALIA, the Empire, and our cause.

I earnestly wish every soldier of the Corps the best of good fortune, and a glorious and decisive victory, the story of which will re-echo throughout the world, and will live for ever in the history of our home land.

John Monash, Lieut.-General Cmdg. Aust. Corps.

It was a sight to remember when the Company moved out of camp at 6 p.m. on the evening of the 7th; to the envy and disappointment of the few officers and men who had been selected to stay behind. All the officers were mounted, and the men were accommodated in G.S. waggons with Company limbers in rear carrying the 16 guns, gear, and ammunition. Captain Drummond was always keen to avoid unnecessary marching, and his efforts on this occasion were greatly aided by Lieutenant Blenkarn's persuasive eloquence with the Army Service Corps. The sight of the loaded waggons brought forth many pleasantries from less fortunate individuals who wanted to know "where's the picnic?" Passing through Glisy, and to the left of Blangy-Tronville, the cheerful party moved on. Away to the left and right could be seen thousands of fellow Australians toiling forward under the setting sun, across the rolling French fields, in battle order, en route to the assault. In spite of the numbers involved and the complexity of the moves, everything was moving with precision and without hustle. "We were lost in admiration," noted one observer, "of the traffic control." The only disturbing note was the spectacle of a large fire raging in a wood adjacent to Villers Bretonneux. A chance enemy shell—it was learned later—had set fire to petrol supplies for the tanks, and the resultant conflagration had destroyed a number of tanks and a large quantity of stores. Meanwhile, the blaze caused many to wonder if the great scheme had been discovered.

In due course, the Company reached the appointed "rendezvous," near the north-eastern corner of Villers Bretonneux, about 9 p.m., and took cover in dug-outs. There the teams remained—snatching some sleep meanwhile—till 2 a.m. on the morning of the 8th, when eight teams and guns moved forward and took up their positions on the "jumping-off" tape. The night continued calm, confirming the impression that the enemy had no knowledge of the impending storm. Three o'clock passed, and a cool fog enveloped the country. An occasional shell from either side whined lazily overhead, and everything appeared normal, though the damp grass and the mist shrouded many thousands of Australians, grim and silent, but with bayonets fixed and ready. To quote Corporal F. L. Fitzpatrick: "With half an hour to go, the eastern sky lightens. Ten minutes to go; men light up their last smoke—for the time being, at any rate—and take a last look at equipment and weapons. A minute to go; forms rise up from the shell-holes in readiness; the word passes round; 30 seconds to go; we glance back to the dark stillness of the western horizon, so silent, but we know, packed with artillery batteries, with the gunners standing tense and ready. With still 10 seconds to go, a red and yellow blaze appears on our right—a vicious boom—the French artillery open up. Still the rear horizon is silent and menacing—then a terrific ripping flash! A thousand guns speak as one; such awe-inspiring roar and rend and flash and crash as surely man never saw or heard before; we're off!" Thus, at 4.20 a.m. the great blow fell.

The artillery preparations included a proportion of smoke-shells which, added to the existing fog, considerably restricted visibility. Direction and formation were hard to maintain, but the attackers pushed on, and were greatly encouraged by the noise of the British aeroplanes overhead, which they could not see, and the noisy tanks, which were not visible unless close at hand. Attackers and defenders alike were hampered by the fog, but the advantage lay with the former because they had the initiative and pressed boldly forward. Although the surprise was complete, enemy parties held out bravely, but the attackers never hesitated to rush them, and the tanks assisted by over-running machine-gun nests and strong points. The general attack was almost a complete success. On the Anzac Corps front, the whole of the objectives were attained with trifling loss, and many prisoners taken, as well as an immense amount of material and guns.

The experiences of the Company's eight teams and guns attached to the 5th Brigade are recorded as follows.

The 20th Battalion was allotted to the left Brigade sector of the first objective which included the enemy front line system and involved a penetration of about one mile. Apart from the common problem of maintaining direction, no particular difficulties appear to have been encountered. The tanks were of great material and moral assistance, and all except one arrived at the objective. With the Battalion were two teams from No. 2 Section, under Lieutenant G. A. Williams, who was assisted by Sergeant D. C. M. Parkhill and Corporal W. E. Peters. At Zero, the party moved off, and at the outset sustained its only casualty when Private H. G. Merry was wounded in the face by a shell splinter. Keeping close to the first wave of infantry, and following the road leading to Warfusee, "more by the feel of our feet than anything else," said Lance Corporal S. H. Deakin, they were brought to a halt by a wounded infantryman who warned them of an enemy machine-gun post directly in front. Williams and Parkhill went forward to investigate. They came upon the post, which contained 16 men and 2 machine-guns. A very irate N.C.O. ordered the gunners to fire, but the two determined officers overawed them with their revolvers, whereupon the whole of the occupants of the post surrendered. For this exploit, Lieutenant Williams received the Military Cross. Resuming the advance, some of the infantry who had lost their bearings in the fog and had turned in a circle, were met, and had to be re-directed. Ultimately, the objective line was reached without further incident, and the guns established as ordered. The complete success of the operation disposed of any possibility of counter-attack, consequently the guns were not called on for action:

To the right sector of the Brigade's first objective was allotted the 19th Battalion, with a task similar to that undertaken by their comrades on their left. The assault was carried out with vigour, despite the fog. Many prisoners were captured, and the objective consolidated. Casualties were light. With the Battalion were two teams from No. 2 Section, under Lieutenant N. F. Wilkinson, with Sergeant J. P. Adams and Corporal L. Barrand as assistants. "Just on Zero," said Wilkinson, "I issued a round of rum to all ranks. Though all of us were particularly subdued, fully realising the nature of the great attack to be launched, the issue of the rum seemed to loosen the tension, and I remember the hum of excitement and quiet handshakes all round as I carefully checked off the last two or three minutes to Zero. My own stimulant was my old favourite—cold tea from my water bottle, instead of rum. Zero at last, and what a pandemonium! The heavens fairly roared. Over we went from the assembly trench, and then our troubles began for there was a very heavy ground mist, and to keep direction

THE BEGINNING OF THE END.

was difficult. However, I knew that to our right lay the main road to Warfusee-Abancourt, and I quickly moved over to it, then crossed it, and kept the men about 100 yards away because I knew it would be shelled by Fritz. We met no serious opposition until nearing the village, when on our right a battery of machine-guns started to spit around us. Following us was a tank, and we quickly got it to charge this nest of guns. Right at them the tank went, firing through the now clearing mist, at the battery. Their fire ceased, and we rushed forward and came upon all the guns intact, but their crews had gone under the shelter of the mist and in fear of the tank, which surely would have mowed them down if they had remained a little longer at their post. We went on again, and there lay the mound which was the limit of our attack, and where we quickly got our guns into position for a counter-attack, should it develop. Some time later, official photographers appeared on the scene, and took a photo of the tank which helped us, and our two teams resting in front of it." The photograph so taken is part of the official records of the A.I.F. During the advance, however, the teams suffered loss. Shortly after moving from the "jumping-off tape," Private A. G. Stewart was wounded just above the right ankle; an injury which kept him in hospital for 15 months. Barrand bound the wound and hurried forward, to be himself hit in the leg, but he carried on. Bullets were whistling past, and one struck Private A. Bingham in the stomach. "Oh! Scotty; Scotty, I'm hit," said he to his mate—Private T. Haggart—as he fell; to die soon after. On reaching the objective, Private H. F. R. Lindsell was hit by a shell-splinter, which shattered his lower jawbone and carried away the teeth on one side. Barrand again rendered first aid, and while so doing, a "dud" shell fell in the same shell-hole in which he was at work—assisted by Private L. Miller. "By G——, that was pretty close," remarked the operator as he continued at work. Corporal Barrand's activities also included keeping his teams together and assisting his officer. His exertions brought him the award of the Military Medal. While the party were deciding on the best place to establish their guns, Private H. D. Stone was struck on the shoulder by a shell-splinter or bullet, which carried away the stud of the fuzee spring of the gun he was carrying. Very soon after, a shell burst a few yards away, and again wounded Stone as well as Privates E. T. Deakin and E. Daniel. Deakin had an artery inside the elbow of his right arm cut, and, in a dazed condition, was bleeding badly, but a tourniquet applied by Daniel, checked the bleeding and probably saved Deakin's life. Daniel was wounded in the heel, but was able to help Deakin to the dressing station. During the advance, Sergeant Adam was, as usual, a cool and capable assistant, and his sterling work (which he again demonstrated three days later in a subsequent advance) was recognised by the award of the Military Medal. Thereafter the sector became quiet, and the teams were not disturbed, neither were they called on for action. Later, they witnessed the passing through of the 5th Division, and were further interested by the passing of armoured cars through the village of Warfusee—Abancourt to exploit—with dramatic effectiveness—the 5th Division's successful attack.

To the left sector of the second objective went the 18th Battalion. After passing their comrades of the 20th Battalion, they carried the advance 2,000 yards further, and co-operated with the 17th Battalion in the capture of Warfusée-Abancourt. Little opposition came from the enemy, and the apportioned section of the Division's final objective was captured and consolidated. With the 18th Battalion were two teams from No. 1 Section, under Second Lieutenant F. G. Hamilton, who had with him Sergeant B. H. Johnston and Corporal A. E. Noonan. Misfortune overtook them at the outset. Private E. Brain was killed by a bullet as he rose to advance. Owing to the fog, some of the party became detached from their comrades, and Sergeant Johnston directed them to wait in a shell-hole while he went forward in an endeavour to trace the others. While he was absent, a shell burst in the shell-hole. Privates A. E. Johnson and E. J. Dunne were killed instantly, and Privates R. J. Howlett and J. Crompton wounded; the former badly. Crompton received several small wounds in the right arm, neck, and chest, and the effect of the burst left him "under the impression that he consisted of numerous different pieces." He managed to crawl to another shell-hole, but soon after another shell landed by his side, inflicting another wound in the neck. Recovering from the double shock, he was able to walk back to the nearest aid post and was there attended to. The stretcher-bearers found Brain lying dead with but a single mark on him. As a result of the disaster, the teams reached the objective without ammunition because the unfortunate party happened to be ammunition carriers. Fortunately, none was required. When the 46th Battalion of the 5th Division passed through later, a supply was obtained from them per medium of Lieutenant Eddy. In spite of the loss of five men and ammunition, the others pressed on, and caught up to a tank which had lost its way. They were

THE BEGINNING OF THE END.

able to direct the occupants of the monster to two enemy machine-guns which were blazing away. "A couple of rounds from his three-pounders (I think they were) brought out all the Huns at the double. They were the first we saw," said Lance Corporal H. J. Bennett, "and they had no fight left in them." The circumstances found Noonan in his element. At one stage, when detached from the infantry, he bombed a trench and forced no less than fourteen of the enemy to surrender; an act for which he received a bar to his Military Medal. "After the objective was reached," continued Bennett, "we entered a German dug-out and found hot stew, warm coffee, cigars, beer, etc., set out ready for breakfast." Except for firing a few rounds at an enemy aeroplane which was forcing a British R.E.8 machine to land, the guns did not come into action. The fog lifted, and after the infantry of the 5th Division had passed through, there was little to occupy the attention of the teams. It was Lieutenant Hamilton's first experience of an infantry action, and in spite of the upset of his plans caused by fog and enemy shell-fire, he acquitted himself with credit.

The 17th Battalion was directed to carry the right sector of the Brigade front in the final objective, including the capture of the joint villages of Warfusee-Abancourt and Lamotte-en-Santerre. The fog hampered operations, but as every man knew his part, the given task was completed in good time. Lively encounters took place. At one point a battery of 5.9 guns in action was captured, as well as a battery of 4.2 guns; a tank assisting in the capture. Both villages were quickly enveloped, and shortly after 7 o'clock elements of all Companies were digging in on their allotted objectives. Two teams from No. 1 Section were allotted to the 17th Battalion. Lieutenant W. S. Clayton was in charge, and had as assistant, Corporal E. D. Saker. To enable the men to arrive at the "jumping-off" tape without undue exertion, pack mules were provided to carry the guns, ammunition, and gear to the assembly position. Lieutenant Newcomen, Battalion Transport Officer, supervised the arrangements, and drivers from the Company Transport Section had charge of the animals. The journey to the tape was effected without mishap, although the mules at times took some urging to induce them to cross trenches. The drivers are worthy of commendation for their efforts. "With every man loaded up and checked off," said Lieutenant Clayton, "we set off in Indian file, following the white directional tape which was plainly visible, and had not gone far when, to our amazement, we came upon lines of tanks drawn up ready for the attack. We hadn't much time to speculate as to how they had got there, but there they were. Their crews were squatting down in groups, quietly smoking and yarning as though nothing at all unusual was afoot. Passing through the lines of tanks, to the cheery greetings of the members of the crews, we soon reached the cross tape which marked the "jumping-off" positions. At Zero, the noise of the barrage was deafening, and the men could scarcely hear each other speak, even when shouting in each other's ears. While so trying, Private B. Caligari was struck in the jaw by a machine-gun bullet, and he found himself spitting blood and teeth. Eight teeth had been shattered. He "reckoned he was dead unlucky not to be in the fun any further," but lost no time in getting out. The party moved off with the infantry, and soon encountered the difficulty of maintaining direction. Occasional glimpses of the trees along the main Amiens-St. Quentin road were obtained, but a thicker fog blotted them out. Clayton halted his party, and taking Private W. J. Cotter with him, reconnoitred ahead. Having ascertained that he was on the right track, he was just on the point of returning when a shell landed almost on top of the two. Clayton received a severe wound from a splinter passing through his right thigh, but Cotter escaped. Though the shelling continued, Cotter bound his officer's wound and set him on the way out. It was Clayton's third wound received during the war, but despite its severity, he rejoined the Company shortly after the Armistice. After disposing of his officer, Cotter went off, as directed, to find his team mates, but was unsuccessful. He appears to have reached the front of the attack by riding in a tank, and afterwards bombing an enemy machine-gun position and capturing two guns and five Germans. When Lieutenant Clayton did not return to his waiting teams, Corporal Saker led the teams forward. As he was thoroughly conversant with the plan and all its details—a precaution taken by his officer—no difficulty was present in that respect. "After a short delay," said Saker, "we moved off again, but there was nothing of a startling nature as the infantry had done their work thoroughly. We passed several enemy machine-guns with their crews 'a la morte' beside them. It was practically a 'walk over' as far as we were concerned. I followed the instructions that Lieutenant Clayton had given me, and gained our objective." "We had scarcely dug in," said Lance Corporal Caldwell, "when the 5th Division infantry went through us, carrying an Australian flag, and a short while after the 18-pounders pulled in, in front of us."

Saker's leadership deserves a word of praise. "He was the coolest man in the party," continued Caldwell, "which was a great thing in keeping us all together." The comparative absence of adventure afterwards apparently left Privates A. McK. Howie and W. H. Wilson unsatisfied, for they set out to explore Warfusee-Abancourt. While so doing, a machine-gun in the village opened fire on some infantry. The pair set out to capture it, and after some manoeuvering, did so; taking four prisoners in the process; and then discovered three more guns in a cellar. Both men received the Military Medal for the exploit.

An hour after Zero, Nos. 3 and 4 Sections who had been held in reserve moved forward to the first objective, and established themselves in readiness for future action. Thus, by 8 o'clock, the whole of the 16 teams and guns were in position in the new area, as planned. Everyone was highly elated by the complete success of the Divisional plan, and greatly impressed by the spectacle of a whole army moving forward over ground which, a few hours before, was enemy territory. The absence of enemy shelling confirmed the favourable reports coming back as to the success of the 5th Division in front; and everyone felt that the war was being won at last. Later in the day, it was known that the Australian part in the attack had been completely successful. A quiet night enabled everyone to obtain a night of undisturbed sleep; welcome after the reaction of the excitement of the day, and sweetened by the thought of a sweeping victory achieved with what appeared trifling loss. It was obvious to all that a decisive blow had been struck, but its effects were not revealed till later. General Ludendorff afterwards admitted that "August 8th was the black day of the German Army in the history of the war . . . the situation was uncommonly serious . . . August 8th made things clear for both Army Commands, both for the German and for that of the enemy." After that date, he himself gave up all hope of a German victory.

The Company losses were: Four other ranks killed in action or died of wounds; one officer and 10 other ranks wounded. In addition to those mentioned in the narrative, Private W. H. Greening was wounded in circumstances which have not been ascertained. Company members were deeply grieved to learn that the Flying Corps casualties included their former officer and comrade, Lieutenant E. J. Bice, who was shot down in flames while observing the progress of the attack.

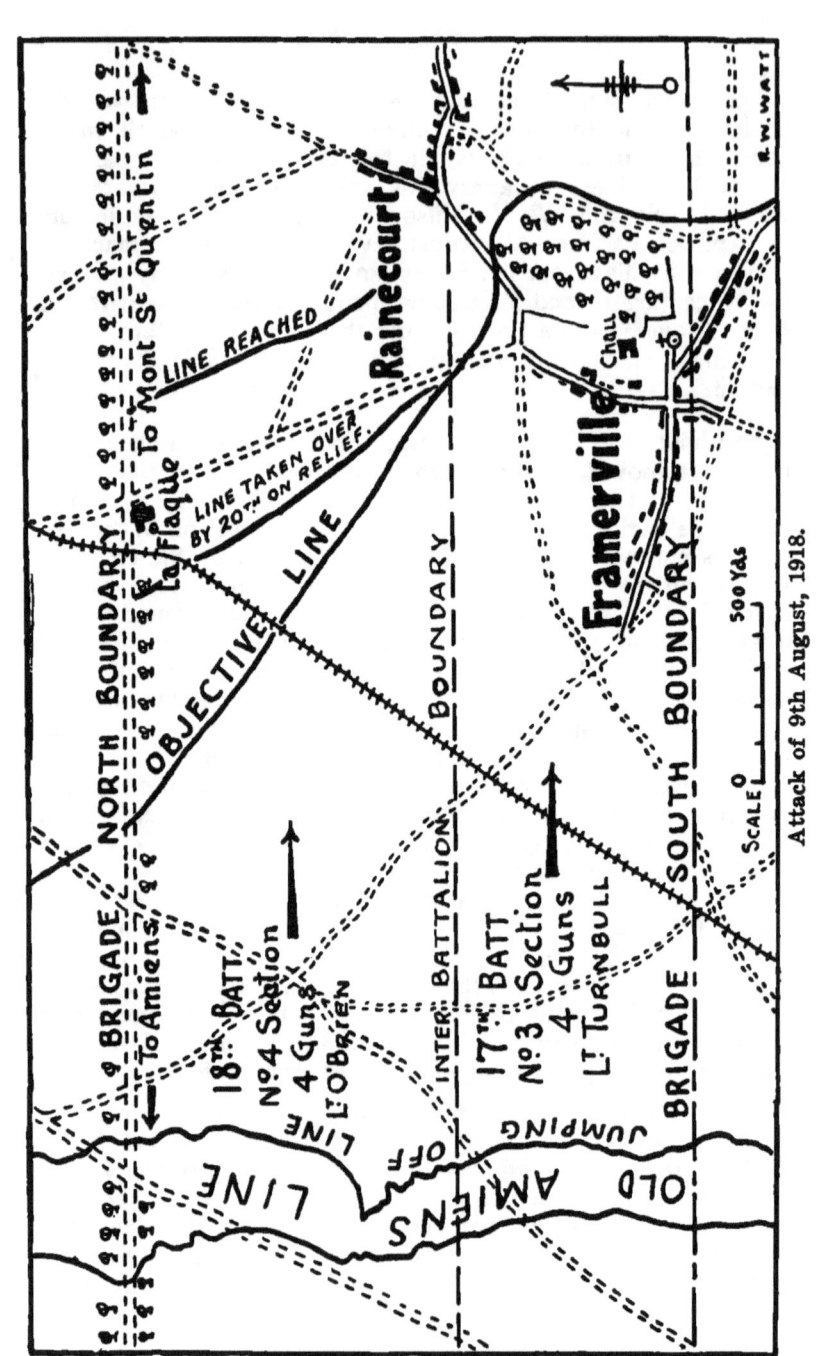

Attack of 9th August, 1918.

THE BEGINNING OF THE END.

After the brilliant stroke of the 8th August, the Fourth Army at once proceeded to exploit its success, and the succeeding day saw the Anzac Corps move forward again. Following a thrust by the 5th Division which included the capture of Vauvillers by midday, the 1st Division (right) and the 2nd Division (left) attacked at 4.30 in the afternoon. The advance of the 2nd Division was made from the front line of the 5th Division which they had captured the previous day. The frontage followed the north and south Old Amiens Line, with its old and wide trenches —a relic of a much earlier stage of the war. From the 2nd Division's position—its final objective of the previous day—to the new front line, a distance of about four miles had to be traversed.

The 5th Brigade continued in its position as the left Brigade of the Division, and was allotted a sector stretching due east, with the main Amiens-St. Quentin road as its left boundary, and was the point on which the left of the Corps attack hinged. The left of the day's objective was nearly a thousand yards distant from the hinge, and bore away, diagonally, to the south-east. To its frontage of 1,700 yards, the Brigade directed its 18th Battalion (left) and 17th Battalion (right). The former moved to its "jumping-off" position—the front line of the 5th Division —shortly before midday.

To the 18th Battalion was allotted four teams and guns from No. 4 Section, under Lieutenant O'Brien, who had with him Sergeant W. Carrick and Corporal F. L. Fitzpatrick and Corporal A. E. Coe. The morning of the 9th found the Section resting in the line of the first objective of the previous day, feeling very satisfied with the results of the attack, and enjoying the bright sunshine and blue sky. About 1 o'clock, they received a rude shock, when orders arrived requiring them to move forward. The Section was hastily assembled, guns and gear placed on the limbers, and then marched along the main road to its assembly position, four and a half miles distant. A little forward of Harbonnieres, the party debouched into a field to the left and forward of that village. Here bursts of machine-gun fire greeted them, so the limbers were unloaded in double quick time. "We moved forward," said Fitzpatrick, "and in a sunken road, found ourselves, to our surprise, in the front line, now occupied by our comrades of yesterday, the 18th Battalion. Captain Graham was in command, but was in doubt as to the precise details of the attack, although he was aware one was to be delivered." No artillery barrage was provided, but tanks were to assist the infantry. Before Zero, two tanks lumbered up, and the senior tank officer reported to Captain Graham for orders, but the latter said he understood that directions were to come from the tank officer. A hurried conference was held, but by that time, 4.30 p.m. had arrived, and it was decided that the attack had better start. In the circumstances, it is not surprising that the left flank of the Battalion over-ran its allotted objective by 1,100 yards, leaving an entirely exposed flank to the enemy in daylight, with disastrous consequences to itself and attached formations. At first, all went well. "As we climbed the bank of the road and advanced, I wondered why the enemy was not firing," said Private A. Chitty. "We crossed our own front line and advanced through a field of oats, nearly waist high, towards the German lines. I looked across to the right and witnessed what I think was the finest sight I saw at the war. As far as I could see were the infantry moving forward in 'artillery formation' with the bright afternoon sun gleaming on their bayonets. Shrapnel puffs were bursting overhead, then hell let loose." No cover was available on the open, level country, and the absence of a supporting barrage allowed the enemy to devote his undisturbed attention to the infantry and tanks. From the open left flank, from the north-east and east, came heavy machine-gun fire which played havoc with the attackers. The tanks did good work—one was seen to attack an enemy machine-gun, shoot the gunners, and finally roll over the gun and dead and wounded—but anti-tank guns got busy and put the three working with the Battalion out of action. The anti-tank shells added to the troubles of the attackers. The infantry fell in all directions. The Company's four teams were in the thick of it, one being almost wiped out. Privates C. Dean and H. Jefferson were killed, and W. Bailey wounded. Corporal J. G. Anderson was badly hit in the left shoulder and, as he was staggering out, a stretcher-bearer went to his assistance, but a shell from a small trench mortar blew them both to pieces. The gun was undamaged, and was recovered by Corporal Fitzpatrick and Private A. N. Bowley and brought into action. Private T. J. Frawley, of Coe's team, was wounded. Meanwhile, the other teams were busy. Coe's gun, handled by Private A. Chitty, helped to dispose of an enemy party as they moved in the high grass, and then became involved in a duel with an anti-tank gun. The latter was well served, but Chitty, by cool firing, shot three of the opposition and disposed of the enemy's fire. By this time fire was coming from the right— from a brewery located near Framerville. Two belts fired

THE BEGINNING OF THE END.

accurately by Chitty caused a number of Germans to leap from the windows, and no further trouble came from that quarter. Then a "whizz-bang" burst nearly on top of the gun, but without result, except to shock the gunner. As if the troubles of the attackers were not enough, the British artillery commenced a desultory fire, and some of the 60-pounder shells fell around the sorely tried party. By this time, nearly all of the infantry officers had become casualties, and a critical situation developed. It was a time for cool heads and ready wits. O'Brien was very active, moving about in spite of the heavy fire, and helping materially to straighten things out. He was ably assisted by Carrick and Fitzpatrick. The former did much to rally the disorganised remnants of the 18th Battalion and induced some of them to dig in in a series of holes, while the two N.C.O.'s walked up and down with their two guns purposely mounted out in front of the diggers, to the obvious encouragement of the latter. The danger was great, in spite of Carrick's allegations that, by turning side on to the enemy, he presented an impossibly narrow target. The situation gradually quietened down, and at dusk the remnants were withdrawn to the approximate line of the Framerville-La Flaque road. By 3 o'clock next morning, the 20th Battalion provided relief, and took over a line parallel to and slightly in rear of the road referred to. The 18th Battalion's losses were reported at 10 officers and 104 other ranks. An anxious night was spent, but the enemy made no attempt to dislodge the garrison from its advanced holding. There is no doubt that the resolute action taken by the Company's quota steadied a very critical situation, and saved almost certain retirement. For their outstanding work, O'Brien received the Military Cross, and Carrick, Fitzpatrick, Bowley, and Chitty (the last mentioned in conjunction with subsequent courageous work at Mt. St. Quentin), the Military Medal.

The 17th Battalion—on the right of the 18th—was entrusted with an advance of about 3,000 yards, and which included the capture of the village of Framerville, the objective including the orchard on the eastern edge of the village. The time of receipt of the orders gave the infantry barely time to get on to the "jumping-off" line—the old Amiens Line—before Zero. As it was, they moved forward in "artillery formation," and went straight into the attack. As with the left Battalion, tanks assisted. "Free from flank disturbance the advance from the 'jumping-off' line went in grand style," said the Battalion diarist, "and was a splendid spectacle; no well trained regiment could have moved with better precision or a more business like appearance." Prisoners and material were captured, and the objectives taken by 5.10 p.m., and touch established with both flanks. A good deal of confusion was caused by the 7th Brigade—on the right —crowding into the territory of the Battalion, but sorting out was attended to when the situation became clear.

With the 17th Battalion were attached four teams and guns, under Lieutenant T. Turnbull, who was accompanied by Sergeant F. Graue and Corporal J. W. Findlay. At first it was understood that the attack was timed for noon, but later, 4.30 p.m. was announced. To assist the teams over the long "carry" of four and a half miles from their location in the first objective of the previous day, the Transport Section provided limbers and drivers. The guns, gear, and ammunition were thus carried to the assembly position, which the teams reached before the assaulting infantry. While the latter were moving into position, two German aeroplanes swooped down, and their pilots peppered them with machine-gun fire. British aeroplanes then appeared, and a spectacular fight followed; two enemy machines being sent down in flames. Advancing over the level ground with the foremost infantry, with Framerville in view, it was not long before heavy machine-gun fire was met. The attackers moved on, and the steady advance of the determined infantry unsettled the enemy outpost line. Parties were seen to jump up and run towards the village—"in a disorganised mob"—as one witness recorded. The guns were hastily mounted, and some "bursts" fired into them, and the advance was resumed. The machine-gun fire became intense, the bullets sweeping the ground, so the attackers took shelter in a sunken road. "This is no good, chaps," called a voice, "so off again." It was too much for the opposition. "The Germans now began to surrender in batches of threes, sixes, and dozens at a time," said Private R. C. Trevan, "and we sent them back on their own. Had no more trouble till we reached Framerville, and entrenched ourselves in an orchard on the far edge of the village, and on the edge of a deep valley, 500 yards or more wide and 100 feet deep. Sergeant Graue ordered me to fire on the enemy who were climbing the far side of the valley. I put one and a half belts of ammunition over, but cannot say with what result, though the target was a first class one, but visibility was poor." "At 4.30 we went over in fine style," said Turnbull, "and were accompanied by tanks . . . Fritz put down a hurried artillery shoot as we started, but this was lifted early. We were, however, met with much machine-gun fire and an anti-tank gun became particularly active. We started with 56 boxes of belted ammunition and arrived at our objective with 48." The only casualty during the advance was Private A. G. Stiles, who was hit in the wrist and face. Two guns were ultimately mounted on the eastern edge of the orchard, and the other two on the northern edge of the village; one, under Findlay, being located in the cemetery.

Thus, by nightfall, eight guns (including one German gun) were mounted in the new front line ready for counter-attack. The night, however, passed without unusual incident. Two hours after Zero, Nos. 1 and 2 Sections moved forward, and placed their eight guns in the old Amiens Line. It is worth noting that the association of No. 3 Section with the 17th Battalion was a happy one, although they were comparative strangers to each other. The infantry expressed their warm appreciation of the gunner's presence in the front line, and hoped for a continuance. The Company losses for the day were three other ranks killed, and two wounded.

During the night of 9-10th, No. 1 Section were disposed in trenches adjacent to what had been a German hospital, on the Amiens-St. Quentin road, and a little in rear of the old Amiens Line. Sergeant B. H. Johnston prevailed on Captain Drummond —against his better judgment—to grant permission to occupy an elephant iron shelter for the night. A little after midnight, a salvo of 4.2 shells fell in the vicinity, and unfortunately, the last shell struck the shelter. Johnston was killed outright, and Privates R. O. L. Ey and W. J. Cotter badly wounded. While rescue parties were at work, Ey, a respected and reliable member, bled to death. Cotter was rescued in a bad way; his left leg was smashed, his right leg was broken at the ankle, and he sustained a wound in the back. Willing hands carried the sufferer to a forward dressing station, where he was attended to. Amputation of the smashed leg was followed by a good recovery. Johnston was a very efficient non-commissioned officer, and highly esteemed for his personal qualities. He was a foundation member of the Company, and it is not too much to say that everyone deeply regretted his passing in his fourth year of active service. In addition to the Company members, about eight infantrymen were in the shelter at the time. One was killed, two wounded, and the remainder shocked.

No further advance from the 2nd Division's front was made or attempted on the 10th, consequently the occupants of the line of posts forming the "front line" were able to strengthen their positions and obtain a measure of rest. Those on the right were not very successful. During the morning, the vicinity of the orchard was steadily shelled by high calibre shells from the British artillery; one of the most demoralising experiences that troops can undergo. "We were subjected to about three hours' fire from our heavy guns, and were glad of the cover," said Lieutenant Turnbull, "which the orchard provided; old French dug-outs built in the early days of the war for the defence of the village. Although the ventilation was dreadful, they were responsible for saving many lives that day. Both the 17th Battalion and myself sent back runners, but mine—Private F. F. Fraser—was wounded, and the Battalion lost two killed in endeavouring to have the shelling stopped.

Later in the day, the enemy paid the village of Framerville much attention. "From Raincourt," said Private Trevan, "which is a little more than 200 yards distant (half left), the enemy shelled the orchard point-blank with 'whizz-bang' (77 m.m. gun), and it was uncanny the frightful way the shell whizzed through the trees. He also concentrated other artillery on the orchard, and almost made it untenable, but the troops discovered some deep and large underground vaults, apparently many years old, and sheltered there, with the exception of a skeleton guard above. Just at dusk on the 10th, the enemy counter-attacked across the valley, supported by intense machine-gun and trench-mortar fire. Private W. E. Lavell, on Sergeant Graue's gun, about 20 yards away, and myself, with Lance Corporal J. C. Muir on the belt, assisted in repelling this attack, having practically no support on about 300 yards of the front. The infantry were forced to keep down in the trench on account of the machine-gun fire from the gulley, which cut the hedge of the orchard to pieces two feet from the ground, a bullet striking the fusee spring of the gun while Muir and I operated it. I have reason to believe that both Lavell's gun and mine accounted for a considerable number of the enemy as they appeared, for fully half a minute, advancing in the teeth of our fire up the near bank of the valley, not more than a hundred yards distant. We had nearly finished the second belt of ammunition when the attack petered out." During the attack, one of the guns sustained a broken lock. Graue dashed across to a dug-out and obtained a spare one. He had just returned when he was struck in the wrist and abdomen by a bullet, and fell across the gun. The area was swept by enemy fire, but four Battalion stretcher-bearers carried the wounded man away; the

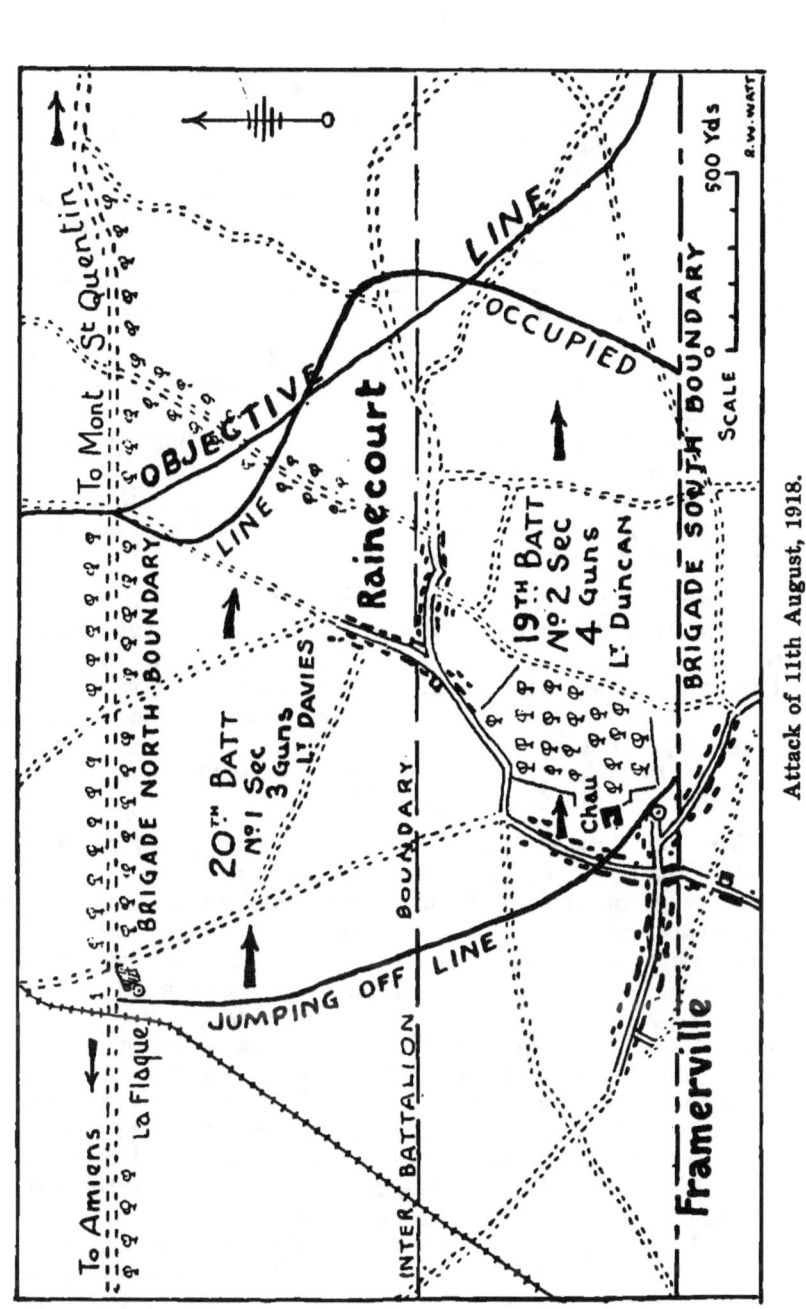

Attack of 11th August, 1918.

enemy showing good spirit in respecting the make-shift white flag carried by the bearers. The two teams on the northern edge of the village were not involved in the attack. Findlay's party, however, managed to get some good sniping practice with rifles during the afternoon. Hostile shelling in the evening caused two casualties; Private J. E. Smith received a shell-splinter in the left eye, and Private J. H. Ford (from No. 4 Section on the left) was wounded in the knee by a machine-gun bullet while paying a visit in search of ammunition.

During the evening of the 10th, the right sector of the Old Amiens Line was heavily shelled; gas shells being used freely. One burst close to Privates V. J. Norman and J. T. Bates, of No. 2 Section. Both were affected before they could put their helmets on, and were sent out to Company headquarters to rest. Norman was evacuated three days later, while Bates recovered after the rest. The losses for the day were: Two other ranks killed, five wounded, and two gassed.

After a day of comparative inaction, the 2nd Division—in conjunction with the 1st Australian Division on its right—continued its advance due east, on the 11th. At 4 a.m., the 20th Battalion attacked on the left, and the 19th Battalion on the right of the Divisional front. No tanks took part, the advance being supported by an excellent barrage provided by our Artillery Brigades. The morning was fine and warm, but a dense fog again made conditions difficult.

The 20th Battalion was required to advance 1,500 yards, and capture the village of Raincourt on its right front. As soon as the barrage opened, the enemy replied vigourously with high explosives and gas shell, but without disturbing the troops on the "jumping-off" tape. The enemy did not offer very stiff resistance, but from the exposed left flank came a good deal of machine-gun fire from the direction of Proyart, which caused many casualties in the flank Company. Practically the whole of the allotted objective was secured, including the village of Raincourt, which fell to the right Company. Twenty-five prisoners were taken, as well as a number of machine-guns. With the 20th Battalion were three teams from No. 1 Section, under Lieutenant W. B. Davies, assisted by Corporals Noonan and Saker. Davies took charge of the two teams with the right of the Battalion, leaving Saker to take the other team close to the main road on the left of the Brigade front. Smoke and fog hampered the advance. Before going far, Lance Corporal

A. V. Caldwell and Private A. McK. Howie were wounded by shell-fire. Saker attended to Howie, but Caldwell carried on till the objective was reached. He was sent out in a weak state due to loss of blood from a leg wound, and collapsed after reaching the dressing station. His courageous effort, combined with previous good work on the 8th, brought the award of the Military Medal. Without further loss, the gun was mounted in the objective line, but was not called on for service as no counter-attack developed. Davies' party also suffered loss. Early in the advance, he was wounded under the left eye by a shell splinter and returned to Company Headquarters, whence he was evacuated. Lieutenant Hamilton was sent up and took over from Noonan, who had been left in charge. The teams had, meanwhile, pressed on and taken up positions in the new front line, but lost two men while so doing; Corporal W. S. Wallin and Private W. H. Wilson. Both were wounded. While Wilson was evacuated, Wallin died shortly after from head wounds. His injuries were bound up, but he realised that the end was near. "Tell Hyland, Chitty, and the rest of the boys," said he, "that I died game." "He was as game as ever when we left him," said one narrator. The guns did not come into action owing to the paucity of targets. Private C. W. Deal evidently found the inaction hardly to his liking, for he crept out a considerable distance in front and, with rifle-fire, managed to silence an enemy machine-gun which was annoying the infantry as they were digging in. Then he devoted his attention to enemy snipers, and finally returned with two prisoners. For his enterprise, he was awarded the Military Medal.

To support the advance of the 20th Battalion, No. 4 Section was withdrawn some distance, and provided indirect fire. Soon after the attack opened, the gunners were surprised to see a party of about 30 of the enemy under an officer—without escort—suddenly appear out of the mist in front of the gun positions. Throwing up their arms, they took shelter near one of the guns located in a disused quarry, for about two hours. When the artillery fire slackened, the officer marched his party to the rear, again without escort. Meanwhile, a peculiar situation arose; the gunners firing their programme while their erstwhile enemies watched with interest. Lieutenant O'Brien examined the officer's papers, and the gun-team "souvenired" about a dozen watches and other things. Some of the Germans were without gas masks, and as enemy gas-shells were falling around, they were allowed to appropriate others from the dead near by.

During the morning, Lieutenant O'Brien and Corporal Fitzpatrick were walking across open ground in rear of the front line when O'Brien was hit in the thigh by a stray bullet, apparently a spent one from an aerial fight going on overhead. Fitzpatrick bandaged the wound and took the sufferer to the nearest aid post. Lieutenant W. A. Carne was sent up and took charge of the Section.

The 19th Battalion—on the right of the 20th—were not troubled by flank consideration. At the outset, the enemy heavily shelled Framerville and the orchard. Troublesome machine-guns encountered in the advance were disposed of, and the captured area consolidated. Over a hundred prisoners were taken, as well as machine-guns. To the 19th Battalion were attached four teams and guns from No. 2 Section, under Lieutenant F. V. W. Duncan, who had with him Sergeants D. C. M. Parkhill and J. P. Adam, and Corporal W. E. Peters. To enable the artillery to make a good start with its barrage, the front line posts were vacated shortly before it fell. Consequently the teams moved off from the left edge of the orchard. Parkhill, with Peters, took the two right hand teams. They moved off independently of the two teams on the left with Duncan, and without getting in touch with the infantry. Moving cautiously in the fog, the party reached the eastern edge of the orchard, and at that point, Parkhill, taking Peters with him, went forward some distance and reconnoitred the front. Returning to the teams, who had separated for safety, they had just decided to take one each in a further advance when Parkhill, after calling to his team to move, fell dead; shot through the heart. Parkhill was a conscientious and efficient non-commissioned officer, and greatly respected by his comrades; one whom the Company could ill afford to lose. Peters took charge and, despite the depressing fatality, the teams moved forward through a hail of bullets, and reached their objective without further loss. Lance Corporal S. H. Deakin's "tin hat" was almost knocked off his head by a bullet, but he escaped injury. It was only after the objective was reached that contact was made with the infantry. With its reduced strength, the Battalion had much ground to cover, and the guns were disposed to cover wide gaps in the line. Use was made of a captured gun, which was placed under Privates P. J. Dinneen and A. E. D. Marsh. This gun came into action several times during the day; Marsh at one time creeping out in front and, from a vantage point, dispersing parties of the enemy who appeared to be collecting in a gully for the purpose of counter-attack. Dinneen was also active, and when four men were buried in a dug-out by shell-fire, he rescued them in spite of the continued shelling. His enterprise brought him the award of the Military Medal. During the evening he was wounded in the hip by machine-gun fire. The other guns were not called on for action.

Lieutenant Duncan moved forward at Zero with the two left-hand teams, in charge of Sergeant Adam. Soon after moving off, Private N. C. Andrews was wounded in the leg by a shell splinter. The fog enabled the attackers, at times, to come in close contact with enemy posts; so close that at one stage, three of the party actually fired at Germans with their revolvers as they scurried to their rear. Further loss was sustained when Private L. Miller was wounded in the right knee by shell-fire; and later, Private S. V. Manypeney was wounded in the head, his steel helmet preventing what might have been a fatal wound. Manypeney came across Miller lying disabled, and after carrying him to the shelter of a sunken road, dressed his wound and, with the aid of two prisoners, carried him to a dressing station. As on the right, the guns were disposed to cover gaps in the infantry line, but had little opportunity for service. Continued shelling of the orchard at Framerville resulted in No. 3 Section sustaining three additional casualties, when Privates G. Savage, E. A. Falkingham, and G. G. O'Meara were wounded. During the morning, while crossing the orchard to obtain ammunition, O'Meara was wounded in the leg. About the same time, Falkingham was struck on the right temple by a large piece of spent shell. He was sent out in charge of O'Meara.

During the night of 11-12th, the Company was relieved in its locations by the 7th Machine Gun Company, and took up reserve positions—with the 5th Brigade—in the Old Amiens Line. The losses for the day were: Two other ranks killed or died of wounds, two officers and 10 other ranks wounded.

Six days spent in Divisional reserve in the Old Amiens Line with the 5th Brigade, were in the nature of a rest. The guns were mounted in defensive positions, but, beyond keeping their weapons in order and performing salvage duties in the area, there was little else to attend to. The area was shelled intermittently but no further loss was sustained. Three other ranks were evacuated sick. At this time, the Company's complement of officers was increased by the arrival of Lieutenant E. F. Armit, M.C., D.C.M., late 7th Machine Gun Company.

During the night of the 17-18th August, the Company was relieved by the 97th Machine Gun Company of the 32nd Division. On completion of the relief, motor omnibuses carried the gun teams to Fouilloy, a village close to Corbie, where billets had been arranged. Lieutenant Carne and eight guides who had been left behind to complete the final stages of the "change over" were not so fortunate, as they found it necessary to tramp nine miles before rejoining their comrades early next morning.

During the period covered by this chapter, the total losses were: 11 other ranks killed or died of wounds, three officers and 27 other ranks wounded, three other ranks gassed. It is significant that, during the period of actual fighting, no one went sick; the five evacuations under that heading and one gassed case took place before and after active hostilities. The decorations were on a generous scale, and totalled two Military Crosses and 12 Military Medals. It is pleasing to note that one of the latter came to the Transport Section. As usual, its members ably seconded the gun teams' efforts by pushing forward their limbers —in advances and on reliefs—thus reducing the long "carries" of the heavy guns, tripods, gear, and ammunition. The decoration in question was bestowed on Driver H. H. T. Harris, and the recommendation—which might be applied to others—said: "During the operations on the 8th and 11th August, Driver Harris assisted the gun sections greatly, when in charge of packhorses, by the promptitude with which he got gun gear and S.A.A. forward to advanced positions. He reconnoitred tracks forward, and brought the fighting limbers to assembly positions, calmly and efficienly working his team, notwithstanding shellfire and casualties. His courage and devotion to duty were always outstanding."

Another pleasing event was the bestowal of knighthood on General Monash by His Majesty the King, on 12th August, at Bertangles. The ceremony took place in the presence of selected parties: a hundred from each of the Five Divisions. Corporal A. E. Coe and Signaller C. Wood were the Company's representatives at a notable gathering.

So ended a remarkable period. Four days saw an advance of more than 8 miles over territory occupied by the enemy, the shattering of the whole of the enemy defensive organisation, the capture of thousands of prisoners and an enormous quantity of guns and stores. Important as were the material gains, the moral effect was—especially at that stage of the war—infinitely greater. The crushing of the front disclosed the fact that the German Army was a spent force, and raised justifiable expectations of decisive victory for the Allies. To members of the Company, it was an exhilarating experience, especially to those who recalled the tragic days at Pozieres—just two years before—when a few hundred yards of ground were won at great cost after ten days of protracted struggle. The overwhelming extent of the victory precluded any serious or general counter-attack, with resultant diminished opportunities for gun work. After eleven days of memorable line duty, everyone felt weary—for even victories become exhausting—and glad of a respite; one which was sweetened by the knowledge of participation in what was probably the greatest and most successful blow of the A.I.F.

CHAPTER XXV.

Mont St. Quentin.

17th August—4th September, 1918.

Once again the Company found itself resting in the valley of the Somme, and on the banks of that familiar river. The hamlet of Fouilloy was but a kilometre from the large village of Corbie, and a few miles to the westward was Amiens. The countryside was well populated by Australians; outward evidence of the ultimate but long delayed union of the five Australian Divisions. Everyone was aware of a feeling of unity and a comfortable atmosphere arising from the thought that the war was being won at last. Almost daily, evidence of the activities and successes of the sister Divisions in the line was presented when large contingents of German prisoners marched by. A diarist noted that 2000 had passed on the 23rd August, and a thousand on the following day. It was an item of interest to visit the "cages" in the vicinity, and inspect the samples detained therein. Continued warm weather rendered bathing a delightful exercise, especially when a trifling walk brought the bather to the water's edge. A diarist noted at this time that "the valley of the Somme is full of naked Australians, enjoying the hot weather and water." The spectacle of a river valley sheltering many thousands of troops, horse lines, dumps, and vast quantities of army accessories was doubtless a tempting target for enemy bombing aeroplanes for the area was frequently visited at night. But in the air, as in other domains, the tide was flowing strongly against the enemy. The troops noted with much interest and satisfaction the measures in being to deal with the nocturnal visitors. When the twin-engined Gotha—as it usually was—droned overhead, with its double throb, searchlights swept the sky for the intruder who, when found, appeared very much like an incandescent dragonfly. As he moved along in the converging beams of the search-lights, anti-aircraft batteries, machine-guns using "tracer" (phosphorescent) bullets, and numerous rifles, opened in a flashing, fiery pandemonium. The target was difficult to hit, and the descent of much metal caused considerable anxiety. Occasionally a white point of light would indicate the approach of a British machine whose pilot would notify his location of the enemy aeroplane by firing a flare as a signal for the ground activities to cease. Thereupon, he would close with his giant antagonist and sometimes send him to earth.

In such conditions, Company training was resumed, but was not of an exacting nature; sufficient to keep all ranks in touch with their particular duties and always with an eye to the training of reinforcements. On the 19th August, 24 reinforcements were taken on strength from the machine-gun base at Etaples, and helped to fill the vacancies caused by the recent line activities. Games were played; cricket being the most favoured. On Saturday, 24th August, the 2nd Machine Gun Battalion held a swimming carnival and aquatic sports at Daours. The eight day spell came to an end on the 25th, when orders were received regarding the preliminary move in the relief of the 1st Australian Division in the line, by the 2nd. Next day was spent preparing to move. The company "nucleus" with packs, blankets, etc., was sent to La Neuville. About 7 p.m. the gun-teams, guns, and gear proceeded by 'bus to a point on the Amiens-St. Quentin road, forward of Lamotte, whence march was made to the Old Amiens Line, just in rear of Proyart, where the night was spent. Next day (27th) the Company moved to and occupied huts in an old German camp near Chuignolles.

Since the 2nd Division had been withdrawn from the line, steady progress eastwards had been maintained by the Australian Corps as part of the advance of the Fourth Army. In conformity with the divisional "change over," and in continuation of the same policy, the 5th Brigade was directed to pass a battalion through the left of the 6th Brigade. The Company was again attached to the 5th Brigade, and in view of Captain Drummond's impending departure for a school of instruction at Camieres, Captain Rae attended 5th Brigade headquarters, where the plans for the move were discussed and settled. Thereafter, Captain Rae kept in close touch with Brigade headquarters, and directed the Company operations detailed in this chapter. Meanwhile, the 18th Battalion was chosen for the task just indicated, with the 19th in support, while the Company was ordered to allot two gun-sections to the 18th Battalion. No. 3, under Lieutenant W. A. Carne, and No. 4, under Lieutenant F. V. W. Duncan, were accordingly detailed. They marched out of camp shortly after midday on the 28th, accompanied by the fighting limbers carrying guns and gear—and joined the Battalion near Salmon Wood, late in the afternoon. Soon after moving off, Private H. W. Berner was wounded in the knee and arm by an odd shell-burst. After waiting for the 21st Battalion (6th Brigade) to clear Frise and the trench system west of Mereaucourt Wood, the 18th Battalion moved off at dusk, accompanied by the two gun-sections, who unloaded their limbers near Frise, and from that point man-handled their guns, gear, and ammunition. Traversing the north of the Wood, and the area lying between it and the Somme, A and B Companies, accompanied by No. 4 Section, with C and D and No. 3 Section in close support, cleared the area. As the leading parties emerged from the Wood, the enemy blew up the bridge at Feuilleres, which immediately took fire. By 10.30 p.m. a line running north and south on the western edge of Feuilleres was established. Up till then, it had been a cautious advance in the darkness without any serious opposition. In the light of early morning, the advance was continued with C and D Companies and No. 3 Section in the lead. The morning (29th) was beautifully fine, with a touch of early autumn in the air, and the advance continued without opposition except enemy shelling from the right front, and machine-gun fire from the north end of Bancourt Wood, also on the right. As the two Brigades—the 7th on the right of the 5th—moved over the gently sloping ground which fell away to the river bank, it looked like a peace-time manoeuvre, with the battalions moving steadily and well spaced in "artillery formation," and an occasional despatch rider arriving with orders. Bursting shells, however, gave a very realistic touch.

In due course, the left of the 18th Battalion, with No. 3 Section close on its heels, reached the left bank of the canal which short-circuits the U bend of the Somme at Clery, without disturbance. On the right, German field guns could be seen firing from the vicinity of Halle, on the eastern bank of the river. Sergeant F. Wigmore had charge of the two right hand teams and, bearing away to the right with D Company, came under the machine-gun fire emanating from Bancourt Wood. While Wigmore was reconnoitring, he received a bullet through the wrist. Lance Corporal R. C. Trevan attended to the injury, and then, in company with an officer and two infantrymen, bombed an enemy party out of an adjacent copse, killing five Germans in the process. Meanwhile, investigation revealed the fact that the centre of the bridge across the canal had been destroyed, but three mines at the near end had failed to explode. These were coolly detached by Lieutenant Duncan who, with No. 4 Section, had now appeared on the scene. A further search down stream located a flimsy suspended footbridge, and over the precarious structure passed three companies of the battalion, as well as No. 4 Section and half of No. 3; the whole party taking cover on the forward bank of the canal. No further move was made during the day. The infantry and gunners spent a quiet time, resting, sniping, and observing from their vantage point, enemy movement across the river, also the efforts being made on the left by the 3rd Australian Division to extend its frontage beyond Clery. At one stage, Lieutenant Carne observed and reported the relief of an enemy party, giving map reference, and some time later was interested to notice that the enemy post was shelled by the artillery. The idle day permitted everyone to enjoy the warm autumn sun, and to study at their leisure their objective, Mont St. Quentin, distant about 2¼ miles. Its gentle slopes—almost bare of cover—reached a height of 360 feet; no great elevation, but it dominated the adjacent town of Peronne, and the valley of the Somme, especially at the Ommiècourt bend, from which point the efforts of the 2nd Division were about to be directed. Possession of the Mount by the British Army would enable it to turn the whole line of the Somme to the south, and, northwards, the line of the Canal du Nord. To the capture of such an important key position, General Monash was now devoting his close attention, and directing the movements of his Corps to that end.

A quiet night followed. About 3 a.m. on the following morning, orders to attack arrived, directing the Brigade to pass over the bridge at Ommiècourt, which had previously been reported as passable. At the same time, No. 3 Section was transferred to the 20th Battalion for the operation. It was discovered, however, that the bridge in question had been so damaged as to be unuseable, and further, that the adjacent village of Clery was still occupied by the enemy. Later orders, therefore, directed the 17th, 18th, and 20th Battalions to withdraw from the canal bank and retire to the vicinity of Feuilleres. The move was completed without mishap shortly after 7 a.m., No. 3 Section transferring to the 20th Battalion as directed. Breakfast was taken, and the three battalions and two gun-sections, sheltering in a sunken road, waited further orders.

While the events just described were taking place, the other Battalions in the Brigade were set in motion, with Mont St.

Quentin as the objective. At 5 a.m. on the 29th, the 19th Battalion advanced on the right of the 18th, with the 17th in support, while the 20th followed in rear of the 18th. No real opposition was encountered by the leading 19th—keeping in touch with the 18th on its left—until it reached the high ground overlooking the canal, with the south part of Bancourt Wood and Ticker Copse in front. From Halle, across the river, came fire from field guns, and from snipers and machine-guns in the Wood and Copse. The two latter places had to be cleared to enable the Battalion to reach the left, or west bank of the river. This was done, and patrols investigated the river bank. An early report indicated a passable bridge, but when the Battalion moved forward to cross on the morning of the 30th, it was discovered that the bridge had been destroyed. A return was then made to its former location near Ticker Copse, where it remained for the day and part of the following night.

To the 19th Battalion were attached No. 1 Section, under Lieutenant E. F. Armit, and No. 2 Section, under Lieutenant G. Williams. Armit was a firm believer in aggressive action, and always insisted that machine-guns were to be shot out of, and shot out of they were. The hidden enemy guns in the Wood and Copse, however, did not afford opportunities, so his aggression sought another outlet. When Bancourt Wood was being cleared, two enemy guns were firing from a point near the river bank and holding up the advance. "It was then that I was presented with a chance to earn a V.C.," said Corporal Riley; "Lieutenant Armit came to me with the question: 'Corporal, would you like to earn a V.C.?' I said I would if I did not have to run any risk, and then settled down to Mother Earth for protection. He did not take the hint, and went so far as to suggest that he and I, armed with bombs, should stalk those guns and capture them. I was not impressed, but after a while agreed to go with him. We crept up a bank, Armit leading, and once on top ran 50 yards across a clearing to get shelter in the wood, the Huns burning the ground under our feet as we ran. After getting our breath, we started to search the Wood. I was never so 'windy' in my life, and wished him to Hell. We found nothing, but strange to relate the Huns never fired from those positions again, and after our return we could move about with safety." Across the river, enemy movement could be observed in the vicinity of Limberlost Wood and the Quarries, so Armit took forward two of his guns as well as a captured German gun, and fired 6000 rounds on enemy troops and a motor Decauville train. Estimated casualties were set down at 40. Thereafter the day passed uneventfully, likewise the one following (30th), the Sections sharing with the Battalion the duty of watching the river bank on their front.

At this point, it is necessary to explain the radical alteration in the Divisional and Brigade plans. Up to the present time, the general advance of the Corps had been due east, along and including the general east-west line of the Somme, but the lie of the river beyond the Ommiècourt bend interposed a frontal barrier to further progress eastwards on the part of the 2nd Division. The natural barrier was rendered more difficult by the enemy's destruction of the river crossings, and his possession of the eastern bank. For the attack on the key position of Mont St. Quentin, General Monash decided to pass three Battalions of the 5th Brigade across the Somme at Feuilleres, thence over the area of the 3rd Division, and launch the 5th Brigade's attack from the eastern end of the village of Clery. The 19th Battalion from its position on the south bank, was to cross the bridge at Ommiècourt, which, it was expected, would be repaired meanwhile.

At a conference held at 5th Brigade headquarters, the new plans were discussed, and details arranged. Briefly stated, the 17th Battalion was to attack the summit of the Mount and the village of St. Quentin; the 20th was given the left shoulder of the Mount and the village of Feuillacourt; the 19th was to secure the right flank of the thrust, while the 18th was held in reserve. On the left of the 5th Brigade, the 3rd Division was to advance its front as part of the general attack. The Company's orders required it to allot a gun-section (4 teams and guns) to each of the four battalions. The attachment of No. 2 Section to the 18th Battalion was the only change needed to complete the distribution ordered.

About 11 a.m. on the 30th a start was made, the 20th Battalion leading the column over the bridge at Feuilleres, with the 17th and 18th following in the order named. No. 3 Section followed in rear of the 20th Battalion, and was in charge of Lieutenant Carne, accompanied by Corporals J. H. Falkingham and J. W. Findlay. No. 4 Section was with the 17th Battalion, and was in charge of Lieutenant Duncan, whose assistant was Sergeant S. Reed. The road parallel to and close to the north bank of the Somme was followed until the west edge of Clery was reached. Here, the limbers which had accompanied the

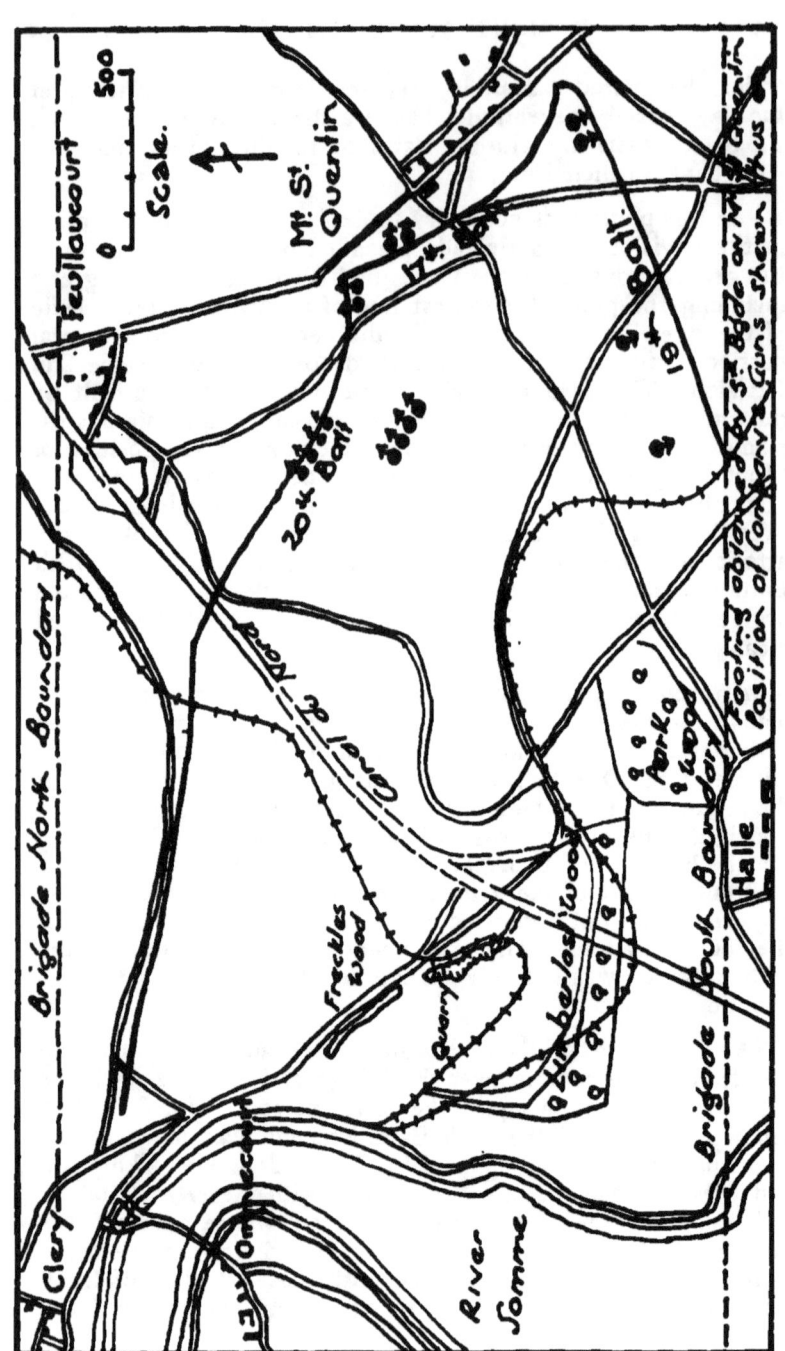

Mont St. Quentin.

Sections were unloaded and sent back. From this point, the teams manhandled their heavy loads—including rations and water—for the remainder of the operation. Meanwhile, the leading Battalion had reached the desolate area which embraced the old trench system of the earlier days of the war. The ground was cris-crossed with trenches, and tangled masses of barbed wire. Contact with the enemy was soon made by the leading 20th Battalion, and the first task was to clear the east side of Clery. Then the trench system forward of the village was entered, and found to be occupied by the enemy. The rest of the day was spent steadily pushing forward, and by skilful bombing and fighting, dispossessing the enemy garrisons; over 100 prisoners and a number of machine-guns being taken by the persistent infantry. The Sections toiled along in rear, but as the fighting was confined to the trenches, they had no opportunities for effective action, although some distant targets were engaged. The only casualty was sustained when Private H. G. Schild (No. 3 Section) was wounded by a well-nigh spent bullet. As the attackers pressed forward, they were steadily shelled by 5.9 shells and sneezing gas shells. By nightfall, the 20th Battalion was well established in the trench system east of Clery, with the 17th in close support. As a result of the general advance over difficult ground, irregular penetration of the enemy's holding had left a confused front "line"; a state of affairs which led to odd members of both sides straying into their opponent's territory at night and being taken prisoner.

While the 17th and 20th Battalions and their associated machine-gun sections (Nos. 3 and 4) were steadily working their way forward on the north bank on the 30th, the 19th Battalion (with Nos. 1 and 2 Sections) remained on the south bank, guarding the Divisional front. During the night, the Battalion moved forward, and about 4 a.m. on the 31st, crossed the river at the Ommiècourt bridge, which had been repaired. The Sections followed, but while No. 1 continued with the Battalion, No. 2 remained in reserve near the east edge of Clery with the 18th Battalion, as ordered. Thus, three of the four Battalions of the 5th Brigade were feeling their way forward in the darkness to attain their allotted "jumping off" places for the assault on Mont St. Quentin. The situation before Zero was such as to test the skill and resolution of officers and men. Each battalion was well behind the artillery "start line" with enemy posts between, firmly established in an old trench system with wire in evidence.

Zero hour was timed for 5 a.m. on the morning of the 31st

August. Before that time, the 20th and 17th Battalions had moved forward and, adopting a bold policy in the darkness, rushed any opposition, making as much noise as possible meanwhile. The ruse was successful; prisoners and machine-guns were taken, and the attackers proceeded to follow the artillery barrage to their respective objectives.

The fortunes of each battalion and attached machine-gun section will now be followed. The bold tactics of the 20th Battalion carried it right to its objective, including the village of Feuillacourt. No touch could be obtained on the left because the advance of the 3rd Division had lagged behind that of the 5th Brigade. From the exposed flank came enemy pressure, and before evening, withdrawal had been made to Gotlieb and Oder Trenches. During the previous night, a conference of company commanders was held, to which Lieutenant Carne was summoned. Very unwisely it proved, he left his tired men without taking one of them with him, and when the conference concluded about 2 a.m., he set out alone for his Section. All was quiet at the time, but in the confused positions of both combatants, he walked into an enemy post in the mistaken belief that it was his own party, and was taken prisoner. His continued absence naturally caused concern among the members of the Section, especially as they were ignorant of the details of the plans of attack. However, soon after dawn, Corporals Falkingham and Findlay decided to seek for the 20th Battalion headquarters, whence they were directed to gaps in the front line. While moving up, they came in contact with Lieutenant Duncan, of No. 4 Section, who took control of both Sections, and saw to the disposal of the guns in defensive positions, two under each corporal. They did not come into action during the day. The falling back of part of the 20th Battalion was observed, but no Germans were sighted. Late in the afternoon, while the positions were being heavily shelled, a shell burst in one gun position, killing Private M. O'Loughlin, wounding Private A. J. G. Stiles, and knocking Corporal Findlay unconscious. O'Loughlin had just relieved Stiles on the gun. The gun was damaged and put out of action. Soon after, Lieutenant T. F. Turnbull arrived and took charge of the Section. He had been sent up earlier, but his guide became lost, and heavy shelling and approaching darkness did not help. However, quite by accident, the 20th Battalion headquarters were discovered, and on reporting, the Colonel said that he was anxious to have a gap in the line covered by two Vickers guns. When Turnbull eventually located the Section, he found that Falkingham had already carried out the Colonel's orders. For his leadership, Falkingham received the Military Medal. A quiet night followed, and the next morning the 6th Brigade passed through the scanty remains of the 5th to complete, after a second attempt at 1.30 p.m., the capture of the Mount. During the second attempt, two of the guns under Falkingham assisted by direct overhead fire; one of the few occasions when it was possible to assist an attack in that way. Late in the evening, the Section withdrew to Florina and Gotlieb trenches, adjacent to Halle, in company with the Battalions of the 5th Brigade, who had withdrawn to the same area.

The 17th Battalion moved off at 3.30 a.m. Adopting the bold tactics of the 20th Battalion on their left, excellent progress was made; parties of the enemy surrendering to the determined infantry. As a result, the "jumping off" position was reached, and a good start was effected under the barrage. Shortly after 6 a.m., two companies reached the village of Mont St. Quentin, while a third formed a defensive flank. A determined enemy counter-attack, supported by field guns firing over open sights, developed, and, as no touch had been established on the left, the line was withdrawn to the trench system a little short of the Mont St. Quentin-Peronne road. The left flank of the Battalion rested on a point close to the bend in the Mont St. Quentin-Feullacourt road. It was strengthened by three of Lieutenant Duncan's guns and a number of Lewis guns. The flank withstood five bombing attacks directed against it, and the line was held till the 6th Brigade passed through next morning. With the Battalion, No. 4 Section advanced in the attack. At first the gunners kept up with their infantry comrades, but the rapid pace set by the latter and the necessity for occasional spells by the heavily laden gunners, caused them to drop to the rear. During the advance, Private H. J. Chewings received a bullet wound in the upper part of the left arm. The wound was attended to, and he was able to find his way to an advanced dressing station. Ultimately, Lieutenant Duncan allotted three of his guns as indicated, keeping the fourth in reserve. The guns joined in repelling the counter-attacks; Lance Corporal Chitty firing six belts in the process. Later, he fired on a German field gun which was being removed by a team and six horses. The range was well over a thousand yards, but although two belts were fired, the gun was got away. Other parties were fired on with effect. No further casualties were sustained by the Section, although enemy shelling—at first badly directed—

became heavy and accurate. For his skilful leadership, Duncan received the Military Cross. The line was held, and the weary holders were well pleased to see the 6th Brigade pass through to complete the storming of the Mount. During the evening of the 1st September, the Section—with the Battalion—withdrew to the vicinity of Florina and Gotlieb trenches, and remained in support positions.

The 19th Battalion made the crossing of the partially repaired bridge at Ommiècourt in single file, about 4 a.m., in spite of artillery and machine-gun fire directed on it, and with little time at its disposal, moved forward to its assembly position. Its allotted objective was on the right of the 17th, and bore away south-west from the Mont St. Quentin-Peronne road, and provided right flank protection for the general attack. Close at hand on the right was the town of Peronne. Assembly was made in adverse conditions of ground and lively shell fire. However, aggressive tactics were rewarded by a measure of success, and a defensive flank was formed almost parallel to the allotted line, but some distance in rear. It became obvious, from the stiff opposition encountered, that the vicinity was held in greater strength than was anticipated. Still, the line was held in spite of enfilade fire, including "pineapple" bombs and rifle grenades.

With the Battalion was No. 1 Section, under Lieutenant Armit, who was still assisted by Sergeant J. H. Hodge and Corporals A. Matthews, W. N. Riley, and E. D. Saker. "After crossing the river," said Saker, "we were lined up and given our instructions. We looked a sorry mob to attack these positions. The 19th Battalion seemed little more than a company strong, and I think our teams were each of five men including the N.C.O. in charge." Before going far, the Section was held up and, as shells were falling, Armit sheltered his men in a dugout and went forward to investigate. Soon after, a passing signaller halted at the entrance to the dug-out and, while standing there, a shell burst and killed him, the explosion blowing his body into the dug-out. The advance continued in face of considerable opposition. While passing the Quarries, Riley noticed a German put up a light machine-gun about 50 yards in front of the advancing Section. Shouting a word of warning to his mates, he dived for shelter, but received a bullet through his leg. "I lay low for a time," said he. "My leg became painful and stiff, so, sensing 'Blighty,' I gave my revolver to Private E. Stokes and took his rifle. I lifted my head to see if the coast was clear to duck out, when I noticed a Hun firing at our troops, about 80 yards to my right. I had a shot at him with the rifle, and saw, by the way he flung his rifle up, that I had got a bull's eye. I lay still, watching the spot, and then up went a bayonet with a white rag on the end. I hobbled over, and got two Huns, an officer and a N.C.O., both slightly wounded. The officer told me that I was the one that wounded him; the bullet striking his wrist and travelling along his forearm and passing out at the elbow. We bound each other's wounds, and they were only too anxious to help me out. I still have the souvenirs they gave me." Without loss of time, the party pressed on and met heavy machine-gun fire. Private A. J. Ball fell, badly hit in the face. It was clear that little could be done for him, so he was bandaged and left. Four days later he died at a casualty clearing station. The reduced party had scarcely moved again when Private H. G. Dawson was shot dead by a bullet through the head. Lance Corporal V. G. Esmond, with two men left in his team, pressed on, and while moving up an old trench, came under a shower of stick-bombs. They threw some in reply, and sighting movement on their right, Esmond hastily placed the gun on the edge of the trench, without the tripod, and opened fire, while Private Stokes watched the belt. At the same time, a Lewis gunner placed his gun by the side of the Vickers, but as soon as he fired he was hit in the head, and died instantly. The result of the fire from Esmond's gun could not be ascertained, but no further trouble came from the opposition and, with the help of some infantry, the trench was barricaded. Esmond's position was on the extreme right of his Section. During the afternoon, an infantry officer came along and asked Esmond to fire on a field gun which was firing from the right flank and causing casualties among his men. Esmond moved his gun into a convenient shell-hole from which the enemy gun and gunners were visible. Opening fire at about 800 yards with the officer observing, Esmond silenced the field gun; the officer declaring that five men had fallen, and apparently remained so. At all events, the gun remained inactive and unattended. Later, a terrific bombardment assailed Esmond's position, and Private E. Stokes was wounded in the leg by a splinter, and retired, leaving Esmond and another man on the gun. They kept watch during the night, and were encouraged when Sergeant Hodge visited them with the news that the 6th Brigade was to pass through. When the latter arrived to attack in the morning, some of them rested near the gun position, and while so doing, Esmond indicated the position of an enemy machine-gun about 400 yards distant. After a consultation, it was agreed that

Esmond would keep the enemy gun under fire while the infantry worked round its flanks. The plan was successfully carried out. On the infantry reaching a prearranged point, Esmond ceased fire, and the infantry rushed the position and disposed of the enemy gunners. Thereafter, the two survivors were not disturbed, and retired with the infantry in the evening.

Corporal E. D. Saker's team was a little more fortunate. Said he: "We ultimately gained a point near our objective. The grass was well grown there, and we had to expose ourselves to see anything. We were getting a lot of machine-gun fire thrown at us, so I got Private G. Nolan to train the gun on to some old brick-work to see if I had gauged the range correctly. The brick-work was just to the right of a clump of bushes where the fire was coming, and to which we saw men running. The range was correct, so we immediately traversed to the bushes and gave them a good issue. We heard no more from that quarter. Later, as we were trying to locate another post and while exposing ourselves, both Nolan and I were wounded. Nolan was hit in the face by a machine-gun bullet, and fell back, saying: 'Sak., the b—— have got me, I've got the b—— lot.'" Saker dressed his mate's wounds, and not till then did he discover that he himself had received a bullet in the right shoulder. Nolan was very distressed when Saker took him out. After Saker and Nolan's departure, two men remained on the gun; Privates M. G. Daffy and T. Stokie. Daffy decided to move forward and place his gun in a trench occupied by some infantry. He took the tripod into the trench and returned to assist Stokie with the gun and gear, but during his absence a shell had so damaged the tripod as to render it useless. The two remained with the infantry, and retired with them without further incident, on the evening of the 1st September.

Another team, under Corporal A. Matthews, had a lively experience. The gun was mounted without loss, but the position was subjected to heavy shelling and minenwerfer fire. Private W. H. Howden was wounded in the right arm by a bomb splinter, and one or two others were hit while the tripod was so damaged as to render it useless. A counter-attack developed, but in spite of the useless tripod, Matthews stuck to his gun and fired as opportunity offered. His fire inflicted loss, and helped to break the attack. Later, a party of the enemy succeeded in moving along a sap until they got within ten yards of the gun, but the determined Matthews bombed them out, and fired on them as they retreated. His spirited conduct brought the award of the Military Medal.

MONT ST. QUENTIN.

The fourth gun also came into action. It was the left hand gun of the Section (close to the village of Mont St. Quentin), and was in charge of Sergeant J. H. Hodge. From a point in front, a German machine-gun was very active, and although under fire from it, Hodge managed to mount his gun and endeavoured to silence it with his own fire. Finding he was not able to get on to his opponent, he resorted to rifle grenades, and was thus able to hold the opposition in check. Next morning, when the 6th Brigade attacked the Mount, he kept his German opponent under fire as the infantry advanced, until parties of the latter moved into line and masked his fire. Prior to the Section being established, he actively and bravely assisted his officer in establishing the guns, and subsequently kept in touch with the other teams. For his good work he received the Military Medal.

The guns of No. 1 Section were emplaced on the Mount, and close to the village. Actually most of them were in territory allotted to the 17th Battalion, for reasons which have not been ascertained. Doubtless, the prospect of effective fighting close to the village appealed strongly to Lieutenant Armit's aggressive spirit. At all events, he was in his element. In addition to handling his four teams, he actively interested himself in the general line in his vicinity and, when it showed signs of giving way under pressure, he threatened to deal drastically with any infantry who attempted to fall back. His determined leadership greatly steadied the hard pressed defenders. During the evening of the 1st September, the Section fell back with the infantry to reserve positions near Halle.

During the morning of the attack, the reserve battalion, the 18th, was ordered to move forward and reinforce the hard-pressed units on the slopes of the Mount. While on the move, two companies were sent to support the left flank of the 19th Battalion and link up with the 20th on its left. The other two companies were sent to the right flank of the 19th in an endeavour to clean up Anvil Wood. In the face of intense machine-gun fire this was found impracticable, so positions in Johannes Trench and Agram Alley were taken up on the right of the 19th. Shortly after mid-day, the Section (No. 2) allotted to the 18th Battalion was also moved forward. Lieutenant G. A. Williams was in charge of the four teams, and had Sergeant A. E. Cameron and Corporal F. T. Schofield to assist him. The guns were ultimately disposed on the right flank of the Brigade's holding. Cameron was detailed to take two teams and guns forward, and found considerable difficulty owing to the activity of enemy snipers. The objective given him was vague, and, leaving his party, he went forward in an endeavour to locate the 18th Battalion. After discovering them, he returned to his teams, just in time to see one of his men shot dead. It appears that, during his absence, an infantry officer came along and prevailed on Private F. A. Woodman to mount his gun and try to dispose of an enemy sniper who had been worrying his men all the afternoon. At the same time, the officer gave as his reason for not using his Lewis guns, that they were short of ammunition. Woodman attempted to mount his gun on the parapet of the trench where the party was sheltering, but while so doing, a bullet passed through his head and he never moved again. Cameron was naturally much distressed by the happening, and was left to the depressing reflection that, had he been present, he would have opposed the mounting of the heavy gun in such an exposed spot for such a purpose. Cameron then took his two teams forward and mounted them in defensive positions in the rear of the 19th Battalion. The move was evidently observed because, shortly after arrival, enemy trench mortars opened fire on the spot with "pineapple" bombs, and two were wounded. Private E. John was hit in the arm, but carried on. Cameron was less fortunate, one hand was broken, and he received wounds in both legs and one foot. The teams remained in position during the night. Soon after the attack of the 6th Brigade was launched the following morning, a large enemy party was observed working up a gully in a direct line with Private D. Lazarus's gun. Lazarus opened fire, using almost two belts of ammunition. Observable loss was inflicted on the attackers, who scattered and took cover. While the firing was taking place, the 23rd Battalion passed through the lines, and the teams had no further call for action. In addition to the part just narrated, Lazarus actively assisted his Sergeant in the general advance, and received the award of the Military Medal. The other half-section apparently did not come into action; at all events, the writer has not been able to trace the teams' movements. As with the remainder of the Company, the Section withdrew to reserve positions with the infantry on the evening of 1st September.

Thus, by the evening of 1st September, the 5th Brigade and the Company were established in reserve near Halle. The relief was more than welcome. For four days and nights, Nos. 3 and 4 Sections had been almost continuously on the move, carrying guns, gear, and ammunition, with little opportunity for rest. Nos. 1 and 2 Sections covered a good deal of ground, but had not been so strenuously employed. Two days after relief, Lance Corporal Trevan noted in his diary: "My shoulders are still sore from carrying the tripod so many days." During the day after relief, Private A. Anders and others netted some huge eels in the adjacent Somme river, and the Section prepared for a feast. The result, however, was very disappointing as, owing to the absence of salt, the fish were not very palatable; one member declaring that "it was like eating vitalised mud." The comparative serenity of the day was followed by intense shelling at night; the Company losing two as a result. Sergeant A. Y. E. Turner and Private A. Anders were badly wounded, and died the following day. Anders was a foundation member of the Company, and had lost a brother—also a Company member—killed in action at Flers, as previously recorded. Turner was a Queenslander, quiet, well-liked, and efficient, and seemed certain of promotion to commissioned rank.

While the operations were in progress, Captain Drummond left under orders (on 31st August) to report to the School of Instruction at Camieres. Following his active and capable handling of the Company during the operations just recorded, Captain Rae, as on two former occasions, assumed command of the unit.

During the period covered by this chapter, casualties amounted to one officer missing, six other ranks killed or died of wounds, 15 wounded, and seven evacuated sick. As usual, "sickness" leading to evacuation fell to a minimum during active operations; in the present instance, all the departures took place a week before moving up to the line. In addition to the losses which have been noted in the narrative, Privates J. N. Jacobson, H. E. Nicholson, and E. R. Owen were wounded, but the circumstances have not been ascertained although diligent enquiry has been made.

For the operations culminating in the capture of Mont St. Quentin, Company members received one Military Cross and six Military Medals. In addition to the five Military Medals referred to in the narrative, the Transport Section deservedly participated. The honour fell to Lance Corporal J. J. Passeri, and the recommendation stated that, following months of excellent conduct in handling men and horses in line work, he had, "during the advance near Peronne in August and September,

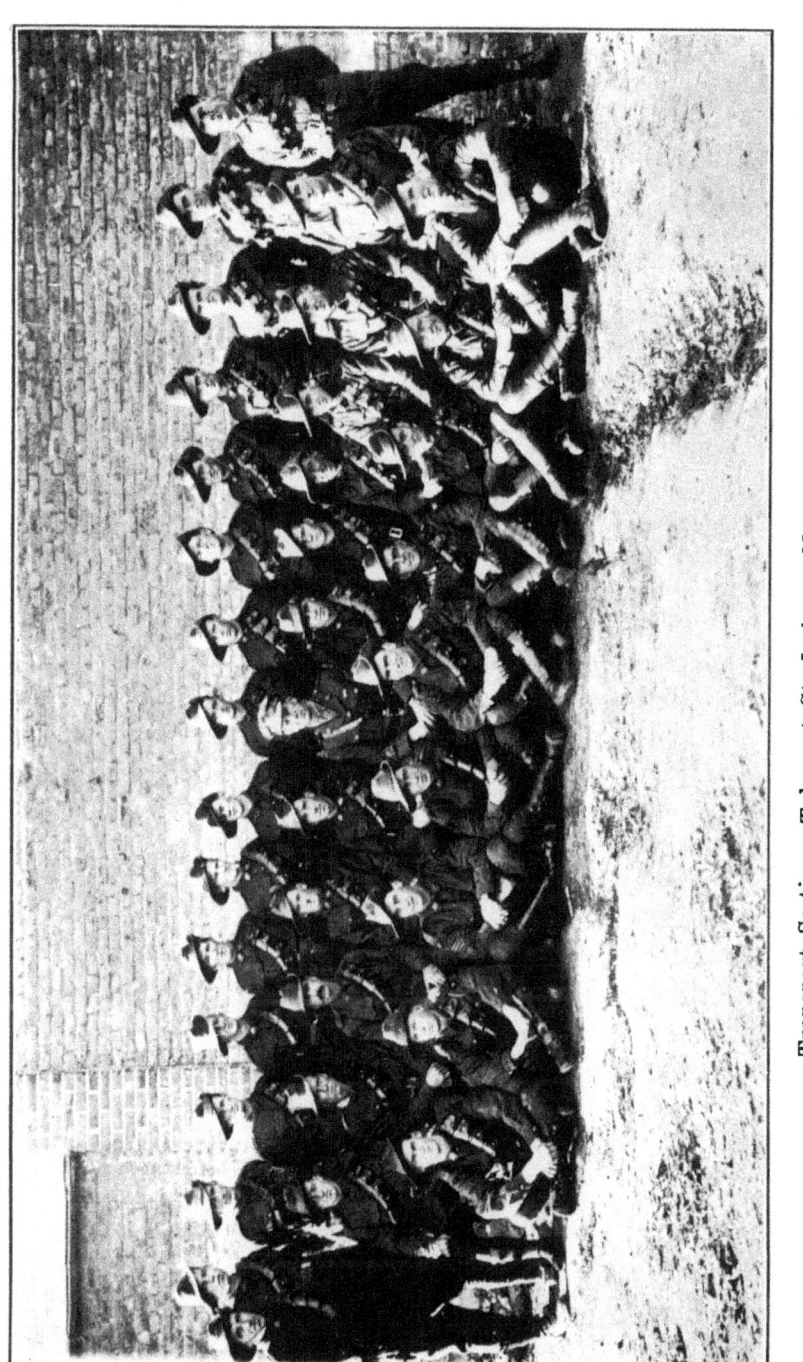

Transport Section. Taken at St. Ledger. November, 1918.

CHAPTER XXVI.

The Last Fight: Montbrehain.

4th September—5th October, 1918.

The withdrawal of the Company just related, was part of a divisional relief, when the Second—after an adjustment of Corps boundaries—was withdrawn for much needed rest and re-organisation. While the Company gun-teams were moving back to Mereaucourt Wood on the 4th September, the "nucleus" and details had retired to the village of Cappy, in which area the Division was congregating. After a night at Mereaucourt Wood, the gunners joined their comrades at Cappy and a reunited Company settled down to "rest," to recount recent experiences, and to attend to its own internal re-organisation. Cappy was situated on one of the many bends of the Somme, and it is hardly necessary to say that its aquatic facilities were again welcomed.

For three weeks, everyone was able to enjoy the early autumn weather—which was generally fine and warm—and the respite from active operations. The "family" life proceeded quietly, with most of the day devoted to the usual Company training when out of the line. In view of possible "open warfare" in the near future, the syllabus was varied by exercises in route marching, when getting into action with limbers was practised. Other variations took place when the whole Battalion assembled for training. On the 7th September, a Battalion parade was held, and several drill movements carried out. It was the first time that the Battalion had drilled together since its formation, seven months before. Other items were route marches of 10 miles, conducted under the direction of the Commanding Officer, Lieutenant-Colonel A. W. Ralston. At this time, Second Lieutenant G. E. Rennie rejoined after obtaining his commission at an officers' cadet battalion in England.

Meanwhile, the course of events on the Western Front proceeded with much satisfaction to the Allies. The German line was being steadily and surely pushed back. Still in the van was the Australian Corps, adding victory to victory. On the 18th September, the 1st and 4th Divisions set the seal on their fame by breaking through the Hindenburg outpost line in an astonishing performance which yielded thousands of prisoners. As events proved, it was the last operation of both divisions. Eleven days later, the 3rd and 5th Divisions began their last fight which ended—in conjunction with American troops—in the breaching of the main Hindenburg Line. While so engaged, the 2nd Division, rested by its spell near Cappy, commenced to move forward to carry on the devastating work of the sister divisions.

On the 26th September, orders were issued for the move eastwards, and in the evening of the following day, the Company moved off with the Battalion at 7 p.m. Marching through the darkness, it reached Buire—on the Cologne River—at 2.30 a.m. on the succeeding morning (28th). During the day, fresh orders were received, directing a further move forward. In view of the impending operations, the 5th and 6th Companies were allotted to their parent brigades and came under their control. The march was again conducted at night. The Company moved out at 7.15 p.m. with the 6th Brigade, and arrived at Hamel—also on the Cologne River—at 8 p.m. After three days at Hamel—resting and awaiting orders—another night march brought the Company to Villeret at 1.15 a.m. on the morning of the 2nd October. Shelter was taken in old trenches and orders awaited. The weather was damp and the roads very muddy. The last move brought the Company to the Hindenburg outpost line, with the actual fighting line no great distance ahead. The 2nd Division was at this time taking over the front of the 5th Division, and when the change was completed, the former was the only Australian Division left in the line. The frontage taken over—6000 yards—was a considerable one for a numerically weak division. The 5th and 7th Brigades—with their respective machine-gun companies—were deployed in the front line with the 6th Brigade—and 6th Company—in reserve. Opposite the divisional front was a section of the Beaurevoir Line—part of the Hindenburg system—with its defensive system fully developed, well wired, and in good order. The two line brigades attacked on the morning of the 3rd October, and broke through the last organised line of the enemy on the Western Front. To exploit the success, the 6th Brigade was sent forward, and after further progress, the Divisional front was reduced to 4,000 yards, on the 4th. The divisional tasks having been completed, the initial steps were undertaken to hand over

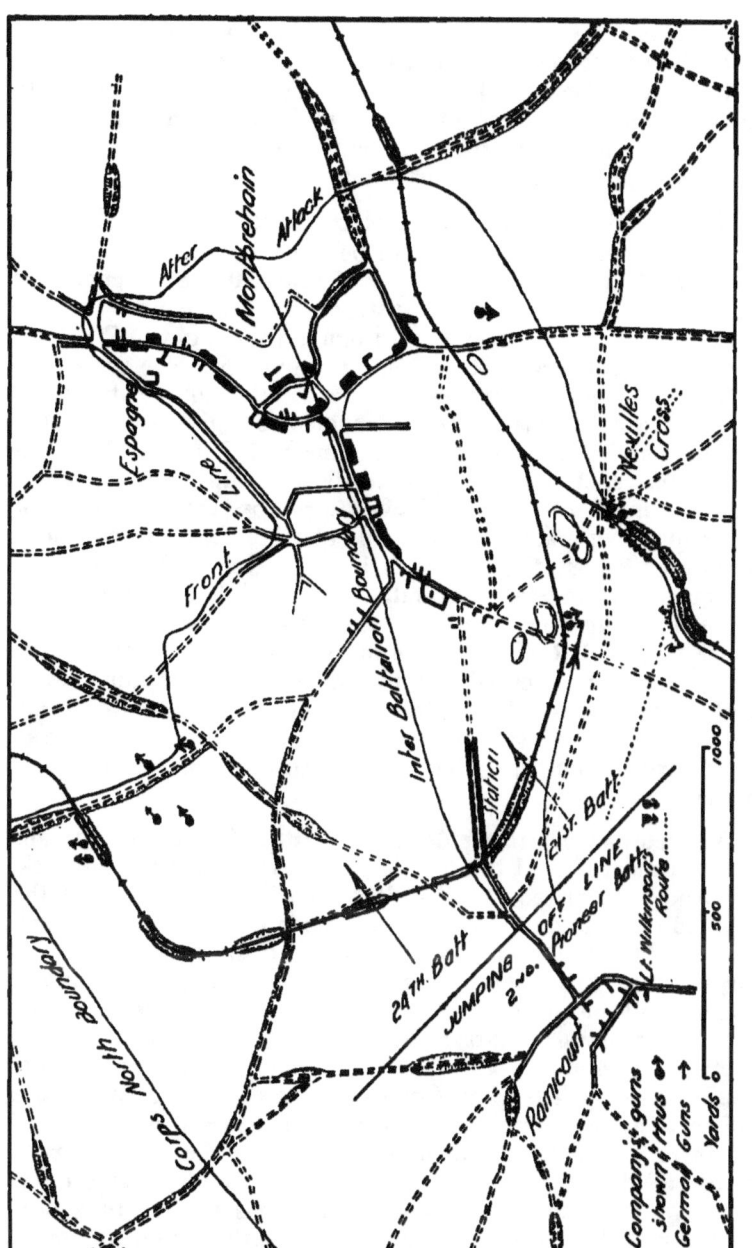

Montbrehain.

the frontage to the 27th and 30th American Divisions. To cover the period required to enable the 30th American Division to take over, General Rawlinson desired General Monash to utilise the time in advancing his line still further eastwards. He accordingly chose for attack the village of Montbrehain, which stood on a plateau dominating any further advance.

The decision had the effect of committing the 6th Brigade and Company to what proved to be the last fight of the A.I.F. Meanwhile Captain Drummond had rejoined the Company on 1st October from School of Instruction at Camieres, and the Company had left Villeret at 9.15 p.m. on the night of 2nd October, and two hours later arrived in the vicinity of Nauroy and took up quarters in trenches close to the Bellicourt entrance to the great canal—constructed in Napoleon's regime—which connects the river systems of the Somme and Scheldt. At Bellicourt, the canal passes for some distance through an underground tunnel. The tunnel was used by the Germans for sheltering troops, and was the scene of a horrible but unfounded newspaper report that in it their dead were subjected to a boiling down process. Naturally, such a place attracted attention from Company members, with others. An extract from Lance Corporal R. C. Trevan's diary reads: "I was one of the first to enter the reputed chamber of horrors, or boiling down works for corpses. I saw the big stew coppers and 17 dead German soldiers lying about the room. I also saw where one of our delayed action shells had penetrated the roof and exploded in the chamber."

In accordance with the decision to attack Montbrehain, plans were formulated, and the 6th Brigade was chosen for the task. In turn, it entrusted the assault to the 24th Battalion on the left, and the 21st on the right. To provide right flank protection, the 2nd Pioneer Battalion was attached to the Brigade for that purpose, and, incidentally, to make its first entry as a combatant unit. Tanks were also attached for the purpose of assisting the assaulting infantry. Early in the afternoon of the 4th, Captain Drummond was called to Brigade headquarters, where details were settled. The Company was directed to provide a half-section (two teams and guns) to go forward with each of the three battalions engaged in the attack; the remaining 10 teams and guns were to be held in reserve. Without any delay, teams were selected and other preparations made. In a now veteran unit the necessary details were quietly and quickly completed.

Accompanied by the limbers, which carried the guns and ammunition, the teams marched out of camp at 5.30 p.m. on the afternoon of the 4th, and two hours later reached the vicinity of Ramicourt where the limbers were unloaded and the teams rested. While the unloading was taking place, a bursting shell wounded Driver J. E. McMahon. In preparation for the attack, other transport was busy, and eighteen-pounder artillery was getting into position. While so doing, a German bombing machine came over, flying low. Some small bombs were dropped, and one fired a dump of eighteen-pounder ammunition, causing it to explode. The explosion lighted up the surrounding country. The aeroplane thereupon swung round and proceeded to drop a line of bombs across the assembling troops; one falling about eight feet from Corporal H. J. Bennett, of No. 1 Section, which was sheltering in some shallow rifle pits. The explosion in soft ground threw up a quantity of earth and stones, and a small splinter went through the compass case carried by Lieutenant E. F. Armit, but caused no further damage.

Meanwhile, the general preparations for the attack proceeded. In accordance with orders, the Pioneer Battalion took over the front line from troops of the 138th British Brigade who were holding it, and then covered the assembly of the 24th and 21st Battalions, and the Company's teams on the "jumping-off" tape some little distance in rear. The tape was laid by the 6th Field Company Australian Engineers without difficulty, and shortly before Zero, the Pioneer Battalion withdrew behind the infantry in readiness to follow the latter; to "mop up," and then to carry out their difficult task of swinging to the south of the village and forming a defensive flank facing south-east. The final moves were made without disturbance from the enemy.

The progress of the attack will now be indicated, and the action of the Company's teams described. On the left of the advance was the 24th Battalion, which allotted three Companies. "D" Company was on the left, "B" in the centre, and "A" on the right. The tanks were late in arriving, so the attack commenced without them. Zero time was 6.5 a.m., and when the British artillery opened fire, the infantry went forward. For a time, the flank companies made good progress, but "B," in the centre, met stiff resistance very early in the proceedings, and much desperate fighting followed. Ultimately, the whole of the northern half of the village allotted to the Battalion was captured, and ground on its left secured. No organised counter-attacks were launched, but the attackers had much to contend with from machine-gun and artillery fire. Turning more particularly to "D" Company on the left flank of the Brigade attack —because the Company was concerned therein—it should be stated that the line of the Montbrehain-Ponchau road was reached. The artillery covering the advance had been very ragged, and on the left, whence so much fire was coming, there was no supporting fire at all. However, the line was held, although every officer became a casualty and the Company Sergeant Major decided to dig in. Ultimately, an officer from the centre company went across and took charge and established touch with the 23rd Battalion on the left. To "D" Company, Lieutenant F. G. D. Hamilton, and two teams and guns from No. 1 Section were attached. They assembled on the J.O.T. in good order and in good time. The morning was cold and calm, and as some gas was lying low in the grass, the men stood up while waiting. An enemy machine-gun was firing on the right front, but the shooting was high. The usual enemy flares were being fired and, while watching them, one member remarked that "the fireworks proper would soon start." When Zero arrived, the teams went forward under what appeared to be a good barrage, keeping close to the infantry. The German counter-barrage was good, but seemed to be composed mainly of small shells. After some progress had been made, the advance was checked by a German machine-gun firing from a hedge near the extreme left of the town, and right in front of the attackers. It was not more than 200 yards away, and had a good field of fire over open ground. Lieutenant Hamilton went forward to reconnoitre and, while walking across the open ground, was shot dead. Sergeant A. E. Noonan, while crawling forward received about eight wounds, mainly along his back, from the same gun. As the party was waiting for the infantry to root out the gun, a heavy tank was seen moving in a line that would take it past the gun. Ultimately the tank located the enemy gun, and one shot from it settled the German gunners. Corporal H. J. Bennet then took the two teams forward to a short, deep German trench, at one end of which was a roomy dug-out, and at the other a small concrete chamber, which was evidently used as an observation post, for it had a small port hole on the side facing the British lines. Being on the top of an elevation, it commanded a great view forward as well as backwards; miles each way. One gun was mounted in the trench and the other, under Lance Corporal C. W. Deal, to the right rear. Meanwhile, the tank had swung away to the left, and when returning in the direction of the trench, caused consternation in Bennett's party by firing two or three shots at them. Tin hats waved on bayonets signalled the identity of the occupants of the trench, and presently a friendly hand waved from the tank in acknowledgment. By this time, a 77 m.m. gun had begun firing at the tank, and ultimately put it out of action by cutting one of its caterpillars; the crew taking refuge in the trench before moving out to the rear. Unfortunately, one of the shells aimed at the tank struck the roof of the dug-out wherein some of the 24th Battalion wounded had been collected as well as spare numbers of the gun-teams. The shell-burst caused the roof to collapse, and a number of the occupants were killed and injured. Two Company members, Privates T. Watson and A. H. Marshall, were resting in the dug-out and, although severely shocked, managed to crawl out. They were sent back to Company headquarters with a message reporting the progress of the half-section, and afterwards evacuated.

Across the north of Montbrehain and in line with the guns, ran a shallow gully. Along the road in the gully several small parties of Germans were seen making towards Montbrehain. The forward gun fired several "bursts" and scattered them. Later, larger parties, in "artillery formation," were seen coming over the far slope and disappeared from view in the gully. Bennett reported for transmission to the artillery, the concentration and map reference to a party of 24th Battalion signallers who, with a Lucas signalling lamp, had established themselves in the observation post. Shortly after, a party of Germans emerged from the gully, and, with maps in their hands and outstretched arms, appeared to be surveying their front. The forward gun again fired—about 80 rounds—and scattered them. Then the artillery opened fire with shrapnel and H.E. on the map reference given. The effect was not observable, but no further movement eventuated. The Company's gun fired about 10 a.m., and thereafter no firing was done by the half-section, and the front became strangely quiet. The only trouble arose out of the action of a British 18-pounder battery which was firing short, and dropped some shells very close to Deal's gun; but another message—again per medium of the invaluable Lucas lamp—soon brought relief. After a long spell of inaction on both sides, a German 4.2 gun commenced firing, and placed a perfect "bracket" over the forward gun position. Then, without damage, the fire was shifted to the position of the rear gun, and became so close that it was deemed wise to move the team into the shelter of the trench. This was done, and no loss sustained. A quiet night followed. Enemy bombing planes came over and dropped bombs near the front line. Each time a red glow appeared on the ground in front, and soon after the bombs dropped in rear. As it appeared to be an enemy signal, an infantryman went out with the declared intention of "shifting him" (the signaller). When another aeroplane appeared, so did the glow. Then a Mill's grenade exploded, and there was no more glow. Very late at night, the half-section was relieved by a party from "B" Company, 114th American Machine Gun Battalion, without mishap. The newcomers took over the Company guns, tripods, and ammunition; an arrangement very acceptable to the outgoing teams. After going a few hundred yards, the party was hailed by a "Yank." Questions showed that "he guessed when his party had halted for a spell he, being the last of the line, had gone to sleep and woke up to find them gone." He was left to guess that, if he went straight on, he could not miss his pals.

On the right of the 24th Battalion, the 21st Battalion was given the task of capturing the southern half of the village. At Zero, the infantry went forward under barrage without the tanks, which were late in arriving. Much enemy machine-gun fire was encountered but, in spite of it, the allotted portion of the village was taken and a line of posts established on its outer edge. With the Battalion were two teams from No. 1 Section, under Lieutenant E. F. Armit and Sergeant J. H. Hodge and Corporals R. J. Saunders and A. Matthews. Their instructions were to establish their guns on the eastern edge of the village. They assembled on the "jumping-off" tape with the Battalion in good order, but sad misfortune attended them at the outset. The party had scarcely moved forward when a shell burst close by and wounded all except Hodge and two men. Armit received a splinter in the foot and was taken out by Private W. T. Brien (unwounded), who was given a report to take to Company headquarters. Corporal Saunders and Private L. H. Burn were badly hit, and succumbed to their injuries, the former the same day, and the latter on the day following. Others wounded were: Corporal Matthews, Privates C. Langford, W. McGown, W. Kavanagh, E. Jones, and M. G. Daffy. After the wounded had been attended to and despatched, Sergeant Hodge was left with one man, Private T. P. Scanlon. It was manifestly impossible for two men to carry out the task given to a half-section, so Hodge decided to make the best of the circumstances. The guns were accordingly mounted on an adjacent point from which they could command much of the ground south of the village. There was no call for action, and in the early evening the two men, guns, and gear, were withdrawn to the Company's reserve.

The important task of establishing and maintaining the right flank of the attack was entrusted to the 2nd Pioneer Battalion. As a preliminary move, it was to take over a section of the front line close to the west edge of Montbrehain, from the 1st Monmouth Battalion and 4th Leicester Battalion of the 138th British Brigade on the night of 4-5th October, and cover the assembly —in its rear—of the attacking 21st and 24th Battalions. When the attacking infantry moved forward, it was to follow in rear, and while its left (A) Company was allotted to "mopping up" work in the village, B, C, and D companies, pivoting on the right of D, were to swing eastwards and then southwards, and make good the right flank. On the right of the Division, British troops were to advance their frontage. The manoeuvre expected of the Pioneers was no light task for a non-fighting unit engaged in its first offensive operation. It need only be said that, in spite of their inexperience, they carried out their tasks as ordered, established and held the right flank, and took some hundreds of prisoners. Their attendant difficulties were increased by the failure of the British troops on their right, which left their flank open to enemy fire all the following day.

With the 2nd Pioneer Battalion were two teams and guns from No. 2 Section, under Lieutenant N. F. Wilkinson, who had to assist him, Sergeant J. P. Adam, Corporals L. Barrand, and F. T. Schofield. Their orders directed them to move to the right flank with the Pioneers and assist in the consolidation of the line; Neville's Cross being indicated as an approximate objective. Leaving camp shortly after 5 p.m. on the evening of the 4th, they reached the trench system in rear of Ramicourt about two hours later, and there they rested. At 9 o'clock, they went forward with the Pioneers, and took up a position in the front line, close to Montbrehain. The night was clear, cold, and quiet. Shortly after 5 a.m. on the 5th, they fell back with the Pioneers to the rear of the attacking infantry. Meanwhile, Lieutenant Wilkinson had reported to the commanding officer of the Pioneers, and in the latter's comfortable dug-out on the forward edge of Joncourt, the details were discussed. The Pioneer officers were naturally concerned as to their duties in their unfamiliar enterprise, and Lieutenant Wilkinson found himself the centre of many and varied questions from the Colonel and his various subordinates. All possible information and advice was given to the enquirers who then departed to their various stations. At Zero, the half-section moved forward, and at once turned obliquely to the right. Round the south edge of Montbrehain runs a somewhat shallow valley, and along this valley they proceeded. No troops were seen on the right, but some Pioneers were close at hand on the left. Before much progress had been made, very heavy machine-gun fire from the front held up the advance, and the gunners and Pioneers went to earth among the remains of a wheat crop, which partially screened them. A way out of the impasse had to be found; so, taking one of his men with him, Wilkinson worked away further to the right till he reached the railway line which approached Montbrehain in a north-easterly direction, and which lay obliquely across the line of attack. Making the best use of the available cover, the two reached the line unmolested at a point where it ran through a cutting. Moving along the cutting to their left, and following the curve of the line, they saw, to their amazement, the reason of the "hold up" of the attack up the valley. About 200 yards distant, the railway ran across an embankment at the head of the valley, and on the embankment were a large number of machine-guns, heavily manned, busily firing to their front and quite oblivious of the intrusion on their left.

It was a dramatic moment. Here was an opportunity which Company gunners had hitherto but dreamed about; a considerable target, in enfilade, and at point blank range. No time was lost. Wilkinson at once sent word for his teams to come forward; but before proceeding to narrate what followed, it is necessary to record what took place before the teams entered the railway cutting. In front of the teams, as they waited, was an off-shoot from the railway cutting in the shape of a small spur, possibly 200 yards distant. As the teams moved forward, two machine-guns opened fire from the direction of the spur. From the right-hand team, Sergeant Adam, Private A. Lazarus, and another crept forward and located one gun on the spur. Dashing over some open ground, Lazarus reached the gun first and shot two of the gunners with his revolver, thereupon six others put up their hands and surrendered. For this courageous act, Lazarus received the award of the Distinguished Conduct Medal. Scarcely had this been done, when the enemy gun on the left was discovered by some members of the left-hand team. Making use of the cover afforded by some straggling wheat, Lance Corporal N. C. Hammon and others got within ten yards, and a final rush and shots from their revolvers induced the five or six occupants of a T-shaped trench on lower ground on the left of the spur to surrender. Immediately they did, one was seen to tie a Red Cross badge on his arm.

The position of the two captured guns indicated that they had been so placed to give left flank protection to the large group situated on the railway embankment. At all events, their disposal had the very important result of permitting the teams to enter the railway cutting and engage the numerous guns on the embankment. The way being clear, Wilkinson then took his teams to the bend in the cutting, and placed his guns at a point where the gunners had a clear view of their target, and at the same time giving a minimum exposure of themselves. Then followed a few hectic minutes. Two belts were fired from each gun, Lance Corporal A. E. D. Marsh operating one and Private J. Bates and Corporal Barrand (in turn) the other. Before such a dreadful concentration, the opposition helplessly and quickly faded out. On moving to the embankment, the annihilating effect of the fire was revealed. No less than fourteen enemy guns had been put out of action, and out of nearly a hundred men estimated to have been on the embankment, about thirty were killed and fifty wounded; the others made good their escape to the rear. The way being now open, the teams proceeded to Neville's Cross. On the right of the embankment they came upon two machine-guns mounted in shell-holes, evidently so placed to give right flank protection to the embankment guns, but the wiping out of the main line of defence appeared to have unnerved their teams, because they retired hurriedly to the rear; some of the Company's gunners taking pot-shots as they ran. Lieutenant Wilkinson fired his revolver at one fat, ungainly German, who sprawled ludicrously into a shell-hole with a wound in his hip, but as others were firing at the time, the successful shooter could not be determined. Other Germans rose from cover and were fired on, the Pioneers appearing at this stage and joining in the shooting.

The low-lying ground at Neville's Cross did not commend itself to Wilkinson, so he took his teams forward till he reached the high ground south-east of Montbrehain, and from that vantage point was able to command a view for miles eastwards and southwards. The guns were mounted without any immediate opposition, and, feeling satisfied with his position, he sent a message to the nearest Pioneer officer on his right rear, proposing that he come forward with his men and establish a line on favourable ground. But the Pioneer could not be moved.

He insisted that he was at his objective, and intended to remain so. Actually, he was correct, but his position on the low ground was not a good one. A quiet period followed, and some of the teams did a little "souveniring," but presently parties of the enemy were observed making their way up the valley on the right of the guns, so Wilkinson decided that his advanced and unsupported position was becoming dangerous, and fell back to an embankment close to Neville's Cross. "We did the return trip in double quick time," said Adam, "as small shells and bullets were rather busy." The guns were again mounted, and fire directed on the parties in the valley, which were scattered. Later, reports indicated that massing was taking place in the same quarter, and again fire was opened. Further reports stated that much havoc had been caused. When the situation quietened down, some of the teams revisited the railway embankment where the 14 enemy guns had been. A few German wounded were attended to, and in conversation with Adam, one of them said that the men on his side were all sick of fighting, and had they known that Australians were attacking that morning, they would not have put up a fight at all.

About 4 p.m., the half-section sustained its only casualty when Wilkinson received a bullet in the leg, and was carried out. Late at night, relief was provided by teams from "B" Company 114th Machine Gun Battalion. The exchange was carried through without mishap, and the teams retired to camp near Bellicourt.

Such was the most effective blow delivered by the Company. The operation was carried through without any assistance from the Pioneers or tanks, and affords a striking example of intelligent initiative in leadership, supported by courageous and dashing team work. Admittedly, an element of good fortune was present, but that would have been of no avail had the leader and teams not seized their opportunities with determination and skill. Attacking emplaced machine-guns in infantry fashion was not regarded as part of the gun-team's training or work, but as no other solution was at hand, the gunners—for the moment—assumed infantry tactics successfully. The disposal of the enemy guns on the embankment was an opportunity for gun work to be seized quickly and skilfully.

As to the effect of the exploit on the Brigade's attack, it appears certain that it was decisive as far as the success of the right flank of the operation was concerned; and it may well have had results wider still because the enemy guns on the embankment and vicinity commanded the whole of the valley on the south of Montbrehain, as well as most of the sloping ground which fell away from the village itself. The reports of the Brigade and Pioneer Battalion made but passing reference to the Company's activities, and it would appear that both units were unaware of the latter's part in the operation. However, generous acknowledgment came from higher sources. In addition to Private Lazarus's Distinguished Conduct Medal, Lieutenant Wilkinson's leadership and enterprise brought him the award of the Belgian Croix de Guerre, while his principal gunners were decorated for their part. Lance Corporal A. E. D. Marsh received the Distinguished Conduct Medal, and Private J. T. Bates the Military Medal. It should be remarked that, throughout the operation, Sergeant Adam rendered invaluable service. Lieutenant Wilkinson subsequently testified to the assistance received, and added that each move was the outcome of consultation with his Sergeant.

While the six "attacking" teams were moving forward on the evening of the 4th, the remaining ten spent most of the night in camp near Nauroy. At 3 a.m. next morning they also commenced to move forward so as to be well advanced should they be required. By 5 a.m. they had reached a point between Joncourt and Ramicourt, where they rested, and where Company headquarters were established. No. 3 Section watched the opening barrage from the roof of a mill. About 10 a.m. orders were received for the Section to move, and under Lieutenant T. F. Turnbull—assisted by Sergeant A. E. Forster and Corporal J. W. Findlay—set out upon a mile and a half trip to the front line, carrying the guns, gear, and ammunition. Its destination was the right sector of the 24th Battalion, and the intention was to make good the deficiency caused by the disaster which befell Lieutenant Armit's party. Passing through Ramicourt, heavy shelling was experienced, but no loss was suffered. The village had been occupied by French civilians, and numbers were hastening back to safer areas, overjoyed on being released after four years' of residence under their German captors. Full use was made of sunken roads during the move, and the front line was reached without loss. At one stage, a lone figure was observed coming from the direction of Joncourt. Shells were falling around, but the figure strolled on quite unconcerned. Presently, as he approached closer, "we recognised Captain Drummond," said Findlay, "I don't think he even had a tin hat on, and he said he had only strolled up to see that we had got to our positions alright. He soon put us on the right track, and calmly strode back. It was one of the most casual things I had seen at the war, and I will never forget it. But that was just like him; he was always concerned about his men, and would never send anyone where he would not go himself."

Section headquarters were established in a quarry, just in rear of the village cemetery, and the four guns disposed on and near the Montbrehain-Ponchau road, with good fields of fire. Lieutenant Turnbull made contact with the commanding officer of the 24th Battalion, whose headquarters were in an exposed position on a forward slope. The latter was amazed that Lieutenant Turnbull had reached him unmolested, because his men had been troubled by snipers, and he pointed out the bodies of four of them who had been shot clean through the middle of the forehead. Owing to the numerical weakness of the battalions, the guns covered gaps in the line without any immediate infantry support. Section headquarters in the quarry and the vicinity were subjected to some shelling, but slits cut in the ground afforded good cover. The only casualty was when Private D. McDonald received a machine-gun bullet in the arm, but he remained with his team, and went out with them on relief. After the shelling had eased, Lance Corporal R. C. Trevan created much amusement by appearing at Section headquarters with an accordeon, a woman's hat, and a litter of pups in a felt hat. As usual, he had been "souveniring," and the trophies were obtained from a few houses adjacent. His only regret was that he could not extract music from the accordeon. "During the afternoon," said Lieutenant Turnbull, "word came through that we were to be relieved by the Americans, and the boys became quite excited for we realised that the much-talked-of Corps rest was to become an accomplished fact. But even with Fritz on the run, we did not realise that we would never again go into action. We all expected about three months complete rest and then an intensive brush-up before we would be called on to give Fritz the final kick; and many were the rewards we promised ourselves when we reached Germany." Some "bursts" were fired at small targets during the day and again near nightfall. In the latter case, the gunners earned the distinction of having fired the last shots from A.I.F. Vickers guns in the line. When the relieving Americans arrived at night they brought six men per team, and their disposal, in the very limited protection available, took some time. At last everything was complete except the relief of the left flank gun; the gear had been placed on the Transport Section limber which had been brought right up along a sunken road under cover of darkness, and Lieutenant Turnbull was talking to the American officer while he awaited Sergeant Forster to report the final relief. Just then, a minenwerfer shell landed close behind Lieutenant Turnbull, wounding him severely as well as injuring Private W. J. Taylor. Forster completed the relief and conducted the Section out without further mishap. Meanwhile, Turnbull had been handed over to the stretcher-bearers, and had an exciting passage owing to enemy aeroplanes bombing the roadways. Ultimately he was put aboard a hospital train, and the first person he saw was his colleague, Lieutenant Wilkinson, who had been wounded earlier in the day. The meeting brought to a fitting conclusion a series of co-incidences. Both left Australia as members of the 2nd Australian Casualty Clearing Station; without mutual arrangement, they were sent for a course at the First Corps School at Aveluy; both passed through the same cadet course at Cambridge and proceeded to the machine-gun school at Grantham; both joined the Company and quitted it per stretcher on the same day from the same cause.

The Company reserves were further depleted at 8.30 a.m., when No. 4 Section (4 teams and guns) was directed to move forward and take up positions on the right of Montbrehain for the purpose of giving additional support to the infantry. The Section was in charge of Lieutenant G. E. Rennie, who had with him Sergeant W. Carrick and Corporal A. E. Coe. Before reaching the reserve position in the rear of Ramicourt, Private A. E. Yates was affected by gas; he took no further part in the advance, and was subsequently evacuated. As the party moved off, Ramicourt and vicinity were being heavily shelled, but Rennie took his teams through the main street of the village because the going was better, and it was a matter of luck as to getting through the barrage of shells. The village was left behind without mishap, and the Section took temporary shelter in the railway cutting on the forward edge of the village. The cutting was rather wide, but fairly deep, and appeared reasonably safe to wait in while Rennie went forward to investigate. As the men were scooping out shelter holes in the forward bank, a heavy howitzer shell fell on the rear bank behind the party, wounding Privates A. Napper and J. P. Vaughan. Napper was badly hit; as well as other wounds, one leg was almost severed at the knee. The medical officer of the 21st Battalion was close at hand, and amputated the damaged limb, but the sufferer died the next day. A brother of Napper's, Private Arthur Napper, was killed in action while serving with the 29th Battalion. In addition to the two wounded men, others were shocked, and sent out, while one gun was badly damaged and rendered useless. The unfortunate happening left sufficient men for the handling of two guns only, so after Rennie had consulted with the 21st Battalion, he took two guns forward and mounted them on the slope south of Montbrehain, where they had command of the ground to the south and south-east. Some detached groups of the enemy were seen, fired on, and scattered. Later in the afternoon, one gun was moved further eastwards and mounted in conjunction with a Lewis gun of the 18th Battalion, a part of which had been sent to reinforce the 21st Battalion. Still later, Rennie was hit by a shell splinter, and rendered unconscious. At the time, he was standing near an old stable when a 77 m.m. shell hit the eave of the building and a splinter from the burst struck him in the back of the neck. Sergeant Carrick and Corporal Coe obtained a stretcher and carried him to an advanced aid post, but he died on the way. Rennie was an original member of the Company, quiet and well-liked, and it was very hard, after long service, to lose his life in the last fight. During the afternoon, Lance Corporal Chitty had been sent out with a report to Company headquarters, and on delivery, was detained to guide in the relief at night. Lieutenant G. Williams conducted the "change over." In the darkness, the gun positions were not easy to find, but Chitty ultimately located them, and the Americans took charge without incident. As the Americans took over the tripods and ammunition, the task of the outgoing men was much easier.

At 12.30 a.m. on the morning of 6th October, Captain Drummond was pleased to report that the relief of his Company was complete, and with Captain Rae (second in command) was able to rest undisturbed with his weary men.

During the operation, the Company losses were: one officer killed, one officer and three other ranks died of wounds, three officers and 15 other ranks wounded. In addition to those recorded, Private E. Daniel was wounded in circumstances which have not been ascertained. It was a remarkable happening that every officer (5) who went into the line became a casualty; two unfortunately meeting their death. During his relatively short sojourn with the Company, Lieutenant Hamilton had won the respect of all ranks by the conscientious way in which he discharged his

No. 4 Section. Taken at St. Ledger. November, 1918.

MONTBREHAIN.

duties. He had the power to will himself to go anywhere or do anything which he conceived his duty demanded. His conception of leadership doubtless prompted him to try to locate the enemy machine-gun which caused his death. Previous to joining the Company, he had served with distinction in the 7th Field Ambulance, and was awarded the Military Medal and Bar before being nominated to an officer cadet battalion in England. During the period covered by this chapter, nine other ranks went sick, but all the evacuations took place before the resumption of hostilities.

Decorations awarded totalled one Belgian Croix de Guerre. two Distinguished Conduct Medals, and one Military Medal; all being gained by members of the two teams from No. 2 Section who went to the right flank with the Pioneer Battalion.

Such was the Company's part in what proved to be the last fight of the A.I.F. Despite the strain of over three years' campaigning, members of the unit entered upon it confidently and in good heart. Everyone had benefited by the spell since Mont St. Quentin, but the spectacle of a beaten foe who was rapidly being pushed out of France was a powerful stimulant for further action. It is worthy of note that an appreciable number of original members of the Brigade (and foundation members of the Company) were present. The fortune of war decreed that the Company's opportunity for striking its greatest blow be reserved for its last fight, but, as previously stated, the chance was seized with both hands. As the Australians did not return to hostilities after Montbrehain, the Company was able to claim the distinction of being the last machine gun company of the A.I.F. to leave the line, and to have fired the last shot.* It will be recalled that it was a close second in making contact with the enemy in April, 1916.

* The only other machine gun company concerned in the operations at Montbrehain was the 7th Company which sent its No. 2 Section forward early in the afternoon of the day of the attack. According to the report of Lieutenant H. O. C. Hunter, who was in charge, indirect fire was brought to bear on reported enemy movement north of the village at 3.30 p.m. from a point close to the village church. Hostile air craft were also fired on. The report further states: "At 30.30 (8.30 p.m.) the C.O. 21st Battalion gave me orders to withdraw, which I did."

CHAPTER XXVII.

Last Days.

St. Ledger, Boulogne-sur-Helpe, Yves-Gomezee, Montignies-le-Tilleul.

October, 1918—May, 1919.

No time was lost in moving backwards to the Corps "rest" area. The morning after the relief at Montbrehain (6th October) the Company, with the Battalion, left Nauroy at 11 a.m. and marched to Hesbecourt, which was reached shortly after 1 o'clock. There the night was spent, and the march was resumed at 9 on the following morning. On arriving at Tincourt, the Company entrained for La Roche. Detraining at 7 p.m., a long tramp of about 12 miles was commenced. It proved to be the worst march in the Company's experience. Everyone was feeling the reaction of the Montbrehain operations, was very weary, and the ration arrangements—a rare occurrence—broke down. One member noted: "We existed upon the mythical iron rations for the day in the train." So a tired and hungry column set out in the darkness with Lieutenant Callister in the lead. Lieutenant-Colonel Ralston marched with his battalion but, although the officers continually urged on the jaded men, many fell out. Some slept in haystacks for the remainder of the night. The main body arrived at St. Ledger at 3.30 a.m. on the 8th, followed by the stragglers, who reported in daylight; their lapse, however, was quietly ignored. The Transport Section, which had journeyed by road, rejoined the unit on the 9th.

St. Ledger was situated in the Somme valley, and N.W. from Amiens. In the valley between Amiens and Abbeville, the Australian Corps was enjoying a well-deserved "rest" while re-organising and training for further line operations. The Company spent 48 days at St. Ledger. The first three were easy ones, devoted to listing of shortages in equipment, making promotions, and re-organising generally. Thereafter, the usual training was resumed with the afternoon occasionally given up

LAST DAYS.

to sport. On Sundays, the only item was the Battalion church parade. On the 17th, Lieutenant E. S. Stephens was allotted to the Company; Lieutenant M. J. O'Brien rejoined after recovery from wounds received on 11th August. A few days later, Sergeant W. Carrick departed to enter an officer cadet battalion in England. He was the last Company nominee, and obtained his commission in due course. Others to join were Lieutenants Cridland and Hickman. Another departure about this time was that of Captain Drummond. He went on English leave, and while in England became ill and was evacuated to hospital. Upon discharge he returned to Australia, and his appointment was terminated. Although he did not have an opportunity to say farewell to his charge, he is remembered with respect and admiration for the way he controlled and directed his Company. A due appreciation of his services as commanding officer has already been noted in these pages.

On the 26th October a Battalion sports was held; a full day being allotted. A long programme of events was arranged, and various heats were decided in the morning. It was nearly 6 p.m. when the last event was concluded in failing light. The Company retained the Battalion Shield in overwhelming fashion, as will be seen from the following table of results:—

```
                                                    Points
Event No. 1—Obstacle Race:
    1st—7th Coy., Driver Nixon .. .. .. .. .. ..       3
    2nd—22nd Coy., Driver Ryan .. .. .. .. .. ..       2
Event No. 2—Hop, Step, and Jump:
    1st—6th Coy., Corporal Trevan .. .. .. .. ..       3
    2nd—6th Coy., Private Walker .. .. .. .. ..        2
    3rd—6th Coy., ——  .. .. .. .. .. .. .. ..          1
Event No. 3—100 Yards Flat Race:
    1st—7th Coy., Driver Dixon .. .. .. .. .. ..       3
    2nd—6th Coy., Sergeant McGaffin .. .. .. ..        2
    3rd—6th Coy., Lieutenant O'Brien .. .. .. ..       1
Event No. 4—Sack Race:
    1st—6th Coy., Private Monk .. .. .. .. .. ..       3
    2nd—5th Coy., Private O'Brien .. .. .. .. ..       2
    3rd—6th Coy., ——  .. .. .. .. .. .. .. ..          1
Event No. 5—200 Yards Flat Race:
    1st—6th Coy., Sergeant McGaffin .. .. .. ..        3
    2nd—6th Coy., Private Meagher .. .. .. .. ..       2
    3rd—6th Coy., Lieutenant O'Brien .. .. .. ..       1
```

Event No. 6—High Jump:
- 1st—5th Coy., Private R. R. Ramage 3
- 2nd—6th Coy., Lance Corporal Chitty 2
- 3rd—22nd Coy., Captain McLennan 1

Event No. 7—440 Yards:
- 1st—22nd Coy., Private N. W. Fairless 3
- 2nd—6th Coy., Corporal Trevan 2
- 3rd—7th Coy., Lieutenant Haydock 1

Event No. 8—Tug o'War:
- 1st—6th Coy Team 4
- 2nd—22nd Coy. Team 2

Event No. 9—Long Jump:
- 1st—6th Coy., Private Walker 3
- 2nd—5th Coy., R. R. S. Ramsay 2

Event No. 10—880 Yards:
- 1st—22nd Coy., Private N. W. Fairless 3
- 2nd—7th Coy., Lieutenant Haydock 2
- 3rd—6th Coy., Lieutenant Callister 1

Event No. 11—120 Hurdles:
- 1st—7th Coy., Private Pickett 3
- 2nd—7th Coy., Driver Dixon 2
- 3rd—22nd Coy., Captain McLennan 1

Event No. 12—Musical Chairs:
- 1st—7th Coy., Private Sandells 3
- 2nd—6th Coy. Private Woods 2
- 3rd—6th Coy., Private Brophy 1

Event No. 13—Relay Race:
- 1st—6th Coy. Team 4
- 2nd—5th Coy. Team 2

Event No. 14—Horse Rescue:
- 1st—5th Coy., Lieutenant Ryan 3
- 2nd—5th Coy., Driver Kelsall 2
- 3rd—6th Coy., —— 1

Event No. 15—Wrestling on Mules:
- 1st—6th Coy. Team 3
- 2nd—5th Coy. Team 2

Event No. 16—Mule Rescue Race:
- 1st—6th Coy., Driver Harris 3
- 2nd—5th Coy., Lieutenant Ryan 2
- 3rd—6th Coy., —— 1

Event No. 17—Horse Hunters:
  Dead Heat:
    22nd Coy., Lieutenant Byatt 2½
    6th Coy., Driver G. Smith 2½
    3rd—7th Coy., —— 1
Event No. 18—Mule Race (2 furlongs):
    1st—7th Coy., Driver Hammond 3
    2nd—6th Coy., Driver G. Smith 2
    3rd—6th Coy., —— 1
Event No. 19—Mule Race (3 furlongs):
    1st—6th Coy., Corporal Passeri 3
    2nd—7th Coy., Driver Hammond 2
    3rd—7th Coy., —— 1
Event No. 20—Officers' Mule Race:
    1st—22nd Coy., Captain McLennan 3
    2nd—22nd Coy., Lieutenant Murray 2
    3rd—5th Coy., Lieutenant Ryan 1
Special Event—Fancy Dress Character:
    1st—Private & Mrs. Piconi as Charlie Chaplin
       and Mrs.. in France; 6th Coy. 1

                              Total 118

AGGREGATE POINTS:
    1st—6th Company 55½
    2nd—7th Company 24
    3rd—22nd Company 19½
    4th—5th Company 19
    2nd Machine Gun Battalion Headquarters .. —

                              Total 118

At this time, much football was played. The grouping of the four companies permitted the formation of Battalion teams; one to play Rugby and another to indulge in the Australian game. From time to time, the composite teams played against units in the vicinity. The village boasted a cinema hall; an amenity which permitted welcome diversions at night. In the hall the Battalion concert party gave a series of performances. On other nights, regimental bands from neighbouring units played to appreciative audiences. A series of debates was also arranged, and it is indicative of the times that the first debate dealt with the question: "Should Australian Soldiers Marry

English Girls?" It should be noted that, far from home, the affirmatives won. An occasional frost reminded all hands that winter was at hand.

Meanwhile, momentous events were taking place. By the end of October an Armistice had been arranged with Turkey, and a few days later Austria ceased hostilities. On the Western Front the German line was reeling under the repeated blows of the Allies. Company members were naturally greatly interested, and the general military position was known. Battalion headquarters were in the Mairie, and the orderly room was a big one on the ground floor and was entered through a large hall. Lieutenant-Colonel Ralston used the walls of the hall to hold big-scale maps, mostly of the Western Front. By means of pins and tapes, the day to day adjustments of the Allied fronts were displayed. Members of the Battalion referred to these maps very frequently, and the Colonel often lectured (impromptu) on the situation. A collapse of the German system appeared imminent, but the majority seemed to think that the Germans would not surrender but, after much manoeuvring, would evade their opponents and make a fresh effort behind the Rhine in the spring. An Armistice was not expected, nor was an unconditional surrender on the part of Germany. Nevertheless, both events came to pass. At 10.30 a.m. on the morning of the 11th November, Battalion headquarters received the official notification. The Company was on parade, and the announcement was at once made to the men, who received it very quietly. Said Lance Corporal A. Chitty: "We were cleaning the guns when Signallers Wood and Swindon arrived with the news of the Armistice. It was taken very calmly, and we just went on with our job. Some of the boys got a bit gay that night. I was Corporal of the town picquet, but had no trouble at any of the estaminets." "In my opinion," said Corporal N. C. Hammon, "the Armistice should have been four days later (pay day), then we could have shown our approval in a better spirit. As it was we were nearly broke, and had to celebrate in French beer. It was rather tame; nobody seemed to realise what it really meant." "I returned from hospital on Armistice afternoon," said Private S. Renshaw, "and got the impression that the mob was not quite prepared to believe it was true." An outstanding memory is a remark made in the Orderly Room by, I think, Lieutenant M. J. O'Brien: "It certainly is the end of a sticky affair, but unfortunately it also ends lots of fine friendships and fellowships." As soon as the morning parade was dismissed, some made for the railway station to obtain newspapers. Others

LAST DAYS.

hurried to the large hall where the maps were hung. It was soon packed with men who, though in a way excited, were also exceedingly quiet. Presently they drifted off, really disbelieving that it was all over. The news was too good to be true, it seemed, and the Germans were arranging for time to slip away, and they (the men) would have to resume operations further east.

Actually, four years of campaigning had trained the Company in arms and mental outlook, and thinking was in terms of combat. The sudden cessation of hostilities required a new mental attitude, and new thinking started very slowly. As realisation is so often different from expectation, so the Armistice —so frequently imagined in very different terms—came to the Company. The French residents—mostly elderly men and women, and children—reacted differently. Excitement ran high; flags were brought to light, and some of the villagers became intoxicated and carried on their celebrations through the night. "They even came near to giving free beer, wines, and spirits for a time," noted one Company observer. But the troops did not participate in the excitement to any extent, and there was little drunkenness or celebration. Rather were they onlookers at the satisfaction of the natives. There was no relaxation of discipline, and the military machine continued to function faultlessly.

Indeed, as far as the Company was concerned, it continued as before. On the very next day, the Company combined with one of its sisters, the 7th, in "tactical operations in open warfare," when the "fighting" limbers accompanied the teams. A week later, field firing on a 400 yard range was carried out. The only relaxation was in regard to the censorship regulations; men could say where they were and what they were doing, and the use of cameras was permitted. Interest was aroused by the issue of preliminary instructions in connection with "Advance to the Rhine" orders, which, however, never eventuated.

Since the withdrawal from Montbrehain, and up to the end of October, no evacuations for sickness were recorded, but, with the advent of the colder weather in the beginning of November, about five per week was the average. Among those sent away was Private G. Neville, who complained of a severe cold. Actually it was acute influenza, and twelve days later he died in the 3rd Australian General Hospital on 15th November. Neville joined the Company shortly after Pozieres. His eyesight was not good, and some time before his illness he had been engaged as assistant Company Clerk. About this time, Lieutenants R. Dodgshun and W. S Clayton rejoined from hospital. Early in October, Company Sergeant-Major J. Brandebura was promoted to Regimental Sergeant-Major on Battalion headquarters staff, and Sergeant A. Payton became the Company's fifth Company Sergeant-Major.

The stay at St. Ledger came to an end on the 24th November, when the Company—with the Battalion—marched out at 5.30 p.m., and reached the entraining station, Hangest-sur-Somme, at 8.30 p.m. The night was spent in the station yard, and entrainment took place at 9.50 the next morning. A most tedious train journey followed. It was 10 o'clock at night before a cramped Company detrained at Bertry, and, after delay at the station, march was made to Maurois—two miles away—which was reached at 1.30 a.m. on the 26th. The temper of the weary men was not improved by the announcement that the blankets had not arrived. The march was resumed the same day, and continued on the two following days, the nights being spent at Rejet-de-Beaulieu and Petit Fayt. The last stage brought the Company to Boulogne-sur-Helpe, in the Avesnes area. During the journey unusual delays occurred in the issue of rations owing to interruptions in supplies. Billets were occupied at Bellevue, about a kilometre from Boulogne, and were poor and rather crowded.

Nineteen days were spent at Boulogne-sur-Helpe. The Company soon settled down to easy training, in which route marching was prominent. Part of the time was devoted to lectures on non-military subjects. Thus Corporal H. J. Bennett discoursed on "Natural History of Australia," and Private S. G. Brameld on "English Literature." Educational classes were also formed. At the end of November, the strength was 11 officers and 184 other ranks.

On the 1st December, the Company, in company with the Division, lined the Avesnes-Landrecies road, near Marilles, and were inspected by His Majesty The King, who was accompanied by the Prince of Wales and the Duke of York. It was a foggy autumn day, and the Royal party looked very cold. Other items included another innoculation and a collection of funds to defray the cost of the 2nd Division's memorial at Mont St. Quentin; 613 francs being raised. Much damp and misty weather was experienced.

During the stay at Boulogne-sur-Helpe, the Sergeant's mess was in the farm-house of Madam Richet. One evening there was a terrific commotion; Madame, Marie the daughter, and the son—aged about 18—all bursting into loud sobbing simultaneously as a tattered, bewhiskered tramp walked in. It was Richet Pere, home after over four years a prisoner in Germany, having been taken in August, 1914, near Maubeuge. The residents were short of many things, a fact which enabled Captain Rae to exchange an old pair of boots for three bottles of old wine which the owner of his billet had kept buried in a field to keep them from the Germans.

On the 17th December, the Company, with the Battalion, left Boulogne-sur-Helpe for Yves-Gomezee, in Belgium. The march extended over four days, the nights being spent at Flaumont, Sivry, and Barbencon. Much rain fell during the journey. At Flaumont, an explosion at a German ammunition dump caused the death of Private A. Johnson and the wounding of Privates T. J. Riddell and W. Hardie. A member of the 7th Company was also wounded. The regrettable accident occurred soon after arrival in the village. British airmen had previously bombed the dump, and most of the ammunition had been destroyed but, as a precaution, Captain Rae placed it out of bounds. However, a number of recent arrivals in the Company made an inspection and, while so doing, decided to have a group photograph taken. To make the picture more effective, a number of big shells were up-ended and, while arranging them, one of the party carelessly threw a bomb or small shell to the ground. It exploded, and the concussion doubtless caused others to burst. The deceased member was buried in the village churchyard.

The sojourn at Yves-Gomezee was prolonged to 48 days. The usual parades were held, but were not of an exacting nature. Before the end of the year, the Education Scheme inaugurated in the A.I.F. was well established, and men who felt disposed were enabled to resume studies which enlistment had interrupted. Corporal H. J. Bennett, who had been engaged in instructional work, was promoted as a Lieutenant in the Education Service. The scheme was subsequently extended to "non-military employment" by which individuals were allocated to various trades and occupations for the purpose of gaining experience. To some it afforded a pleasant escape from the Army routine, and therefore came to be known as "non-military enjoyment." Leave was given to visit Brussels, and parties were taken to the large centre of Charleroi, distant 15 miles, to inspect the industrial establishments.

Four awards to Company members should be noted. Lieutenant R. Dodgshun was Mentioned in Despatches for consistently good work, and Sergeant J. McGaffin received the Meritorious Service Medal. The latter award was in recognition of services rendered as Transport Section Sergeant practically over the whole of the Company's existence. During that time the recipient had maintained the horses and limbers in a high state of efficiency, as well as supervising the staff of drivers and the internal economy of the Section. Driver G. O'Gorman and Private H. A. Hanley also received the Meritorious Service Medal. Hanley's decoration was in recognition of an act of rescue performed by him at Charleroi, about the end of March. An English soldier, while walking along the canal bank, slipped and fell into deep water which was surrounded by steep concrete walls. He was unable to swim and, while in imminent danger of drowning, Hanley, without hesitation, dived into the canal and, after a severe struggle, brought the greatly distressed man to safety.

On the 24th December, H.R.H. The Prince of Wales, presented medals to members of the Division. The only Company participant was Signaller C. Wood, who received the Military Medal and Bar.

The same day saw the beginning of the dissolution of the Company. Since the signing of the Armistice, thoughts of the return to Australia were uppermost in all minds. The impending breaking up of a close-knit unit, of course, tinged the thoughts of home and loved ones, but now the task for which each had enlisted was completed, little time was lost in idle regrets. So, after the selected ones had made preparations, and much handshaking had taken place, Lieutenant F. V. W. Duncan marched out with his party of 14 other ranks on the first stage of the long journey homewards. There was an anti-climax, however. Owing to some hitch in the transport arrangements, the party—after spending the night at Marchienne-au-Pont, near Charleroi—returned next day. A second attempt made a few days later was quite successful, and in due course they reached England to await transport to Australia. It is worth noting that the first batch landed at Port Melbourne (after a week's quarantine at Portsea owing to the influenza epidemic) on 30th April, eight days short of four years spent oversea on active service.

LAST DAYS.

The fourth Christmas away from Australia was spent at Yves-Gomezee. The day was very cold, and a slight fall of snow took place. After church parade in the morning, a distribution of parcels from Australia was made, and everyone settled down to enjoy a Christmas dinner free from the sound and thoughts of war. To mark the occasion, the menu comprised boiled mutton, potatoes, cabbage, plum pudding, and custard, to which an issue of rum was added.

The casualty list to 31st December totalled 45, and was made up by two deaths, two wounded, and 39 evacuations due to injuries and sickness, all being "other ranks"; while two officers went sick. Records have not been compiled after the end of 1918 by the writer.

On the 17th January, Lieutenant-Colonel Ralston donated 200 francs for competition among the Transport Sections of the Battalion. As usual, the Company's Section was well to the fore, and secured half of the prize money. Another noteworthy item was the presentation of a silver watch and gold locket to Quartermaster-Sergeant A. H. ("Boss") Smith by the "other ranks" of the Company. The watch was suitably inscribed, and indicated that it had been given "as a token of esteem." Such a mark of favour must be unique among the records of the Quartermaster-Sergeants of the A.I.F.

The month of January saw further departures of officers and men for England, homeward bound; Captain Rae, Lieutenants Callister and Blenkarn leaving on the 9th. A few days before, Captain Rae received the award of the Military Cross for his capable direction of the Company, both as Second in Command and Commanding Officer. Still further departures left a shrunken unit, and consequently on the 21st, the Companies in the Battalion were reduced from a four to a two Section formation; the Company conforming to the order by amalgamating Nos. 1 with 3 and 2 with 4. A more drastic change took place on 2nd of February, when the Companies in the Battalion were reduced to two, the 6th being amalgamated with the 7th to form "B" Company. Thus, the Company officially ceased to exist a month short of its third birthday. The "strength" at the time was stated to be 9 officers and 116 other ranks. All gun gear had been returned to store by this time. The process of dissolution extended to the horses and mules of the Transport Section, except that they were not returned to Australia. Some were sent to the base, some were sold in Charleroi, and some of the mules, alas, were sold to local butchers. By mid-March, the remnants in the Battalion were amalgamated in one Transport Section.

On the 6th February, the Battalion marched out of Yves-Gomezee to Walcourt, and entrained for Bouierre. From the latter place it proceeded by route march to billets in the Montignies-le-Tillieul area. It was a bitterly cold day, and the horses and mules had great difficulty in maintaining a foothold on the frozen roads. Parades were held, but little drill was imposed; much time was given to the educational classes. Paris leave was obtained by a few, and Brussells leave by others. One member noted that the latter "was quite equal to Paris leave." To the dwindling remnants, even easier times were vouchsafed. Practically all had secured quarters with the local families. It was a very convenient arrangement for individuals, but imposed difficulties in the way of obtaining labour for the incidental fatigues. Acting Company Sergeant-Major F. L. Fitzpatrick had no easy task when he made the rounds of the dwellings, and a dialogue something as follows, took place:

C.S.M. (calling at door of house): "Any soldiers here, Madame?"

Madame: "Soldiers all partis, Monsieur."

C.S.M. (hearing voices at back with a decidedly Collingwood flavour): "Tell the soldiers I wish to speak with them, Madame."

Madame: "Absolutely no soldiers here, Monsieur."

(The C.S.M. usually lost the argument.)

It is pleasing to add that the relations of soldiers and civilians appear to have been of the happiest, and as the drafts of soldiers left, the local populace attended in hundreds to see their late guests depart.

At this time, the remnants frequently co-operated with the 24th Battalion and held dances. Every one of the locals, from 5 to 95 turned up, and it was pathetic to see the eager reception of the supper, which usually consisted of tins of cocoa and biscuits. The badly nourished civilians died like flies of pneumonic influenza; funerals occurring almost daily, but the war-hardened and better-fed soldiers appeared to be immune.

By mid-May, the Battalion itself had dwindled to one officer and 43 other ranks, who were attached to the 5th Brigade Battalion before final dissolution. With Quota 55, which departed about 15th May, was Lieutenant H. C. Thomas (Batta-

LAST DAYS.

lion Adjutant), Sergeant Anderson (Battalion Orderly Room Sergeant), and Acting Warrant Officer S. Renshaw (6th Company), who proceeded to Administrative Headquarters, Horseferry Road, London, and handed over the final documents of the Battalion and Company.

Meanwhile, the earlier parties from the Company had arrived in the Homeland, and the majority were en route for the same destination. So, by various transports and different routes, small parties helped to form assorted boat-rolls on the long journey home. Older in years, deeply experienced, and with a better appreciation of the favoured state of their native country, the survivors landed; their mission accomplished and crowned with hard-won victory. Before long, the A.I.F. ceased (officially) to exist, and in the dissolution, Company members returned to their homes, to loved ones and friends, and—to what appeared to be, after years of excitement and change—the hum-drum pursuits of civilian life.

In all, about 650 officers and men passed through the ranks of the Company up to the end of 1918. This figure includes an appreciable number who were "attached" from infantry battalions for varying periods; in some cases the stay was of short duration. Nearly 100 laid down their lives, while a mere handful escaped wounds and sickness. The complete figures are stated in the Appendix.

* * * *

Twenty years have elapsed since the "Euripides" and "Ulysses" sailed from Port Melbourne, carrying with them the battalions of the 6th Brigade and their associated machine-gun sections. The survivors of the latter and later formed Company meet each year in Melbourne in happy reunion. The passing of time but adds to the enthusiasm observable at large gatherings, as, with a better perspective, each one lives again, for a few brief hours, those associations distant in years but so readily renewed. Much had happened since. Some have answered the Final Roll-call; though young in years, the burden imposed by their service having become too heavy to be borne. The remainder view a disturbed world with clouded skies. But to them remains a treasured and imperishable possession: the memory of their allotted part in the shining story of the A.I.F., linked with and overshadowed by those great and splendid comradeships and associations in what will always be to them—THE COMPANY.

APPENDICES

APPENDIX.

APPENDIX A.

ROLL OF HONOUR.

OFFICERS.

2nd Lieut. F. W. H. Matthews, D.C.M.	Killed in action	8/11/16
2nd Lieut. A. L. Newland	Killed in action	8/11/16
Lieut. A. Palling	Died of wounds	3/5/17
Lieut. R. D. Desmond	Killed in action	3/5/17
Lieut. A. P. Earle	Died of wounds	24/7/17
Lieut. J. D. Campbell	Killed in action	9/10/17
2nd Lieut. F. G. D. Hamilton, M.M. and Bar	Killed in action	5/10/18
2nd Lieut. G. E. Rennie	Killed in action	5/10/18

OTHER RANKS.

419	Pte. J. F. Gribble	Killed in action	30/6/16
1740	Pte. K. J. Mackenzie	Killed in action	2/7/16
201	Pte. B. E. Gale	Killed in action	4/7/16
475	Pte. A. F. Matthews	Killed in action	4/7/16
10445	Pte. H. H. Matthews	Killed in action	4/7/16
1337	Pte. E. O'Neill	Killed in action	4/7/16
916	Pte. R. O. H. Wood	Died of wounds	28/7/16
70	Sgt. C. F. Murrell	Killed in action	30/7/16
2719	Pte. A. Hunt	Died of wounds	28/7/16
1123	L/Cpl. T. J. Milnes	Died of wounds	5/8/16
2474	Pte. A. J. Skelly	Died of wounds	22/8/16
2491	Pte. T. J. Ryan	Killed in action	22/8/16
144	L/Cpl. W. Dutton	Died of wounds	4/8/16
2007	Pte. J. B. Smith	Killed in action	26/8/16
462	Pte. E. R. Smith	Killed in action	26/8/16
457	Sgt. J. W. Taylor	Killed in action	8/11/16
1280	Pte. F. A. Anders	Killed in action	8/11/16
94	Pte. H. Buckley	Killed in action	8/11/16
1936	Pte. W. H. George	Killed in action	18/11/16
1298	Pte. G. Scott (Parsonage)	Killed in action	22/11/16
246	Pte. T. H. Smith	Killed in action	22/11/16
827	Pte. J. S. T. Dale	Died of wounds	24/11/16
1084	L/Cpl. A. Robinson	Killed in action	24/12/16
1579	Pte. H. Stebbing	Died of wounds	16/1/17
730	Pte. W. D. Watson	Died of illness	5/3/17
712	Pte. H. Wood	Killed in action	12/4/17

1039	Pte.	W. Compton	Killed in action	12/4/17
345	Cpl.	J. J. O'Gorman	Killed in action	3/5/17
277	Pte.	C. W. Dalitz	Killed in action	3/5/17
344	Pte.	C. W. Franklin	Killed in action	3/5/17
2668	Pte.	J. German	Killed in action	3/5/17
2134	Pte.	W. J. W. Clark	Killed in action	3/5/17
426	Pte.	W. Hayward	Killed in action	3/5/17
5328	Pte.	A. W. Dean	Killed in action	3/5/17
1200	Sgt.	G. B. Crerar	Died of wounds	20/5/17
1227a	Pte.	A. W. Hamond	Killed in action	20/9/17
1139	Pte.	W. H. Lucas	Killed in action	21/9/17
3800	Sgt.	A. E. Duncan	Killed in action	26/9/17
4984	Pte.	J. S. Boland	Killed in action	4/10/17
260	Pte.	W. Porteus	Killed in action	8/10/17
2132	Sgt.	H. J. Cook	Killed in action	9/10/17
1762	Sgt.	G. T. Guinea, M.M.	Killed in action	9/10/17
716	T/Cpl.	G. Pollock	Killed in action	9/10/17
1679	L/Cpl.	R. C. G. Greig, M.M.	Killed in action	9/10/17
145	L/Cpl.	H. L. Delandes	Killed in action	9/10/17
2394	L/Cpl.	E. J. Lyons	Killed in action	9/10/17
784	L/Cpl.	J. B. R. Horne	Killed in action	9/10/17
2010	L/Cpl.	C. F. Skead	Killed in action	9/10/17
2125	L/Cpl.	J. Bone	Killed in action	9/10/17
2173	Pte.	C. P. Jeffery	Killed in action	9/10/17
458	Pte.	W. H. Burns	Killed in action	9/10/17
336	Pte.	W. J. Morris	Killed in action	9/10/17
1667	Pte.	W. J. Bell	Killed in action	9/10/17
3689	Pte.	J. B. Wrigley	Killed in action	9/10/17
345	Pte.	R. J. Selkrig	Killed in action	9/10/17
427	Pte.	W. J. Richards	Killed in action	9/10/17
2189	Pte.	H. Jephcott	Killed in action	9/10/17
2127	Pte.	T. Britt, M.M.	Died of wounds	11/10/17
5049	Pte.	P. J. Mahoney	Killed in action	3/11/17
331a	Pte.	J. Williams	Died of wounds	7/11/17
621	Pte.	W. Flintham	Killed in action	17/3/18
730	Pte.	J. Watson	Died of wounds	7/4/18
726a	Pte.	W. Sage	Killed in action	15/5/18
622	Pte.	F. H. Lockwood	Killed in action	15/5/18
1731	Pte.	G. H. Mayell	Died of wounds	16/6/18
753	Cpl.	W. J. Jarvis	Killed in action	14/6/18
2216	Cpl.	J. J. Riley	Died of illness	12/7/18
8812a	Pte.	A. E. Johnson	Killed in action	8/8/18
2630	Pte.	E. J. Dunne	Killed in action	8/8/18
548	Pte.	A. Bingham	Died of wounds	8/8/18

APPENDIX.

634	Pte. E. Brain	Killed in action	8/8/18
704	Sgt. B. H. Johnston, M.M.	Killed in action	9/8/18
237	Pte. R. O. L. Ey	Died of wounds	9/8/18
777	Pte. C. Dean	Killed in action	9/8/18
3829	Pte. H. Jefferson	Killed in action	9/8/18
1658	Cpl. J. G. Anderson	Killed in action	9/8/18
1593	Sgt. D. C. M. Parkhill	Killed in action	11/8/18
4237	Cpl. W. S. Wallin	Died of wounds	11/8/18
6260	Pte. H. G. Dawson	Killed in action	31/8/18
6324	Pte. M. O'Loughlin	Killed in action	31/8/18
86	Pte. A. F. Woodman	Killed in action	31/8/18
343	Sgt. A. Y. E. Turner, M.M.	Died of wounds	3/9/18
6537	Pte. A. J. Ball	Died of wounds	4/9/18
1581	Pte. A. Anders	Died of wounds	4/9/18
4891	Pte. L. H. Burn	Died of wounds	6/10/18
299	Cpl. R. J. Saunders	Died ot wounds	5/10/18
5169	Pte. A. Napper	Died of wounds	6/10/18
458	Pte. G. Neville	Died of illness	15/11/18
4734	Pte. A. Johnson	Accidentally killed	17/12/18

APPENDIX "B."

DECORATIONS AND MENTIONED IN DESPATCHES.

(Out of the recommendations sent in by the Company and endorsed by Brigade headquarters, the following were accepted. After March, 1918, 2nd Machine Gun Battalion endorsed or otherwise.)

The names of the recipients are arranged alphabetically, and the rank stated is that at the time of the award. An asterisk denotes those who are deceased.

Military Cross (M.C.):

*Lieut. E. J. Bice.
Lieut. F. J. Blenkarn.
Lieut. R. C. Callister.
Capt. J. H. Drummond.
Lieut. F. V. W. Duncan.
Lieut. J. E. Hopper.
Major L. F. S. Hore.
Lieut. M. J. O'Brien.
Capt. D. F. Rae.
Lieut. G. A. Williams.
Lieut. F. L. Wright.

Distinguished Conduct Medal (D.C.M.).

19	Sgt. A. P. Hitchcock.	513	L/Cpl. A. E. D. Marsh.
418	Pte. D. Lazarus.	21	Sgt. F. W. H. Matthews.*

Military Medal (M.M.).

102	Sgt. J. P. Adam.	563	Pte. A. McK. Howie.
1075	Cpl. L. Barrand.	1526	Pte. H. L. Heyne.
3777	Pte. J. T. Bates.	704	Pte. B. H. Johnston.*
290a	Pte. J. C. Berriman.	418	Pte. D. Lazarus.
2124	Pte. A. D. G. Bone	442	L/Cpl. A. Matthews
1324	Pte. A. N. Bowley	1799	Pte. A. McDonald.
5307	L/Cpl. A. V. Caldwell.	592	Pte. A. E. Noonan.
843	Sgt. W. Carrick.	1768	L/Cpl. J. J. Passeri.
1594	Pte. H. G. Carthew.	239	Pte. W. H. Roberts.
935	Pte. A. Chitty.	682	Cpl. H. A. Robinson.
3507	Pte. P. W. Dale.	1032	Pte. S. S. Smith.
1531	Pte. C. W. Deal.	543	Pte. H. Stevenson.
3509	Pte. P. J. Dinneen.	518	Cpl. A. St.G. Tuohy.
1108	Pte. F. V. W. Duncan.	343	Cpl. A. Y. E. Turner.*
814	Pte. A. G. Elliott.	732	Pte. W. Ward.
2365	Pte. J. H. Falkingham.	281	Pte. S. Watts.
4483	Cpl. F. L. Fitzpatrick.	1273	Pte. F. Wigmore.
1762	Pte. G. T. Guinea.*	2438	Pte. W. H. Wilson.
508	Dvr. H. H. T. Harris.	2453	Sig. C. Wood.
2704	Sgt. J. H. Hodge.		

APPENDIX.

Bar to Military Medal.

592 Cpl. A. E. Noonan. 2453 Sig. C. Wood.

Meritorious Service Medal (M.S.M.).

509 Pte. H. A. Hanley. 2083 Sgt. J. A. McGaffin.
468 Dvr. G. O'Gorman. 1731 C.Q.M.S. A. H. Smith.

Mentioned in Despatches.

Lieut. R. Dodgshun. Capt. D. F. Rae.
Capt. J. H. Drummond. Lieut. F. Windsor.

FOREIGN DECORATIONS.

Croix de Chevalier, Legion of Honour.
Lieut. F. Windsor.

Belgian Croix de Guerre.
Lieut. N. F. Wilkinson.

Serbian Gold Medal.
1753 L/Cpl. M. J. O'Brien.

SUMMARY.

M.C.	11
D.C.M.	4
M.M.	39
M.S.M.	4
Foreign Decorations	3
Bars.	
M.M.	2
Mentioned in Despatches	4
Total	67

APPENDIX "C."

LIST OF OFFICERS WHO SERVED WITH THE COMPANY.

Note.—Rank stated is that on transfer, death, or discharge.

Major L. F. S. Hore, M.C.
Captain J. H. Drummond, M.C.
Captain R. C. Webb, M.C.
Lieutenant W. J. Darley.
Lieutenant A. J. Noall.
Captain D. F. Rae, M.C.
Lieutenant A.N. McLennan.
Lieutenant D. Mc. Lilley.
Lieutenant C. M. Williams.
Lieutenant R. C. Callister, M.C.
Lieutenant F. Windsor, C. de G.
Lieutenant R. F. Bennett.
Lieutenant F. J. Blenkarn, M.C.
Lieutenant J. D. Campbell.
Lieutenant E. S. Everett.
Lieutenant R. Douglas.
Lieutenant E. F. Armit, M.C., D.C.M.
Lieutenant E.J. Bice, M.C.
2nd-Lieutenant F. W. H. Matthews, D.C.M.
2nd-Lieutenant E.N.S. Lawrence.
2nd-Lieutenant A. L. Newland.
Lieutenant A. Palling.
Lieutenant R. D. Desmond.
Lieutenant A. P. Earle.
Lieutenant F. V. W. Duncan, M.M., M.C.
Lieutenant H. DeB. Newcomen.
Lieutenant E. J. Hopper, M.C.
Lieutenant H. A. Robinson.
Lieutenant A. P. Hitchcock, D.C.M.
Lieutenant F. L. Wright, M.C.
Lieutenant F. J. Nixon.
Lieutenant R. Dodgshun.
Lieutenant W. B. Davies.
Lieutenant W. Elliott.
Lieutenant T. F. Turnbull.
Lieutenant N. F. Wilkinson, C. de G. (Belgian).
Lieutenant G. A. Jeffery.

Lieutenant M. J. O'Brien, M.C., Serbian Gold Medal.
Lieutenant W. S. Clayton.
Lieutenant G. A. Williams, M.C.
Lieutenant W. A. C. Carne.
2nd-Lieutenant F. G. Hamilton, M.M. and Bar.
2nd-Lieutenant G. E. Rennie.
Lieutenant A. D. G. Bone, M.M.
Lieutenant W. Carrick, M.M.
Lieutenant E. S. Stephens, M.M.
Lieutenant E. D. Cridland.
Lieutenant Hickman.

APPENDIX "D."

MEMBERS OF THE COMPANY WHO WERE BROTHERS.

(Rank stated is that on death, transfer, or discharge.)

1581 Pte. Anders, Alfred.
    (Died of wounds, 4/9/18.)
1280 Pte. Anders, Francis Arthur.
    (Killed in action, 8/11/16.)

    Lieut. Bennett, Roy Frederick.
    Lieut. Bennett, Harold James.

    Lieut. Bone, Arthur David Gordon, M.M.
2125 L/Cpl. Bone, John.
    (Killed in action, 9/10/17.)

503 Pte. Britt, James Michael.
2127 Pte. Britt, Thomas Chas. Herbert, M.M.
    (Died of wounds, 11/10/17.)

2352 Pte. Carne, Henry Frank.
    Lieut. Carne, Wm. Albert Claude.

139 Pte. Daniel, Edward.
2337 Pte. Daniel, J.

2365 Sgt. Falkingham, Joseph Henry. M.M.
3110 Pte. Falkingham, Eric Alexander.

418a Pte. Greaves, George.
1158 T/Sgt. Greaves, Stanley Arthur.

1227 Pte. Hamond, Alfred William.
    (Killed in action, 20/9/17.)
399 Pte. Hamond, Robert Henry.

39 Pte. Letson, Alfred John.
    (Died since discharge.)
2693 Pte. Letson, Charles Arthur.
    (Died since discharge.)

APPENDIX.

   475 Pte. Matthews, Arthur Francis.
            (Killed in action, 4/7/16.)*
 10445 Pte. Matthews, Henry Hooper.
            (Killed in action, 4/7/16.)*
 2nd. Lieut. Matthews, Frederick Wm. Hordern, D.C.M.
            (Killed in action, 9/11/16.)

    53 Pte. McMahon, Charles Frederick.
  1874 Pte. McMahon, John Edward.

   468 Pte. O'Gorman, George.
    45 Cpl. O'Gorman, John James.
            (Killed in action, 3/5/17.)

  1084 Pte. Robinson, Albert.
            (Killed in action, 24/12/16.)
  4897 Pte. Robinson, Clarence Rupert.

  1342 Sgt. Reed, Samuel.
 6873a Pte. Reed, William.

  2216 Cpl. Riley, Joseph James.
            (Died of illness, 12/7/18.)
  2218 Pte. Riley, William Bates.

  2446 Pte. Stebbing, Alexander.
  1579 Pte. Stebbing, Harry.
            (Died of illness, 16/1/17.)

FATHER AND SON.

     6 Pte. Burtonclay, Arthur Edward (Father).
  4453 Pte. Burtonclay, Ernest James (Son).

   707 Pte. Deakin, Edwin Thomas (Father).
  1221 Cpl. Deakin, Sydney Henry (Son).

* By the same bomb.

APPENDIX "E."

Statement of Service of Corporal R. L. M. Cox.

Enlisted	5/2/15
Embarked as an original member of 22nd Battalion	8/5/15
Served with 22nd Battalion at Gallipoli	Sep.-Dec., 1915
Transferred to 6th Machine Gun Company in France	20/7/16
Promoted Lance Corporal	17/5/17
Promoted Corporal	26/11/17
Transferred to Machine Gun Depot, Parkhouse, England	Sep., 1918
Discharged	6/6/19

During the whole period of service, Corporal Cox was never absent from his unit except on two occasions when he went on leave. It so happened that he obtained his leave—the first, 2½ years after enlistment—when the Company was resting, and was with the Company in every engagement except the last attack of the A.I.F. at Montbrehain.

He was never present at a sick parade, and no entry appears on his record for breach of the regulations.

Born in London, England, 12/1/1893.

APPENDIX "F."

THE OLDEST MEMBER OF THE COMPANY TO FALL.

No. 726—PRIVATE WALTER SAGE.

When the Federal Conscription Referendum of 1916 met with an adverse vote, one of those Australians who deplored the result was Mr. Walter Sage, of Curlwaa.

Descended from sterling Devonshire stock, he was the grandson of early pioneers who arrived in South Australia in 1836, and was born at Angaston (S.A.) on 30th April, 1861. His father—Thomas Radford Sage, who had fought in the Crimea War—purchased for him an apprenticeship as a petty officer on the sailing ship "Hesperus," trading between Australia and England. Later, he was transferred to and served in the "Helen White," another sailing ship. At the age of 14 he deserted and obtained employment with a farmer at Millicent (S.A.), working on a threshing machine which toured the district threshing the farmers' crops. While so occupied he fell from the machine and broke his leg. The accident disclosed to his parents his whereabouts, and they took him to their home at Angaston, and in that district he remained for many years.

About 1907 he migrated from South Australia, and with his son to aid him, took up a block of land on the "Wentworth Irrigation Area" in New South Wales, near the confluence of the Murray and Darling rivers. The location was about four miles from Wentworth. Up to the time of Sage's entry, the scheme had not proved a success, but as a result of his practical experience as an orchardist at Angaston, combined with his ability to inspire optimism in others, the settlement obtained a new lease of life, and is to-day one of the most successful in the Murray Valley. The name was altered to Curlwaa about 1912. Meanwhile, Sage had, by his intelligence and industry, converted ugly bush land into a fertile orchard. A passing journalist at this time described him as a "bronzed, broad-shouldered, and successful orchardist." In memory of his community labours, the settlers have planted an avenue of trees through the area, and named it: "Walter Sage Memorial Avenue."

The outbreak of the war found him eager to help his country, but he was past the maximum military age, and for that reason was rejected when he offered himself for enlistment.

Not disposed to accept the decision, he put his case to the then Minister for Defence (Senator Pearce), who told him that he could serve his country equally well by helping to get volunteers. This he did, travelling the Riverina districts in his efforts.

The rejection of the Referendum proposals again turned his thoughts to enlistment. Without mentioning the matter to his friends and relatives, he proceeded to Melbourne on the 7th December, 1916, and was accepted for active service on declaring his age at 43. The medical officer in passing him remarked on his fine physical condition, and placed his years at probably 48. Actually, they were 55 years and 7 months.

On enlistment, he obtained three months leave for the purpose of harvesting his fruit crop, and in due course entered the camp at Broadmeadows on 16th March, 1917. Three months later (21/6/17) he embarked, and reached England as a reinforcement of the 22nd Battalion. After a period of training he was sent to France, and joined the Battalion on 1st January, 1918. It is understood that, up to that time, various Army officials attempted to side-track him into useful positions which offered an escape from the rigours and perils associated with a fighting unit. He, however, resisted all attempts, and joined the Battalion as stated.

After nearly three months' service with the Battalion, he succeeded in obtaining a transfer to the Company, and joined on 23rd March, 1918. Shortly after transferring, inducements were again made to have him accept a position of comparative security and exemption from line work. Finally, Captain Drummond called him before him and, as a preliminary question, enquired his age (nearly 57). "Excuse me, sir," said he, "but are you asking for military or private reasons?" "For private reasons," replied the Captain, seeing the import of the counter-question. The correct age was given. On hearing it, the Captain put his pre-conceived suggestion that he should accept a position in the Quarter-master Sergeant's store, or, as an alternative, a transfer to the Army Service Corps. Straightening himself up, the recipient declined the proposal in the following terms: "I thank you, sir, but my manhood will not permit me to accept it." He went on to explain that his death would not be a matter of great loss as he had lived most of his life, whereas so many of his comrades had theirs to live. Before such pleading, the Captain gave way, and he was allowed to resume his place in a gun-team in No. 2 Section. Subsequently, Captain Rae refused to allow him to go into the line, and again the persistent one won his point by declaring: "I cannot go home without having been in the front line."

Possessing a cheerful nature, and maintaining a dignity natural to him, he soon became a favourite with his comrades, who affectionately christened him "Dad," and conspired to make his path easier by sundry little acts of consideration and help. He, in turn, loved to tell of his orchard and experiences.

And so it went on till a soldier's death claimed him in his 58th year. As related in the narrative, the end came on the 15th May, 1918, at the morning "stand to" in the sunken road near Treux. As he and a comrade were leaning side by side against the wall of the gun position, an odd shell fell between them, killing both instantaneously.

An only son of the deceased, Private A. L. Sage, served in the 60th Battalion, and at the time of his father's death, a transfer was being arranged so that the son might join the father. It is worthy of note that a brother of the deceased (George Sage) and his three sons served in the New Zealand Expeditionary Force. Private A. L. Sage's three brothers-in-law (Haven Ainley, Alex. Borthwick, and Charles Penglase) served in the Australian Imperial Force, likewise three cousins (Charles, Tom, and Jim Sage) who took up land at Curlwaa. Tom Sage was killed at the landing on Gallipoli.

APPENDIX "G."

SUMMARY OF CASUALTIES.

Table A.

	Officers	Other ranks
Killed in action; died of wounds or illnesses; or accidentally killed	8	89
Wounded or gassed	25	208
Sick or injured	13	376
Prisoner of war	1	—
Total	47	673

Table B.

	Five times	Four times	Three times	Twice	Once	Total
Wounded or Gassed	—	—	5	30	158	233
Sick and Injured	1	4	22	59	184	389

APPENDIX "H."

NOMINAL ROLL OF MEMBERS.

(a) Supplied by Defence Department, Melbourne.

Rank stated is that on transfer, death, or discharge.

Asterisk indicates Foundation Member.

102	Sgt. Adam, J. P.		291	Pte. Birch, W. A.
591	Pte. Adams, A. J.		1502	*Cpl. Black, H. G.
321a	Pte. Alderson, A. J.		2119	Pte. Black, J. C.
457	Pte. Allan, G. G.		94	Pte. Blackman, W. H.
4655	Pte. Allen, S. F. S.		4137	Pte. Blackwell, G. D.
1659	Cpl. Allen, W.E.		5307	Pte. Blair, E.
1581*	Pte. Anders, A.		6538	Pte. Blake, E. R.
1280	Pte. Anders, F. A.			*Lieut. Blenkarn, F. J.
1658	Cpl. Anderson, G.		1790	Pte. Bliss, V. E.
1655	Pte. Andrews, N.C.		4984	Pte. Boland, J. S.
2105	Pte. Armstrong, N. W.			Lieut. Bone, A. D. G.
2107	*Far. Sgt. Armstrong, R. A.		2125	L/Cpl. Bone, J.
11	*Sgt. Bailey, O. H.		4135	Pte. Botten, A. E.
141	*Pte. Bailey, Wm.		1785.	*Sgt. Bowden, C. M.
6537	Pte. Ball, A. J.		1324	Cpl. Bowley, A. N.
1	*Dvr. Barnett, E. W.		634	Pte. Brain, E.
1075	Sgt. Barrand, L.		4366	Pte. Brakenwagen, L.
633	L/Cpl. Barrett, T. O.		993	*C.S.M. Brandebura, J.
794	*Dvr. Bartlett, Wm.		1517	Cpl. Braithwaite, F.
67	Pte. Bastable, F. E.		6539	Pte. Brien, W. T.
3777	L/Cpl. Bates, J. T.		503	*Pte. Britt, J. M.
328	Pte. Baudinette, A. S.		2127	Pte. Britt, T. C. H.
2	Pte. Beardmore, H.		505	Pte. Brown, T.
564	*L/Cpl. Bell, P. D.		94	Pte. Buckley, H.
1667	Pte. Bell, Wm. J.		4269	Pte. Burn, C. G.
322	Pte. Bennett, D. C.		458	Pte. Burns, H. W.
	Lieut. Bennett, H. J.		6	*Pte. Burtonclay, A. E.
	*Lieut Bennett, R. F.		4453	Pte. Burtonclay, E. J.
290a	Pte. Berriman, J. C.		3785	Pte. Butterworth, A. W.
	*Lieut. Bice, E. J.		4	*L/Cpl. Butterworth, W. H.
548	Pte. Bingham, A.		1056	Cpl. Byrnes, L. G.

5307	Pte. Caldwell, A. V.	829	*Sgt. Davies, L.
237	Pte. Caligari, B.		Lieut. Davies, W. B.
3318	Cpl. Callaghan, C.	2358	Cpl. Davis, B.
	*Lieut Callister, R. C.	1221	*Cpl. Deakin, S. H.
769	Sgt. Cameron, A. E.	1531	Cpl. Deal, C. W.
5316	Pte. Campbell, A.	777	Pte. Dean, C.
	*Lieut. Campbell, J. D.	145	L/Cpl. Deslandes, H. L.
2265	T/Cpl. Campbell, J. S.		*Lieut. Desmond, R. D.
2352	*Pte. Carne, H. F.	3509	Pte. Dinneen, P. J.
	*Lieut. Carne, W. A. C.	1059	Sgt. Dixon, R. H. E.
1692	*Dvr. Carrick, L. T.		*Lieut. Dodgshun, R.
	*Lieut Carrick, Wm.	1534	*Dvr. Donovan, T. J.
1594	Cpl. Carthew, H. G.	1598	Pte. Doyle, G. F.
345	*Cpl. Chalmers, A. C.		*Capt. Drummond, J. H.
935	*L/Cpl. Chitty, A.	3800	Sgt. Duncan, E. A.
2134	*Pte. Clark, W. J. W.		*Lieut. Duncan, F. V. W.
	*Lieut. Clayton. W. S.	17	Pte. Dunn, H. H.
15	*Cpl. Coe, A. E.	144	*Pte. Dutton, W.
5325	Pte. Coleman, J.	1535	Pte. Earey, F.
1505	*Pte. Commerford, E.		*Lieut. Earle, A. P.
1039	*L/Cpl. Compton, W.	814	*Pte. Elliott, A. G.
14308	Pte. Cook, H. H.		Lieut. Elliott, Wm.
2132	*Sgt. Cook, H. J.	2166	L/Sgt. Esmond, V. G.
4999	Pte. Coote, T. H.	237	Pte. Ey, R. O. L.
1025a	Pte. Cotter, W. J.	371	*L/Cpl. Fair, A. E.
3785	Pte. Coulston, T.	3110	Pte. Falkingham, E. A.
136	Cpl. Cox, R. L. M.	2365	Sgt. Falkingham, J. H.
356	Pte. Cox, R. M.	5581	Pte. Farrell, A. B.
1200	*Sgt. Crerar, G. B.	71	*Cpl. Findlay, J. W.
2253	Pte. Crisp. A. W.	624	Pte. Fitch, F. J.
1896	Dvr. Crowley, G.	4483	Sgt. Fitzpatrick, F. L.
1531a	Pte. Cullen, J. V.	621	*Pte. Flintham, Wm.
389	Pte. Curran, L. A. A.	886	L/Cpl. Ford, H.
323	Pte. Cuthbert. H.	622	Pte. Ford, J. H.
324	Pte. Daffy, M. G.	1714	Sgt. Forster, A. E.
827	*Pte. Dale, J. S. T.	344	Pte. Franklin, C. W.
3507	Pte. Dale, P. W.	326	Pte. Fraser, A. J.
277	Pte. Dalitz, C. W.	1587	Pte. Fraser, F.
828	*Pte. Dalton, J.	560	Pte. Frawley, T. J.
139	Pte. Daniel, E.	1677	*Dvr. Gadd, R. B.
	*Lieut. Darley, W.	201	*Pte. Gale, B. E.
399a	Pte. Davidson, G. E.	2180	*Pte. Gamble, G. E.
1665	*L/Cpl. Davies, C. A.	1936	*Pte. George, W. H.
5335	Pte. Davies, J. P.	2666	Pte. Georgeson, B. C.

APPENDIX. 415

2668	Pte. German, J.	2173	Pte. Jeffery, C. P.
606	Pte. Gilbert, J. H.		*Lieut. Jeffrey, G. A.
727	*Pte. Gornall, W. A.	2189	Pte. Jephcott, H.
1029	*Sgt. Graue, F. M.	1559	*Pte. Johnson, F. G.
418a	*Pte. Greaves, G.	2288	*Pte. Johnson, F. W.
1158	*T/Sgt. Greaves, S. A.	704	Sgt. Johnston, B. H.
1514a	Pte. Greenwell, R.	1125	Pte. Jolly, A.
1679	L/Cpl. Greig, R. C. G.	1528	Pte. Jury, L. J.
419	*Pte. Gribble, J. F.	7270	Pte. Kay, M. E.
2248	Pte. Griffiths, A.	2755	Pte. Keane, J.
3829	Pte. Grip, H.	4971	Pte. Keer, D.
1762	Sgt. Guinea, G. T.	3853	Pte. Knott, D. R.
826	*Cpl. Hall, S. F.	897	*Dvr. Laity, P. C.
962	T/Cpl. Hammon, N. C.	644	Pte. Langford, C. A.
1227	*Pte. Hamond, A. W.		*Lieut. Lawrence, E. N. S.
399	*Pte. Hamond, R. H.	2199	Pte. Layton, E. T.
509	Pte. Hanley, H. A.	905	*Dvr. Lee, E. J. M.
286	Pte. Harapeet, E. A.	333	Dvr. Legge, O. F.
507	Dvr. Harris, E. F.	938	Pte. Leishman, W. T.
508	L/Cpl. Harris, H. H. T.	171	*Pte. Lello, E.
598	Pte. Hatton, M. J. V.	39	*Pte. Letson, A. J.
462	Pte. Hayward, W.	2693	Pte. Letson, C. A.
3347	Pte. Hefferman, W. T.		Lieut. Lilley, D. McM.
1526	*Cpl. Heyne, H. L.	217	*Dvr. Lindsay, G.
148	*Cpl. Hickey, F.	2681	Pte. Lindsell, H. F. R.
	*Lieut. Hitchcock, A. P.	64	*Pte. Littler, G. A.
2704	Sgt. Hodge, J. H.	622	Pte. Lockwood, F. H.
3180	Pte. Hogan, H.	56	Pte. Logan, G.
650	Pte. Hollywood, E. A.	561	Pte. Louis, G. H.
2389	Pte. Holt, C.	1210	Pte. Loveless, W. J.
	*Lieut. Hopper, J. E.	1139	Pte. Lucas, W. H.
	Major Hore, L. F. S.	2394	*L/Cpl. Lyons, E. J.
784	L/Cpl. Horne, J. B. R.	334	Pte. Mackay, J. G.
642	Hon. Sgt. Horner, H. E.	1740	*Pte. Mackenzie, K. J.
2457	*Pte. Howard, D. C.	20	*Sgt. Mackley, E.
595	Pte. Howe, J. R.	3082	Pte. Madden, S.
563	Pte. Howie, A. McK.	5049	Pte. Mahoney, P. J.
1524	Pte. Hutcheson, C. J.	1928	Pte. Malcolm, G.
510	Pte. Hyland, W. J.	470	Pte. Maloney, J. A.
4321	Pte. Idam, H.		Lieut. Malpas, H. E.
514	Pte. Jackson, J. D.	918	Pte. Manning, G. R.
2257	Pte. James, L.	379	Pte. Many-Peney, S. V.
753	A/Cpl. Jarvis, W. J.	513	L/Cpl. Marsh, A. E. D.
3829	Pte. Jefferson, H.	645	Pte. Marshall, A. H.

2223	Pte. Marshall, W. E.	2417	*Dvr. Nash, E. J.
428	*Sgt. Masters, A. E.	458	Pte. Neville, G.
442	*Cpl. Matthews, A.		Lieut. Newcomen, H. DeB.
475	*Pte. Matthews, A. F.		*2/Lieut. Newland, A. L.
	2/Lieut. Matthews, F. W. H.	798	*L/Cpl. Nicholson, H. F.
			*Lieut. Nixon, F. J.
10445	Pte. Matthews, H. H.		*Lieut. Noall, A. J.
1942	Pte. Maughan, J. P.	592	*Sgt. Noonan, A. E.
1731	Pte. Mayell, G. H.	604a	Pte. Norman, V. J.
1799	*Sgt. McDonald, A.		*Lieut. O'Brien, M. J.
2083	*Sgt. McGaffin, J. A.	3909	Pte. O'Donoghue, J. J. A.
471a	Pte. McGinnis, F. J.	468	*Dvr. O'Gorman, G.
2413	Pte. McHenry, H. E.	345	*Cpl. O'Gorman, J. J.
614	*Pte. McIntyre, W. M.	703	*Pte. Oldham, H. G.
1695	Pte. McKay, T. A.	1337	*Pte. O'Neill, E.
	*Capt. McLennan, A. N.	2366	Pte. Ostle, T.
53	Dvr. McMahon, C. F.	484	Pte. O'Sullivan, D.
2084	Pte. McMahon, J.	563	Pte. Owen, E. R.
1874	Pte. McMahon, J. E.		*Lieut. Palling, A.
1047	*Dvr. McManus, J.	3987	Pte. Palmer, J. R.
436	*Pte. McNaughton, L.	1593	Sgt. Parkhill, D. C. M.
339	*Pte. McPherson, A.	1594	Pte. Parsons, E.
518	Pte. McPherson, J.	1768	*Cpl. Passeri, J. J.
2377	Pte. McPherson, R. H.	292	Pte. Paulig, W. O.
524	Pte. Merry, H. G.	1985	*Pte. Paull, N. A.
2993	Pte. Miles, J. H.	7	*Sgt. Payton, A.
241	L/Cpl. Millar, T.	675	*Dvr. Peacock, E. W.
1592	Pte. Millett, A. W.	564a	Pte. Penfold, H. H.
1123	*Pte. Milnes, J. T.	669	Cpl. Peters, W. E.
300	Pte. Mitchelson, C.	1548a	Pte. Phillips, E.
928	*Cpl. Moffatt, E.	13634	Pte. Pittendreigh, J. F.
1730	Cpl. Moran, T.	716	T/Cpl. Pollock, G.
859a	Pte. Morey, L. C.	2353	*Pte. Price, C. N.
469	Pte. Morris, C. C.	720	*Pte. Price, W. P.
1737	*Dvr. Morris, R. W.	259	*Pte. Purchase, J. W.
336	Pte. Morris, W. J.	1761	*Cpl. Quinn, M.
459a	Pte. Morrison, H. J.		Capt. Rae, D. F.
460	*Pte. Moss, N. B.	338	Dvr. Rawson, H. W.
935	*Pte. Mounsey, P.	951	Pte. Ray, F. J.
2186	Cpl. Muir, J. C.	1342	Sgt. Reed, S.
70	*Sgt. Murrell, C. F.	890	*Pte. Reeves, E. D.
289	Pte. Mustard, R. S.	4758	Pte. Reid, H. C.
	*Lieut. Myers, J. N.		*2/Lieut. Rennie, G. E.
5169	Pte. Napper, A.	4319	Pte. Rice, G. A.

APPENDIX.

427	Pte.	Richards, W. J.
565	Pte.	Ridley, G. W. J.
2216	Cpl.	Riley, J. J.
2218	Dvr.	Riley, W. B.
193	Cpl.	Riley, W. N.
2370	Pte.	Ritson, J. C.
266	*Pte.	Roach, R. G.
239	Pte.	Roberts, W. H.
380	Pte.	Robertson, A.
1084	* Pte.	Robinson, A.
4897	Pte.	Robinson, C. R.
	*Lieut.	Robinson, H. A.
525	Dvr.	Rodda, E.
2436	Pte.	Rollinson, H. M.
570	Pte.	Rolls, E. B.
3618	Cpl.	Russell, W. B.
2102	Pte.	Ryan, J.
5078	Cpl.	Saker, E. D.
299	Cpl.	Saunders, R. J.
340	Pte.	Schild, H. G.
1950	T/Sgt.	Schofield, F. T.
1298	Pte.	Scott, G. (stated to be Parsonage, William George).
345	Pte.	Selkrig, R. J.
4213	Pte.	Sharp, H.
698	Cpl.	Sharp, Wm.
1415	Pte.	Shirer, F. G.
456	Pte.	Simmons, F. E.
5089	Pte.	Simmons, T. J.
2010	L/Cpl.	Skead, C. F.
2474	*Pte.	Skelley, A. J.
522	Pte.	Smith, A.
1731	*C.Q.M.S.	Smith, A. H.
72	*Pte.	Smith, A. H.
1615	*C.Q.M.S.	Smith, H. L.
2256	Pte.	Smith, J. A.
56	Pte.	Smith, J. E.
72	*Pte.	Smith, R. J. V.
1032	T/Cpl.	Smith, S. S.
57	*Dvr.	Smith, T.
246	Pte.	Smith, T. H.
1549	Pte.	Spearman, W. J. N.
4199	T/Sgt.	Spittle, J. N.
284	*Pte.	Stait, H. H.
198	*Sgt.	Stapleton, J. L.
2446	*Pte.	Stebbing, A.
1579	Pte.	Stebbing, H.
298	Pte.	Steen, W. G.
244	Dvr.	Stephenson, F. W.
1039	*Sgt.	Stevens, A. G.
543	*Pte.	Stevenson, H.
1344	*L/Cpl.	Stewart, A. C. L.
339	Pte.	Stewart, A. G.
521	Pte.	Stone, H. D.
2259	Pte.	Stott, F. E.
2458	*L/Cpl.	Swindon, N. S.
607	Pte.	Taylor, C.
1183	Pte.	Taylor, J. H.
256	*Pte.	Taylor, J. M. R.
457	*Sgt.	Taylor, J. W.
749	L/Cpl.	Taylor, W. J. T.
4937	Pte.	Telford, L. W.
5097	Pte.	Thomas, H.
2475	Pte.	Thomas, W. H.
476	Pte.	Thompson, P. L.
609	Pte.	Thomson, A.
	*2/Lieut.	Torrens, J. W.
5104	L/Sgt.	Trevan, R. C.
518	*T/Cpl.	Tuohy, A. St.G.
	Lieut.	Turnbull, T. F.
343	Sgt.	Turner, A. Y. E.
2465	Sgt.	Turner, G. R.
1562	*Pte.	Upton, M.
5702	T/Cpl.	Varney, A. F.
2271	Pte.	Vincent, S. H.
1981	*Pte.	Vonarx, F. J.
1786	*Dvr.	Wakeley, C.
432	Pte.	Walker, F. L.
538	*Pte.	Wallace, W. H.
4237	Cpl.	Wallin, W. S.
732	Pte.	Ward, Wm.
611	Pte.	Warner, C. J.
730	Pte.	Watson, W. D.
1567	*C.Q.M.S.	Watt, R. W.
281	Pte.	Watts, S.
731	Dvr.	Weatherhead, G.
1748a	Pte.	Weight, W. S. J.

418   IN GOOD COMPANY.

473	Pte. Wells, A.		2438	*T/Cpl. Wilson, W. H.
1985	Dvr. Wells, H.		1754a	Pte. Wollin, C.
231	Pte. West, H. C.		2453	*Pte. Wood, C.
1273	*Sgt. Wigmore, F.		712	Pte. Wood, H.
	Lieut. Wilkinson, N. F.		2245	Pte. Wood, H. E. A.
2818	Pte. Wilkinson, R. N.		916	*Pte. Wood, R. O. H.
60	*C.S.M. Wilhelm, L. H.		4334	Pte. Wood, W. R.
	Lieut. Williams, C. M.		62	*Pte. Woodburgess, G.
10	Sgt. Williams, E. C.		86	Pte. Woodman, A. F.
331a	Pte. Williams, J.		1752	*Pte. Wormald, H.
2015	Dvr. Wilmot, E. W.			*Lieut. Wright, F. L.
	*Lieut. Windsor, F.		3689	Pte. Wrigley, J. B.
1008	*Pte. Wilson, R.		3672	Pte. Yates, A. E.

(b) Compiled by the author from records in Australian War Memorial.

NOTE :- Seperate Company records were not compiled after the formation of the 2nd Machine Gun Battalion in mid-March 1918

	Lieut. Armit, E. F.		211	Pte. Hardie, W.
3969	Pte. Ball, A. E.		4446	Pte. Hannan, J. F.
632	Pte. Barrass, B.		139	Pte. Hartley, T.
695	Pte. Bate, R. A.		5030	Pte. Healey, T.
4365	Pte. Beanland, G. D.		5843	Pte. Henderson, A. T.
672	Pte. Berner, H. W.		796	Pte. Heriot, E.
694	Pte. Bradley, T. W.		675	Pte. Hibbs, J. W.
238a	Pte. Brophy, J.			Lieut. Hickman.
1665	Pte. Brown, A.		1813	Pte. Howlett, R. G.
1022	Pte. Brown, R.		394	Pte. Howden, W. N.
1655	Pte. Bull, F. E.		683	Pte. Jacobson, J. N.
4891	Pte. Burn, L. H.		677	Pte. John, E.
4992	Pte. Campbell, C. R.		4734	Pte. Johnson, A.
8838	Pte. Chewings, H. J.		8812a	Pte. Johnson, A. E.
2349	Pte. Cresdee, L. J.		6368	Pte. Jones, E.
	Lieut. Cridland, A. E.		6574	Pte. Jones, E. W.
8799a	Pte. Crompton, J.		2927	Pte. Kavanagh, W.
6260	Pte. Dawson, H. G.		3859	Pte. Kennelly, M. O.
707	Pte. Deakin, E. T.		679a	Pte. Knox, A.
1048	Pte. Dickson, J. C.		4726	Pte. Lavell, W. E.
3140	Pte. Donohue, R. M.		418	Pte. Lazarus, D.
2630	Pte. Dunne, E. J.		3130	Pte. Lean, A.
4104	Pte. Green, V. W.		718	Pte. Lewis, A.
4720	Pte. Greening, W. H.		5896	Pte. Meagher, M. H.
2373	Pte. Gibbons, D. T.		1083	Pte. Miller, L.
	2/Lieut. Hamilton, F. G. D.		5658	Pte. Morris, W. F.
1707	Pte. Haggart, T.		7276	Pte. McDonald, D.

APPENDIX.

6861	Pte. McGown, W.		2436	Pte. Savage, G.
6847a	Pte. McKenzie, K. J.		505	Pte. Scanlon, T. P.
2245	Pte. McLellan, R. S.		8802a	Pte. Shillabeer, W. H.
721	Pte. McLennan, W. R.		3459	Pte. Shanley, F. A. C.
722a	Pte. McNamara, L. J. P.		6119	Pte. Short, W. E.
5446	Pte. Nelson, K. B.		826	Pte. Smith, G. J.
2126	Pte. Nicholson, H. E.		2314	Pte. Stiles, A. J. C.
4772	Pte. Nolan, G. P.			Lieut. Stephens, E. S.
697	Pte. Owen, H. C.		502	Pte. Stokes, E.
723	Pte. O'Brien, F.		1146	Pte. Stokie, T.
6324	Pte. O'Loughlin, M.		1817	Pte. Stokoe, P. H.
622	Pte. O'Meara, G. G.		5693	Pte. Sullivan, W. H.
4766	Pte. Pickering, T.		3643	Pte. Taylor, W. J.
808	Pte. Piconi, A.		6145	Pte. Terry, T. G.
6371	Pte. Redman, E. W.		2848	Pte. Waterman, J.
6873a	Pte. Reed, W. J.		730	Pte. Watson, J.
1784	Pte. Renshaw, S.		6931	Pte. Watson, T.
1420	Pte. Robbins, N. R.		6407	Pte. Wright, H. S.
50134	Pte. Riddell, T. J.		731	Pte. Welsford, G. R.
6106	Pte. Rookyard, E.		6419	Pte. Williams, M.
726a	Pte. Sage, W.			

(c) List of names of men who were temporarily "attached" to the Company.

5539	Pte. Adams, G. A.		4404	Pte. Dorsett, W.
5540	Pte. Anderson, C. R.		1707	Pte. Fennelly, T. J.
5293	Pte. Anthony, R. L.		880	Pte. Fraser, P.
98	Pte. Bonella, J. H.		3809	L/Cpl. Fuller, W. R.
	Pte. Borland, S.		5122	Cpl. Goldsmith, R. O.
3776	Pte. Blundell, G. A.		1225	Pte. Green, V. G.
5308	Pte. Bourke, J. H.		4104	Pte. Green, V. W.
5305	L/Cpl. Brown, W. E.		626	L/Cpl. Gregson, T.
2335	Pte. Brien, A. R.		5355	L/Cpl. Henshall, E. E.
6295	Pte. Burrell, W. H.		5034	Pte. Holt, E.
1891	Pte. Calder, R.		2719	Pte. Hunt, A.
610	Pte. Campbell, A.		1577	Pte. Hunter, L. G.
5568	Pte. Cheel, A. C.		5359	Pte. Hyams, W.
4286	Pte. Cobatt, T. H.		6100	Pte. Ivory, T. W.
5332	Pte. Cumming, A. W.		2162	Pte. Jones, P.
2620	Pte. Daly, P.		900	Pte. Leonard, L.
2337	Pte. Daniel, J.		4578	Pte. Leslie, J.
5328	Pte. Dean, A. W.		592	Pte. Lorimer, R.
2138	Pte. Dolan, T.		2857	Pte. Loudon, J.
3804	Pte. Dooley, T. J.		5381	Pte. Martin, J. P.

210	Pte.	Mew, W. W.	2491	Ptc.	Ryan, T. J.
1729	Pte.	Moore, W. A.	1766	Pte.	Ryan, W.
866	Pte.	McDonnell, P.	1583	Pte.	Sandells, S. W.
2245	Pte.	McLennan, R. L.	5091	Pte.	Sharp, W. J.
4289	Pte.	Newling, P.	5716	Pte.	Slade, W. B.
2278	Pte.	O'Callaghan, A. J.	460	Pte.	Smith, E. R.
5424	Pte.	O'Rourke, C. J.	2207	Pte.	Smith, J. B.
2231	Pte.	Oxley, S. J.	951	Pte.	Smith, R. W.
806	Pte.	Pearce, D.	5967	Pte.	Smyth, D.
6363	Pte.	Peters, W. J.	2043	Pte.	Spark, E. W.
6107	Pte.	Phibbs, W.	3910	Pte.	Stewart, L.
4016	Pte.	Phillipson, J. R.	6395	Pte.	Thomas, C.
260	Pte.	Porteus, W.	2408	Pte.	Thomson, A.
4754	Pte.	Quelch, A.	723	Ptc.	Thomson, H. A.
5411	Sgt.	Rail, R.	719	Pte.	Tregonning, H. P.
5708	Pte.	Rankman, J. R.	2022	Pte.	Wightmann, C.
380f	Pte.	Robertson, F.	3968	Pte.	Williams, E.
380	Pte.	Robertson, F.	5444	Pte.	Wilson, F. G.
3238	Pte.	Rickman, A.	1756	Pte.	Wright, E.

APPENDIX "I."

THE HORSES AND MULES OF THE TRANSPORT SECTION.

(A Tribute.)

The Allied Cause was well served—on the Western Front as elsewhere—by an immense number of horses and mules. Indeed, without them, it is difficult to conceive how the Army could have functioned. Faithful, and at times heroic service by dumb servitors, surely warrants more than the passing allusions which have been made to them in the preceding narrative. For that reason, space has been found to acknowledge their labours with gratitude.

In that vast army, the Company's establishment originally provided for 11 "riding" and 47 "light draught" horses; the former being reduced to 7 in March, 1917; while the latter suffered a diminution to 44 when the Machine Gun Battalion was formed in March, 1918. It was not always possible to maintain the "light draughts" at the prescribed weight, and the wastage of war required the deficiencies, at times, to be made good with mules. This complement provided for the whole of the Company's transport requirements (apart from personnel) for the greater part of the three years of its existence. At times, assistance was rendered to other units in the Brigade.

Throughout the changing conditions of summer and winter, the stresses of offensive operations, and the less exacting intervals of "rest," that service was maintained without interruption. The conditions in summer did not make heavy demands on the animals, but the winters imposed severe strain on both man and beast. When cover was available, or could be improvised, it was used, but more often the lines were on open ground, and frequent rain added enormously to the difficulties in the way of maintenance. The chief problem was to keep the lines dry, and it was never ending. Bricks, chalk, or any solid substance was used in the endeavour to obtain a dry base. Standing in wet lines induced the complaint known as "greasy heels." Heels so affected became cracked and sore, and unless the complaint was checked, the horse could not be worked. The remedy was to put the horse on a dry line and apply an ointment which was supplied by the Vetinerary Sergeant. Another complaint was the presence of lice in the hair of the legs, causing the horse to bite his legs and stamp on the ground. The remedy in this case was to clip the heels and apply a lotion, also supplied by the Vetinerary Sergeant, and then the feet were dipped in a prepared solution. In the cold weather, rugs were used, each rug bearing the name of the horse to which it belonged.

The frozen roads in winter added another difficulty, that of maintaining a foothold on the slippery surface. This was met by the issue of cogs or spikes, which were screwed into holes previously made in the shoes; three in the front shoe and two in the rear. Each spike had four points which could be sharpened with a file. It was the custom among the drivers to carry a few spare spikes in the pocket in case of loss or breakage when in use. As the horses came off the roads and were placed on the lines, the spikes were withdrawn to prevent possible injury to other horses. The removal and replacement of the spikes was often a difficult business, and caused much work.

Apart from the difficulties arising out of the winter conditions, single horses sometimes presented problems which had to be dealt with individually. For instance, one horse had to be tethered to a single post so that he could continually circle it as he gazed upwards at aeroplanes, day or night. If left on the line with other horses, he would upset the whole party in his frantic endeavours to look skywards.

It should be added that the drivers used every effort to maintain their charges in working condition. Each driver kept to his own pair and used them continuously; one incentive to effort being the fact that, if his horses went "sick," they were sent away to hospital and he never saw them again. Consequently much attention was given to the horses' feet when they came back to the lines after work. "In the winter," said Corporal J. J. Passeri, "we were never finished trying to get them on dry footing, and would wash their heels when they came back to the lines." The use of corduroy tracks led to many broken shoes, and sometimes part of the hoof came away with the shoe. These losses called for much ingenuity on the part of Farrier R. A. Armstrong. Said Corporal Passeri: "He always had some patent shoe that would enable us to keep our horses on strength and allow the horse to walk in comfort. If a horse lost a shoe on the march, he always had one to fit, and had it on in no time." The efforts of the Farrier-Sergeant were well seconded by the saddler, Private G. R. Manning, who invariably kept the leather work in good order. Later in the campaign, when enemy bombing machines paid greater attention to horse lines, the drivers built earthern walls round the lines to minimise the effects of bursting bombs.

APPENDIX. 423

When the supply of horses was insufficient to meet the demands of the service, mules were issued. The presence of two kinds of animals naturally afforded comparisons. On the lines, horses required more care, and their behaviour was better than mules. The latter needed less attention, would eat almost anything, but, on the other hand, would "kick from any angle, and fight on the lines all night." When rugs were first placed on mules, unforseen loss occurred. The next morning it was discovered that nothing remained of their coverings but the buckles, metal rings, and clips. The animals had eaten the whole of the fabric from the backs of each other. Thereafter, they had to be muzzled to save the rugs.

In line work, horses proved superior; their higher intelligence appearing to help them. They could be got in and out of positions quickly; an important consideration in shelled areas and in congested traffic where speed was essential. Furthermore, they were easily led, would go almost anywhere, and were better for pack work. Generally, horses behaved well under fire, although after frequent trips in forward areas, they appeared to be conscious of danger, as evidenced by a lather of sweat when in dangerous localities. Once hit, they were inclined to flinch and try to get away. When shells were falling, they would follow readily into any sheltered place or trench and stay there, and would even try to enter dug-outs.

On the other hand, while mules would stand a lot of work, they were sluggish in heavy traffic, and sometimes caused traffic jams. In pack work they were slow and had to be pulled about. Under shell-fire they appeared to be more difficult to handle, and had to be pulled and flogged to get into positions.

Horses were preferred to mules by all drivers with, perhaps, the solitary exception of Driver C. F. McMahon, but as he had charge of two exceptionally good mules, his judgment was possibly biassed. He admitted that his charges were "as tractable as two small ponies," and that one, "Bob Up," won every flat race for which he was entered, and returned his driver about 800 francs. In addition, "Firefly," the other mount, won two hurdle races with his driver aboard, who collected about 100 francs.

In this brief notice, it is not possible to make extended references to individual horses, but as two mules have been specified, two horses will be selected for mention. In the early days of the Company, the water cart was drawn by "Hippo" and "The Little Mare." They were an oddly assorted pair. The presence of the two, one on each side of the pole, was regarded as a standing joke in the Company, and an oft-seized opportunity for outsiders to comment with very pointed remarks. Beside her ungainly mate, "The Little Mare" was a well-shaped animal and rather dainty in her actions, but her companion's form broke all the rules of equine beauty. A large, round body was mounted on strong legs, while a pronounced Roman nose was joined to a large head. In action, he displayed a "paddling gait." While Nature was niggardly in bestowing good looks on "Hippo," she compensated him with enormous strength and good temper. "Hippo" was never known to fail at a pinch, and his tremendous strength was requisitioned for other vehicles of the Section when in difficulties. Though never known to display bad temper, he was the most clumsy of horses. He would thoughtlessly step on his driver's feet, and if not checked instantly, would literally walk over him. As indicating his great strength, an incident is worth recording. After being securely pegged for the night (as was thought) he was found next morning a considerable distance from the horse lines, dragging the stout peg and line after him in his search for extra food. The peg which he drew from the earth by his massive neck was the regulation type, and had been driven well into hard ground. In his wanderings he had traversed a good deal of Sausage Valley, amongst batteries of artillery ranging from 18-pounders to the roaring and rearing 60-pounders, but he escaped scathless. During the days at Pozieres, the water-cart, its horses and driver, bore charmed lives, and it is believed that the outfit was the only one in the Brigade to come through without loss.

Although the horses and limbers were always sent well forward in line work to help the gun-teams as much as possible, and many risks were run, few losses were sustained owing to enemy action.

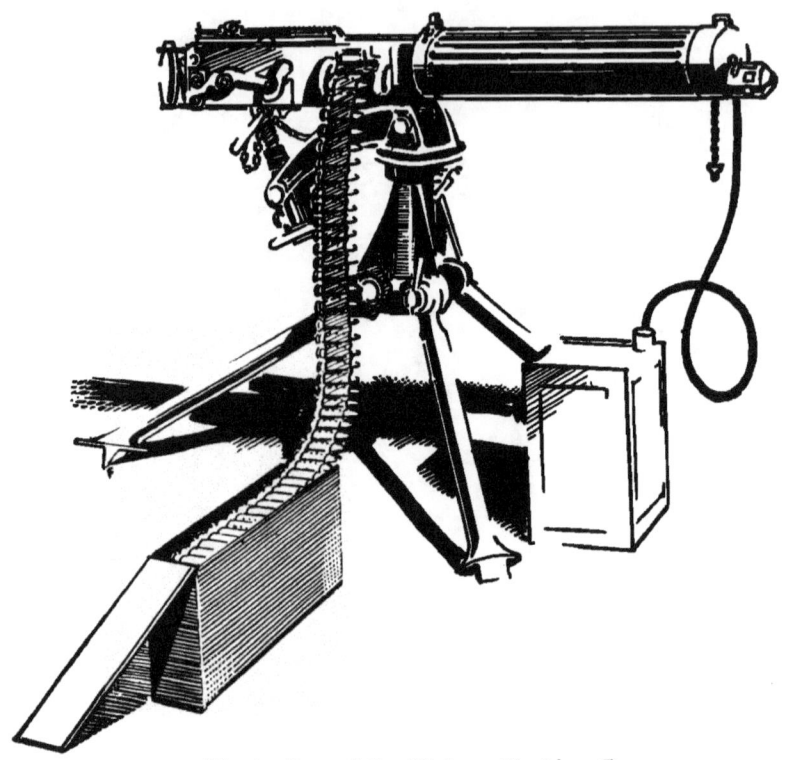

Illustration of the Vickers Machine Gun.
The gun is mounted ready for action.

APPENDIX "K."

Short Specification of the Vickers Machine Gun.

THE GUN.

DESIGNATION	.303 Vickers Light Machine Gun.
WEIGHT	With barrel casing filled with water—38 lbs.
RANGE	Up to 2,900 yards.
RATE OF FIRE	Up to 750 rounds per minute.
ACTION	Automatic.
ACTUATING FORCES	(a) The force of the explosion of the charge which carried the recoiling parts to the rear.
	(b) The force of the "fuzee spring" which carried the recoiling parts forward.
FEED	By medium of fabric belt (holding 250 rounds) passing through automatic feed block.
COOLING FACTOR	Water filled jacket or casing.

THE TRIPOD.

DESIGNATION	Tripod Mark IV.
WEIGHT	About 56 lbs.
DESCRIPTION	Three adjustable legs attached to a pillar upon which the gun was mounted.

AMMUNITION.

DESIGNATION	.303 Small Arm Ammunition, Mark VII.
BOXES	Of steel. Each box held one filled belt weighing 21 lbs. (Formerly of wood.)

APPENDIX "L."

THE ITINERARY OF THE COMPANY.
EGYPT.

1916

Mar. 1 ⎱ Mar. 9 ⎰	Canal Zone (Sinai Desert)	8 days	Company in process of formation
Mar. 9 ⎱ Mar. 19 ⎰	Canal Zone (Moascar)	10 days	Company formed and in training.
Mar. 19 ⎱ Mar. 20 ⎰	Alexandria (On Transport)	1 day	"H.M.T. Minnewaska"

MEDITERRANEAN SEA.

Mar. 20 ⎱ Mar. 25 ⎰	At sea	5 days	En route to France

FRANCE.

Mar. 25 ⎱ Mar. 27 ⎰	En route to Northern France	3 days	Per rail.
Mar. 27 ⎱ April 4 ⎰	Rincq	8 days	In billets. Training
April 4 ⎱ April 5 ⎰	Haverskerque	1 night	En route to the Line
April 5 ⎱ April 7 ⎰	Sailly	2 days	En route to the Line
April 7 ⎱ April 29 ⎰	Fleurbaix	22 days	In the Line
April 29 ⎱ June 10 ⎰	Erquinghem	42 days	In Brigade Reserve (Training)
June 10 ⎱ July 4 ⎰	Bois Grenier	24 days	In the Line
July 4 ⎱ July 8 ⎰	Steenwerck	4 days	Training
July 8 ⎱ July 9 ⎰	Strazeele	1 night	En route to Somme area
July 9 ⎱ July 11 ⎰	Renescure	2 days	En route to Somme area
July 11 ⎱ July 16 ⎰	St. Sauveur	5 days	Training
July 16 ⎱ July 18 ⎰	Rainville	2 days	En route to Pozieres
July 18 ⎱ July 20 ⎰	Toutencourt	2 days	En route to Pozieres (Training)

APPENDIX.

Date	Place	Duration	Activity
July 20 – July 26	Varennes	6 days	En route to Pozieres (Training)
July 26 – Aug. 7	Pozieres	12 days	In the Line. (Relief commenced night 5-6th)
Aug. 7 – Aug. 10	Warloy	3 days	Resting
Aug. 10 – Aug. 11	La Vicogne	1 night	En route to Berteaucourt
Aug. 11 – Aug. 18	Berteaucourt	7 days	Training
Aug. 18 – Aug. 19	La Vicogne	1 night	En route to Pozieres (marching by day)
Aug. 19 – Aug. 20	Toutencourt	1 night	En route to Pozieres (marching by day)
Aug. 20 – Aug. 21	Vadencourt	1 night	En route to Pozieres (marching by day)
Aug. 21 – Aug. 22	Albert	1 night	Bivouac in open field
Aug. 22 – Aug. 27	Pozieres	5 days	In the Line
Aug. 27 – Aug. 28	Albert	1 night	In billets in Albert
Aug. 28 – Aug. 29	Warloy	1 night	En route for Ypres (Belgium)
Aug. 29 – Aug. 31	Herissart	2 days	En route for Ypres (Belgium)
Aug. 31 – Sept. 3	Bonneville	3 days	En route for Ypres (Belgium)
Sept. 3 – Sept. 5	Gezaincourt	2 days	En route for Ypres (Belgium)

BELGIUM.

Date	Place	Duration	Activity
Sept. 5 – Oct. 19	Ypres Salient	44 days	In the Line. (Details at Erie Camp)

FRANCE.

Date	Place	Duration	Activity
Oct. 19 – Oct. 20		1 night	Entraining and marching
Oct. 20 – Oct. 22	Oudezeele	2 days	Resting
Oct. 22 – Oct. 23	La Meneqat	1 night	Marching by day to Somme area

Oct. 23 Oct. 24	Eperlecques	1 night	Marching by day to Somme area
Oct. 24 Oct. 25	St. Omer to Brucamps	1 night	Travelling by train to Somme area
Oct. 25 Oct. 27	Brucamps	2 days	Training
Oct. 27 Nov. 3	Buire	7 days	Training
Nov. 3 Nov. 4	Mametz Wood	1 night	
Nov. 4 Nov. 21	Flers	17 days	In the Line
Nov. 21 Nov. 22	Flers	1 night	
Nov. 22 Dec. 1	Dernancourt	9 days	Training
Dec. 1 Dec. 17	Flesselles	16 days	Training
Dec. 17 Dec. 20	Ribemont	3 days	Training
Dec. 20 Dec. 21	Fricourt Camp	1 night	Moving to the Line
Dec. 21 Dec. 22	Bernafay Wood ("E" Camp)	1 night	Moving to the Line
Dec. 22 1917 Jan. 17	Le Transloy	26 days	In the Line
Jan. 17 Jan. 18	Bernafay Wood ("C" Camp)	1 night	Moving to "Rest" area
Jan. 18 Jan. 29	Ribemont	11 days	Training
Jan. 29 Feb. 1	Becourt Camp	3 days	Moving to Line (Training)
Feb. 1 Feb. 5	Shelter Wood Camp	4 days	Moving to Line (Training)
Feb. 5 Feb. 14	Between Le Sars and Eaucourt L'Abbaye	9 days	In the Line
Feb. 14 Feb. 17	Shelter Wood Camp	3 days	In Divisional Reserve
Feb. 17 Feb. 24	Between Le Sars and Eaucourt L'Abbaye	7 days	In the Line

APPENDIX.

Date	Location	Duration	Activity
Feb. 24 – Mar. 1	Shelter Wood Camp	5 days	In Divisional Reserve
Mar. 1 – Mar. 21	Albert-Bapaume Rd., Grevillers, Avesnes-le-Bapaume, Favreuil, H'denburg Line	20 days	Following the German Withdrawal
Mar. 21 – Mar. 26	Warlencourt	5 days	Training
Mar. 26 – Mar. 30	Mametz Camp	4 days	Training
Mar. 30 – April 8	Becourt Camp	9 days	Training
April 8 – April 10	Beugnatre	2 days	Moving to the Line
April 10 – April 12	Bullecourt	2 days	In the Line
April 12 – April 15	Beugnatre	3 days	Training
April 15 – April 19	Bullecourt	4 days	In the Line
April 19 – April 24	Beugnatre	5 days	Training
April 24 – April 26	Bullecourt	2 days	In Reserve Line
April 26 – April 27	Beugnatre	1 day	Training
April 27 – April 29	Bullecourt	2 days	In Reserve Line
April 29 – May 1	Beugnatre	2 days	Training
May 1 – May 4	Bullecourt	3 days	In the Line
May 4 – May 6	Bullecourt	2 days	In the Reserve Line
May 6 – May 8	Beugnatre	2 days	Partial relief in Reserve Line
May 8 – May 9	Kookaburra Camp	1 day	Moving to "Rest" area
May 9 – May 17	Mametz Camp	8 days	Training and Resting
May 17 – May 20	Millencourt	3 days	Training and Resting
May 20 – June 15	Warloy	26 days	Training and Resting

June 15 July 24	Reincourt-les- Bapaume	39 days	Training and Resting
July 24 July 28	Aveluy	4 days	Training and Resting

FLANDERS.

July 28 Sept. 11	Wardrecques	45 days	Training and Resting
Sept. 11 Oct. 12	Ypres area	31 days	Camp, Belgian Chat. Prep. for and part. in 4 attacks
Oct. 12 Oct. 26	Steenvoorde	14 days	Training and Resting
Oct. 26 Nov. 3	Ypres area	8 days	In reserve
Nov. 3 Nov. 12	Ypres area	9 days	In the Line
Nov. 12 Nov. 18	Steenvoorde	6 days	Training and Resting
Nov. 18 Dec. 15	Locre	27 days	Training and Resting
Dec. 15 1918 Jan. 13	Neuve Eglise	29 days	Training and Resting
Jan. 13 Jan. 27	Warneton	14 days	In the Line
Jan. 27 Jan. 30	Kent Camp, near Neuve Eglise	3 days	Training and Resting
Jan. 30 Jan. 31		1 night	Travelling
Jan. 31 Mar. 6	Watterdal	34 days	Training
Mar. 6 April 2	Warneton	27 days	In the Line
April 2 April 3	Lark Camp	1 day	Moving to the Somme
April 3 April 4	Rouge Croix	2 days	Moving to the Somme

FRANCE.

1918 April 5 April 6	St. Sauveur	1 night	
April 6 May 1	Near Albert	25 days	In the Line
May 1	Montigny	1 night	

APPENDIX.

Dates	Location	Duration	Activity
May 2 – May 2 – May 10	Querrieu	8 days	Training and Resting
May 10 – May 21	Ville-sur-Ancre	11 days	In the Line
May 21 – May 31	Near Franvillers	10 days	Training and Resting
May 31 – June 15	Ville-sur-Ancre	15 days	In the Line
June 15 – June 28	Querrieu	13 days	Training and Resting
June 28 – July 21	Villers-Bretonneaux	23 days	In the Line (Centre Sector)
July 21 – July 28	Villers-Bretonneaux	7 days	In the Line (Right Sector)
July 28 – Aug. 7	Lamotte	10 days	Resting and Training
Aug. 7 – Aug. 17	Moving eastw'ds from Villers-Bretonneaux	10 days	Active Line Operations
Aug. 17 – Aug. 26	Fouilloy	9 days	Resting and Training
Aug. 26 – Aug. 27	Proyart	1 night	Moving to Line
Aug. 27 – Aug. 28	Chuignolles	1 night	Moving to Line
Aug. 28 – Sept. 1	Moving east in active operations	4 days	Advance to and attack on Mt. St. Quentin
Sept. 1 – Sept. 5	Halles	4 days	In Reserve
Sept. 5 – Sept. 27	Cappy	22 days	Training and Resting
Sept. 27 – Sept. 28	Buire (on Cologne River)	1 night	Moving to Line
Sept. 28 – Oct. 1	Hamel (on Cologne River)	3 days	Moving to Line
Oct. 1 – Oct. 2	Villeret	1 night	Moving to Line
Oct. 2 – Oct. 4	Nauroy	2 days	Moving to Line
Oct. 4 – Oct. 5	Montbrehain	1 day	Attack on Montbrehain
Oct. 5 – Oct. 6	Nauroy	1 night	Moving to "rest" area

Oct. 6	Herbicourt	1 night	Moving to "rest" area
Oct. 7			
Oct. 7	St. Ledger	48 days	Training and Resting
Nov. 24			
Nov. 24	Hangest-sur-Somme	1 night	Moving to Belgium
Nov. 25			

BELGIUM.

1918

Nov. 25	Maurois	1 night	Moving to "rest" area
Nov. 26			
Nov. 26	Rejet-de-Beaulieu	1 night	Moving to "rest" area
Nov. 27			
Nov. 27	Petit Fayt	1 night	Moving to "rest" area
Nov. 28			
Nov. 28	Boulogne-sur-Helpe	19 days	Training and Resting
Dec. 17			
Dec. 17	Flaumont	1 night	Moving to Charleroi area
Dec. 18			
Dec. 18	Sivry	1 night	Moving to Charleroi area
Dec. 19			
Dec. 19	Barbencon	1 night	Moving to Charleroi area
Dec. 20			
Dec. 20	Yves-Gomezee	48 days	Training and Resting
1919 Feb. 6			
Feb. 6	Montignies-le-Tilleul	22 days	Training and Resting
Feb. 28			

www.ingramcontent.com/pod-product-compliance
Lightning Source LLC
Chambersburg PA
CBHW052041220426
43663CB00012B/2393